The Ordeal
of the Constitution
THE ANTIFEDERALISTS
AND THE RATIFICATION STRUGGLE
OF *1787–1788*

The
Ordeal
of the
Constitution

THE ANTIFEDERALISTS
AND THE
RATIFICATION STRUGGLE
OF 1787–1788

By Robert Allen Rutland

UNIVERSITY OF OKLAHOMA PRESS

NORMAN

125277

BY ROBERT ALLEN RUTLAND

Birth of the Bill of Rights, 1776–1791 (Chapel Hill, 1955)

George Mason, Reluctant Statesman (Colonial Williamsburg, 1961)

The Ordeal of the Constitution (Norman, 1965)

LIBRARY OF CONGRESS CATALOG CARD NUMBER: 65–24203

Copyright 1966 by the University of Oklahoma Press, Publishing Division of the University. Composed and printed at Norman, Oklahoma, U.S.A., by the University of Oklahoma Press. First edition.

TO

Fayette Copeland

FOR HIS GENTLENESS, SCHOLARLY MANNER,
ENCOURAGEMENT, AND FRIENDSHIP

Preface

ORIN G. LIBBY'S PIONEER WORK on Constitutional history late in
the nineteenth century revealed new insights that seriously
challenged his contemporaries' polarized view of the Federalists and
the Antifederalists. Thereafter, the Antifederalists were not simply
blockheads standing in the way of progress, but were recognized as
serious, oftentimes brilliant, citizens who viewed the Constitution in
1787–88 with something less than awe. Professor Charles A. Beard
followed Libby's advance in 1913 with *An Economic Interpretation
of the Constitution of the United States.* Much time has been spent
since then attempting to prove that Beard was wrong or right in his
major thesis: that the Constitution was the handiwork of a skillful
group "whose property interests were immediately at stake." Indignant lawmakers denounced the implications of Beard's book when
it first appeared. A score of able historians have since been provoked
either to attack Beard's propositions or to defend them.

This book is neither a defense nor an attack on Beard. Instead, it
attempts to tell readers something of the Antifederalists' personalities, their problems, and their hopes. Federalist sources provide
much information about this area of inquiry; they also reveal how
politically sophisticated the Founding Fathers really were in analyz-
ing their adversaries' maneuvers and motives. When this work was
in its final stages, Professor Jackson T. Main's excellent book *The
Antifederalists* appeared. Both books cut across the same pathways in
a good many instances, however, a difference in interpretation and
emphasis is markedly evident. Other studies about the Antifederalist
movement are in progress, and hopefully, each will illuminate our
understanding of that period when American politics rapidly emerged
from infancy to childhood.

My indebtedness to the many organizations and people that assisted me in this enterprise is staggering. The University of Cali-

fornia, Los Angeles, was generous with funds for research, as was the American Philosophical Society. Individuals who were particularly helpful include Robert E. Cushman, Curtis P. Nettels, Wilmer Leech, Stephen Riley, and Savoie Lottinville. Indispensable aid came from the library staffs at U.C.L.A., Massachusetts Historical Society, Boston Public Library, New York Public Library, Library of Congress, Historical Society of Pennsylvania, New-York Historical Society, Yale University, Harvard University, Maryland Historical Society, University of Virginia, Virginia State Library, Colonial Williamsburg, and the Manuscripts Division, Library of Congress. The patience of Esther Sassa and Mrs. Arletta Gentile was inexhaustible. And some acknowledgment should go to an American official who saved me hours and weeks of worry by depositing Max Farrand's *Records of the Federal Convention* in the Library of the University of Innsbruck, Austria, at the end of World War II.

ROBERT ALLEN RUTLAND

Los Angeles, California
September 15, 1965

Contents

Illustrations

A Guide to the Footnotes

Short Titles

Works cited with great frequency are carried in an abbreviated form, with the full identification listed below.

LCC. Edmund C. Burnett (ed.), *Letters and Correspondence of Members of the Continental Congress* (8 vols., Washington, 1921–36).

DHC. *Documentary History of the Constitution* (5 vols., Washington, 1894–1905).

Elliot. Jonathan Elliot, *Debates in the Several State Conventions on the Adoption of the Federal Constitution* (5 vols., Philadelphia, 1901). Cited thus: Elliot, *Debates*, II, 136.

Farrand. Max Farrand (ed.), *Records of the Federal Convention* (3 vols., New Haven, 1911–37). Cited thus: 2 Farrand 43, i.e., page 43 of volume II.

Jefferson Papers. *The Papers of Thomas Jefferson*, ed. by Julian P. Boyd (Princeton, 1950–). Cited thus: 12 *Jefferson Papers* 232, i.e., page 232 of volume XII.

Locations of Documents

Symbols similar to those used in the National Union Catalog of the Library of Congress indicate the location of documents used and cited.

DLC. Library of Congress
MHS. Massachusetts Historical Society
NYHS. New-York Historical Society
NYPL. New York Public Library
BPL. Boston Public Library

The Ordeal
of the Constitution
THE ANTIFEDERALISTS
AND THE RATIFICATION STRUGGLE
OF *1787–1788*

*"It is obviously impracticable in the federal government
of these states, to secure all rights of independent sovereignty to each,
and yet provide for the interest and safety of all: Individuals
entering into society, must give up a share of liberty
to preserve the rest."*

—Washington's letter of transmittal
to the Continental Congress,
September 17, 1787

☆ I ☆

The Dissenting Trio

THE POLITICAL ORDEAL that produced the Constitution in 1787 and brought about its ratification in 1788 was unique in human history. Never before had the representatives of a whole nation discussed, planned, and implemented a new form of government in such a manner or such a short time. In little more than a year, Americans established a political framework which enlightened Europeans viewed with skepticism, for it was an age of theories that had seen few accomplishments. The unprecedented struggle to write and ratify a document affecting millions of citizens in the new nation revealed divergent views of the nature of republicanism. Nonetheless, a written constitution manifested an American willingness to experiment— even to gamble.

The Founding Fathers were practical men, but life as well as politics had been a risky business for them since 1765. They were also impatient men. If the Constitution had been drafted in the usual tedious legislative manner, slowly debated, and more slowly ratified (to replace the Articles of Confederation), then the process would not have brought Americans to a political crossroads. With only limited experience and native intuition as their guides, Americans were asked to make a hurried decision. To some, the speed of the maneuver was overwhelming. "The malady of human nature in these States now, seems to be . . . a temporary Insanity," Richard Henry Lee observed with alarm. Constitution-making was too serious a business to be hurried through, Lee insisted. But Hamilton and his friends believed that urgency was proper at a time when the main question of the day was whether "men are really capable or not of establishing good government from reflection and choice, or whether they are forever destined to depend for their political constitutions on accident and force." Racked with doubt and distrust, Lee spoke for powerful forces when he charged that the rush to ratify the Consti-

3

tution was "certainly the most rash and violent proceeding in the world," for even in an emergency prudence was justified in "a business of such infinite moment."[1]

The Constitution had barely reached public attention when Lee raised his storm warnings. The first national political campaign, the ratification struggle of 1787–88, moved American political battles from dozens of local arenas into the national coliseum. The contest became a desperate fight between powerful local forces and a mighty (and for the times surprisingly sophisticated) national organization. Long only a vague memory with the general public and sometimes glossed over by historians, the exciting period when Federalists contended with Antifederalists was the seedtime of American party politics.

The principal issue seemed simple enough: shall the Constitution proposed by the Federal Convention be adopted or not? But what was clear in September became cloudy by October, when the first gushes of enthusiasm were spent, giving way to gnawing doubts and fears. Exploiting those fears and doubts were the Antifederalists— the "Grumbletonians" who proved during the first party contest in the new Republic that contention and strife are the healthy, natural state of American politics.

The common ground for opposition to ratification in 1787–88, as in most political struggles, was the distribution of political power. The Revolution had transferred the seat of power from Britain to her former colonies, and then distributed it among thirteen sovereign states, occupying a thousand miles of coast line. Jealousy and fear of a strong, centralized government prompted the thirteen states to surrender so few powers to the national government that the Articles of Confederation barely kept the loose alliance intact during the war years. The whole structure began to creak and groan in the peacetime that followed. A dozen incidents, some trivial and some serious, focused attention on the weaknesses of the shimmering theory that

---

[1] Richard Henry Lee to Dr. William Shippen, Jr., October 2, 1787; Lee to George Mason, October 1, 1787, *The Letters of Richard Henry Lee* (ed. by James C. Ballagh), II, 440, 444; "Publius," *New-York Independent Journal*, October 27, 1787.

political sovereignties may coexist with scant regard for their neighbors' interests or aspirations. Many struggles for power took place before the Revolution—within cities and colonies, and among colonies and regions. The Revolution provided a lull as energy was directed toward the battlefield, but with the return of peace came renewed rivalries and scrambles for power. Since widespread confusion was the result, desperate measures seemed necessary. The Constitution was conceived by its framers, as Madison was to state with such clarity, as a means of throttling all the power struggles by placing the highest authority in a national government under "the supreme law of the land." For some citizens this quick transition of power from local or regional levels to a national or federal level was simply a matter of moving too fast and going too far.

Thus, when Lee spoke of the madness that seized men in the late autumn of 1787, it was his fearful expression of a sentiment well nurtured in his own mind. Power, wrested from Great Britain at a terrible price, was not a trinket to be tossed about recklessly. Rather, each citizen, after careful study of the proposed Constitution, should determine for himself whether or not too much control over his affairs was being shifted to a distant federal authority. For the next ten months the issue of local interests versus national powers overshadowed all other considerations in the ratification struggle. Implicit in every battle cry of the emerging Antifederalist movement was the message: a strong national government will in time weaken and destroy local governments. A further corollary was that local governments preserved democratic institutions, while a national government would become an aggrandizing aristocracy. Despite the emotional trappings draped over the antifederal cause, the political nexus was clear to Antifederalist leaders. However, the means whereby that bond of interest could be crystallized in effective action was not.

The Antifederalists unfortunately fell heir to a party label that had already become unpopular by the time they were identified with it. In 1787, they were burdened with the unenviable reputation of being a disorganized but sizable political group that existed in nearly every state at the close of the Revolution. When the wartime Continental Congress was desperate for a means of collecting revenue, its members who opposed a tax on imports collected on behalf of the Confederation rather than on behalf of the state where the goods landed were subsequently branded "antifederal." The prevailing system of the Continental Congress was to send each state a requisition for money—this money was the source of Continental revenues. When states failed to send funds—as they often did—printing presses and foreign loans supplied the difference. By 1783 political figures who favored an independent source of revenue for Congress instead of the unreliable source provided by the quota system became known as "federal" men. State political figures who considered proposed requests for funds a threat to their own sources of income made no secret of their antifederal views. Officials in New York and Rhode Island, where the state tax collectors kept themselves busy, withheld their assent to a national revenue repeatedly—a kiss-of-death, because the Articles of Confederation required unanimous support by the state legislatures for any change in the revenue system.

Seemingly indifferent to insinuations of being avaricious opponents to real union, the rank-and-file Antifederalists of 1781–87 defended the Articles of Confederation against the cries of calamity and ruin that were heard with increasing frequency after a postwar recession began. With an effort that was to be its death rattle, the Continental Congress in 1785 asked the states to approve a 5 per cent levy on imports to bolster the shaky national treasury. Powerful Virginia assented to the plan, but New York and Rhode Island guarded their privileges adamantly. But for their stubborn localism, one shrewd observer later noted, "in all human probability the Federal Constitution would not have been called into existence."

Coupled with the ineptitude of the national government—which in practical terms was the Continental Congress, a corpulent general, a harassed postmaster, and a fundless treasurer—was widespread postwar disillusionment. Hopes for a prosperous postwar life gave way in 1783–86 to the hard realities of humdrum existence. The economy of areas dependent upon shipping and commerce suffered more than those dependent upon agriculture. The new nation was no match for her erstwhile sovereign when it came to manufacturing and carrying goods to far-flung ports. But in time the farmers felt as pinched as the merchants. Businessmen were troubled by the variety of currency issued by the groaning public presses, with fluctuating values that vexed even the most patient. The farmer, and particularly the back-country yeoman, saw little hard money of any variety. In too many cases his soldier certificates, issued during the war, had long been sold for a fraction of their nominal value, often to some speculating town dweller.

Blame for all ills soon fell on the state politicians. "Could a general convulsion, which might correct the hellish habit of our political system, take place—I care not how soon we spasmodise," lamented a Revolutionary veteran of 1784.[2] The idle secretary of war Henry Knox used his time to spread news of recession and unrest, cursing "the vile State governments." But when prominent figures in Massachusetts suggested in 1785 that the Articles of Confederation be revised, Elbridge Gerry and his fellow congressmen raised objections. Not only might a revision of the Articles be premature, but republican institutions were already under attack by plans "artfully laid, & vigorously pursued, which had they been successful, We think, would inevitably have changed our republican Governments, into baleful Aristocracies," and the Society of the Cincinnati, unless soon abolished, "will have the same fatal Tendency."[3] This direct attack on the Cincinnati, a powerful organization of officers in the late Continental Army, must have offended many discontented veterans. Yet Gerry dismissed the cry for "more power in Congress" as the slogan of schemers who desired "lucrative Employment, civil & military."

Gerry's plea for patience found little support from disillusioned colleagues. "There is a langour in the States that forebodes ruin," David Ramsay wrote. "In 1775 there was more patriotism in a village than there is now in the 13 states."

The troubled times quickened political interest. "We are all become politicians in Virginia,—Men Women & Children have learnt to discuss some particular subjects of State importance—Paper Money—British Debts and the encrease of Congressional Power are

---

[2] William Jackson to Horatio Gates, August 6, 1784, Emmet collection, *NYPL*.

[3] E. Gerry, R. King, and S. Holten to Governor James Bowdoin, September 3, 1785, Emmet collection, *NYPL*.

the principle Topicks," Bushrod Washington reported. His uncle, shrouded in pessimism after reading doleful letters from wartime companions, was shaken by postwar realities. "No morn ever dawned more favourably than ours did; and no day was ever more clouded than the present!" he lamented. "We are fast verging to anarchy and confusion!" What could save the Republic he had nurtured? Instead of thirteen "Sovereignties pulling against each other, and all tugging at the federal head," there must be a "literal, and energetic Constitution, well guarded and closely watched, to prevent encroachments."[4]

Washington echoed the young nation's shock when reports of Shays's Rebellion in Massachusetts flowed north and south. General Knox, with a handwriting that almost defied reading when he was calm, excitedly noted that Shays's forces "have never paid any, or but very little taxes." Their goal was "to annihilate all debts public and private . . . by means of unfunded paper money which shall be tender in all cases whatever."

As the bugaboo of Shays's insurrection frightened some men, others talked about revising the Articles of Confederation. The ill-fated Annapolis Convention of 1786 seemed further proof of a national malaise. But astute delegates Alexander Hamilton and James Madison, perceiving the temper of the times, helped fashion a call at the abortive interstate parley for a general convention to revise the Articles. The suggested meeting was to be held in Philadelphia the following May. Coincidentally, the national convention of the Society of the Cincinnati was also set for a May date in Philadelphia. Some delegates planned to attend both meetings.

Meanwhile, the general policy of penniless drift was enfeebling the Continental Congress to such a degree that Madison feared the Confederation was about to "tumble to the ground." Suspicion and distrust seemed to be the order of the day. The French chargé d'affaires in New York placed much of the blame on an aristocratic clique which withheld support from the tottering Confederation. Among those who refused their support the French diplomat numbered "rich men, the merchants, the public officers, the Cincinnati"

[4] Washington to Madison, November 5, 1786, *The Writings of George Washington* (ed. by John C. Fitzpatrick), XXIX, 51–52.

8

and the holders of depreciated public securities.[5] Nothing seemed to be greater evidence of knavery to many Federalists than the paper-money schemes that had been adopted throughout the land. Rhode Island was held in reproach as the most wanton offender, but the taint was only a matter of degree. Paper money, in its fluctuation and depreciation, made a mockery of private contracts in many states. In a society that lived on credit, printed money of uncertain value threatened to disembowel the whole financial structure. Businessmen of the no-nonsense stripe readily ignored the successful emissions of New York and South Carolina. Thus many Federalists were all too willing to burn down the barn to kill the paper-money rat.

Enemies of the paper-money acts, pine barren acts (that allowed worthless lands to be offered as legal tender), and similar schemes came to regard Rhode Island as the scourge of sound credit. In that tiny state drastic measures had accomplished more than businessmen cared to admit. By 1787, Rhode Island had extricated herself from a staggering public debt, and except for the noisy town merchants the people demonstrated their approval by re-electing the proponents of paper-money schemes. The success of Rhode Island officials in public finance was glossed over by out-of-state newspaper essayists, who attacked them as *"leaden headed legislators"* with black hearts and empty pockets. The most provoking aspect of the Rhode Island scheme was its apparent success, which Federalists scorned as they considered drastic remedies to curb "Rogue-Island." After viewing matters at first hand in Newport, Judge Francis Dana of Boston reported his delight that Rhode Island had not chosen delegates for the Federal Convention or the Continental Congress, "as their neglect will give ground to strike it out of the Union & divide their Territory between their Neighbours." Dana elaborated on his scheme, which gave the territorial spoils to Massachusetts and Connecticut. Never one to overlook a prime opportunity, Dana proposed that the commercial area be grafted onto Massachusetts, since it would "best accord with the spirit & genius of our People." Dana was sure that a dissection of Rhode Island "wou'd meet the general approbation of the Commercial part of it, tho' they are afraid to take any open

[5] M. Otto to Comte de Montmorin, April 10, 1787, 3 Farrand 17.

measures in the present state of things, to bring it about." All that was needed, according to Dana, was "a bold politician [who] wou'd seize upon the occasion their abominations and antifederal conduct presents for annihilating them as a separate Member of the Union."[6] Since no Federalist champion appeared, the Rhode Island commercial men and their friends elsewhere had to be patient, although the whole experience was mortifying.

The clamor raised by the Federalists discouraged sympathizers in other states from showing their support of Rhode Island's antifederal legislation. Fearing some taint, they avoided any kind of alliance with kindred souls there. This aloofness was characteristic of scores of men with antifederal leanings who watched with awe as the Federalists out-maneuvered them by gloomy outcries and dire predictions.

The somber winter of 1786–87 was a prelude to a spring that blossomed with pleas for corrective action. The Federal Convention delegates trudged to Philadelphia, uneasy about the pathway before them. "The prevailing apprehension among thinking people is that the Convention," Hamilton observed, "from a fear of shocking the popular opinion, will not go far enough."[7] Suspicious William Grayson surveyed opinion in the Continental Congress and predicted that northern delegates would push for "a very strong government, & wish to prostrate all the state legislatures . . . but I don't learn that the people are with them!"[8]

The moving spirits behind the Convention had no further use for the Articles of Confederation, but it would have been imprudent to bare this attitude publicly. In a rare display of unanimity, the delegates voted to keep their debates secret. The precaution was taken "to prevent mistakes and misrepresentation until the business shall have been completed—the final result would read better than piece-meal newspaper reports of several crude and indigested parts."[9]

[6] Francis Dana to Elbridge Gerry, September 2, 1787, L. W. Smith collection, Morristown National Historical Park.

[7] Hamilton to Washington, July 3, 1787, Hamilton papers, *DLC*.

[8] Grayson to Madison, May 29, 1787, Madison papers, *DLC*.

[9] Mason to George Mason, Jr., May 27, 1787, Kate Mason Rowland, *The Life of George Mason*, II, 103–104.

Fifty-five delegates participated in the Convention business in some way, and thirty-nine of them signed the Constitution.

Since antifederalism in the Federal Convention was always on the defensive, its defenders found themselves continually fighting a rear-guard action. Governor Edmund Randolph handed delegates a framework of ideas which served as a working draft, but later he became vexed by doubts that slowly turned him against the whole proceeding. His fellow Virginian, George Mason, became a watch-dog for southern interests. Elbridge Gerry drifted into their company because he feared that republicanism could not survive under a strong national government. Arrayed against them was a collection of talent, the like of which the world has seldom seen gathered under one roof.

Randolph's plan, which favored the large states, plunged the Convention into an atmosphere of tension. But compromises were inevitable if ideological and regional differences were to be resolved. What increasingly alarmed Randolph and Mason was that the concessions always seemed to be southern ones. The basic idea of a federal union with legislative, executive, and judicial branches seemed proper, but the two Virginians, fearing domination of agricultural interests by northern commercial interests, opposed the idea of a single president and insisted on a triple-headed executive board. Their demand for representation by the northern, middle, and southern areas on an executive council—so that each executive might safeguard his regional interests—had no serious support.

Despite repeated frustrations, Mason hinted that the "energetic government" outlined by the delegates would be a northern-dominated oligarchy. A strange alliance was created in late July when Gerry joined the Virginians in their uncompromising position. Gerry and Mason opposed the popular election of a president, fearing not the people but the wartime heroes who might prove to be popular demagogues at election time. Mason said he respected the Society of the Cincinnati, but "he never wished" that body "to have a preponderating influence in the Govt." Since nearly every state delegation had at least one Cincinnati member, Mason and Gerry ruffled many prominent members. Delegate William Pierce noted that

Mason was "undoubtedly one of the best politicians in America," but nobody praised Mason's diplomacy.

Merchant Gerry was proof that politicians do not choose their company from self-interest alone, for he sided with the Virginia planters, because they, too, distrusted a strong national government. Obviously a friend of the commerce which had built his fortune, Gerry on more than one occasion noted that the country was divided into two groups—those with land and those who lived by trade. When it came time to determine a method of selecting senators, Gerry joined Mason and Randolph in insisting that the power be vested in state legislatures. To the Virginians this power preserved a vestige of their state legislature's sovereignty, but to Gerry it supplied the means to "provide some check in favor of the commercial interest agst. the landed; without which oppression will take place."[10] Thus, despite the ends sought, the trio often found themselves in agreement.

On the other hand, none of the three men were obsessed by the idea of preserving state rights. When dissension over small-state and large-state representation threatened to dissolve the Convention, both Gerry and Mason labored to hold tempers in check, and they served on the committee which shaped the final compromise. Gerry served as chairman of the committee after he reminded hotheaded delegates that "Something must be done, or we shall disappoint not only America, but the whole world." Gerry had a higher regard for the Union than Mason, who distrusted most northern delegates and seemed to fear their aims more than a loose-jointed confederacy. Mason gained some support for his contention that Congress must be prohibited from taxing exports, since such a tax would burden the farmers and planters. Surely, Mason said, the North "did not mean to deny the Southern [states] this security."[11]

Before the matter was settled, Mason unveiled his worst suspicions. He went into a tirade on the potential oppressive majority which the eight northern states might exercise by having "in one branch of the legislature 36 votes agst 29, and in the other, in the proportion of

[10] 1 Farrand 66.
[11] 2 Farrand 284.

12

8 agst 5." Even closer to Mason's heart was his proposal that limited the power of Congress to regulate shipping. He proposed that no act interfering with a shipper's right to select his vessels and ports should be passed without the concurrence of a two-thirds majority in Congress. Great Britain had long exercised such control, and Mason could visualize northern shipowners clamoring for protection of their industry. Randolph joined Mason in demanding passage of this check on Congress as a scrap salvaged from the surrender of state sovereignty to a federal union. However, some northerners had equally strong feelings. In one of the most candid remarks uttered at the Convention, Nathaniel Gorham reminded delegates "that the Eastern States had no motive to Union but a commercial one."

Mason and Randolph lost their fight in the committee, perhaps because a powerful delegate reminded others that protection for shipping would be a means of "encouraging american bottoms & seamen" and, moreover, lay the foundation for a much needed navy. Besides, Gouverneur Morris argued, the shipping trade "was the worst & most precarious kind of property, and stood in need of public patronage." Mason, equally certain that such laws would spell disaster for the South, said that without competitive shipping the "Southern States . . . will deliver themselves bound hand & foot to the Eastern States, and enable them to exclaim, in the words of Cromwell on a certain occasion—'the lord hath delivered them into our hands.'"

Frustration greeted the Antifederalists at every Convention session. Mason expressed concern over the clause on fulfilling "the obligations of the United States," which he feared would set off another round of "speculations and increase the pestilent practice of stock-jobbing." The original holders of depreciated securities issued by Congress and the states probably had long since sold their holdings out of ignorance or distress. Surely, those who bought the stocks at depreciated prices were not entitled to enormous profits. Mason, ever vigilant and as frugal in public affairs as in private, wanted the government to give full payments only to the original holders of securities. On this point Mason and Madison were in rare agreement, but Mason's proposal was rejected by the Convention. Gouverneur Morris liked the implications of the expression that the United States "shall fulfill" all obligations, and Morris was not one to be coy. A strong statement would be salutary here because "it would create many friends of the plan."[12] Plain-spoken Morris thus told Mason what he was to hear again and again, that the *commercial* interests of the country would have to be won over to the Constitution by special favors. To Mason's mind, the terms "commercial" and "northern" were synonymous.

By August 31, Mason was so upset that he indignantly declared that "he would sooner chop off his right hand than put it to the Constitution as it now stands." Mason then uttered the threat that was to haunt Federalists for the next ten months. If fundamental changes were not made, Mason warned, it might be necessary to call another Federal Convention to finish the work now improperly fashioned. Morris was quick to ridicule Mason's idea of a second convention. Another convention would have his approval, Morris said, provided it had the courage to give America "vigorous Government, which we are afraid to do." Randolph, still siding with his senior colleague, suggested that state conventions might make amendments which could be submitted to a second convention.

In the final weeks of the Convention, Mason and his small following were able to gain acceptance of only a few of the propositions which they considered fundamental. New York delegates Yates and Lansing had long since left Philadelphia, making no secret of their opposition to the proposed Constitution. Luther Martin had returned to Maryland in a huff. It is indeed surprising that the Mason-Gerry-Randolph entente secured any concessions at all. The exclusive right of the House of Representatives to originate appropriation bills was finally approved, but other antifederal propositions found scant support.

Before the Convention adjourned, Mason reviewed the proceedings since May and concluded that the Constitution as it stood was swollen with dangerous doctrine. Showing belated concern over the personal rights of citizens, Mason came forward with an eleventh-hour proposal for a bill of rights that "would give great quiet to the people." Time was short, but by using any of the state declarations

[12] 2 Farrand 412.

14

of rights, "a bill might be prepared in a few hours." A few delegates sided with Mason, but most agreed with Sherman, who attacked Mason's proposal by stating that the Constitution was not repealing any of the state bills of rights, which remained "in force" and were sufficient. A last-minute effort to accomplish the same goal through piecemeal provisions became a fiasco.

In the final hour of debate, Mason resurrected the navigation act clause. Certainly, he pleaded, it was only fair that southerners should insist that a two-thirds majority of Congress be required to pass legislation that favored one section over another. As matters stood, Congress by a simple majority could allow "a few rich merchants in Philada N. York & Boston, to monopolize the Staples of the Southern States & reduce their value perhaps 50 Per Ct."[13] He wanted the same twenty-year trial period for this idea that his colleagues from South Carolina had gained for the importation of slaves, but only Maryland and Georgia joined Virginia in favoring Mason's doomed proposal.

Reviewing the work of the Convention, Randolph said that his basic plan with its "republican propositions" had been twisted until it was barely recognizable. The Governor declared he was duty-bound to propose that the state conventions be permitted to offer amendments to the Constitution for the consideration of another body which would have "full power to settle the Constitution finally." The hostility of most delegates to the second-convention scheme, which had undoubtedly been discussed over dining-room tables in Philadelphia for some time, was apparent. Brought to a vote, the idea was rejected by an impatient majority. Undaunted, Randolph droned on with a list of faults, ranging from the failure to limit the size of the standing army to "the Authority of the general Legislature to interpose on the application of the *Executives* of the States."

Most of the delegates, now impatient and ready to prepare a final draft that could be sent to the Continental Congress, found the complaints of the dissenting trio tiresome. When Gerry suggested that the Convention had assumed too much power by "dissolving in so slight a manner, the solemn obligations" of the Articles of Confederation, the atmosphere must have chilled on that warm September day.

[13] 2 Farrand 626.

Two days before the Convention adjourned *sine die*, Gerry, Mason, and Randolph served their final warning. Gerry's list of objections encompassed fears concerning the "unlimited power of Congress" and the treatment of slaves as freedmen on the census rolls. These and other matters Gerry might have swallowed "if the rights of Citizens were not rendered insecure." The only remedy, Gerry suggested, was the calling of another convention. A vote on Randolph's final motion to secure this end brought a reverberating "No!" from the delegates.

Although plagued with some misgivings, Randolph assured the Convention that he would not become a troublemaker. The Federalists, anxious to snuff out the tiniest flame of opposition at this crucial moment, pleaded with the antifederal trio to reconsider. Morris assured them that he himself had reservations about the Constitution, but as it stood it was the best that men could agree upon. Once it was broadcast throughout the country, the burning question would be "shall there be a national government or not?" Hamilton's anxiety caused him to add that by refusing to sign the document at this point, "A few characters of consequence . . . might do infinite mischief . . . by kindling latent sparks." The recalcitrant trio was unmoved.

After the Constitution was signed, the delegates moved to the City Tavern for a round of toasts and more speculation on the prospects of ratification. Three of the delegates who viewed the proceedings with pessimism, however, did not feel that spirit of compromise that moved delegate McHenry of Maryland. McHenry signed despite some reservations because he distrusted his own judgment, "especially as it is opposite to the opinion of a majority of the gentlemen whose abilities and patriotism are of the first cast."[14] Perhaps Randolph began his wavering course in the midst of the camaraderie at the City Tavern. But Mason and Gerry apparently believed they had lost only the first skirmish.

[14] 1 Farrand 645.

☆ II ☆

"The Less of Two Evils"

WHEN THE CONTINENTAL CONGRESS received the Constitution with Washington's accompanying letter which seemed to be a ringing endorsement, a brief political honeymoon ensued. Everywhere the great patriot's name was associated with the document. "I have observed that your name to the new Constitution has been of infinite service," the General was informed. "Indeed I am convinced that if you had not attended the Convention, and the same paper had been handed out to the world, it would have met with a colder reception, with fewer and weaker advocates, and with more and more strenuous opponents." Who would be so foolish as to range himself against Washington's public image? A false report from Alexandria related that Mason had been publicly denounced there because he had refused to sign the Constitution. Randolph returned home to tell intimate friends that the Constitution needed amending, but was still "the less of two Evils." Gerry remained in New York as a delegate to the feeble Continental Congress, and was so bedeviled about his recent conduct that he was driven to write a defense of his convention behavior.

Newspaper fanfare and jovial toasts in taverns where Federalists congregated were deceiving, however. Ahead lay the often cantankerous Congress, which had to give the Constitution its blessing, and then at least nine state conventions. No matter how much enthusiasm was generated in a newspaper essay, in a pamphlet, or at a public rally, it was in the legislative halls that the Constitution would be approved or defeated.

In the Continental Congress there was the same undertone of sectional opposition that had marked the debates in the Federal Convention. When Richard Henry Lee visited Philadelphia during the Convention sessions, he had sympathized with the prevailing sentiment that a strong federal government was needed. The change was dictated, he wrote, by "the injustise [*sic*], folly, and wickedness of the State Legislatures" so "that the people in general seem ready for any thing."[1] But once Lee had the Constitution before him, he saw much that he did not approve. Moving swiftly to counteract the Federalists, Lee worked with Gerry, Grayson, Nathan Dane of Massachusetts, and a few other delegates in an effort to throw fetters on the Constitution. Lee would have simply allowed the Constitution to lie stillborn, ignored on the ground that the Convention had exceeded its powers. But not even Grayson would go that far, although he was "at best for giving it only a Silent passage to the States."

Thwarted in their effort to make the Constitution appear as a usurpation of authority, Lee and his followers fell back to a second scheme in an attempt to deprive the Constitution of the tacit approval of the Continental Congress. They unsuccessfully tried to persuade fellow delegates that they had the power to alter the Constitution themselves. Finally, Lee insisted that a set of amendments from Congress should accompany the Constitution in its passage to the states, to be acted upon in state conventions along with the Constitution. These efforts were confounded when Madison and a contingent of Federalists resumed their seats. Moreover, Lee's churlish action seemed inconsistent, for as even he had admitted earlier, some radical change in the structure of the Union was vital to its continued existence.

Lee's efforts availed the Antifederalists nothing, but again demonstrated the Federalists' ability at parliamentary maneuvering. By juggling words at the Philadelphia Convention, Federalists made it appear that harmony pervaded the final session. The unanimity of state delegations was stressed again in the Continental Congress, so that even Lee and Grayson were outvoted by their Virginia colleagues. First, Lee's proposals were overwhelmed; then, the Constitution was passed on with a "unanimous" state vote. "The people do not scrutinize terms," Virginia delegate Carrington observed. "The unanimity of Congress in recommending a measure . . . naturally implies approbation." Washington dropped some of his usual reserve

[1] Lee to Francis Lightfoot Lee, July 14, 1787, Ballagh, *Letters of Lee*, II, 423–24.

to applaud the Congressional tactician's success. "This apparent unanimity will have its effect," he commented. "Not every one has opportunities to peep behind the curtain; and . . . the appearance of unanimity in that body on this occasion will be of great importance."[2]

Lee fumed but could do nothing beyond report his failure. "It was with us, as with you," he dolefully complained to Mason, "this or nothing; and this urged with a most extreme intemperance." Lee visualized the Federalists as a coalition "of monarchy men, military men, aristocrats and drones whose noise, impudence and zeal exceeds all belief." Lee hoped his amendments had upset their timetable, "for the plan is to push the business on with dispatch, and with as little opposition as possible."[3]

The disorganized Antifederalists had lost two battles, and both by overwhelming margins. Moreover, the general public knew virtually nothing of their efforts because of the closed-door rule at Philadelphia. Gouverneur Morris, probably the chief architect of the Federalist plan to rush the ratification process along wherever possible, had predicted that when the Constitution "first appears, with the sanction of this Convention, the people will be favorable to it." Then, he warned, "By degrees the State Officers, & those interested in the State Govts. will intrigue & turn the popular current against it." Crusty Luther Martin of Maryland agreed, but for a different reason. Martin told the Convention that the people "would not ratify it unless hurried into it by surprise." Convinced that he was right (and Martin was dogmatic if nothing else), the acidulous Maryland delegate had left the Convention before the final signing ceremonies. Once home, Martin lauded an essay written by Samuel Chase which urged citizens to consider the Constitution with deliberate care "because you want information, and have not had time yourselves to examine the proposed system." With news drifting in from other states of Federalist efforts for speedy adoption, Chase declared "time is not given for your countrymen in this, and the other States, to consider the subject . . . you are not pressed in point of time . . . to decide, therefore, in a few days will be rashness and folly." The

[2] Washington to Madison, October 10, 1787, *DHC*, IV, 321.
[3] Lee to Mason, October 1, 1787, *LCC*, VIII, 652–53.

headlong rush for ratification made Chase question the Federalists' motives, "and it is not uncharitable to suspect that they are improper."[4]

Thwarted in the Continental Congress, Antifederalists looked at Pennsylvania and saw their suspicions confirmed. Indeed, overbearing tactics never seemed more obvious. Before the Pennsylvania legislature had received the recommendation for a state convention, over-anxious Federalists proceeded to expedite the ratification of the Constitution. In alarm, Assemblyman Whitehill of Cumberland County tried to apply the brakes of legislative procedure. He knew the majority favored speed but as a matter of propriety, he asked, "why not allow time to consider of it?" There ought to be a cooling-off period before the state called a convention, he said, adding "and I don't know any reason there can be for driving it down our throats, without an hour's preparation."

On September 28, the Congressional resolution arrived. Knowing that they were outnumbered, sixteen Antifederalists of the Pennsylvania legislature simply failed to return from the noon recess, hoping to prevent a quorum and to suspend business while they might marshall some strength. The legislature's sergeant at arms was ordered to seek out absent members. Assisted by a mob, he found two Antifederalists and forced them into the chamber. One refused to keep his place, but after a brief struggle a quorum was declared present. Before the day was over, the state convention had been scheduled to meet early in November. A feeble Antifederalist motion to move the site from Philadelphia to Lancaster was easily outvoted. Even arch-Federalist Tench Coxe conceded that his friends had been imprudent. "I am sorry for any thing that appears irregular, or looks like an interruption of peace," Coxe lamented.[5]

Federalists' versions of the Philadelphia violence made it appear the just deserts of a truculent, disappointed band of sordid men. While Federalists hailed the accomplishment—only twenty hours had elapsed between the approval of the Continental Congress and

---

[4] "Caution," Baltimore *Maryland Journal*, October 12, 1787. Quoted in *Essays on the Constitution* (ed. by Paul L. Ford), 328.

[5] Tench Coxe to Madison, September 28, 1787, Madison papers, *DLC*.

that of the Pennsylvania legislature—their adversaries gasped, but for another reason. Such unnatural speed, Antifederalists held, was unquestionable proof of a plot to bamboozle citizens out of ordinary caution.[6] Henceforth, Antifederalists insisted that convention calls be delayed. The roughshod tactics used in Philadelphia deserved wide publicity. Given enough time, the antifederal argument ran, the people will see the Constitution for what it really is: a "consolidating" machine designed to destroy the state governments. Thereafter, tactics of delay, albeit unco-ordinated in contrast to the efficiency of Federalist maneuvers, would characterize antifederal efforts to thwart ratification.

Gerry and Lee, observing their opponents in New York and piecing together such information as drifted their way, believed time was working to their advantage. The New England delegate privately declared the Constitution was a master plan to erect "a Government of *force* & *fraud*," with the wealth of America destined for the coffers "in Pensylvania, where the Seat of the foederal Government is proposed to be, & those who will use the greatest address in obtaining an acceptance of this despotic System, will hereafter scourge the people for their folly in adopting it." Gerry expressed his belief that the Federalists were determined "to carry it thro by Surprise," a device which made it imperative "that the Legislature of Massachusetts will not propose a Convention till the next Session, & thus give to the people an opportunity to consider of the Constitution before they are called on to adopt it."[7]

Sensing a Federalist scheme to conduct a whirlwind campaign, Lee matched speed with speed. Early in October he began writing essays which he titled "Letters of a Federal Farmer." Hamilton and Governor Clinton were already abusing each other in newspaper articles that reflected more heat than light. Although the city of New York had nine newspapers, all of their publishers except one soon fell under the sway of Federalist partisans. The lone Antifederalist, Thomas Greenleaf, left his columns open to attacks on the Constitu-

[6] *Pennsylvania Packet*, October 8, 1787; Litchfield, Connecticut, *Monitor*, October 15, 1787.
[7] Gerry to [James Warren?], October 18, 1787, Gerry papers, *DLC*.

tion; and it was his *New-York Journal* that Lee favored with his charges. In the first letter Lee hinted that an aristocratic plot had been hatched to hurry the Constitution along by suppressing open discussion of its merits. The "Federal Farmer" admitted that several state legislatures, with their paper money and legal-tender laws, had "prepared many honest men for changes in government, which otherwise they would not have thought of." But who had dreamed that the ultimate goal of a certain set of men was to destroy the state governments and form "one consolidated system"? The Federal Convention had been called to revise the Articles of Confederation, and few then suspected "that the old ship was to be destroyed, and [the people] . . . put to the alternative of embarking in the new ship presented, or being left in danger of sinking."[8]

Lee warned readers that the country was not in such an alarming state as the Federalists claimed. "It is natural for men, who wish to hasten the adoption of a measure, to tell us, now is the crisis—now is the critical moment which must be seized, or all will be lost; and to such the door against free inquiry." Lee lamented the failure of a handful of men who had been elected to the Convention to actually serve—a veiled suggestion that Patrick Henry, Willie Jones of North Carolina, and a few others might have stemmed the tide toward consolidation at Philadelphia. "Had they attended I am pretty clear that the result . . . would not have had that strong tendency to aristocracy now discernable in every part of the plan." Lee also vaguely hinted that the driving force behind the Constitution had come from city-dwelling merchants who had thrown the landed interests off their guard by talking about commercial regulations which farmers "had little or no concern about" when something far more sinister was really contemplated.

Nor was Lee alone in sounding the alarm. In Boston, the antifederal hue and cry came from the only local newspaper that was consistently antifederal, printer Edward Powar's *American Herald.*

---

[8] A hint of the importance of these essays is given by the treatment accorded them by the Federalist *Poughkeepsie Country Journal*. Lee's essays were the first lengthy articles by an opposition writer to appear there, and the whole series was published between November 14, 1787, and January 2, 1788.

Instead of acting in a blind panic, the *Herald* urged readers to consider that citizen "a TRAITOR to himself and his posterity, who shall ratify it . . . without first endeavouring to understand it." Still the Federalists tried to rush the convention call along, but their hopes of beating the calendar with a session in December were thwarted by a handful of Antifederalists in the Massachusetts House of Representatives. Dr. James Kilham of Essex said that many people suspected the Constitution "would not go down, if not suddenly pushed." A Maine delegate suggested that the Constitution be submitted directly to the town meetings, because many smaller communities "were too poor to support a delegate to the Convention." This idea must have sent chills down Federalists' spines, for they hurriedly added an amendment that provided for salary payments by the state treasury. Opposition to a January convention then ebbed. The only solace for Antifederalists was the lengthened "cooling-off" period that they deemed essential.

Weak as the antifederal vote appeared, their cause gained ground outside the state house after Gerry's explanatory letter was made public shortly after the convention date had been set. Gerry's apologia for not signing the Constitution—like Mason's "Objections"—was intended as much to persuade as to vindicate the author's conduct. "Conceiving as I did, that the liberties of America were not secured by the system," Gerry wrote, "it was my duty to oppose it." Specifically, Gerry charged that the Constitution inadequately provided for the representation of the people, that their right of election was not secure, and that the executive and legislative branches were dangerously blended. The latter mixture, Gerry explained, was caused in part by the treaty-making provisions, which armed the executive with too much influence in Congress. As for the judiciary, it "will be oppressive"; the whole system lacks "the security of a bill of rights." Attempting to rise above sectional interests, Gerry asserted that these faults "are not local, but apply equally to all the states."[9] He concluded with an indicting summary: "The constitution proposed has few if any federal features; but is rather a system

[9] Gerry's letter was widely reprinted in New England; one of its first appearances was in the Boston *American Herald*, November 5, 1787.

23

of national government." Still, rather than reject it outright, Gerry suggested that "by proper amendments, [the Constitution] may be adapted to the 'exigencies of government, and preservation of liberty.' " The final sentence was disquieting to the Federalists because it hinted that the Constitution did not have to be ratified as it stood—that amendments might be proposed in the state conventions.

Gerry took great pains to see that New England newspapers printed his letter. Henry Jackson, General Knox's confidant in Boston, became indignant as he saw much of the Federalists' hard work apparently subverted by this publicized censure. Gerry, he reported to Knox, "has done more injury to this Country by that infamous Letter than he will be able to make atonement in his whole life & by this act he has *damn'd* himself." The letter had possibly stemmed the tide of enthusiasm which had been rising steadily in their direction, and nobody could discern his motives. In fact, Jackson insisted, Gerry had promised Rufus King that he would not stir up trouble in their home state. As he wrote, Jackson seethed all the more. "*Damn him —damn him*—everything look'd well and had the most favorable appearance in this States, previous to this—and now I have doubts."[10]

However, Gerry's apologia did more than merely check the rising tide of the Constitution's acceptance in his home state. Antifederalists hailed its appearance in Boston as the first home-devised argument to influence the people noticeably. Its effectiveness seems obvious from the manner the letter was denounced by the opposition. "It is indeed possible, that our *news-paper zealots*, who extol this performance above the reach or necessity of examination, may very much lessen the majority of the people in favour of it," the Federalist "Observer" noted. Virginia congressman Edward Carrington heard his friends lament the effectiveness of the letter, and surmised that Gerry's intention was "to work some probable Mischief." How much damage Gerry had done was still uncertain, "but the circumstance occasions alarm to the Friends of the measure."

Boston Federalists began to prepare their slate for the state convention even though the letter continued to rankle them. Men who

[10] Henry Jackson to General Henry Knox, November 5, 1787, Jackson papers, *BPL.*

24

had been friendly to Gerry since Revolutionary days and who had helped his rise in politics a decade earlier now turned their backs as Gerry announced that he was a candidate for the convention. Gerry "has gone for the *Vote*, as this measure will either *damn* him, or place him at the head of a *restless and uneasy* junto in the government." If some old friends scorned him, Gerry took refuge with James Warren, James Winthrop, and other Antifederalists who seemed overwhelmed in the environs of Boston, but they expected the western counties to supply allies for the state convention.

Thus, less than a month after the Federal Convention had made public its work, the Antifederalists and their opponents had drawn up their strategies. That which was mercury to the Federalists was molasses to the Antifederalists. At the top echelons of both groups, men thought in terms of days and weeks, with the clock or calendar cast either as friend or villain.

To the south, Mason and Randolph voiced their opposition with varying degrees of animosity. Mason had scribbled some "Objections" in Philadelphia, which now appeared in pamphlet form. The flaws Mason saw ranged from a failure to include a bill of rights to the omission of checks on discriminatory shipping laws. Randolph watered down his protests, complained that the second-convention idea had found little support, and expressed hope that amendments might somehow be made in ratifying conventions. Despite its innocuous tone, Randolph took three months to make the letter public. With braver hearts, Pennsylvania Antifederalists tried to turn their scapegoats into heroes by publishing "An Address . . . to their Constituents" which claimed that Federalists were hell-bent on ratifying with a minimum of public discussion.[11] The essay charged that city-dwelling Federalists had consistently ignored the desires of farmers at every stage of the ratification process. As friends of the Pennsylvania Constitution of 1776, they were alarmed that the Federalist party as it coalesced was being composed of undemocratic elements. Caution, they advocated, was necessary since the proposed Constitution "would in its consequence affect or perhaps annihilate our own [state] constitution" and would raise taxes.

[11] *Pennsylvania Evening Herald*, October 4, 1787.

To allay fears created by the "Address," Philadelphia Federalists held a public meeting where James Wilson verbally flayed the seceding sixteen for their obstinacy. Antifederalists raged about direct taxes and a bill of rights without cause, Wilson charged, for the Constitution was one of expressed powers. What the framers left unmentioned was done so intentionally, to leave unmolested wide areas within the jurisdiction of the state governments where they belonged.

Wilson's argument was masterfully conceived, and so delighted Federalists that they never tired of quoting it. But in the faraway Maine country, newspaper publisher Thomas B. Wait read Wilson's speech without being converted to the Federalist cause. Some of Wilson's points were good, Wait conceded, "and some, in my opinion, were very good for nothing." Wilson had not convinced Wait that the states would retain their "right of Sovereignty," and only "this will secure them from the encroachments of *Almighty* President and Congress." Wait also deemed desirable a bill of rights.[12]

The Maine editor had touched on the two items that were to be the chief issues of the ratification campaign in every section of the country. Declaim as they would against the corruption of state officials and insist as they would that a bill of rights was an extra and needless trapping, the Federalists always found themselves on the defensive when the debate turned to the remaining powers of states or to the necessity for some guarantees of personal liberties. No matter how much of the lawyer's logic the Wilson speech retained in rebuttal, the amendments proposed in the state ratifying conventions and those ultimately added to the Constitution proved that the Federalists were vulnerable on these key issues.

The Federalists, armed with examples of the weaknesses of state government, never grew weary of pointing out the corruption of local politicians. Who were the first to take the field against the Constitution, their argument ran, but the caviling placemen who feared their jobs would be lost? Was this right—the right to be governed by corrupt officials—the vaunted right that states wanted to

[12] Thomas B. Wait to George Thatcher, November 22, 1787, Thatcher (the name is also spelled "Thacher") papers, *BPL*.

preserve? "Away ye spirits of discord! Ye narrow views! Ye local politics! Ye selfish patriots, would damn your country, for a six penny duty! In the present state of America, local views are general ruin!" It was time to oust "many pettifogging antifederal scribblers in offices of great public trust and confidence," a Federalist writer warned. "Put it out of the power of any factious penny-wise politician to mar the welfare of our country (for the sake of their private interest and fear of their consequence being lessened)."[13] In New Jersey, where antifederal opposition proved to be little more than token resistance, state officials were besieged with vehemence. "These insects and worms are seen on their own dunghill. There are minds whose narrow vision can look over the concerns of a state or town, but cannot extend their short vision to Continental concerns." Barbs at the entrenched officials of New York were gleefully hailed in New Jersey and Connecticut, where the imposts collected by their larger sister state were regarded as a means of making her wealthy at their expense. "Shun, my countrymen, the sham patriot, however dignified [*sic*], who bids you *distrust the Convention*," a Hartford Federalist advised. "Mark him as a dangerous member of society . . . Fix your eyes on those who love you . . . on those whose views are not bounded by the town or country which they may represent, nor by the state in which they reside, nor even by the union—their philanthropy embraces the interest of all nations."

Privately, the Federalists were no less insistent that state interests must give way to the national good. The petulant Benjamin Rush of Philadelphia was no less restrained. "The new federal government like a new continental wagon will overset our state dung cart with all its dirty contents (reverend and irreverent) and thereby restore order and happiness to Pennsylvania." To a man, the Federalists agreed that "the monsterous system of State governments" must be shorn of much of their power. Only in this fashion could they "make the Revolution a blessing instead of a curse."[14]

For their part, the Antifederalists saw a counterrevolution shaping that would give them the curse of a consolidated national govern-

---

[13] "Cato," Philadelphia *Independent Gazetteer*, November 17, 1787.
[14] David Humphreys to Alexander Hamilton, September 1, 1787, *DHC*, IV, 269.

ment. In his "Letters of A Federal Farmer," Lee seemed to be disarmingly nonpartisan, but he subtly injected a casual phrase—"there are many good things in the proposed constitution"—before a damaging thrust. "This subject of consolidating the states is new: and because forty or fifty men have agreed in a system, to suppose the good sense of this country . . . must adopt it without examination . . . is truly humiliating." Lee's technique was to begin a paragraph with a sentence like a zephyr, then conclude with a tornado. "The guards against those evils we have experienced in some states in legislation are valuable indeed," but the Constitution goes to the other extreme and would deprive states of their taxing power, so that they will be "annihilated."

The appeal to state pride was emotional, and to a people who had long identified themselves as Virginians or New Yorkers rather than as Americans, it doubtless had some effect. But arguments based on the taxpayers' pocketbooks probably struck home with more force. "The phantom of sovereignty" left to the states by the Constitution would lead to two sets of taxgatherers, readers of a Richmond newspaper were warned. "Unhappy situation where two rival excisemen battle at your doors for precedence in seizing these spoils!" Are you willing, the Antifederalist asked, "to see the state of Virginia dwindle into the insignificance of a town corporate"?[15] Another predicted that a greedy Congress would grab every source of revenue, and "will not have as much to spare for the separate states to collect as Lazarus picked up of the fragments from the rich man's table." The citizen who favored the Constitution was helping divide "the public cake to the last crum[b]."

No Antifederalist was more certain that the Constitution would be the engine of destruction for state rights than Luther Martin. Martin harangued the Maryland legislature and private audiences with the same dire forebodings. The object of the Federalists, he warned, was "the total abolition and destruction of all state governments," with the subsequent elevation "far above the common herd of mankind."[16] In truth, the acerbic Martin continued, the Consti-

15 "Cato Uticensis," Richmond *Virginia Independent Chronicle,* October 17, 1787.

tution was "neither wholly federal, nor wholly national—but a strange hotch-potch of both." It was federal enough to deceive the "unsuspecting multitude," and so constructed that once ratified its promoters could drop appearances "to render it wholly and entirely a national government." Not far behind Martin in hoisting storm signals was Robert Yates, the New York delegate who had also left the Federal Convention in a black mood. Yates insisted that the "general welfare" clause would enable the federal government to take over "the most trifling concerns of every state" under a benevolent guise.[17] "In a word, the new constitution will prove finally to dissolve all the power of the several state legislatures, and destroy the rights and liberties of the people."

These fears of an all-powerful national government were not the Macedonian cries of a people merely seeking to preserve old forms for the sake of tradition. Rather, the concern over the status of state governments represented a genuine apprehension that local matters could not be handled justly by some distant tribune. An antifederal poet dwelt on a tender point when he wrote:

> *When* thirteen *states are moulded into* one
> *Your rights are vanish'd and your honors gone;*
> *The form of Freedom shall alone remain,*
> *As Rome had Senators when she hugg'd the chain.*[18]

Richard Henry Lee had been among the first to note the immense size of the country, a factor he asserted as propably incompatible with a concentrated national government based on republican principles. With a territory extending from the Maine country to Georgia, Lee had argued in his "Letter No. II," the remote regions would never be represented adequately. He insisted that the two main features of a free government—equality of representation and trial by jury—would be demolished under the proposed constitution. "It would be

---

[16] *Maryland Journal*, March 21, 1788, quoted in Ford, *Essays on the Constitution*, 366–67.

[17] "Sydney II," *New York Journal*, June 14, 1788, quoted in *ibid.*, 313–14.

[18] Charleston *South Carolina State Gazette*, January 28, 1788, quoted in L. M. Miner, *Our Rude Forefathers*, 204.

impossible to collect a representation of the parts of the country five, six, and seven hundred miles from the seat of government."

In New York, Yates took the theme and painted a doleful picture of that day when the United States would have not three, but thirty million souls. Could such a vast empire elect representatives who were known to the people and who could "speak their sentiments without their becoming so numerous as to be incapable of transacting public business?" He said that in a far-flung republic it would be practically impossible to call wayward congressmen "to account for their misconduct, or to prevent their abuse of power." Another critic of the Constitution predicted a membership of 3,733 in the House of Representatives by 1887.[19]

An even more disconsolate view was spread before readers of the Boston *Massachusetts Gazette*. "Large and consolidate empires may indeed dazzle the eyes of a distant spectator with their splendour, but if examined more nearly are always found to be full of misery," an Antifederalist observed. Playing on sectional prejudices, New Englanders were told that people in the southern states were "more dissolute in their manners, and less industrious, than in colder countries. A degree of severity is, therefore, necessary with one which would cramp the spirit of the other . . . It is impossible for one code of laws to suit Georgia and Massachusetts."[20]

It was only a step from this proposition to another early target of the Antifederalists, the proposed district for the national capital. The Constitution provided for control of the ten-square-mile area by Congress. Writing under the pseudonym "Cato," Governor George Clinton ripped into this seemingly innocuous provision. Since the president would have the powers of a monarch, it was certain that a court would be established there marked by all the trappings of a royal entourage—including idleness, pride, flattery, "the thirst of riches without labor . . . but above all, the perpetual ridicule of virtue." Hints that an area along the Susquehanna River was favored by leading Federalists fed the fires of antifederal suspicion. A northern

[19] "Tullius," Philadelphia *Freeman's Journal*, October 10, 1787.
[20] "Agrippa," Boston *Massachusetts Gazette*, December 3, 1787, quoted in Ford, *Essays on the Constitution*, 64.

30

writer predicted that a national capital would attract "all the men of genius and wealth," making it the "center of revenue, and of business, which the extremes will be drained to supply." New Hampshire citizens were said to be alarmed by "the idea of a 'Federal city' . . . what a tremendous cost must this be—and to be walled in too, and these walls are to be as high as those of Jericho." Where the walled-city story first originated was anybody's guess, but it gave the Constitution an Oriental flavor among its opponents. The district would have to be carved from existing states, Pennsylvanian John Nicholson observed, "so that we shall be parcelled out to nabobs."

The Federalists had undoubtedly underestimated the attachment of citizens to their states, either out of sentiment or self-interest. Speculation on the federal district was ludicrous, but the concern over state sovereignty was not. Hamilton became aware of the problem when the first *Federalist* came from the pen of "Publius." Noting the charge that the United States was "of too great extent for any general system," Hamilton presented the issue in black and white. Either the Constitution was adopted or the Union would split into fragments with "the certain evils, and the probable dangers, to which every State will be exposed from its dissolution." Another supporter of the Constitution, less bent toward polarized arguments, appealed for a spirit of Union born out of "*amity, and mutual deference and concession.*" Washington was reluctantly dragged into the controversy when his private letter with a gloomy prediction became publicly circulated. If the Constitution was not ratified, Washington speculated, the Union would soon fall apart. "General government is now suspended by a thread." Gleeful Federalists urged editors to reprint the letter, even though Washington complained that printing it would be an invasion of his privacy.[21]

To their opponents' chagrin, Federalists found that associating Washington's name with the Constitution was an incontestable endorsement. It was common knowledge that he would be called forth to serve as the nation's first president. "The *Foederalists* should be distinguished hereafter by the name of WASHINGTONIANS, and

[21] Washington to Madison, February 5, 1788. Fitzpatrick, *Writings of Washington*, XXIX, 404.

31

the *Antifoederalists* by the name of SHAYITES, in every part of the United States," a New Jersey newspaper propagandized. Faced with such tactics, Antifederalists began to question Washington's judgment. A New York partisan denied that Washington or Franklin was a demi-god, or that anything those two agreed upon "would be such as all good men ought to approve, and none but bad men would disapprove." A nod from these patriots was not an unassailable argument for the Constitution, since even the best men could err.

An unescapable truth was, however, that the people trusted Washington. His endorsement of the Constitution was an argument that Antifederalists could never surmount. A back-country editor who was not a friend of the Constitution admitted this. "The honest and uninformed *freemen* of America entertain the same opinion of those two gentlemen as do European *slaves* of their Princes,—'*that they can do no wrong.*' " "Grate use has bin made of his name to deceive the people & make them content," was another antifederal judgment, "& much time has bin spent in our Legislative bodyes, & sacred pulpets, in the most fulsome & sickish praise & adulation of Warshington."[22] The charm of Washington's name sometimes drove the Antifederalists to despair, and, consequently, in defense they too fell back on "great names." Lee, Randolph, Mason, Henry, Gerry, and Governor Clinton, "who reprobate the system," were cited as equally respectable public figures. Like the martyrs of old, they were now bearing abuse because "they have come forward to protect" the people "from the chains forged for them in secret conclave." Still the Antifederalists must have squirmed when a smug opponent closed his case with the quip: "Well, Washington is for it."

Amidst a multitude of frustrations, the Antifederalists stumbled upon one oversight in the Constitution that bore the appearance of an Achilles' heel. This was the failure of the Federal Convention to include a bill of rights in the Constitution. Mason was the first to sound the alarm outside of the state house in Philadelphia, when he began to list his objections with, "There is no Declaration of Rights." Mason passed the infectious slogan on to the Antifederalists in Philadelphia, who assiduously promoted the idea that the failure to in-

[22] William Manning, *The Key of Libberty*, 56.

32

clude a bill of rights was not an oversight, but a studied bit of
Federalist deception.

In time the Federalists grudgingly admitted their tactical error
in the Federal Convention of scuttling a bill of rights. Conversations
in countinghouses and on courtyard squares proved that this issue,
above all others, was vital to the public. Wilson's counterargument
that all rights not vested in the national government were reserved
to the states was ineffective, particularly in the western counties,
where logic lost much of its force in rough-and-tumble debate.
Friends of the Constitution labored under an unnecessary burden, a
southerner noted, "as some of the greatest men I ever knew have
objected to the government for no other reason but because it was
not buttoned with a Bill of Rights."[23]

Only in a rare moment did an Antifederalist admit himself un-
sympathetic with the bill-of-rights issue. Silas Lee shared James
Winthrop's disdain for the Constitution, but he could not follow his
fellow Yankee's reasoning that a bill of rights was essential. "I am in
doubts whether such a Bill would not of itself make the Constitution
far more dangerous than it now is," Lee wrote, for a bill of rights
"would give up the controlment at least of every right not expressly
granted away, [and] instead of lessening the powers of Congress
such a Bill would actually enlarge them." Another branch of the
Lee family tree, however, found that the bill-of-rights issue possessed
the strength of gnarled oak. Richard Henry Lee, writing to his old
friend Samuel Adams in Massachusetts, urged the venerated patriot
to consider the calamities that might befall the nation if the Constitution had no bill of rights.[24]

Try as they did, the Federalists never succeeded in convincing the
populace that a bill of rights was a needless trapping. From the outset, Hamilton condemned the howl for a bill of rights as "the stale
bait for popularity at the expense of the public good." But Hamilton's verbose effort to dispel the objection in the concluding issues
of the *Federalist* fell on a disbelieving public. The spirit of compro-

[23] William Pierce to St. George Tucker, September 28, 1787, quoted in *American Historical Review*, III, 315.
[24] Lee to Samuel Adams, October 27, 1787, Ballagh, *Letters of Lee*, II, 457-58.

mise that prompted the Federalists to meet their opponents halfway on this issue undoubtedly won them much belated support. If a bill of rights were added to the Constitution, one ardent Antifederalist promised to "fall down, and worship it." When leading Federalists eventually conceded that a bill of rights should be added to the Constitution, the ground was cut from beneath the most appealing issue exploited by the Antifederalists.

The Federalists were not inclined to capitulate easily, however. Months before the Federal Convention adjourned, General Knox predicted that if the Convention proposed "an efficient National government," their offering "would be ridiculed in the same [way] as was the ark of old, while building by Noah. . . . Demagogues and vicious characters will oppose for a while. But reason will at length triumph."[25] The adjective "wicked," which rolled easily from some New England tongues, was often considered synonymous with antifederalism. Antifederalists were only once removed from anarchists, "who never were for any government but such as their ignorant and wicked hearts" had conceived.

Jefferson may have read with some wonderment a Federalist correspondent's view of the opposition. The scheming Antifederalists were determined to discredit the Constitution, come what may. "These subtil, dextrous, long-train'd, Systematical opponents well knowing the Constitution recommended must be approv'd of in toto, or not at all, therefore would seem to approve of it as highly as any of the most Zealous for it," Christopher Gadsden reported.[26] These hypocrites tempered their approval "only with an *All But*, which *But* alter'd wou'd gain they wou'd pretend universal Satisfaction, that it might be defer'd for that mighty reasonable *But* to another Convention hoping that will never happen & so the Bubble burst of Course."

Gadsden was exaggerating, but he had discerned a cardinal point in the patchwork Antifederalist program. The second convention call, which Randolph had sounded in the dying moments of what he hoped to be the first, found leading Antifederalists receptive in

[25] Knox to Mercy Warren, May 30, 1787, *MHS, Collections*, Vol. 73, p. 295.
[26] Christopher Gadsden to Jefferson, October 30, 1787, 12 *Jefferson Papers* 297.

RICHARD HENRY LEE

OBSERVATIONS

LEADING TO A FAIR EXAMINATION

OF THE

SYSTEM OF GOVERNMENT,

PROPOSED BY THE LATE

CONVENTION;

AND TO SEVERAL ESSENTIAL AND NECES-
SARY ALTERATIONS IN IT.

IN A NUMBER OF

LETTERS

FROM THE

FEDERAL FARMER TO THE REPUBLICAN.

◄◄◄◄◄◄◄◄◄◄◄◄◄◄-◊-►►►►►►►►►►►►

PRINTED IN THE YEAR M,DCC,LXXXVII.

TITLE PAGE OF LEE'S
"Letters from the Federal Farmer"

every state. Ridiculing the Federalist argument that "such an agreement could not be again be produced even by the same men," their adversaries insisted that a second convention could perfect the Constitution. If the plan was bold, the times seemed to cry for audacity. The people would not awaken to such a cry unless the Constitution as it stood was discredited. Seeds of doubt had to be sown—and soon.

☆ III ☆

The Antifederalists Attack

I N MID-JULY, 1787, the possibility of a second convention was discussed among Federal Convention delegates when matters seemed
to be at a crisis. Then Edward Rutledge pleaded for a compromise
that would keep the Confederation together "a little longer, hoping
that another Convention will supply our omissions, [rather] than
abandon everything to hazard." Although Federalists soon dismissed
the idea as impracticable, Randolph decided the second-convention
notion had merit. With little urging from Mason, Gerry, and a few
others, the second-convention scheme became a firm antifederal tenet.
Federalists discerned in this effort a conspiracy to destroy the Constitution by operating behind the façade of a drive for amendments.[1]
"It would be difficult, if not impossible," one Federalist charged, "to
point out the difference between a public attempt to amend this new
system, and a secret design to destroy it."

Federalists were vexed, but so, too, was Randolph. Upon his return from Philadelphia he began to have misgivings. Meanwhile,
the second-convention spark transmitted to others had lessened in
Randolph's own breast. The mercurial young governor lacked confidence in his judgment. With little effort he might have helped
wield the Antifederalists into a united force working for a revising
convention. Instead, Randolph lapsed into a hemming-and-hawing
course of nonaction.

So far as Virginia was concerned, the matter was already out of
Randolph's hands. Lee eagerly seized leadership. "The plan for us
to pursue will be to propose the necessary amendments, and express
our willingness to adopt it with the amendments; and to suggest the
calling of a new convention for the purpose of considering them,"
Lee confided.[2] Patrick Henry, Mason, and a few lieutenants in the

---

[1] "A State Soldier," *Virginia Independent Chronicle*, February 6, 1788.
[2] Lee to Randolph, October 16, 1787, *LCC*, VIII, 658.

Virginia House of Delegates squelched Federalist protests to guide such a measure through the legislature. Ostensibly a call for a state convention, the bill as finally approved also provided expenses for delegates to a second federal convention, and other states were asked to join in an implicit endorsement of a second convention. It was the first clear-cut Antifederalist victory.

While Randolph procrastinated, Lee marched into the lion's den with the demand for another convention. In a letter to Washington, Lee declared it was "among the first distresses that have happened to me in my life, that I find myself compelled . . . to doubt about the new System." The prospect of a second convention appealed to him as the best means of securing amendments that would "give security to the just rights of human nature, and better secure from injury the discordant interests of the different parts of this Union." To soften Washington's opposition to another convention, Lee explained that with "so great a part of the business well done already," the necessary amendments "could not long employ another Convention."

As the campaign wore on, it became obvious that a second federal convention was the rock to which all the Antifederalists' hopes were anchored. In the demand there was implicit criticism of every feature of the Constitution as it stood. The caution against hasty ratification and the clamor for a bill of rights were meaningless gestures, in the eyes of leading Antifederalists, if another meeting were not called to implement their program. Thus a direct attack on the Federal Convention seemed propitious as well as expedient.

The tone of the antifederal attack was set in the city where the Convention had taken place. Colonel Eleazer Oswald, a swashbuckling editor with friends in New York political circles, quickly made his Philadelphia *Independent Gazetteer*, or *Chronicle of Freedom*, the organ of the antifederal offensive. As the leading metropolis of the young nation, Philadelphia boasted eleven weekly and daily newspapers during the ratification struggle, while New York and Boston combined had only seventeen. Oswald's antifederal sympathies were supported for a while by two allied newspapers, the *Freeman's Journal* and the *Pennsylvania Evening Herald*. In New York, Oswald also maintained a business alliance with Thomas Greenleaf,

37

who brought his *New-York Journal* into the antifederal camp. These four newspapers, along with Edward Powar's Boston *American Herald*, formed the pillars of Antifederalist journalism during the ratification struggle.

Colonel Oswald flung his newspaper's columns open to both factions in the weeks immediately following the adjournment of the Federal Convention. By mid-October, however, the *Independent Gazetteer* began favoring the antifederal writers with columns of space while the opposition began receiving sparse coverage. Not more than a dozen other newspapers in the entire country could be classed as avowedly antifederal, but these ranged from the Maine woods to tidewater North Carolina, and their editors relied on Oswald's bombastic journalism for political guidance. Moved to action by the points queried in the "Federal Farmer's" letters, Oswald's contributors pounced on the call for another convention. Why did the Federalists insist that the Constitution had to be accepted without alteration? "Centinel" asked. The Federal Convention could not have known the wishes of the people, since its business was conducted in secrecy. High-pressure tactics, "Centinel" asserted, caused many good men in the Convention "to give their sanction to this system of despotism."[3]

The only way to curb the work of the *"artful* and *designing"* Federalists, "Centinel" urged, was to call a second convention. Public discussion would serve a useful purpose, for "a future general Convention being in possession of the objections," could make the necessary amendments. Other Antifederalist writers joined the attack, scorning the assertion that amendments were inadmissible. Vexed by these screeds, Robert Morris assured Washington that the Antifederalists were "not Numerous altho they fill the News Papers every day." As the weeks passed, the antifederal writers repeatedly pricked their opponents with barbs labeled "CONSPIRACY" and insisted that the Constitution was being foisted on the citizenry through "systematic fraud and deception."

Periodically embarrassed by the connotation of their party label, some Antifederalists became etymologists. Using the pseudonym "None of the Well-Born Conspirators," one such penman insisted

[3] "Centinel IV," Philadelphia *Independent Gazetteer*, November 30, 1787.

that "federalism" was derived from "foedus," meaning a league entered into by various groups for the mutual advantage of all. To identify supporters of the Constitution with that name was a great abuse of language "for our modern federalists . . . evidently aim at nothing but the elevation and aggrandizement of a few over the many." The federalism of 1787–88, he continued, was a league against the liberty of the people, "that is in plain terms a conspiracy; and this is the fifth signification of the word Foedus, given by Ainsworth in his excellent Latin dictionary."[4]

To citizens who were still on the fence because of discouraging experiences under the Confederation and doubts about the Constitution, the conspiracy charge had meaning. A Massachusetts politician regretted that the Federal Convention had so swiftly disposed of the Articles of Confederation, contrary to its instructions, with a contemptuous wave of the hand. "But altho compossd [*sic*] of the first characters in the Continent I, by no means, think it the less unwarrantable on that account—when Officers throw aside their commissions, or Servants their orders, then the liberties of the people depend entirely upon the humour of the one, & the property of the Master on the uncertain conduct of the other."

Despite widespread criticism of the Articles of Confederation by the Federalists, the more temperate Antifederalists took their cue from Lee and admitted that conditions under the Articles had been less than salutary. Reviewing the situation when the Federal Convention was barely under way, the Philadelphia *Freeman's Journal* paid homage to the Confederation as a device "made for the temporary purposes of the war . . . as wisely drawn as the then situation in the country would permit." In time it became apparent that "the confederation, that appeared so perfect in its original state," was nothing more than "a loose, incomplete agreement," and that Congress "may declare every thing, and can do nothing." A more forthright Antifederalist admitted that few states had shown magnanimity in surrendering their power to collect duties. "If the continental treasury had been so far assisted, as to have enabled us to pay the interest on our foreign debt, possibly we should have heard little,

[4] Philadelphia *Freeman's Journal*, April 23, 1788.

very little, about a new system of government," he suggested.[5]

But antifederal extremists were loathe to admit that the Confederation contained irreparable weaknesses. "For years past, the harpies of power have been industriously inculcating the idea that all our difficulties proceed from the impotency of Congress," "Centinel" charged. The real cause of hard times was wartime devastation and excessive postwar imports of luxuries that drained America of hard money and increased foreign debts. Regulation of commerce and treaty powers could make Congress a virile agency, but in the Constitution these items were clothed with despotic powers. "The gilded bait conceals corrosives that will eat up their whole substance" unless the people bestirred themselves. "Two new articles," James Winthrop observed, could mend everything. One would give Congress a "limited revenue . . . with a right to collect it," and the other "a limited right to regulate our intercourse with foreign nations." The idea that the Confederation might be saved by nailing these two planks on its battered sides died hard with many Antifederalists. Of course, Federalists winced when the opposition suggested that the Confederation might be rejuvenated. "Conciliator" claimed that Antifederalists only harped about a second convention but offered no positive program of their own. "Where is the man, who after having drawn a prize, would put his ticket into the wheel again?"

Unlike many Antifederalist writers who matched sneer with sneer, Richard Henry Lee made his points by delicate concessions. He neither claimed that the Confederation might be saved nor held that a second convention could unravel all the good in the Constitution. Federalists had insisted that state conventions could not alter or amend the Constitution before adopting it. This idea of all or nothing, Lee insisted, was inadmissible. Until the state ratifying conventions had discussed amendments, the matter was worth considering; and if the state conventions "cannot agree in amendments, it will then be an important question before the people of the United States, whether they will adopt or not the system proposed in its present form." Dispassionately, Lee charted a course for the several states. Let each state convention leisurely debate the Constitution

[5] "Alfred," Boston *American Herald*, December 31, 1787.

candidly, determined to "examine coolly every article, clause, and word in the system proposed." Lee dropped a few hints as to what amendments this procedure would cover—internal taxation, the militia, "and the want of a more perfect bill of rights." Then Lee threw in his clinching argument. "I think the honest and substantial part of the community will wish to see this system altered."

Contrast Lee's gentle persuasion with the strident tones of Mercy Warren's scorching pamphlet issued a few months later. Railing against the "partizans of monarchy" who led the Federalists in their "fraudulent designs," she warned against the "deceptive appearance of unanimity." She alluded to the Federal Convention as "the fraudulent usurpation at Philadelphia" and called for "the most prudent exertions for a new general Convention, who may vest adequate powers in Congress, for all national purposes, without annihilating the individual governments, and drawing blood from every pore by taxes, impositions and illegal restrictions."[6] Tenaciously the Antifederalists grasped the second-convention straw as the *sine qua non* of their makeshift program.

To gain popular approval for the second-convention proposal, Antifederalists worked overtime at undermining Federalist reputations. They poured torrents of abuse on the Federalists, insinuating that theirs was the party of aristocratic, would-be royalists. The charge had enough basis in fact to be damaging. During the winter of 1786–87, Madison discerned a "propensity towards Monarchy . . . in some leading minds." However, most citizens would probably prefer "the lesser evil of a partition of the Union into three more practicable and energetic Governments." Respectable New Englanders had toasted the Bishop of Osnaburgh in "half jest, half earnest" as their second choice (following Washington) for an American throne.

John Adams' *Defence of the Constitutions of the United States* was published in the midst of grave doubts about the maxim, "*Vox populi, vox dieu.*" "Democracy never has been and never can be so desirable as aristocracy, or monarchy," Adams wrote. Adams' yankee Calvinism expressed itself in an innate distrust of human nature and

---

[6] Mercy Otis Warren, *Observations on the New Constitution* (Boston, 1788), *Old South Leaflets*, No. 226.

in an exaltation of property as the means of creating a group capable of public service. No "well ordered commonwealth ever existed" without a nobility, and Americans would in time create one. "We have believed that the Citizens of the United States were better than the rest of the world," a disillusioned veteran told Washington, "and that they could be managed in Society without compulsion."[7]

Ultimately, there were warnings posted in the Federal Convention against this trend. John Dickinson foresaw that "when this plan goes forth, it will be attacked by the popular leaders. Aristocracy will be the watchword; the Shibboleth among its adversaries."[8] Luther Martin called the Constitution "a mutilated unsistematick Imitation of the british Constitution," that would offend the people who "snuff Tyranny in every tainted Gale." The American plowman liked the government he now lived under, which was "as energetick as . . . ought to be framed." George Mason had rushed from the state house as fast as his gouty legs could carry him to denounce the threatened aristocracy. His objections included the prediction that the Constitution would erect at the outset a "moderate aristocracy." From that point, Mason bristled, the Constitution would evolve into either a monarchy or a corrupt, tyrannical aristocracy. "It will most probably vibrate some years between the two," he pessimistically observed, "and then terminate in the one or the other."

So the Antifederalists seized upon the "monarchy and aristocracy" cry with enthusiasm. It stirred the emotions of a people long taught to hate kings and lords. A Boston wheelwright or two must have seen Mercy Warren's admonition to infatuated Federalists that monarchy appealed only to those "too much corrupted by luxury, avarice, and a passion for pleasure," but not to honest Americans. The solid yeomen farmers of Massachusetts were told to eschew advice from those who by "chicanery, intrigue, and false colouring . . . plume themselves, more on their education and abilities, than their political, patriotic, or private virtues." A ruffled Rufus King complained that "a distrust of men of property or Education" had "a more powerful

[7] David Humphreys to Washington, January 20, 1787, *DHC*, IV, 64.
[8] 4 Farrand 27–28.

Effect upon the minds of our Opponents than any specific Objections against the Constitution."[9]

Richard Henry Lee's calm analysis of the factions interested in ratification came as a gentle breeze amidst a hurricane of abuse. And, because Lee had a good dramatic sense that led him to underplay his part, he brought points home with force. In his fifth "Letter," which became a primer for the Antifederalists, Lee counseled caution in the ratification process because of dangers arising "from the conduct and views of two very unprincipled parties in the United States—two fires, between which the honest and substantial people have long found themselves situated." One group was composed of debt-burdened, lawless men like those who joined Captain Shays. The other party had fewer, "but more dangerous men." Without bombastic language, Lee declared that the latter group was motivated by avarice. Their goal was simple: the command of all power and property. They were not satisfied with the libertarian status quo. These men, Lee said, "are called aristocrates [*sic*], m[onarch]ites, &c. &c." On the middle ground stood most of the people, neither debt-burdened nor unhappy with republican institutions, "and not aiming at immense fortunes, offices, and power." The outbreaks of 1786 had furnished the aristocrats with a pretext for political action in 1787, and they were busy promoting the Constitution. "The fact is, these aristocrats support and hasten the adoption of the proposed constitution, merely because they think it is a stepping stone to their favorite object." Lee's innuendo needed little elaboration. He was referring to their alleged desire for a king.

Thus Lee warned citizens against pellmell ratification after a cursory examination. While haste was advised by "licentious, assuming, and overbearing men," Lee called for wariness. "I consider the field of enquiry just opened," he said. A second convention was the solution that appealed to virtuous, republican-minded men everywhere. With disarming frankness, Lee admitted that the Antifederalists had been overzealous, but not to the degree that their opponents had been. Imprudent men had already closed debate in the Pennsyl-

[9] Rufus King to J. Madison, January 20, 1788, Madison papers, *DLC*.

vania legislature by rash proceedings. It was rumored that high-handed Federalists had attempted to throttle opposition newspapers in Boston, and in Philadelphia the leading antifederal newspaper accused *"high-flying tools, pigmies and tiffanies of power"* of canceling subscriptions out of political malice. "The very attempts create suspicions, that those who make them have secret views," Lee added.

When the Antifederalists wearied of the aristocracy charge, they had another accusation of equal tenor. This secondary assault was directed toward the Society of the Cincinnati, an organization for officers in the Revolutionary army that had more European trappings than some of its members cared to admit. The handful of prominent military men amongst the Antifederalists were indeed bitterly critical of their quondam tentmates. While the complaints about an aristocratic conspiracy at some times smacked of campaign oratory, the attacks leveled at the Cincinnati were based on real apprehensions. Much of the feeling against the Cincinnati was summarized in bitter retrospect by Mercy Warren. Ordinary citizens were "dissatisfied with the high pretensions of the officers of the army, whose equality of condition previous to the war, was, with few exceptions, in the same grade with themselves." The airs assumed by men who had recently held scythes or pounded anvils were obnoxious, she went on, and it was suspected that the Cincinnati would join with "several other classes of men" to erect a government "too splendid for the taste and professions of Americans."[10] There was a germ of truth in her rancor. The society, founded in 1783, nurtured wartime associations in a spirit of camaraderie, with the grandest plowman-soldier of them all—Washington—as the nominal chief. Foreseeably, the Cincinnati soon agitated politically for wartime promises of half-pay for life. Congress, in an attempt to pacify the veterans, substituted the promise of a lump-sum grant of five years' full pay, but lacked the funds to make the so-called commutation meaningful. Neither veterans nor taxpayers were happy with the measure.

Disenchanted with the Cincinnati, Governor Clinton predicted trouble when he stalked out of the New York chapter of the society

[10] Mercy Otis Warren, *History of the Rise, Progress and Termination of the American Revolution*, III, 359.

after serving as its vice-president. At approximately the same time, diligent Cincinnati members in Connecticut promoted a scheme in the state legislature to convert their pensions into a single final payment. The howls of protest resulted in a convention held in March, 1784, where the commutation bill was vehemently denounced as an effort to create "orders of Peerage and Knighthood." The controversy was reduced to its simplest terms: farmers were to pay their taxes so that the Cincinnati could feed on their vitals. A critic-poet entered the fray with a quip.

> *Forbear noble statesmen give up your estates,*
> *And establish Cincinnati by paying your rates.*

A Massachusetts legislative committee investigated the society and reported that its existence was "unjustifiable" and "may be dangerous."

By 1784 the storm centering around the society reached such proportions that the Rhode Island legislature threatened to disfranchise its members. Similar rumblings in Virginia made Washington threaten to resign from the society unless it toned down its caste-system aspect. When the Cincinnati recommended the abolition of their hereditary membership rule, some fears were allayed. Aedanus Burke of South Carolina wrote a stinging attack, *Consideration on the Order of the Cincinnati*, in 1783. "Burke's address has sounded the alarm, and the Order, however innocent the plan . . . is thought to contain dangerous designs, pregnant with mischief," lamented General Nathaniel Greene.[11]

Burke's wrath shifted from the Cincinnati to the Constitution in 1787. Another civilian headed along the same route was Gerry, who had often voiced his alarm over the society's activities. Late in 1785, Gerry told John Adams that "there are no parties in America, but such as are produced by clashing Interests . . . [although] the Cincinnati indeed may be considered as an Exception." The indefatigable promoter of the society's business was General Knox, who used his franking privilege to keep the society's news circulating. Shays's Rebellion had shocked the corpulent former bookseller to the mar-

---

[11] Greene to Joseph Reed, May 14, 1784, W. B. Reed, *Life and Correspondence of Joseph Reed*, II, 409.

row. Trying to sooth Mrs. Warren, he assured her that "mad democracy" had caused "reason Law, and patriotism" to flee from every state legislature. "Granted says candor, but the remedy? pardon me, the convention is sitting—and shall one of the cincinnati presume to give his opinion?" Knox knew what would correct the evils—"an efficient National government."

Some envy may have been mixed with the accusations hurled at the Cincinnati, for they represented an entrenched elite with social positions or business connections in the leading cities. Was an impartial judgment rendered? A foreign observer, well schooled in the intrigues of vested interests, looked on the society as a body intent upon destroying the Confederation. They, along with the public creditors, were the aristocrats (the French chargé d'affaires in New York reported) who desired a national government that could pay its obligations. While the Convention was sitting, Monsieur Otto sent on further word, assuring the Quai d'Orsay that these two groups wished an amalgamation of the states into a consolidated government. They would elevate to a throne "the gallant Washington with all the powers and prerogatives of a crowned head."[12] To a European this might have made a great deal of sense (if true), but to Americans, who since 1776 had come to regard kings as loathsome creatures, even the suspicion of a Cincinnati-directed government appeared sinister. A letter circulating in private circles in Connecticut, had it been made public, would have confirmed some of the worst fears. Addressed to "a Person of eminence" in the Nutmeg State, the letter suggested that the United States ought to give up the game and seek its former place in the British Empire. The writer "mentioned, among other things, how instrumental the Cincinnati might be & how much it would redound to their emolument," a leading light in the society informed Alexander Hamilton.

Hamilton admired the British system but recognized the vague proposal as too harebrained for serious study. Some of this reckless talk had undoubtedly reached the ears of men whose imaginations easily ran riot. During the Indian summer of 1787, the Antifed-

[12] M. Otto to Comte de Montmorin, April 10, 1787, and June 10, 1787, 4 Farrand 17, 43–44.

eralists persistently tried to identify their adversaries with the Cincinnati in an early instance of "guilt by association." The Federalist-inclined but fair-minded Providence newspaper printed a prayer of deliverance: "O Lord have mercy upon us . . . and deliver us, we pray thee, from STANDING ARMIES, and CINCINNATI OFFICERS." Oswald's newspaper printed what appeared to be damaging answers to the query, Who is to profit from Constitutional ratification? "The military profession will then be respectable, and the Floridas may be conquered in a campaign—The spoils of the West-Indies and South America may enrich the next generation of Cincinnati." This drumfire of criticism did not force the Cincinnati to retreat from their Federalist strongholds, but they obviously adopted the tactics of private work and public silence. Wily Gouverneur Morris, writing to a staunch Cincinnati in Connecticut, jested with him for reported disappointment in the Constitution. The information was "that certain People called Cincinati [*sic*] do not think it sufficiently energetic . . . but . . . take it for the present in Hopes of Something better by and bye." Morris interpreted this public statement to mean "we do in our Hearts approve but fear that Grains from our Lips would give offence or at least alarm to our weaker Brethren."[13]

Whether the Society of the Cincinnati deserved all of the abuse poured upon it is doubtful. But in politics, as in many other walks of life, what people believe to be true at a given time becomes a historical fact for that time; and in this sense the Antifederalists fashioned an effective propaganda weapon in their repeated and sometimes wearisome charges of a Cincinnati conspiracy. A decade after the ratification battle was over, a tough old Antifederalist recalled that through the Cincinnati "their was a continual noys & wrighting from one end of the Continent to the other against the badness of the publick credit, & the weekness & insefitiancy of the Federal Government." Once the Federal Convention adjourned, "a hard tusel was made chiefly by this order to establish a monorcal government in ordir to have their president made a King." The judgment of this unlettered New England farmer might not have been historically accurate, but to him

---

[13] Morris to Jeremiah Wadsworth, October 26, 1787, Wadsworth papers, *DLC*.

and to thousands of his contemporaries the Cincinnati was a discredited antirepublican organization.

So far we have seen how the Antifederalists, in a manner that can best be described as desultory, began to shape a campaign to impede ratification. Among the prominent Antifederalists, at any rate, the avowed goal was not total rejection but a second convention—a meeting where the objections from thirteen state conventions could be considered and probably added to the first proposal. The Federalists were not unduly alarmed, however. In fact, they applied a gilt finish to their imposing bandwagon, readying it for a hopeful continental tour.

☆ IV ☆

Pennsylvania—"the Current Set Strongly"

THE FEDERALISTS LAID a clear-cut strategy in the fall of 1787. They would press for early state conventions, hoping to gain momentum with each victory until the tide was irresistible. Their tactics were so transparent that the Antifederalists counseled caution and delay almost from the outset. In some states, where a combination of circumstances and expediency worked against them, the Antifederalists had to allow ratification almost by default. These were small states, however, and the bigger game lay ahead. Meanwhile, Federalist victories were discounted, and Antifederalists even believed that they might boomerang, provided the propaganda tools at hand were used properly.

Using all the intellectual resources at their command, however, the Federalists went into the fray forearmed with a fairly accurate evaluation of their own weaknesses and strengths. Knox, Madison and Hamilton worked overtime checking the mail and relaying good news. Astute Gouverneur Morris read the reports carefully and made his assessment of the situation. Morris believed the states above New York, except for Rhode Island, were inclined to favor the Constitution. He attributed this to the favorable attitude of the ministers, coupled "with the steady support of the property and other abilities of the country [that] makes the current set strongly." New Jersey would easily ratify and could be relied upon for "more than votes should the state of affairs hereafter require the application of more pointed arguments." Strong words from a strong man. New York would probably go Federalist unless she had backing from other important states. The New York Antifederalists "cannot assign to the people any good reason for not trusting them with a decision on their own affairs, and must therefore agree to a convention." Pennsylvania seemed to be a toss up. Between "the cold and sour temper of the back counties, and still more the wicked industry" of entrenched state

49

officials, all was confusion. Prudently, Morris was noncommittal about the southern states.[1]

Morris' perceptive analysis proved essentially correct. His veiled hint of violence—the possible use of "more pointed arguments" or bayonets—indicates that a few Federalists had at least considered what alternatives were open if the Constitution were rejected. Hamilton agreed that the main opposition would come from petty politicians trying to save their hides and thus "oppose the quiet adoption of the new government." Madison was more concerned about the situation in Virginia. Most disturbing was the confirmation of an earlier report: Patrick Henry was working hand-in-glove with Mason to block ratification.

Before the first snow flurries of winter, the Antifederalists and their rivals agreed on one point—the Constitution would be won or lost in a few large states. If Massachusetts, New York, Pennsylvania, and Virginia ratified, certainly the other nine states would join in a headlong rush. Soon it was obvious that Pennsylvania would be the first testing ground. A discreet delay postponed the Massachusetts convention until after the new year began, and Patrick Henry had convinced the Virginia legislature that an early summer convention would be best. New York legislators took their cue from Governor Clinton and played a waiting game.

The Federalists' decision to proceed with all possible speed in Pennsylvania was a calculated risk. In politics it has often been wise to strike with a hot iron, and plenty of irons were in the Federalist fires in Philadelphia. For a decade Pennsylvanians had argued over the merits of the state constitution of 1776. Far from abating after the Constitution was brought forward, the internecine state party battles seemed "to have collected additional vigour and virulence." An observer saw that few supporters of state constitution sang hosannas for the Federal Convention product, while the staunchest Federalists had long been outspoken critics of the state political machinery.[2] "The controversy certainly rests upon the original founda-

---

[1] Gouverneur Morris to George Washington, October 30, 1787, *DHC*, IV, 357–58.
[2] *Pennsylvania Evening Herald*, October 20, 1787.

Courtesy of Russell W. Knight

ELBRIDGE GERRY

Objections to the Constitution of Government formed by the Convention

There is no Declaration of Rights; and the Laws of the general Government being paramount to the Laws & Constitutions of the several States, the Declarations of Rights in the separate States are no Security. Nor are the people secured even in the Enjoyment of the Benefits of the Common-Law; which stands here upon no other Foundation than its having been adopted by the respective Acts forming the Constitutions of the several States.

In the House of Representatives there is not the Substance, but the Shadow only of Representation; which can never produce proper Information in the Legislature, or inspire Confidence in the people: the Laws will therefore be generally made by Men little concern'd in, and unacquainted with their Effects & Consequences. (1.)

The Senate have the Power of altering all Money-Bills, and of originating Appropriations of Money, & the Sallerys of the Officers of their own Appointment in conjunction with the President of the United States; altho' they are not the Representatives of the People, or amenable to them.

These, with their other great Powers (viz. their Power in the Appointment of Ambassadors & all public Officers, in making Treaties & in trying all Impeachments) their Influence upon & Connection with the supreme Executive from these Causes, their Duration of Office, and their being a constant existing Body almost continually sitting, joined with their being one compleat Branch of the Legislature, will destroy any Balance in the Government, and enable them to accomplish what Usurpations they please upon the Rights & Libertys of the People.

The Judiciary of the United States is so constructed & extended, as to absorb & destroy the Judiciarys of the several States; thereby rendering Law as tedious intricate & expensive, and Justice as unattainable, by a great part of the Community, as in England; and enabling the Rich to oppress & ruin the Poor.

The President of the United States has no constitutional Council (a thing unknown in any safe & regular Government) he will therefore be unsupported by proper Information & Advice; and will generally be directed by Minions & Favourites—or He will become a Tool to the Senate—or a Council of State will grow out of the principal Officers of the great Departments; the worst & most dangerous of all Ingredients for such a Council, in a free Country; for they may be induced to join in any dangerous or oppressive Measures, to shelter themselves, and prevent an Inquiry into their own Misconduct in Office; whereas had a constitutional Council been formed (as was

GEORGE MASON'S
"Objections to the Constitution"

tion," he added, which was to say that either state officials had too much power or the national government far too little.

Farmers in central and western Pennsylvania had fared well under the benevolent tax provisions toward landowners under the state constitution. But Philadelphia businessmen smarted under agrarian domination and complained that they were drained of tax money and were kept in fear of an obnoxious paper-money act. When Gouverneur Morris had said on the Convention floor that he hoped to see all the state constitutions "thrown into the fire," there was doubtlessly a particular one he had in mind.

Although some Federalists regretted the overbearing methods used in the legislature to obtain and keep a quorum, they approved the convention call of November 20. This maneuver shortened the election campaign to a matter of a few weeks—allowing sufficient time to canvass thoroughly the city-dominated eastern part of the state. Frustrated by this fire-wagon approach, Antifederalists decried the process as one of indecent speed. For the next eight months, they continually argued that "cool-thinking men" had been made the dupes of unseemly Federalist haste.

Cool heads were scarce in the City of Brotherly Love by mid-October. Antifederalist attempts to cast doubt on the collective wisdom of the Federal Convention drew scorching counterblasts. The perpetrators of newspaper hints that Franklin and Washington had been tools in the hands of clever manipulators were denounced for using "corrosive ink, extracted from an antifederal heart." John Nicholson, the state controller-general, rashly published a detailed criticism of the Constitution. Although popular in the western counties, Nicholson was publicly insulted in Philadelphia—perhaps hung in effigy—shortly after the pamphlet appeared. Antifederalists consoled him as they wondered why local officials had done nothing to stop the mob. "The moment a person is liable to insult for his Sentiments on public affairs that Moment liberty is at an end," a friend commented.[3] Another acquaintance was certain that a delay of four or five weeks in the voting would have reversed the election results.

[3] Samuel Baird to John Nicholson, November 9, 1787, Nicholson papers, Pennsylvania State Archives.

51

Mason heard of the hasty convention call and thought it scandalous. "They dread a thorough Knowledge & public Discussion of the Subject," Mason wrote Gerry, "& wish to hurry it down."

While the Antifederalists stewed in their frustration, their opponents visualized a twofold advantage in an early ratification. Not only would early ratification give the Constitution important national momentum, but its swift passage and acceptance would also deal a deathblow to the state Constitutional Party. It was an opportunity that would not occur twice. Steadily the Philadelphia Federalists promoted the idea that the Antifederalists were simply opportunists grasping political jobs, masking their real motives with a veneer of alleged faults in the Constitution. Fearful of assaulting the Constitution itself (this was early in the struggle), "they object to the TIME of calling the Convention to adopt it," a Carlisle newspaper charged. The truth was that Antifederalists "had rather, the Union went to Destruction, than lose their hold of dominion and office in Pennsylvania."

Mounting opposition, mainly in the form of newspaper tirades, prompted the Federalists to re-examine the Pennsylvania situation. The Antifederalists harried the opposition at every turn, writing letters "to the frontier counties, where the people is most easily deceived," and alarming back-country voters "with a number of hard words, such as *aristocracy, monarchy, oligarchy*, and the like, none of which they will understand."[4] The Federalists, anxious about the temper of the western counties, made a bid to Chief Justice Thomas McKean of the state supreme court to accept a position on their convention ticket, and he accepted. Although McKean earned his judgeship as a state Constitutional Party man, his Federalist leanings were known, and the Federalists wanted to exploit them. Coxe reported some opposition to McKean from among the stauncher Federalists, "but as he has a western influence and as he will be proof that the federalists do not go upon party distinctions," he will make a good candidate. McKean, no friend of the unicameral legislature that dominated Pennsylvania politics, was ready to cast his lot with former

4 "To the antifederal junto in Philadelphia," Springfield *Hampshire Chronicle*, October 23, 1787.

adversaries. "Those, who have the least at stake and who know the least about Government, are the most busy," he assured a friend.[5] A few stragglers came over with McKean, encouraging the Federalists at a propitious moment. "The Seceders are from the upper Counties, have carried their discontents home with them," and will cause some trouble, Jefferson heard. But the Pennsylvania Federalists became more confident as defectors from the old state Constitutional Party joined their cause.

While canvassing for the state convention went on, attacks on the sixteen antifederal seceders reached a boiling point. Robert Whitehill, John Smilie, and William Findley, all western legislators, were singled out for special vents of wrath. Findley's stand was ridiculed, for had he not turned down a seat on the Pennsylvania delegation to the Federal Convention? Findley snapped back with a plea of poverty, claiming he could not afford to serve, since the delegates received no salary. The Federalists' implication was that Findley's niggardly views kept a westerner off the Pennsylvania delegation. And where were all of the blustering Antifederalists during the war? Snug in offices or padding out militia muster rolls. "These insects and worms are seen on their own dunghill," a Federalist reported. "There are minds whose narrow vision can look over the concerns of a state or town, but cannot extend their short vision in Continental concerns," and the seceding sixteen were manifestly of this disposition.

Prodded by such attacks, the Antifederalists converted zealous energy into the appearance of widespread opposition to the Constitution. At Colonel Oswald's coffee house they poured over newspaper exchanges that Oswald received from other cities, seeking new ammunition for their battle. Findley, aroused by aspersions cast on his wartime role, wrote an essay from "An Officer in the late Continental Army," which Oswald rushed into print. Findley turned Federalist barbs about officeholders into a boomerang by listing federal jobs the Constitution would create making "a burden beyond the utmost abilities of the people to bear."[6] Findley and the Anti-

[5] Thomas McKean to William A. Atlee, October 22, 1787, Atlee papers, *DLC*.
[6] "Federal Constitution," Philadelphia *Independent Gazetteer*, November 6, 1787.

federalists gathered at Oswald's also hatched the plan to flay the Federalists for not including a bill of rights in the Constitution.

Apparently, the Antifederalists hoped to capitalize on the fears harbored by many Pennsylvanians regarding religion and military service. In the minds of Quakers and the German-speakng Mennonites, their religious propensities allowed them freedom from militia duty under their state constitution. By shouting that freedom of religion would be swept away and standing armies maintained, Antifederalists made an obvious effort to play upon the emotions of sizeable voting blocks. Nor were Quakers allowed to forget the portions of the Constitution that protected slavery. What part of the Constitution would save a Quaker from "being dragged like a Prussian soldier to the camp and there compelled to bear arms?"

The standing army bugaboo alarmed Quakers, Mennonites, and other sects. Despite unpleasant memories of wartime disasters brought on by panicky militiamen, there was a blind faith in the citizen-soldier. Standing armies are unnecessary when every farmer could be "quickly converted into a Soldier," Mason had said at the Federal Convention. Nobody had challenged him, though many present could recall the unreliable quality of sunshine patriots. "A Prussian militia" and "five-fold taxes" were blessings promised by the Constitution, Antifederalists insisted.

As election day neared, the hard-pressed Philadelphia Antifederalists assembled a ticket headed by Franklin, although this appears to have been a ruse made without Franklin's approval. The attempt to ride on Franklin's coattail was futile, however, for the Federalists swamped the opposition by a five-to-one margin. Although the Federalist landslide in Philadelphia did not extend to every part of the state, the over-all results gave them a clear two-to-one margin over the Antifederalists.

As news of the complete Federalist victory swept through the metropolis on election night, celebrants emptied tankards with relish. While they toasted friends of the Constitution, their animosity toward the opposition rose. By midnight a sizeable throng, emboldened by success and drink, sought out Major Alexander Boyd's home. Boyd kept an informal antifederal headquarters, where five or six opposition leaders had their lodgings. The mob rammed at the door, broke windows, and called the Antifederalists names that do not ordinarily go into print.[7] Despite Antifederalists' protests, local officials viewed the incident casually. A weak-kneed proclamation offering a three hundred dollar reward for capture of the offenders seems to have been ignored.

When the delegates gathered for the Philadelphia convention, their political attachments followed a familiar pattern. The city delegates were mainly lawyers and merchants, well-known to each other through college associations, business dealings, and social ties. Opposed to tender laws or paper money, they were certain that public confidence and prosperity could return only under a strengthened national government. In contrast, the rural areas sent sometimes articulate but usually unlettered men who more often than not were uneasy in the company of eloquent, learned lawyers or sophisticated commercial men. The delegates who were of Scotch–Irish ancestry, hailing from counties where the Presbyterian Church had its strongholds, were predominately antifederal. Even in western Pennsylvania, the city-against-country alignment held. In Pittsburgh, a disgruntled Antifederalist observed, editor Brackenridge drew Federalist support from "some other Petty foggers with a few discharged officers *Military,* who in all Countrys I find never fails to embrace dispotick [*sic*] principles." Thus antifederalism took hold everywhere "in this country except in this depraved place."

After all the criticism hurled at the Federal Convention's "closed doors" policy, the Pennsylvania delegates set a precedent by opening the state house to spectators. This denied Antifederalists the chance to denounce secrecy in public affairs, and at the same time gave the Federalists an opportunity to keep the galleries full of friends. Once the formalities of the convention had been cleared, McKean formally moved for the adoption of a simple statement of ratification. Although the Federalist disclaimed any hope of "an instantaneous decision," the move was a transparent attempt to block any amendments or long delays. Smilie asked for Federalist forebearance, since the topic deserved "a few days" discussion. A prophetic sign came when

[7] Philadelphia *Freeman's Journal*, November 21, 1787.

the Antifederalists sought unlimited debate, but were outvoted, forty-three to twenty-four.

The Federalists were anxious to get the debates under way with deliberate speed, but their opponents would have none of it. Smilie would not budge from the preamble, particularly the first words—"We, the people of the United States." What had become of the United States? As the Confederation of states was being reduced to nothingness, a consolidated government was offered in its stead. Flattering language was used simply to "disguise the baneful purpose . . . like the dazzling polish bestowed upon an instrument of death." Smilie also rekindled all the arguments over the omission of a bill of rights. McKean noted that the Antifederalists were good at pointing out defects in the Constitution, but were poor in suggesting remedies. If a bill of rights were necessary, "why do they not show us one, that we may judge of its necessity?" Back on his feet, Smilie said he welcomed the idea, since he had the impression that the Federalists were bent on admitting neither amendments nor additions. Smilie offered to bring in a bill of rights and "such other amendments, as would conciliate the opponents of the plan . . . who wished not to reject it altogether."

Smilie's impression about Federalist plans was, of course, quite correct. Therefore McKean's call for tangible antifederal propositions must have been stated in a petulant "put up or shut up" tone. Indeed, amendments or alterations from the opposition would have watered down the impact of the Pennsylvania ratification. The suggestion for amendments was quickly squelched.

Impatiently the Federalists listened as hour after hour dragged by while Antifederalists conducted what has since become known as a filibuster. Faced with inevitable defeat, they tried to place a justification for their votes in the convention journal. The Federalists demurred. "Shall we employ the whole winter in carrying on a paper war, at the expence of the state, in spreading clamour and dissention, not only among our own citizens, but throughout the United States?" Wilson asked.[8] A chorus of nays gave the answer.

Time and again the Antifederalists returned to their favorite

[8] *Pennsylvania Evening Herald*, December 5, 1787.

56

theme—there is no bill of rights. But if Federalists grew weary of that argument, they must have been fatigued by constant aspersions cast on their hasty convention call. The antifederal trio insisted that many voters had been ignorant of the polling because of its hurried circumstances. Why had only thirteen thousand out of seventy thousand eligible voters bothered to cast ballots? Some citizens had stayed away from the polls, because they either considered the Constitution a threat to their liberties or resented the questionable Federalist tactics. Nettled by the gallery cheers for Federalist speeches and by grumbles for their own, Smilie and his friends insisted the visitors' applause was not the voice of Pennsylvania. Findley, who seems to have been a favorite whipping boy, also objected to laughter from the gallery every time he rose to speak.

Admittedly fighting a rear-guard action, the Antifederalist delegates kept the debates going as long as possible. When Federalists pushed for a vote, Whitehill voiced his chief objection. The whole design of the Federal Convention was the destruction of state sovereignty. That, in a nutshell, was what the fight was all about, and the last shot was by no means fired. Knowing the talents of the men who had framed the Constitution, he went on, it could not have been a careless mistake for them to have elaborately plotted ways to enfeeble the states. "I cannot hesitate to impute to them an intention," Whitehill surmised, to emasculate the state governments.

Outside the convention doors Antifederalists kept their presses creaking with industry. In an eleventh-hour appeal, they called for immediate alterations in the Constitution as an alternative to outright rejection. "If you adopt it in toto," warned Benjamin Workman, "you will lose every thing dear to freemen, and receive nothing in return; but misery and disgrace."[9]

Actually, the antifederal cause in Philadelphia was already beyond hope. Nothing could prevent a final roll call in the state convention on the great question. At the last moment petitions arrived from the back countries, beseeching the delegates to adjourn until spring. "The election of delegates was rushed into before the greater part

[9] "Philadelphiensis No. 4," Philadelphia *Independent Gazetteer*, December 12, 1787.

of the people had sufficiently recovered from their surprise to know what part to take in, or how to give their suffrages," one statement from chagrined voters charged, "they therefore remained inactive." Unperturbed by these frantic efforts, Federalists pushed ahead. Doctor Rush tried to calm fears by suggesting he was as certain that "the hand of God was employed in this work, as that God had divided the Red Sea . . . or had fulminated the ten commandments from Mount Sinai!" Whitehill regretted "that so imperfect a work" should be blamed on God. A petition from 750 Cumberland County residents was offered to delegates with entreaties that ratification be based on acceptance of certain amendments—and they conveniently appended fifteen articles that amounted to a bill of rights, along with limitations on taxation powers and federal court jurisdictions. Wilson persuaded other Federalists to deny the petition even the courtesy of entry into the official journal. Smilie then pleaded for a brief adjournment. A short delay would give citizens a chance to catch their breaths and delegates the opportunity to talk with their constituents. Federalists listened in scornful silence.

Finally, the Federalists would brook no further delay. They passed a resolution offering the United States a land cession for a federal district, despite cries from Antifederalists that such action was clearly a violation of the state constitution. The crucial ballot revealed that neither side seemed to have made a single convert, for the 2-to-1 Federalist margin was maintained, overriding any motion for amendments and ratifying the Constitution as it stood. The 46 to 23 vote seemed conclusive proof that Pennsylvania was a Federalist stronghold.

In a surly mood, Antifederalists took no part in the parade their opponents hurriedly assembled to celebrate their triumph, for the last thing in their minds was acceptance of ratification with good grace. While the cheers still rang in the streets, bitter Antifederalists held a rump session, drafted a bill of exceptions, and sent it to the newspapers. Titled "The Address and Reasons of Dissent of the Minority of the Convention of the State of Pennsylvania to their Constituents," the report was replete with sarcasm and dire predictions. It asserted that the 46 ratification votes came from men elected by only 6,800 voters out of 70,000 eligible citizens. "Gilded chains" had been forged by an aristocratic minority which intended to erect a consolidated government that would destroy the states, substituting "an iron handed despotism" backed with a standing army. Mainly the work of Samuel Bryan, the screed charged that without a bill of rights, the Constitution was the foundation of a system of injustice where "the poor man must . . . submit to the wealthy."[10]

Antifederalists hailed the "Address," but one Pennsylvania newspaper derided those who fashioned it as "incendiaries" who had refused the preferred hand of friendship from the victorious Federalists, and then "strove to spread dissension, and to raise rebellion amongst their constituents." Antifederalists doubtlessly intended to broadcast copies of the "Address" in an attempt to cause grave concern about ratification news, but this hope was somewhat thwarted by the temporary breakdown of public mail service. Federalist Boston knew in a few days that Pennsylvania had ratified, but it was months before the "Address" found its way to the slopes of Beacon Hill. Delays in the publication of Lloyd's debates and their final appearance in the form of a Federalist tract did nothing to ease tensions in Philadelphia. Antifederalists denounced the edition as the spurious product of a "party implement."

The pride of Pennsylvania Federalists was in no small measure diminished by all these events, but as it developed, the procrastinating Antifederalists had robbed them of the honor of being the first ratifying state convention. In neighboring Delaware, Federalists had convened in what had the appearance of a love feast. Actually, politics in Delaware were no less complicated than in sister states, but there was a temporary lull in factionalism while the ratification process was in motion.

On the eve of the Delaware convention, a Philadelphia newspaper printed a report from Sussex County, denying that "Shayites" were in control there. Delaware politics represented a constant struggle between the conservative former loyalists, which was to say about half of the voting population, and the radicals who had favored independence. Classed as Tories and Whigs, these factions still struggled

---

[10] *Pennsylvania Packet*, December 18, 1787.

for political power. The correspondent noted that in recent contests the Tory faction had "carried the election, and excluding every whig or friend to the liberties of America, from all offices in government." The tone of the proposed Constitution pleased this crowd—the small states would preserve their identity in the Senate, and imprudent men would find it difficult to vote themselves out of debts sanctified by contracts. Exasperated by the success of their opponents, the Delaware Whigs also decided to support the Constitution, hoping their state government would be swallowed "into a *general federal government*, which would be *more impartial and less expensive*." Local conditions therefore determined that antifederalism would not have the slightest hope in Delaware. Indeed, a bitter opponent of the Tories conceded in 1788 that both parties tried to outdo each other in their praise of the Constitution.[11] The Whigs appear to have won most of the convention seats in New Castle County, while in Kent County they were indifferent to the whole procedure and made no opposition to the Tories. In Sussex County the situation was a bit more complicated. The Tories were accused of spreading false stories that imminent Whigs there were actually Antifederalists. Matters came to a head when Whigs banded together and headed for the polling place at Vaughan's Furnace, where a cannon was reported mounted to prevent their voting. Later testimony on the fray indicated that the Whigs had not been able to vote and "that sundry persons were insulted and violently assaulted . . . because they were whig . . . that some huzzahed for the King, and others expressed a hope, that they might again come under the old [British] government."[12] In a petition to have the election set aside, the Sussex County Whigs declared that the Constitution would not be binding on them without their consent. At least seven petitions came before the convention, but the convention delegates agreed that an inquiry into the irregularities would have been a waste of time "as all were agreed in ratifying the federal constitution; and it could be an object with

---

[11] Timoleon (Dr. James Tilton), *Dionysius, Tyrant of Delaware*, Philadelphia, 1788, and reprinted in *Delaware* Notes, 31st Series (ed. by John A. Munroe), 123–24.

[12] "Papers relating to Vaughan's Furnace Riots," Delaware State Archives.

nobody to set the election aside." Accordingly, the tempest in the Delaware teapot presented no encouragement for the Antifederalists.

December, 1787, was in fact a discordant, discouraging month for the Antifederalists. On the heels of the disheartening news from Pennsylvania came word that New Jersey had joined Delaware in an unanimous ratification. However, the news was hardly startling. In the fall of 1786, open suggestions were made to dissolve that state and to seek a union with New York or Pennsylvania as the only way out of mounting difficulties. Hard hit by the postwar depression and strangled by the New York impost policies that kept her treasury nearly empty, New Jersey citizens were ready to grasp straws. By late October, 1787, a resident of Salem County reported that the Constitution was avidly discussed there, opposed only by penurious debtors who staked their hopes of recovery on a paper-money act. Influential Jersey men agreed, however, that neither "the religion of nature, nor even the pure religion of Jesus Christ . . . can make men honest." Hence it was "absolutely necessary to guard against the great instrument of fraud, viz. the omission of paper money."[13]

Looking across the broad Hudson, Antifederalist William Grayson contrasted the atmosphere in New Jersey with that in New York. "The one was determined to adopt & the other to reject the new constitution before it had made its appearance," Grayson noted. The state convention met for only nine days. The country members, who might have furnished at least a shade of opposition because of their flirtations with paper-money acts, suffered because Abraham Clark was not present. Clark, then a delegate to the Continental Congress, later admitted an initial uneasiness over parts of the Constitution. "I considered it from the first, more a Consolidated government than a federal, a government too expensive, and unnecessarily Oppressive in its Opperation," he confided. Leaderless, the agrarian party offered only token opposition during the convention debate.

Understandably, the Antifederalists quickly discounted the early victories of their opponents in small states. Their delegations at the Federal Convention had eagerly joined the pro-Constitution forces after it became known that they would have equal voices in the

[13] *Pennsylvania Evening Herald*, October 27, 1787.

Senate. From that moment, William Paterson of New Jersey became "for the rest of his life a federalist of federalists." The loss in Pennsylvania was another matter, however. Angered by the crushing vote of December 12, Antifederalists scarcely slackened their drumfire of criticism or tempered their views toward political conciliation. Since Federalists had insisted on ratification without amendments, the militant opposition began criticizing the notion that amendments were inadmissible. Federalists were taunted as the society of "Totos," whose fraternal emblem was "a man gaping very wide and training hard to *swallow fish, tail for[e]most.*" The slight regard given to petitions from western counties was deemed another insolent act of the *"well born and their parasites."* Never one to mince his words, Workman denounced the "self-important nabobs; whose diabolical plots and secret machinations have been carried on since the revolution, with a view to destroy your liberties."[14] Another die-hard Antifederalist demanded that a second state convention be called to consider proper amendments.

The newspaper invectives continued, in the midst of which Antifederalist editors charged that their mails were being deliberately delayed. The *New-York Journal*, one of the few northern links in the Antifederalists' newspaper chain, was missing from mail pouches arriving in Philadelphia. The *Herald* editor charged that seven consecutive numbers of the New York newspapers had disappeared while the state convention was sitting. On December 26, Oswald noted that not a single southern newspaper arrived in the preceding weekend mails. Since newspaper exchanges were the printers' chief source of dispatches, any delay not only gave the news a stale quality but also denied partisan printers a fresh supply of essays. The Antifederalists first assumed that post-office inefficiency was at fault; but as the situation steadily worsened, they linked the mail stoppage with an over-all conspiracy, hatched by Federalists to keep citizens ignorant of persistent opposition.

As Philadelphia Antifederalists pondered the mail snarl, a dramatic event took place one hundred miles to the west. The day after Christmas had been set aside by Federalists in Carlisle to celebrate

14 Philadelphia *Independent Gazetteer*, December 19, 22, 1787.

the Pennsylvania ratification. That much is certain, but beyond that point the evidence conflicts. The Carlisle Antifederalists charged that the Federalists had ordered all windows lighted, "with a menace, that such windows as would not be illuminated should be broken." The town cannon was wheeled out to fire a salute, but a large mob challenged the Federalists' right to use public property in that way. A pitched battle of stones, fists, and clubs ensued, with the Federalists finally forced to scatter.

For Antifederalists, the fun had only begun. "It was laughable to see Lawyers, Doctors, Colonels, Captains, &c., &c., leaving the scene of their rejoicing in such haste," an Antifederalist joyfully noted. The assembled farmers and tradesmen then put the torch to a bonfire that Federalists had prepared, adding the cannon carriage and a copy of the Constitution for good measure. The next day Major John Armstrong, a Federalist whom most townsmen respected, led the pro-Constitution elements as they assembled for a second time with muskets on their shoulders. After a few wild shots had been fired, an antifederal drummer beat a "call to arms." Perhaps the Federalists did not scurry homeward as their opponents claimed, but they did disperse when a band of Antifederalists headed toward the town square.

The matter might have ended there, except that the Federalists decided that their pride had been damaged too severely. Federalists charged that the mob was made up of johnny-come-lately's, former British soldiers, and men "equally void of credit, character, and understanding." The mob leaders fabricated the "broken windows" story to justify "their wicked, abandoned and unprovoked attack." An Antifederalist declared that lawyers had kept the incident alive and the community in a turmoil by constant attacks. "The most contemptuous and degrading ephitets, is given to all such as are not of their faction . . . rabble, mob, chimney sweeps, ragamuffins." Street fights occurred, and one combatant lost an eye-gouging match.

The upshot of the affair was that warrants were sworn out against twenty Antifederalists for breaking the public peace. All but seven were released on bail, but these citizens obstinately refused to post bond, claiming that their arrests were made "to gratify party spite."

As the men were marched to the county jail, the news swiftly swept across the town and surrounding country. Soon a body of over one thousand militiamen gathered, formed a committee to negotiate with the sheriff, and delivered an ultimatum to release the prisoners. The sheriff unhesitantly complied, and the men were released with no harm done "except two balls which were fired through a tavern-keeper's sign who is said to be a warm federalist." All sides appeared anxious for a détente. The state executive council was soon asked not to prosecute the charged men, with ten Federalists joining eight Antifederalist leaders as petitioners. The accused men never stood trial, but the ruffled feelings in Carlisle were not easily soothed.[15]

While dispatching an Antifederalist version of the rioting to Philadelphia, John Jordan pleaded for more co-operation among those opposed to the Constitution. "We are determined here to do everything in our power to retain that liberty without which life is not worth the enjoying," he added. Many Carlisle Antifederalists were determined to have no relations with "the Sticklers for new Constitution . . . either Social or Comercial [sic]," hoping thereby to bring "some of the Federal Merchants and Tavern-keepers to a state of repentance." Lest Antifederalists elsewhere doubt their zeal, an embattled partisan at Sheppersburg informed Controller-General Nicholson that he easily obtained ninety-nine signatures on a petition asking the state legislature to rescind the ratifying convention's work. Many signers "Declairs they will defend their Established Constituonal [sic] Liberty with the risk of their Lives." No Antifederalists gave ground more stubbornly than those who lived in middle Pennsylvania. In time, the extremists around Carlisle hinted that they were prepared to use a few "pointed arguments" of their own. "I am almost certain that the Fœderalist by their mad fury is preparing a fattle Blow both for themselves and Constitution," a ringleader asserted, as he kept his musket handy and advised others to follow suit.[16]

The clogged mail channels kept news of the Carlisle imbroglio confined to the immediate area for some weeks. As news of the incident

[15] *Carlisle Gazette*, January 2, 9, 16, 23, and February 27, 1788.
[16] Benjamin Blyth, Sr., to Nicholson, February 11, 1788, Nicholson papers, Pennsylvania Archives.

drifted slowly to the far reaches of the Republic, Federalists had a ready answer for such lawlessness. "We understand," a Providence newspaper reported, "no county in the State is so much in arrear for taxes. That is, none have no much avoided to pay *the soldiers* who have *fought* for us, the *ally* who has assisted us, and *the public creditor* who has *lent* us money *in the time of need*."[17] Oliver Ellsworth's widely reprinted "Landholder" assured readers that Pennsylvanians loved a good quarrel. "The dispute there is not upon the merits of the subject, but it is their old warfare carried on with different weapons, and it was an even chance that the parties had taken different sides from what they have taken, for there is no doubt but either party would sacrifice the whole country to the destruction of their enemies." Thus the Carlisle incident was dismissed as a local quarrel.

Still, every troublespot caused concern among the top Federalist strategists, for political ships sail best in calm waters. "The minority in Penna. is very restless under their defeat," Madison observed. "If they can get an Assembly to their wish they will endeavor to undermine what has been done there. If backed by Massts. they will probably be emboldened to make some more rash experiment." Accordingly, the focus of both factions shifted northward. If the Antifederalists carried Massachusetts, they would sweep all of New England. The momentum for ratification had to be stopped in Boston, or it could not be halted. Reports from the town meetings encouraged the Antifederalists. Insofar as numbers were concerned, they appeared to be gaining a majority of seats in the forthcoming ratifying convention. All they lacked was leadership.

[17] Providence, Rhode Island, *United States Chronicle*, April 17, 1788.

☆ V ☆

Lawyers *vs.* Farmers—*No Contest*

PROVIDENCE NEVER SEEMED TO SMILE on the Antifederalists. When they made their own luck, it always seemed to be bad. They were desperately in need of a leader in Massachusetts who could whip their undisciplined legions into a determined force, but never found him. Consequently, their strength lay in numbers rather than in organization. Warren, Gerry, Kilham, and other potential leaders all lived in the wrong part of the state, so that in the election for delegates they got lost in a Federalist shuffle. Federalists regarded the Constitution as the work of demigods "as sacred as the Commandments delivered from *Sinai*," but frustrated Antifederalists found no Moses to lead them.[1]

It was a time for action, but the Antifederalists in Massachusetts did not act. They talked. They wrote. But there was no clearinghouse for information, and the Antifederalists established no Committees of Correspondence in New England to promote an opposition program. Instead, they trudged along, hoping somehow that things would turn out well even though most newspapers fought them, most professional men reprobated them, and most prominent public figures scorned them. Yet, the Antifederalists believed that in numbers there was strength—indeed, there was little else in which to believe, unless they intended to allow ratification by default. And Massachusetts was too important a state to surrender without a fight.

"The example of Massa. has a very Great influence upon the o'r State[s]," congressman Dane boasted.[2] Massachusetts was to the North what Virginia was to the South. She had provided leadership in American political affairs since the Stamp Act crisis. Gerry, with his long record of public service, was the logical man to assume Anti-

---

[1] "Candidus" [Benjamin Austin], Boston *Independent Chronicle*, December 6, 1787.

[2] Nathan Dane to Thomas Dwight, February 11, 1787, *LCC*, VIII, 303.

federalist leadership in Massachusetts, but he worked himself into the unenviable position of an insider-turned-outsider. Gerry was a qualified leader; he was wealthy, formally educated, a man of commerce who dabbled in politics, but it became increasingly apparent that it would have been incongruous for him to have become the inspired leader of yeomen farmers who took their politics more on instinct than on reason. In 1787–88, Gerry's lot was to be their friend and sympathizer, but not their leader.

Gerry had turned his back on former well-wishers—the merchants, lawyers, and divines who had respected Gerry's bank balance if not his deep intellect. Although Gerry had been a lonesome New Englander in Philadelphia, he believed that there was support at home for his dissent. James Warren, speaker of the Massachusetts House of Representatives, was dependable and influential with the country party—that is, the legislators from the farming areas.[3] Samuel Adams, his name still magic in state politics, was eagerly courted by the Antifederalists. The failure of the state legislature to lash vindictively at Shays's followers was one of several signs indicating that the majority there was moderate, susceptible to arguments that if the Constitution were adopted "their liberties will soon be terminated." Indeed, the farther one traveled away from Boston, the more apprehensive one would find citizens of any scheme that merchants, bankers, lawyers, and stockjobbers in the cities seemed to favor.

The growth of commerce in the seaboard towns and cities had led to the creation of political alliances in Massachusetts that were also found in other northern states. "Our country deputies are determined to ruin the trading part of the state," a Newport merchant complained in the spring of 1787. It was a familiar cry, and one that explained why Boston, Providence, Portsmouth, and Newport merchants supported the Constitution as one with their brethren in New York, Philadelphia, Charleston, and Baltimore. "The Sea Coast seems everywhere fond of it," Madison could report with accuracy and enthusiasm. Indeed, Antifederalists in the Boston environs pru-

---

[3] Charles Warren, "Elbridge Gerry, James Warren, Mercy Warren and the Ratification of the Federal Constitution in Massachusetts," *MHS, Proceedings,* Vol. 64, pp. 155–56.

dently made concessions to the commercial crowd in their desultory campaign for local support. "The PEOPLE of *the several states are convinced of the necessity of adopting some Federal Commercial Plan*," Benjamin Austin admitted.

The town-country hostility was founded on grounds both real and imaginary. Farmers sold their products to town merchants, and what farmer ever believed he was paid full value for his produce? Not only did more profits seem to accumulate for the handlers rather than for the producers of farm goods, but the holders of mortgages were townsmen who knew the threat of a debtor's prison was at their beck and call. Farmers also suspected that an undue tax burden was shifted to their already overloaded shoulders by city delegates in the state legislatures that served the merchants who had elected them. Hints of this hostility appear in nearly every state, but nowhere more than in New England.

At the outset, many New England farmers had ambivalent feelings toward the Constitution. A Rhode Island farmer who was an early supporter of ratification believed the Constitution would destroy "the aristocratic influence in the Seaport Towns." This attitude soon gave way to a more widespread feeling that farming and commercial interests would always be in conflict "while human nature remains the same that it ever has been." At election time, farmers became the pawns of city-based manipulators. A country gentleman who would go to Congress "must form his connections, and unite his interests with those towns." Control of the federal government would slide into the hands of merchant-dominated groups, while the farmers would be "unrepresented, forlorn, and without hope."[4] The frugal farmer deserved more respect than the "speculating merchant, who, after having drained the country of cash, becomes a bankrupt himself." The only city dweller who merited consideration was the man who toiled for wages. Such ideas must have been deeply ingrained among rustic plowmen who regarded the cities as fleshpots, where bankers and lawyers hatched their schemes of iniquity. It was men of this stamp who unsuccessfully tried to move the state con-

[4] "Cornelius," Springfield *Hampshire Chronicle*, December 18, 1787.

vention away from Boston to a site "less exposed to dangerous mercantile and aristocratic influences."

Lawyers were another pet peeve of the Antifederalists. In that Bible-quoting society, who did not recall that Jesus had said, "Woe to you lawyers . . . for you load men with burdens hard to bear, and you yourselves do not touch the burdens with one of your fingers"?[5] Farmers and mechanics saw "Boys Issue forth from the Writing Shops of attorneys With only their Cloaths to their Backs, with no more Law knowledge than Just to Enable them to Draw a Common Writ . . . Acquire larger Fortunes in the Space of five years than they and their Predecessors, With their utmost Industry frugality and economy, have been able to acquire in five Successive Generations."[6] Testy Theodore Sedgwick, a bitter foe of Antifederalists at Stockbridge, reported that an adversary was spreading anti-Constitution doctrine by saying that "it will be a government for great men & law[y]ers." Indeed, these assertions were strengthened by the undeniable fact that droves of lawyers were supporting the Federalist movement, as General Knox reported to Washington in a survey of the Massachusetts situation.

Tirelessly the northern Antifederalists sought to identify in the public mind Federalist lawyers and merchants with a third set of men—the stockjobbers or speculators in public securities. Nowhere did this tactic have greater impact than in New England, where thousands of veterans had long since disposed of their soldier's notes at depreciated prices. In the Federal Convention, King had uttered sentiments calculated to delight Boston speculators who had been buying all types of state-issued securities for nominal sums. King had suggested that the public debts of all the states should be consolidated into one national debt. The enterprising soul who bought public securities at depreciated prices after September, 1787, not only had the thrill of speculation but also the hope of their eventual redemption at par value. Earlier in the year, when loan certificates had been

[5] Luke 11:46.

[6] Quoted in Stephen T. Riley, "Dr. William Whiting and Shays' Rebellion," American Antiquarian Society *Proceedings*, October, 1956, p. 143.

selling in Boston for less than three shillings on the pound, Stephen Higginson yearned for "an efficient Government" in one breath, and panted in the next for advance news on public finance that he could turn into a profit.[7] General Knox, who knew more about artillery trajections than stockjobbing gyrations, learned in late October that his friends expected the value of public securities to rise as constitutional prospects brightened.

The cleavage between Antifederalists and their adversaries on the matter of redeeming public securities at par value was not, however, so clear-cut. Mason had warned the Federal Convention that vague promises to fulfill national obligations would "beget speculations and increase the pestilent practice of stock-jobbing." He wanted public securities redeemed at their market value unless still held by the original creditors. But Gerry had defended the speculators, since "They keep the value of the paper up." And Randolph had introduced the clause which heartened speculators everywhere—Article VI, section 1—which made all debts contracted under the Confederation binding on the new government. The door was thus left open for whatever program the Federalists, if they were successful, could pass.

Undoubtedly, vast numbers of citizens considered speculation in securities as downright dishonest, particularly since "almost the *whole* of the *widows*, *orphans*, *soldiers*, and other *distressed public creditors*, have sold their certificates." Citizens recalled that mustered-out soldiers had been preyed upon by smooth-talking speculators who insisted their paper "was not worth more than 2s. for 20s."[8] While town meetings discussed the Constitution, one observer recalled that stockjobbers regarded the Constitution as a signal for "legal robbery, such as the history of civilized nations can scarcely produce a parallel to. There were mail stages . . . but their snail-like pace did not answer the views of the speculators; they kept expresses continually on the road."[9]

The antifederal newspapers never tired of reminding readers that

[7] Stephen Higginson to Samuel Osgood, February, 1787, Osgood papers, *NYHS*.

[8] *Massachusetts Centinel*, March 20, 1790, quoted in Joseph S. Davis, *Essays in Earlier History of American Corporations*, 180.

[9] Ebenezer S. Thomas, *Reminiscenses of the Last Sixty-Five Years*, II, 11–12.

there was a speculator-Federalist entente, but the voices of some leaders were all but muted. As a prudent businessman, Gerry held a large number of public securities, and yet he seemed more interested in political principles than in huge profits. When Oliver Ellsworth accused Gerry of "barefaced selfishness" in the Federal Convention debates over redemption schemes, the Antifederalist branded the charges utterly false. The truth was, Gerry explained, that if he were hoping for gain by speculating, he would be a Federalist "because the Constitution held out the hopes of redemption [of public securities] at par."[10] Nor did James Warren pin much hope on the efforts to identify Federalists with avaricious stockjobbers. Warren, involuntarily retired from the legislature in 1778, had been politically inactive for nearly a decade. With Shays's Rebellion as a steppingstone, Warren made a political comeback as the legislative champion of the back-country elements. Chosen speaker of the House, Warren supported a paper-money act that sent shudders down the spines of Boston bankers. Warren was capable of matching the Federalists with verbal brickbats, which they threw at him incessantly. But Warren was hesitant to brand these Federalists as unfeeling moneylenders who grabbed bread from the mouths of widows and orphans.

Warren was wary of making an attack on the seemingly vulnerable Federalist speculators, but to the over-all Antifederalist strategy, if anything so loosely organized deserves the name, he was faithful. He continually exhorted localism and campaigned for a second convention. Perhaps the Warrens realized that the seaboard financial community had more than self-interest behind its Federalist leanings. Indeed, Antifederalist James Winthrop declared that security holders and shipbuilders had suffered greatly in recent times, "and they ought to, and will be provided for" regardless of ratification. Winthrop's argument took a strange twist, however, when he insisted that unconditional ratification would bring an orgy of public-spending and "the increase of expense will be death to the hopes of all creditors, both of the continental [debt] and of the state." Anti-

---

[10] "Landholder," *Massachusetts Centinel*, January 2, 1788. Gerry's reply, *ibid.*, January 5, 1788.

federalists never pushed such an argument much beyond the Back Bay marshes of Boston.

A relentless hue-and-cry over the security holdings of Federalists might have been no more successful than were the mild public attacks, but a Connecticut veteran claimed that the press in his state was shackled by the Federalists, "who it is said has their Chests & trunks &c filled with public securities bought up by their emmissaries heretofore from 1/3 to 6/8 on the pound."[11] A Rhode Islander's argument for a direct referendum on the Constitution, rather than a ratifying convention, was in part based on a similar outlook. In a convention gullible delegates would be manipulated by lawyers, "FULL BLOODED CINCINNATI," and "the present holders of public securities, who have defrauded the honest soldiers of their just dues."[12]

Even when Antifederalists hit upon a popular issue, they found it difficult to broadcast their message. Yet they were not so much inept as they were stymied by Federalist sympathizers. In Connecticut, Federalists converted editors with such dispatch that one chagrined Antifederalist complained that there was never space in newspapers for any attacks on the Constitution. "Every thing huggermuggered & suppressed that was truly alarming against it," he wailed. Whatever the voting habits of her people, Rhode Island newspapers offered little, if any, opportunity for the publication of Antifederalist articles. A frustrated Antifederalist lamented that the *Newport Herald* printed all manner of praises for the Constitution, but only "scurrilous Pieces . . . against all who do not agree in political Opinion with a certain *Junto* in that Town." The Rhode Island printers admitted Federalist leanings, although the outstanding Providence *United States Chronicle* exerted some effort to be fair to the opposition. New Hampshire newspapers were similarly inclined to follow the example of the influential seaboard merchants.

About half of the New England newspapers were published in Massachusetts, and with eight journals Boston was a major news-

[11] Hugh Ledlie to General John Lamb, January 15, 1788, Lamb papers, *NYHS*.
[12] "Extract of a letter to a gentleman in Providence," Philadelphia *Independent Gazetteer*, July 5, 1788.

gathering and distribution center in the Republic. The Constitution had scarcely reached Boston when the *Massachusetts Centinel*, edited by Benjamin Russell, ran up the Federalist flag. Consistently, the *Centinel* characterized the opposition with rasping tones, using that inclusive word so long flung from New England pulpits: wicked. The Antifederalists were "malignant, ignorant, and short-sighted triflers," pitied for "the weakness of their heads, and the badness of their hearts." Russell's hint of an alliance between Antifederalists and the devil apparently found ready believers. An antifederal editor chided an old acquaintance who was thoroughly federal for charging "all who do not think as you do with sorcery, witchcraft &c."[13] But a reader in Rehoboth, Rhode Island, denounced Russell's partisan policy. "Why, if the proposed Constitution is a good one are its Supporters afraid to have any Thing said against it? Why are they for hurrying it down our Throats, before we have opened our mouths?" asked "ARGUS."

While most Boston newspapers allowed an occasional antifederal article to slip into print, the *American Herald* remained outspokenly opposed to the Constitution. Edward Powars kept the flagging hopes of Antifederalists alive as he fired hot salvos into the opposition. Powars insisted that his columns were open to all factions and did occasionally, but halfheartedly, print Federalist essays. Readers knew that the Boston *Independent Chronicle* was solidly behind the Constitution, but it still declared that Federalists should not imitate the dogmatic Lord Peter, who denounced opponents as "blind, positive, conceited sons of bitches" who deserved roasting in Hell.[14]

Some Bostonians doubtless would have enjoyed seeing Powars turning slowly on a spit, however. When Powars showed no signs of antifederal backsliding, Federalist advertisers employed economic pressure. Advertising revenue fell, and by mid-December the subscription list dwindled as the result of cancellations by supporters of the Constitution. As Powars squirmed, the leading Federalists appeared to enjoy the imminent prospect of his bankruptcy. What kind

---

[13] Thomas B. Wait to George Thatcher, January 8, 1788, Thatcher papers, *BPL*.

[14] Boston *Independent Chronicle*, November 8, 1787.

of logic was it, asked a Federalist, that demanded a citizen's support of a newspaper that lambasted his political belief? If men must finance attacks on their own opinions, then "printers of newspapers" had a unique privilege "enjoyed by no other set of men upon earth, of making the public pay for what they neither wish to purchase nor to read."

Despite the slender newspaper resources and the handful of public figures ready to do battle for the Antifederalists in Massachusetts, their adversaries were anything but glowingly optimistic. A Salem Federalist believed that the Constitution was backed "by the thinking & disinterested part of the Community" and opposed by wretches both ignorant and selfish.[15] Oliver Ellsworth, with his facile pen and loose regard for the niceties of fact, included among the opposition debtors "who have no resolution to be either honest or industrious" and pompous local politicians who feared a comeuppance under a federal government. "An Association of CHRISTIAN MINIS-TERS" urged all towns to pray for guidance so that delegates could be sent to Boston who had "the best understanding of the times," men who could see that a well-established, energetic government would re-store trade, stimulate "manufactures, husbandry, and the like." Great weight was given to the influence of ministers with their flocks, as the Federalists marshaled public opinion leaders in every community, pleased that "the Judges & Lawyers, the Clergy, and men of property furnish only here and there an adversary."[16]

Gerry's disaffection was still worrisome. Warren's presence in the "wronghead" camp was considered the ploy of an opportunist, as Federalists spoke his name in hisses. "Detractor! we can trace thee like a snail upon the rock, by the slime of defamation, which thou leavest behind thee." Gerry was not so easily dismissed. Henry Jackson, who was privy to the innermost Federalist councils in Boston, could not forget the Gerry letter. "Every thing went on firm & well untill that damn'd Letter," Jackson huffed.[17]

[15] Henry Gibbs to Simeon Baldwin, October 31, 1787, Baldwin papers, Yale University Library.

[16] Madison to Jefferson, December 9, 1797, Madison papers, *DLC*.

[17] Henry Jackson to Knox, November 18, 1787, Knox papers, *MHS*.

Federalist wrath was partially dampened by the first election results for convention seats. "Mr Gerrys Letter has done infinite mischief," Nathaniel Gorham (who had been a delegate to the Federal Convention) observed, ". . . & I ought to have answered it." The returns coming in now gave affairs a more hopeful aspect, however, as "the disposition of Boston & indeed the whole of the Seacoast is right—that if the Country is divided will turn the scale." Gerry, dismayed by the personal attacks flung his way, sought to win converts by private letters. To one correspondent he predicted that even if the Constitution were adopted, "the Eastern States will soon rebel against it, for it is not a Government adapted to their genius, habits, or aversion to arbitrary powers." Cautiously, Gerry left the door open slightly. If the citizens of New England are "of a different opinion, I have no objection to their trying on the Federal chains." He stated further that he would support the Constitution if it were ratified.[18] Although many old friends shunned Gerry like a leper, at least one compatriot with Federalist inclinations gave him a friendly nod. "I am not by any means of opinion, if your dissent & influence, should stop the progress of the new System, that all would be lost, and no Government adopted," Samuel Otis wrote. If anything had made New Englanders suspicious of the Constitution, it was "the eagerness, avidity, and illiberality of some of the States, in their modes of adoption."

From his desk in Hartford, conveniently near the post road to Boston and New York, Ellsworth sent forth his "Landholder" essays—slashing attacks on the motives and personalities of the Antifederalists. Reckless of fact and given to exaggeration, Ellsworth delighted friends with sallies into the midst of the enemy ranks. Gerry became his favorite whipping boy, but nearly every prominent Antifederalist felt the "Landholder's" lash. In a pessimistic moment, Ellsworth doubted that nine states would ratify the Constitution "at the first trial" in state conventions, but he took consolation in desultory Antifederalist efforts to block ratification. The Antifederalists "betrayed great ignorance of the true spirit and feeling of the coun-

[18] Elbridge Gerry to John Wendell, November 16, 1787, *LCC*, VIII, 680*n.*

75

try, and they have failed to act in concert with each other."[19] Antifederalists, he wrote, were beset with great difficulties "arising from their disunion: in the different states where the opposition rages the most, their principles are totally opposite to each other, and their objections discordant and irreconcilable." Antifederalists were taunted—"no regular system can be formed among you, and you will betray each other's motives."

Ellsworth was not the only Federalist who saw the opposition drifting in a rudderless ship, without a captain on the main deck or a well-charted course. "It is a little singular that three of the most distinguished Advocates for amendments . . . appear to be pointedly at variance with each other on one of the capital articles of the System," Madison observed. Lee, Mason, and Randolph had different ideas about the executive council they demanded. "It is pretty certain that some others who make a common cause with them in the general attempt to bring about alterations differ still more from them, than they do from each other," Madison told Washington. When Mason's "Objections" made its appearance in the North, Antifederalists carefully deleted the barbs aimed at northern shipping interests. Ellsworth and other Federalists leaped on the deletion, exposing the emendation with glee. The net effect was an antifederal boomerang.

What struck the opposition as singular must have also struck the Antifederalists in a similar manner. In his day, Gerry had cast his share of slings toward the South as the good New England man he was. But to his discomfort, Gerry found that in the chorus chanting "The States will be Swallowed Up" he was the only prominent northern public figure. Samuel Adams was said to be sympathetic but was notoriously undependable. Lee had beseeched Adams to make common cause with the Antifederalists from the start, suggesting that the popular Bostonian join in seeking a second convention. Adams seemed impressed with Lee's arguments, but walked circumspectly. "The Seeds of Aristocracy began to spring even before the Conclusion of our Struggle for the natural Rights of Men, Seeds which like a Canker Worm lie at the Root of free Governments," Adams wrote

19 "Landholder VIII," Hartford *Connecticut Courant*, December 24, 1787.

dolefully. But in bidding for a convention seat, Adams held his cards close to the waistcoat. He managed to get elected, then stepped back to see how other political hands were being played.

Gerry and Warren were less fortunate. Both were humiliated at the polls, and their defeat robbed the Massachusetts Antifederalists of tested leadership. Whatever guidance they would have was to come from men whose names had local significance, but not much in the rest of Massachusetts, and none at all elsewhere. Around Boston the antifederal cause had been little more than hopeless, despite lurid appeals to self-interest and the bugaboos of aristocratic lawyers and Cincinnati society fops. In vain the Antifederalists had warned that ratification would divert "commerce and political importance" from Boston to the proposed federal district, which rumors placed near Philadelphia.[20] Business was bad, James Winthrop conceded, but what guarantee was there that ratification would bring a magic revival of trade? Boston merchants looked at their stocks of unsold goods and turned a deaf ear to Winthrop's warning.

The local news was discouraging, but the Boston Antifederalists were heartened by the results of their efforts in the hinterlands. Editor Wait of the *Cumberland Gazette* warned readers against adopting a consolidated federal system. "You might as well attempt to rule Hell by Prayer" as to save republican institutions with a federal system; but still this was the system which "King *George*, and the Convention over which he lately presided, has prepar'd." Another Maine man was equally blunt. He opposed the Constitution "because Sir I think a Continental Collector at the head of a Standing army will not be so likely to do us justice in collecting taxes, as the mode of collecting now practiced." At Biddeford, Antifederalists first denied any need to participate in the state convention. "A dumb Devil seized a Majority & they voted not to send," an enraged Federalist reported. A second town meeting was contrived, and an Antifederalist who had announced he would not serve if elected received thirty votes to his opponent's eighteen. "Horrinda dictu!!!! how are the mighty fallen! Shaysism appears to me to opperate the

[20] Boston *American Herald*, November 19, 1787.

77

same in the Body politic, as epidemic's do in the human body," the dejected Federalist noted.[21]

Although the Federalists in Maine tried to "be wise as Serpents & harmless as Doves," they cut across the grain of local sentiments. William Widgery was said to be waging war against the Constitution with religious zeal, "the same as a *new light* fighting the *Devil.*" Nonetheless, "as we are very calvinistic, I have hopes the preaching of the *Righteous* will convert many from the Errors of their way," an uneasy Federalist wrote. Although antifederal candidates usually lost along the seaboard, few back-country Maine men were converted to federalism. Rumors, spread by Antifederalists ready to believe the worst, made the Constitution seem like another boulder in the pathway of Maine's statehood aspirations. But Federalists insisted that statehood would be more easily gained after ratification. The result was a standoff, with the Maine delegation almost evenly divided.

The news from Berkshire County, however, was more encouraging to opponents of the Constitution. Since that area had been the heartland of the Shays's Rebellion and abounded with citizens whom Federalists had recently labelled as "insurgents," Berkshire offered little hope for advocates of energetic government. As was often the case in Massachusetts town meetings, the elected delegates were given specific voting instructions. Fifteen of the twenty-two Berkshire delegates either had such instructions or had proclaimed their antifederalism in the town meeting. A sixteenth Antifederalist was denied a seat by some fast and clever Federalist maneuvering. At Great Barrington, the center of resistance in 1786, a judge who had sympathized with the armed farmers was elected as an Antifederalist.[22] However, Federalists contrived an adjournment that left the result in doubt, for they could not stomach the thought that Dr. William Whiting, who had been found guilty of seditious libel for his part in the Shays's affair, was to be their chosen delegate. While waiting for another town meeting, Theodore Sedgwick warned that Antifederalists were

[21] Thomas B. Wait to George Thatcher, November 22, 1787, Thatcher papers, *BPL.*

[22] Riley, "Whiting and Shays' Rebellion," American Antiquarian Society *Proceedings,* 119–116.

using "the meanest and basest arts" to arouse "publick passions."[23] "For God Sake come down" and aid the Federalists, he pleaded.

Sedgwick and his friends found sufficient succor at the second town meeting to deprive Dr. Whiting of his credentials. While the Federalists basked in their triumph, other events began to unfold. Four petitions alleged that the first meeting had been conducted in a high-handed manner after Whiting had been elected. "It was aboundantly Evident that the Selectman & their pertizans ware determined to Imbarris the Meeting & if possible to nulify Every thing which had been done," the petitioners declared. The Antifederalists claimed that many unqualified citizens, "whose whole Estates put together would not be Sufficient to Qualify one Vote," were allowed a voice; and finally the majority, in disgust, stalked out of the meeting. Angry and confused, they circulated petitions asking the forthcoming convention to seat Dr. Whiting.

Frustration spread to other town meetings where Antifederalist strength seemed preponderant. At Sheffield, they saw themselves again outmaneuvered by "a certain Set of Men among us not only ravenously greedy to swallow the new Constitution them Selves but making the greatest exertions to ram it down the Throats of others without giving them time to taste it." These Antifederalists thought it passing strange that John Ashley, Jr., the Federalist candidate and a selectman himself, had "held the hat" for the collecting votes. "But Insted of Seting it fair & open on the Table as usual, [Ashley] held it in his Left hand Pressed Close to his breast, Receiving the Votes . . . in the hat himself."[24] When the votes were counted, humble but happy Ashley found himself elected. At the Taunton town meeting, where Antifederalist selectmen had control, a single delegate was chosen. Their opponents then called a rump session where the delegation was enlarged and two Federalists were added amidst cries from their adversaries that the whole business had taken an illegal turn.

Williamstown was the scene of another discordant town meeting. The first gathering picked Antifederalist William Young "by a grate

---

[23] Theodore Sedgwick to Van Schaack, November 28, December 5, 1787, Sedgwick papers, *MHS.*

[24] "Petition of Sheffield Freeholders," Massachusetts Archives.

Majority," but the opposition lingered until "but few people were Present" and called for an adjournment. The next meeting began promptly at the stroke of the hour "and the Moder[a]tor turned the hat Before the people from the Remote parts of the Town could come in . . . and declared Thompson Skinner elected." Seventy-three petitioners vowed their rights had been usurped and called for the seating of Young.

As reports of these heated town meetings reached Boston, Winthrop saw a parallel between what had happened in Pennsylvania and what was happening in Massachusetts. "Means no less criminal, but not so flagrantly indecent, have been frequently mentioned among us to secure a majority," he observed. "But those who vote for a price can never sanctify wrong, and treason will still retain its deformity." Sometimes outright indignation harmed the Antifederalist cause, as at Sandwich where an avowed anti-Constitution delegate resigned after he was instructed to vote in the negative. In high dudgeon the Antifederalist said the Boston convention would meet without him since "the greatest ideot [*sic*] may answer your purpose as well as the greatest man."[25] In Newburyport, James Kilham's support dwindled after his strong anti-Constitution speech in the state legislature. Sympathetic with Kilham's ideas, young John Quincy Adams complained that although "religious bigotry is almost entirely done away, yet the same principle, in another garb, appears in all our political manoeuvres." Adams' employer, Theophilus Parsons, was advocating political orthodoxy at that moment as he wrangled for a convention seat himself. Parsons managed to win enough votes despite Antifederalist attempts to prove that he was far removed from any contact with the *hoi polloi*. Whether Parsons campaigned "as a *British Nobleman* would have done with the most persuasive arguments in his pockets, we are not to say," the leading spokesman of Boston's Antifederalists reported.

Although New Englanders avoided ostentation at Christmas time, Gerry and his friends had several reasons for a mild celebration. The election returns showed that although three-fourths of the seacoast

[25] *Salem Mercury*, January 15, 1788, quoted in Samuel B. Harding, *The Contest over Ratification of the Federal Constitution in Massachusetts*, 57*n*.

delegates were Federalists, the Antifederalists had routed the opposition in central Massachusetts and held a fair majority in the western counties. There were other favorable signs as the ratification convention drew nearer. Sam Adams, still hiding his vacillating antifederalism under a bushel, contributed a few newspaper screeds for the cause. Disgusted Federalists inveighed against his "venom and gall against the Constitution," which "savors more of the politician than the patriot." But to Richard Henry Lee, Adams openly confessed his disdain of the Constitution. "I stumble at the Threshold. I meet with a National Government, instead of a Federal Union of Sovereign States."

For all his suspicions, Adams was moving cautiously. Nor was John Hancock certain of his course. When Governor Bowdoin gave a dinner party for the Boston delegates, the Constitution was a lively topic of discussion. During the course of the evening, Adams "disclosed sentiments opposed to the Constitution" and told the diners "that *the tradesmen were against it.*" Adams threw salt in the festering wound by supporting his antifederalism with "such arguments & such only as appear in the pieces of Brutus & federal farmer."[26] Although the party broke up on a cordial note, the Federalists discerned that Adams' exposed flank was his desire for popularity with the local merchants and artisans. Little time was lost in organizing a meeting to refute Adams' assertion on the opening day of the convention.

If Adams needed nudging, he got it. "A number of Boston tradesmen," who resented allegations that "the Tradesmen of the Seaports, and our bretheren, the Yeomen of the country," were antifederal, gathered at the Green Dragon tavern to protest. Chandlers, cordwainers, and other laborers—guided by men whose principles were harder than their knuckles—approved an attack upon Antifederalists as sowers of discord for "their own wicked purposes." Rejection of the Constitution would bring ruin to the little remaining commerce, the tirade (written by Paul Revere and Benjamin Russell) declared. If Antifederalists triumphed, working men would grub for

[26] Christopher Gore to Rufus King, January 6, 1788, King, *Life and Correspondence of Rufus King*, I, 311.

jobs and swell the ranks of the poor. Clear-thinking laborers wanted the Constitution approved "in all its parts, without any conditions, pretended amendments, or alterations whatever."[27] Sam Adams was impressed.

As the main New England attraction took shape in Massachusetts, a side show in neighboring Connecticut was about to close. In selecting delegates, Connecticut town meetings in the hinterland had favored Antifederalists, but more had either supported Federalists or, what is more likely—if the dry-as-dust meeting minutes are accurate—left their delegates unfettered by instructions. The campaign had been in progress since early July, 1787, when a Fairfeld newspaper noted that attempts were then made to convince Antifederalists "that the most disastrous consequences are to be expected, unless we shall accept the Proceedings of the [Federal] Convention." The real villain in the Federalist tale was New York—pictured as a greedy neighbor with its avaricious customs collections on goods destined for Connecticut farms. Under the Constitution, all would be changed. A vote for ratification was a ballot cast against New York. It was an inkling in 1787 of what was to become an old, old story in American politics: vote against your enemies, rather than for your friends.

If any son of Connecticut was inclined to forgive New York and forget, it was not Ellsworth. He labored prodigiously to foster a spirit of revenge against the neighboring state. With the Hartford ratifying convention only days away, he unleashed an attack on Richard Henry Lee, the "Federal Farmer," that played on every string of discontent and prejudice in Connecticut hearts. Ellsworth noted that Lee had allied himself with Clinton "and a train of collectors of impost and excise, tide waiters and bailiffs, to instruct us poor and despised Yankees in the arts of government." Ellsworth expressed surprise that the owner of several hundred slaves should be anxious over the liberty of northerners. Lee's remarks were proper if addressed "to the people of New Zealand . . . but being accustomed to despise New England, you probably thought we were as dull as the negroes of Virginia."

Although Ellsworth's harangue would make no Federalist con-

[27] *Massachusetts Centinel,* January 9, 1788.

verts below Philadelphia, it was cleverly calculated to weaken anti-federalism in Connecticut. Lamb and other New York Antifederalists were notorious, a Connecticut admirer wrote, "in some of our publick newspapers [and] handled in a very rough ungentlemanlike manner." Since the hostility of Connecticut printers was ill-concealed, the Antifederalists scarcely bothered to submit newspaper articles which "must run the gauntlet through all these inferal grubstreet hireling scourilious scriblers, that watch & gaurd [*sic*] the posts of the printers doors in this town."[28]

Connecticut also had been, as noted earlier, the scene of bitter quarreling over the scheme to commute the pensions of her Revolutionary officers. The issue was still seething. David Humphreys, a choleric Cincinnati, thought that America was ruined unless "popular Demagogues who are determined to keep themselves in office at the risque of every thing" were politically unfrocked. General Jeremiah Wadsworth apparently played down his feelings in public, knowing that his position as president of the Connecticut Cincinnati made him suspect. Jonathan Trumbull was disappointed in his desire for a place at the state convention. Trumbull said he was "not honored with the appointment . . . being . . . under the Cloud of Commutation & Cincin[nati]."

Extreme Federalists of Humphreys' or Wadsworth's stamp had been disturbed when the Federal Convention call for delegates first went out, because local politicians wanted no part of that grand conclave. Amos Granger of Suffield thought the royal charter of 1663, which still furnished the machinery of state government, and the Articles of Confederation were instruments aplenty for the God-fearing people of Connecticut to live by. One legislator even had the effrontery to suggest that Connecticut might join Rhode Island in refusing to send a delegation. But few men of these sentiments had been chosen as convention delegates. The returns showed that Anti-federalists had elected only one acknowledged public man, General James Wadsworth. Thereafter, Wadsworth was the target of unmerciful attacks that finally drove him from public office. Wadsworth's cronies, a Federalist charged, "love him for his kindred

[28] Hugh Ledlie to General John Lamb, January 15, 1788, Lamb papers, *NYHS.*

qualities, viz. for selfish, mean, narrow, antifederal and mobbish principles." When Wadsworth continued his criticism of the Constitution, a somber warning assured him "that underhand opposition to federal measures is the direct road to infamy, and political annihilation."[29]

Connecticut Federalists planned a short convention. A few Antifederalist gadflies "are holding up their Heads," a Federalist observed, but this only meant that "our Majority will be less than was at first expected." There were persistent reports that New York Antifederalists were sending bundles of pamphlets "under Cover to our Wrong Heads—& every under hand [*sic*] measure taken to prevent our adopting it." Ellsworth's Christmas present for Antifederalists was a report that they were fast losing strength, supported only by the most stubborn citizens—"the same blindfold party" that had fought against a federal impost. These "wrongheads" had almost ruined Connecticut, had paid New York an annual tribute of £40,000, and had left farmers begging for fair prices for their products. It was time for a change.

Assured of their majority, Federalists gathered in the handsome Hartford State House early in January. A short, businesslike, and victorious session would impress the Antifederalists in Boston. At the outset the debate took an almost comic aspect when William Williams of Lebanon, who was thought to be a die-hard Antifederalist, "rose, & talked a great while part[l]y on one side & partly on the other, & finally observed with striking propriety that *his arguments concluded nothing*." Judge Eliphalet Dyer lessened his prospects for future political honors by joining James Wadsworth in an attack on the Constitution that Federalists regarded as "ridiculous & disgustful."[30] A few Antifederalists with temerity enough to take the floor complained over the lack of safeguards for personal rights, and Colonel Williams was sorry to see that a man might hold office without "explicit acknowledgment of the being of a God." "But," a delighted

29 "To the Head of the Wrongheads," Hartford *American Mercury*, November 26, 1787.

30 Ebenezer Perkins to Simeon Baldwin, January 15, 1788, Baldwin papers, Yale University Library.

Federalist observed, "the objections & the objectors were weak."

Another version of the debates came from an Antifederalist who admitted that his partisans "were far from being the best Orators (a few excepted)." Despite their shortcomings, the Antifederalists had tried to speak, but "they were brow beaten by many of those Cicero'es as they think themselves & others of Superior rank." The minority also suffered rude inattention to their remarks, "which together with Shuffleing & Stamping of feet, caughing Halking Spitting & Whispering, as well by some of the Members as Spectators" made a shambles of their efforts.[31]

General James Wadsworth's leadership of the Connecticut Antifederalists, mortifying as it was to his kinsman Jeremiah, was also discomfiting to the opposition generally. Without him, the anti-Constitution cause would have been hopeless. With Wadsworth, the Antifederalists caused perhaps a day's delay in their adversaries' timetable. Wadsworth leveled his attack on the broad taxing powers granted to the national legislature. One part of the Constitution granted Congress the purse, another gave the legislators the sword; "and that authority, which has the power of the sword and purse, is despotic." It was the northern echo of George Mason's objections in Philadelphia of the preceding summer. But the scene and speaker were vastly different, for in the next breath Wadsworth claimed that the levying of imposts and excises would favor the South at northern expense. Congress simply had no right to usurp state prerogatives to levy taxes. More plainly, federal taxation was only one step removed from federal coercion.

Ellsworth rose to answer Wadsworth. He scolded the Antifederalists for hinting that the delegates at Philadelphia "were inattentive to their duty, and made a sacrifice of the interests of their constituents" in favor of the South. "We live in a cold climate and want warming. Do not they live in a hot climate, and want quenching?" The North was already turning to manufacturing, while the South was agricultural and "hence they import almost everything."[32] Ellsworth then lectured the Antifederalists on "energetic government."

[31] Hugh Ledlie to General John Lamb, January 15, 1788, Lamb papers, NYHS.
[32] Elliot, Debates, II, 190–97.

Under the Confederation a single state might veto the most urgent public business. "I am for coercion by law—that coercion which acts only upon delinquent individuals." On that chilly January day, delegates must have shivered as Ellsworth's oratory was interspersed with allusions to "an armed force . . . the innocent and the guilty . . . [and impending] calamity."

By January 9, the Antifederalists had exhausted their meager oratorical resources. Although the outcome had never been in doubt, a few Antifederalists probably defected at the last moment. Certain delegates "who it is said were decidedly against it untill they came to this town . . . were told plainly, that if they did not turn & Vote for it they must not expect any place either of trust or profits under the New Constitution, thus this capital stroke was reserv'd for the finishing blow," a disgusted Antifederalist reported. Even so, forty good men "did not bow the knee to Baal but in the midst of all the storms of reproaches &c &c stood their ground firm." What else could have been expected, when the vast majority of delegates were "Lawyers rag tag & bobtail with some Revd. Divines," and other "self Interested gentry"?

While the defeated Antifederalists vented their wrath, their newspaper supporters soon claimed that the vote was contrary to the Connecticut citizens' wishes. Devious delegates used "every sophistical reasoning they were masters of, to deceive the less designing, and dragoon them into it," Annapolis readers were assured.[33] Reports from New York took more sting out of the drubbing. Within less than a fortnight after the adjournment, Federalist war horse Jeremiah Wadsworth was changing his tune. "The Antifederalists in our House of Assembly are gaining ground hold up their Heads & since the news of ——— day last week [confirming that] the New York Assembly are mainly & decidedly *antifedt* they are now more open," Wadsworth wailed. "Indeed my Friend," he wrote General Knox, "we are in Jeopardy after all."[34] The Antifederalists, tired of conceding states that fell to federalism with little or no struggle, searched eagerly for signs of resistance. As Connecticut toppled,

[33] Annapolis *Maryland Gazette*, February 21, 1788.
[34] Jeremiah Wadsworth to General Knox, January 20, 1788, Knox papers, *MHS*.

General Lamb in New York was reassured that Antifederalists' hopes lay "in the Virtue & wisdom of your State together with that of Virginia & Massachusetts not adopting" the Constitution.[35]

Although Antifederalists belittled ratification by the small state conventions, each defeat was as meaningful in the process as New York, Virginia, or Massachusetts. Then on January 2, a ship from Georgia arrived in New York with an authentic report that the southernmost state was eager to ratify the Constitution unanimously. On that same day Georgia had in fact become the fourth state to ratify, after less than a week's debate, with every delegate present voting "aye." This latest blow to antifederal hopes could hardly have been unexpected, but tactically the news came at a bad time.

The plight of Georgia was well known, of course. Since Spaniards in the Floridas and Indians on the frontier had forced Georgians to throw up defenses, the little capital of Augusta was an armed camp when the state ratifying convention met. The Constitution held the promise of aid from a federal army at a time when Georgia was sorely pressed for able-bodied militiamen. Still, there had been some lingering doubt among Georgians. A week before the *Georgia State Gazette* printed the Constitution, it had carried an item from South Carolina which cautioned citizens to be on guard against political quacks. Public men, the article cautioned, "are busy in their secret recesses, like spiders laying their baits, furnishing and fixing an extensive political subtle net, to entangle your wings of liberty." The Augusta printer soon became a rabid Federalist, however, and on the eve of the ratifying convention, he carried Washington's admonition that the Constitution had to be accepted immediately. It was idle and vain to talk about a better constitution than this, for "the next will be drawn in blood!" Printer Smith, declaring that two-thirds of the delegates appeared to be federal in sentiment, predicted that all would be converted when "they hear their objections . . . removed by the gentlemen who have studied it attentively." Smith's ear-to-the-ground prediction was accurate, for four days later the convention ratified unanimously. In a hasty celebration that followed, two rusty fieldpieces fired thirteen salvos. The noise faded quickly, but the

[35] Hugh Ledlie to General John Lamb, January 15, 1788, Lamb papers, *NYHS*.

event had distant rumblings of greater significance. One more state had unanimously moved on the highroad to ratification. With little real information to go on, Antifederalists still thought that the pill went down too easily.

The Federalists were doing well, indeed, better than anyone had expected. Dismayed Antifederalists to the southward gleaned every scrap of news from Massachusetts, hoping to find comfort there after a run of bad news. If the reported antifederal victories in the western counties were true, perhaps they could gain enough bargaining power to halt the snowballing ratification process. An adamant Antifederalist block might even force Federalists to concede a few conditional amendments. Such was their hope.

☆ VI ☆

The Specter of Sectionalism

As DELEGATES HUSTLED down old Milk Street in mid-January of 1788, Boston wore a wintry haze, a proper garb for the tense struggle shaping in the convention hall. In the great room back-country delegates in their homespun sat beside Suffolk County gentlemen wearing tailored broadcloth. The shrewd political veteran and the greenest delegate shared a common anxiety—neither knew what was going to happen. There was speculation everywhere in the convention anterooms, nearby taverns, and down by the wharves. Moreover, thoughtful men in every part of the Union kept a weather eye turned in their direction. Dutch bankers, French ministers, and London merchants were far from disinterested. Americans abroad also strained for news of ratification.

From his post as the American minister to Louis XVI's court, Thomas Jefferson read every scrap of information from his home-land, eagerly awaiting news from the Federal Convention. Jefferson saw defects in the American system but "the comparison of our government with those of Europe are like a comparison of heaven and hell," he insisted. Then the long-expected Constitution arrived, and in a penetrating commentary Jefferson spelled out his views—ideas that the leaderless Antifederalist delegates gathered in Boston would have embraced.

Jefferson favored the separation-of-powers concept, approved the taxing power granted Congress, and was "captivated by the compromise of the opposite claims of the great and little states" in the two branches of the legislature. Congressional voting by individual members rather than by states and the presidential veto power pleased him, along with some "other good things of less moment." "I will add now what I do not like," he told Madison. "First the omission of a bill of rights," which freemen need to protect themselves from "every government on earth, general or particular, and what no just

89

government should refuse, or rest on inference." The American minister had other objections that were a prescient antifederal doctrine. There was no provision for rotation in office, which in the President's case would tend to make him "an officer for life." As with the good parts, there were a few bad things of minor importance. Then Jefferson showed that his intellectual processes were in the same channel as the leading Antifederalists. In the mixture of good and bad, Jefferson was perplexed, but he leaned toward the call for a second convention. The public debate would expose more weaknesses, and the reassembled delegates could say, "We see now what you wish."

As for the energetic government which Federalists sought, Jefferson was not sympathetic. He confessed himself no friend of "a very energetic government," for their tendency was "always oppressive."[1] The next day, however, Jefferson proclaimed himself a neutral in the party contest over ratification, and then came up with another objection. "Would it not have been better to assign to Congress exclusively the article of imposts for federal purposes, and to have left direct taxation exclusively to the states?" No Antifederalist pamphleteer framed the question more cogently.

With his perspective altered by time and distance, Jefferson was to make several revisions of his earlier position. But at the outset, Jefferson raised objections which were so universally held among Antifederalists that the coincidence of viewpoints was striking and prophetic.

The second-convention chorus was indeed swelling as the Massachusetts convention began. Not only were the leading Antifederalists promoting it in private, but there was Lee's pamphlet (now spread to every crossroads meeting place) and a battery of antifederal essayists in Boston. Federalist tacticians in Boston had their orders—the Constitution must be ratified without any qualifications, additions, or deletions.

In the Massachusetts convention, far more than in any other ratifying body that had met, there existed a silent undercurrent. This was the prejudice that existed between the northern and southern sec-

[1] Jefferson to Joseph Jones, August 14, 1787, 12 Jefferson Papers 33–35.

tions of the Union. Sectional pride and prejudice were not unique in American history by 1788. The seeds had been planted more than 150 years earlier and continuously nurtured by every difference between the North and South: climate, geography, attitudes toward religion, dialect, and, of course, slavery. The Stamp Act crisis had forced the sections to make common cause of their grievances. The Revolution had prolonged the alliance, but when the military crisis passed, the tendency was to backslide into the old prejudices. The long overland distances between the sections hampered communication, discouraged all but the adventurous from travel, and promoted an insular spirit in regions where great valleys and deep rivers separated men's interests as surely as a variation of tongue or ethnic origins.

In New England, the tendency had increasingly been to look toward the ocean for a livelihood. Ships were built and provisioned, loaded with cargoes, and sent to the ends of the earth. There exotic products were crammed into holds and borne back to Mystic, Salem, Marblehead, or Boston. The men who raised the pork that was salted for sailors and the men who bought that pork for their crews met together at that Massachusetts convention. Although the one man's mortgage might have been in the other's strongbox, both had firm faith in New England institutions. For the most part they distrusted southerners, who—in the popular mind at least—lived a desultory life, supported mainly by the grudging labor of slaves. It was this prejudice that Ellsworth had exploited in the Connecticut convention, and this same bias pervaded the Massachusetts assembly. Regardless of the higher appeals to unite, the important local political battles were often won on the basis of sectional interests.

Months before the Federal Convention met, influential public men were at odds over the value of union. Theodore Sedgwick was not so sure that the Union was worth saving in August, 1786. Piqued by the decline in northern commerce and shipping, which southerners shrugged off in favor of cheaper foreign endeavors, Sedgwick thought that continued union "will sacrafice [*sic*] everything to a meer chimera. Even the appearance of a union cannot in the way we now are long be preserved." A suspicious southerner had opinions equally certain. The North was interested only in protecting its own commerce, Virginian William Grayson insisted, and some northerners wanted to prevent the southern states "from importing any more of the seed of Cain."[2] One of the significant pieces of legislation under the Confederation, the Northwest Ordinance of 1787, had been the result of a partial compromise between the two sections. The clause prohibiting slavery in the territory "was agreed to by the Southern members for the purpose of preventing Tobacco and Indigo from being made on the N.W. side of the Ohio as well as for several other political reasons," Grayson admitted.

It was now common knowledge that the northern delegates in the Continental Congress, chiefly the Massachusetts delegation, had favored a surrender of navigation rights on the Mississippi River for commercial advantages with Spain. The Mississippi concession was but one of several smoldering issues that Congress pigeonholed in May, 1787.

The North-South schism was beyond the embryonic stage at the Federal Convention. Madison frankly discussed sectionalism in Philadelphia, declaring at one point that the Union was endangered by *"the great southern and northern interests . . . being opposed to each other."* He then minimized all but one difference between the small and large states above or below an invisible divider. Madison was blunt. "The institution of slavery & its consequences formed the line of discrimination."[3]

Both Federalists and Antifederalists exploited prejudice against the South, because both knew they were tilling fertile soil. After the Federalists praised the union concept in one breath, they preached antisouthernism in the next. Ellsworth's readiness to capitalize on sectional bitterness was notorious. King spoke of the prominent southern Antifederalists as the "Nabobs of Virginia." Samuel A. Otis declared that a united New England "will forever counterpoise any cabals & manoeuvres of the South."[4] Yankee Nicholas Gilman believed the southern Antifederalists based their opposition on "an ill-

[2] William Grayson to Madison, May 28, 1786, *LCC*, VIII, 373.
[3] 2 Farrand 10.
[4] Samuel A. Otis to George Thatcher, March 18, 1788, Thatcher papers, *BPL*.

founded jealousy of New England on the subject of commercial regulations."[5]

Above the Susquehanna, Antifederalists took few pains to conceal their disdain of southern conditions, while still welcoming aid and comfort from Lee and Mason. How can southern slaveholders given to "dissipation, and a passion for aristocratic distinctions" understand the northern love of frugality, equality, and freedom? Governor Clinton asked (writing as "Cato"). Warren harped on the three-fifths compromise, which was bound to be unpopular in New England. The formula that apportioned direct taxes and congressional seats according to the number of freemen in each state plus "three-fifths of all other persons" was an affront to Massachusetts. There was no more validity "in admitting the *beasts* of the field, or *trees* of the forest, to be classed with *free electors*." James Winthrop took time from his librarian's chores at Harvard to point out the incompatibility of the two great sections. Not only slavery but "the ignorance and poverty of the lower classes, the softness of the climate and dissoluteness of manners" marked the southern character. Maine editor Thomas Wait foresaw Congress divided along the usual North-South lines with every man ranged "upon one side or the other," contending "with as much earnestness and warmth as if at an Olympic Game." At Springfield, newspaper readers were told the Presidency was a political plum that would bring North and South into "the most violent competitions" with "sufficient pretences for recourse to arms."[6]

There were other appeals made by New England Antifederalists which were no less subtle. Already conscious of their ancestral background, Yankees were warned that the efforts of certain states "to keep their blood pure" might be thwarted when Congress controlled immigration and naturalization. Unchecked immigration, New England bluebloods were told, came at the expense of religion and morality. "The eastern states have, by keeping separate from the foreign mixtures, acquired their present greatness in the course of a century

[5] Nicholas Gilman to John Sullivan, October 31, 1787, Charles E. L. Wingate, *Life and Letters of Paine Wingate*, I, 213.

[6] "Cornelius," Springfield *Hampshire Chronicle*, December 18, 1787.

and a half, and have preserved their religion and morals."[7] All of these advantages of blood and birth would be swept away, citizens of Massachusetts were assured, if the Constitution became the supreme law of the land.

Slavery countenanced, direct taxes, overbearing southerners in Congress, foreigners swarming our shores, local laws crushed under a federal monstrosity—such arguments gave the Antifederalists a ready store of ammunition for the Massachusetts convention debates. Politically naïve, many Antifederalists believed their work in Boston would take only a few days, that after a brief discussion and vote they would soon be on their way home. The Federalists, however, had an altogether different conception of the upcoming convention.

In the mind's eye it is easy to visualize Federalist leaders scrutinizing the list of delegates, checking off the certain votes, the doubtful delegates, and the men beyond redemption. Not far away, Antifederalists were indulging in the same exercise. The most optimistic Antifederalist figured that 222 delegates "was Desidedly against it, out of 360" attending the convention. Federalist Harry Jackson, who knew his men as well as he knew the current price of soldier's certificates, calculated 194 federal votes, 166 antifederal—a remarkably accurate preview of the final ballot. If the voting were to be close, on at least one score the Federalists could be smug. "It is astonishing to see the weight of *respectability, integrity, property*, & ability on the Side of the proposed Constitution," Jackson marveled, "and on the other side the ——— ——— Characters that oppose it ——— my god the contrast."[8]

Antifederalists talked of a forty-vote majority, but it was difficult to discern who was holding the whip in hand needed to maintain party discipline. Samuel Adams' flirtation with antifederalism was still worrisome to the opposition. But where was the man of recognized abilities ready to lead the Antifederalists? The political truism—that a disciplined minority can defeat an unorganized majority—was soon to be verified again.

[7] "Agrippa," *Massachusetts Gazette*, December 28, 1787, quoted in Ford, *Essays on the Constitution*, 79.
[8] Henry Jackson to General Knox, January 20, 1788. Knox papers, *MHS*.

The restless Antifederalists had few outstanding men who had survived the elections and might have assumed party leadership. Dr. Samuel Holten, who was highly regarded by the Antifederalists, became ill and finally withdrew from the convention altogether. Dr. John Taylor, the darling of the paper-money crowd, was a shrewd but a second-rate leader. Charles Turner of Scituate was a man of parts, but he, too, became ill, failed to attend most of the debates, and finally switched political horses. Benjamin Randall was a country politician of the old school, a would-be Demosthenes who cared little for grammatical niceties. These men tried to carry the day for antifederalism, aided by a trio of Maine men—William Widgery, General Samuel Thompson, and Samuel Nasson. Widgery knew the Antifederalists needed a well-known public figure on the convention floor. Lacking one, he did what little he could to fill the vacancy. Widgery himself was a back-country politician, with obvious native abilities, but little education or property. Thompson, in contrast, had some share of the world's goods, a military title, and not a little self-confidence. Nasson was from the same mold as Widgery—an unlettered veteran of the Revolution who took up politics as a side line. Conspicuously absent from the Antifederalist benches were college graduates, lawyers, merchants, or men who felt more comfortable on a countinghouse highboy than on a milk stool.

Every circumstance worked against the Antifederalists' hopes for a short convention. Because of the large number of delegates, there was not a hall with adequate seating in the Massachusetts metropolis; after wasting some days in moving around, they finally decided to stay in "mr. Mooreheads Meeting house" on Milk Street. By a public subscription, stairs were built and seats were provided for six to eight hundred spectators. Then the newspaper editors asked for and received a special press gallery. Popular Governor Hancock was chosen president of the convention, but he excused himself on account of illness and turned the dubious honor of chairmanship over to William Cushing.

On January 12 the delegates shuffled into the meeting house, "the air unwholesome" inside, while much too cold outside. It was high time for action, as business was suffering from the excitement gen-

95

erated by the convention. "We are in that kind of suspense now which is injurious to all private pursuits," Nathan Dane commented after he had dolefully concluded that the Constitution probably lacked "monarchy enough in it for some of our Massachusetts men or democracy enough for others."[9] The Federalists strengthened their position by managing to get their men chosen chairmen of the committees designated to investigate election irregularities. Increasingly disturbed by their lack of guidance, the Antifederalists finally made a gain. Unpredictable Sam Adams moved that Gerry be permitted to sit in the convention to "elucidate the Business by Information &c., that *possibly* had Escaped the memory of the other Gentlemen of the general Convention."

Momentary confusion gave Antifederalists an opening. The convention voted to invite Gerry to join them as an observer and commentator. A few Federalists were struck dumb by the audacious move. "Sam Adams is an arch Devil," Winthrop Sargeant gasped. Another Federalist thought Gerry was dragged into the convention "as a dictionary to use occasionally" because of his known opposition. Others may have agreed with Madison, who had feared that Gerry's defeat for a convention seat would leave him angry enough to become a vindictive political busybody. Placing Gerry in the convention actually played into the Federalists' hand, as Madison saw it. "On the floor of the Convention he could only have urged bad arguments, which might be answered & exposed by good ones," while his insinuations in public places could not be so easily put down.[10] Time was to sustain Madison's judgment, proving once more that even when the Antifederalists appeared to have made a gain, it was in reality a loss.

Adams' position during these days was agonizing. On the one hand, his son was gravely ill. On the other, he was beset by doubts which political expediency magnified. From his old friend Samuel Osgood, caretaker of the empty Continental treasury, Adams received a shocking analysis of the Constitution. Osgood, who usually played his political cards discreetly, bared his bosom to a fellow Yankee. Con-

---

[9] Nathan Dane to General Knox, December 27, 1787, Knox papers, *MHS*.

[10] Sargeant to General Knox, January 12, 1788, Knox papers, *MHS*; Madison to Tench Coxe, January 3, 1788, Madison papers, *DLC*.

fessing that the Constitution "has scarcely been out of my Mind since it first made its Appearance," Osgood said he was "more & more persuaded, that it is a Plan, that the common People can never understand—That if adopted—The Scribes & Pharisees only will be able to interpret, & give it a Meaning." "It has cost me many a Sleepless Night to find out the most obnoxious Part of the proposed Plan," Osgood tortuously wrote. "And I have finally fixed upon the exclusive Legislation in the Ten Miles Square." Then Osgood stated another fear. "I believe if the new Government should take Place, it would prove true, that the first Rebellion against it, would break out in the Town of Boston."[11] Why? Because Boston would scarcely be represented in the new Congress. Could Boston surrender its commercial privileges to a disinterested and perhaps inimical body?

Racked by personal doubts that Antifederalists had already nourished, Adams could not have taken Osgood's words lightly. Yet Adams lacked the confidence and ardor that he had in full measure a decade earlier. While he brooded and fretted, the Antifederalists floundered in a political quagmire. And if Gerry's arrival was supposed to have saved the day, then this was another disappointment. Gerry took his seat, more or less instructed to speak only when spoken to, and an observer noted that for some days he "had been sitting, and biting the head of his cane." The careful selection of committee members to investigate contested seats resulted in reports that favored the Federalists in every case. With experienced chairmen reporting that the Antifederalists petitions were "not supported by evidence," the Federalists acquired votes from Taunton, Williamstown, Great Barrington, and Sheffield.[12]

The Antifederalists seemed to have been weakened by informants who attended their private strategy sessions. The Federalists, who at first were afraid to test their strength on the issue of allowing Gerry a seat, grew bolder with knowledge of their opponents' strategy and of their own growing strength. "Tomorrow we are told certain Enquiries are to be moved for by the Opposition, & that Mr. Gerry under the Idea of stating Facts is to state his reasons," Rufus King

[11] Samuel Osgood to Samuel Adams, January 5, 1788, Adams papers, *NYPL.*
[12] "Convention of 1788," Massachusetts Archives.

noted, ". . . this will be opposed and we shall on the division be able to form some Idea of our relative strength."

After a desultory debate over the necessity for annual elections, General Thompson was called to order for backhanded praise of the Shays's affair. Then the Antifederalist attack shifted to the consolidation scare. "Our manners," Randall said, "were widely different from the southern States—their elections were not so free and unbiassed" as those of New England. In a consolidated government this would inevitably "introduce manners among us which would set us at continual variance." The sword of sectionalism, however, had two edges. When an Antifederalist complained that Congress would impose unreasonable taxes, the opposition had a ready answer. Dawes asserted that land bore the brunt of taxation. He added that foreign vessels were as welcome in southern ports as those "built, navigated and freighted from Salem or Boston." Thus foreigners, especially the British, were making huge profits on southern freights—profits which rightfully belonged to New England. Ratify the Constitution, Dawes implied, and a flow of southern specie would make its way northward as the tax burden was shifted from the land to imports.[13]

Since a short session was precisely what the Federalist board of strategy had decided against, they pushed through a resolution to debate the Constitution paragraph by paragraph. At times, Theophilus Parsons and other Federalists became petulant when their opponents upbraided the lawyers and other educated men for their well-reasoned speeches that were in marked contrast with the back-country harangues. At one point, Judge Dana asked if an educated man ought to be considered an enemy to the rights of his country. "Are there any among this honorable body . . . possessed of minds capable of such narrow prejudice?" Dana knew there were, but he had a word for them. With such delegates "it is in vain to reason," and as some of the Antifederalists had suggested "we had better come to a decision and go home."

While the session labored onward, the Antifederalists took some consolation from the *American Herald* columns, where Warren and

[13] *Debates of the Massachusetts Convention of 1788* (Boston, 1856), 156.

other favorites continued their raking broadsides on the Federalist camp. Although their newspaper fusilades did little damage, some psychological sustenance doubtless was provided by the outpourings of printer Powars' newspaper. Powars' paper, sold on the narrow streets of Boston, proclaimed the "DISADVANTAGES OF FEDERALISM, *Upon the NEW PLAN*," listing thirteen arguments that ranged from the "*Trade of Boston* transferred to *Philadelphia*" to "*Religion abolished*"—all of which bore the signature "TRUTH."[14] While the Antifederalists fired daring, but futile, shots at their adversaries, Sam Adams was placed under further strain by the death of his only son.

Warren and Gerry kept busy after hours, stubbornly refusing to accept the political facts confronting them. After the Federalists won the right to prolong debate, some Antifederalists apparently began promoting the idea of adjournment. Warren wrote an essay favoring the scheme "until the sense of Virginia can be known." The Virginia convention was still months away—proof that her leading men were "not *extravagantly* zealous in this matter." "The great danger in this business is, from *precipitation, not* from *delay*," Warren counseled. Adjournment would not only allow time to "ripen the judgment of our own citizens," but also permit an exchange of opinions with states, where headlong ratification was not the order of the day.

Outside of New England, partisans from both sides yearned for hints as to the progress of the engagement in Boston. The Philadelphia *Independent Gazetteer*, hoping that Massachusetts Antifederalists could somehow turn the tide, printed reports that the back-country delegates in Boston were anti-Constitutional in sentiment. Mindful of the Federal bastion in Boston, the writer declared that "the old jealousy seems to prevail, viz. that the *Boston folks* aim to rule and govern as they please, and are always setting themselves up as *patterns* for, and *dictators* to, the whole state." Postmaster-General Hazard, about to step into a hornet's nest because of the snarled mail service, sat in New York and pondered the situation in Boston. "What will your Convention do?" he asked Belknap. Even if Massa-

[14] Broadside collection, *MHS.*

chusetts ratified, would it be "by such a majority as to secure the peaceable adoption of the new Constitution?"[15] "The intelligence from Massachusetts begins to be very omnious to the Constitution," Madison wrote Washington. His informants reported that the Antifederalists were gaining strength from the old Shays's crowd, plus the Maine men who feared their dreams for statehood would either be shattered under the Constitution, or at least given low priority. "The operation of such an event on this State may easily be foreseen," he added. "The decision of Massachusetts either way will involve the result in this State."

Madison's information came from reliable sources. "Our prospects are gloomy," Rufus King wrote ruefully, "but hope is not entirely extinguished." On January 19, Gerry, perhaps bored by his do-nothing role, asked for the floor to throw some light on the particular point then being debated. The Federalists were in no mood to give Gerry a hearing, for they were already disturbed by the report that he was taking notes, "which is considered as very indelicate on his part." Judge Dana immediately questioned Gerry's propriety. Noisy calls for order and arguments over Gerry's privileges ensued, until the distraught chairman finally heard a motion to adjourn and seized the opportunity to end the session. Gerry and Dana chanced to meet at the hall entrance, where Gerry charged Dana with conduct somewhat less than gentlemanly.[16] Dana made a caustic reply, and it seemed the two were ready to let canes and fists settle the matter. "We were in danger of the utmost confusion," King told Madison. "However, the Gentlemen separated."

Gerry stalked away, vowing he would not return to the convention. A committee of disheartened Antifederalists soon called on Gerry, trying to unruffle his feelings so that he would rejoin them. These Antifederalists, General Lincoln sneered, were men "whom six months since Mr. Gerry & evry [*sic*] good man heartily despised, as devoid of principle & fomenters of faction—men who are indebted to the late tumults in this Commonwealth for their present situation."[17] Thoroughly disgruntled, Gerry was in no mood to

[15] Hazard to Belknap, January 16, 1788, *MHS, Collections*, 5th Series, III, 2–3.
[16] Rufus King to Madison, January 20, 1788, Madison papers, *DLC*.

comply with their pleas. He wrote the acting president of the convention, Judge Cushing, that Dana's attack had "an appearance of party virulence which I did not expect, and he followed one misrepresentation with another."[18] Gerry said his opposition to the Constitution was no secret, but he had not expected to be abused by men "so deficient in liberality, as to bear animosity towards me on this account." Gerry included his recollections of the slavery compromise at Philadelphia and added that he would no longer appear where his conduct was impugned by men who wanted him kept silent.

The incident removed Gerry from the scene, but it left a bad taste all around. "His absence will be a great point gained by the other side," a disturbed Federalist noted. Although most Federalists were delighted by any comeuppance for Gerry, they regretted his being made a hero. To Gerry, the personal attacks came from political enemies determined "to hunt down all who remain attached to revolutionary principles."

Almost forgotten in the acrimonious welter of the Gerry–Dana incident was the spark that ignited the fireworks—the issue that populous Massachusetts was to have only eight representatives in the proposed Congress, while undernourished Georgia would have three. Asked to explain the disparity, Gerry gave a fairly accurate statement. At the Federal Convention it had been pointed out that Georgia was growing and also "that the appointment was made, not, by any fixed principle, but by a compromise." Antifederalists charged that the North was simply truckling to the southern slaveholders. Dana and King had ready apologies for the concession. Put the matter the other way, King said, and the compromise had perspective. Five Negro children in South Carolina "are to pay as much tax as the three governors of New Hampshire, Massachusetts and Connecticut."[19] Antifederalist Nasson had a different view, for "three of our infants in the cradle are to be rated as high [for tax purposes] as five of the working negroes of Virginia."

[17] Benjamin Lincoln to Washington, January 20, 1788, *DHC*, V. 451–52.

[18] Elbridge Gerry to Judge William Cushing, January 21, 1788, "Convention of 1788," Massachusetts Archives.

[19] *Debates of the Massachusetts Convention*, 135.

After two weeks of debate, the Antifederalists seemed to have recovered some strength, contrary to their opponents' strategy. Perhaps the Federalist plan to debate the Constitution item-by-item had been a mistake. A fear that a freeman's rights were endangered, plus "a distrust of men of property or Education have a more powerful Effect upon the minds of our Opponents than any specific Objections," Rufus King admitted. "If the Opposition was grounded on any precise Points, I am persuaded that it might be weakened if not entirely overcome—But every attempt to remove their fixed and violent Jealousy seems hitherto to operate as a confirmation of that baneful passion." In short, the Massachusetts Antifederalists were not responding in the desired manner—they refused to grasp the loaves of logic offered them. King thought the Antifederalists still lacked a majority but admitted that "their Adversaries . . . are not entirely confident of their own" strength. Frustrated by the stubborn attitude of the opposition, the Reverend Jeremy Belknap resorted to layman's language. "The anti-federal speakers are very clamorous, petulant, tedious, and provoking . . . men whose only force lies in noise and opposition." With sagging spirits another Federalist told General Knox of the unexpected turn in affairs. "The prospects [are] not very good—numbers are at present against us—& the Opposition leaders say they are sure of the Victory." Still, Federalists knew what had to be done. "We know all is at stake & work accordingly."[20]

Meanwhile, the Antifederalists began seeking a way out of their predicament. Samuel Nasson, a hard-shelled Maine Antifederalist, thought his side was ahead by forty-eight votes. But the opposition was indefatigable and making inroads. "Mr. Oatis Can tell you what Influance [*sic*] the Boston Members has over that of the Country therefore it is impsable to Read its doom at Present time," Nasson wrote a friend.[21] One way out, the Antifederalists reasoned, was to ratify an amended version of the Constitution. Federalists ridiculed this proposal and were dead-set against the second antifederal suggestion that the convention might adjourn to await the call for a

[20] Nathaniel Gorham to Henry Knox, January 16, 1788, Knox Papers, *MHS*.
[21] Samuel Nasson to George Thatcher, January 22, 1788, Thatcher papers, *BPL*.

second federal convention. The *American Herald* urged the latter course, pointing out that another convention probably would avoid the mistakes of the first. If the Constitution were ratified as it stood, amendments would be as hard to enact as it would be "to remove the ark from the mountain of Ararat . . . for the least attempt . . . may be construed into treasonable practices."

The Maine Antifederalists tried to hold the opposition together. Gerry was gone and Adams silent, but Thompson renewed the cry for an adjournment. Why not wait for a few months, he asked, "and see what our sister States do?" If Massachusetts played a waiting game, she might help dictate terms for a revised version of the Constitution. "Some say, swallow the whole now, and pick out the bone afterwards. But I say, let us pick off the meat and throw the bone away." Nasson stated other reasons for the necessity of a speedy adjournment.[22] The convention had to adjourn, Nasson declared, because the delegates from the distant towns were nearly broke. The paragraph-by-paragraph debate had taken too long, affairs at home had to be attended, and many delegates found their purses perilously flattened. Federalists countered that funds for the delegates' expenses were coming from the state treasury and would soon be ready, but on January 24 the irritated Widgery said a motion for adjournment had been made, and he objected "to the motion's being winked out of sight." The Antifederalists now began pressing for a showdown.

Undoubtedly the Federalists were frightened by this maneuver. Unable to postpone a vote, they gave their lungs a workout and shouted "nay" until the rafters vibrated. Cushing declared the motion defeated without a roll-call ballot. Relieved Federalists discreetly made no joyful demonstrations, but an enthusiast in the gallery started applauding. "Some who were [near] by cried *hush*, with a continued sound of the *sh*: this was interpreted [by the Antifederalists as] a *hiss*," spectator Belknap reported. "They said they were insulted, and were for removing, or shutting up the galleries; and it was above an hour before they would let the matter subside."[23] Tem-

[22] *Debates of the Massachusetts Convention*, 97–98; see also T. Parsons, *Memoir of Theopolius Parsons*, 97–98.

[23] Jeremy Belknap to Hazard, January 25, 1788, *MHS, Collections*, 5th Series, III, 9.

pers were indeed short. The Antifederalists, as the peeved Belknap said, *"will* not be convinced, they *will* not be silenced."

The inevitable bribery charge had erupted earlier that week when an anonymous article in the Boston *Gazette* appeared on the streets with the incendiary headline "Bribery & Corruption!!!" The report declared a "diabolical Plan" was afoot to buy Antifederalist votes. The vote-buying cash came "from a neighboring State," and more collections were probably being made closer to Boston for this evil purpose, the exposé hinted.[24] Their faces flushed by anger, Federalists held the newspaper aloft in the convention hall and ordered an immediate investigation of the charges. Federalist newspapers pounced on the incident, and attention was focused not upon the truth of the charges but upon exposing the author of the bombshell. Within a few days a penitent local citizen admitted his authorship. He had overheard a statement that efforts were being made to silence delegate Nasson, and another report that in Providence "a *bag of money* had been sent down to Boston to quiet the Antifederalists." Perhaps a few of the most impecunious Antifederalists secretly hoped that there was truth in the charges, but the investigating committee branded the report totally false. Unofficially, the affair produced some bad aftereffects. As with most accusations, the story had spread faster than the retraction.

Nonetheless, the signs in favor of ratification seemed to be decreasing. Clearly, an adjournment would derail the Constitution. "It will be a total distruction of it," said a saddened Henry Jackson. His confidant, General Knox, became so alarmed that he wrote a note to the one man who could save the Constitution in Massachusetts—Governor John Hancock. Influential Antifederalists "in almost every state" wanted a second federal convention, Knox wrote, but inquire into the motives of the Antifederalists and in each case there was some sectional grievance, or perhaps a personal speculation. Then Knox gave his screws a last turn. "Every thing depends on Massachusetts."

The defeated motion for adjournment gave the Federalists time

[24] Samuel Phillips Savage to George Thatcher, January 24, 1788, Thatcher Papers, *Historical Magazine*, VI, 2nd series, 268; Harding, *Ratification in Massachusetts*, 103; *Massachusetts Centinel*, January 30, 1788.

to revise their strategy. When debates resumed in the established tenor, with slurs cast at lawyers and the lawyers replying a little more gently, Federalists realized that to demand immediate ratification of the Constitution, unamended, was too risky. After going over the list of delegates time and again, federal strategists still found a substantial number with questionable allegiances—the prospect of defeat moved them toward compromise. "We are now thinking of amendments to be submitted not as a condition of our assent & Ratification, but as the opinion of the Convention subjointed to their Ratification," King told Madison. A month earlier, the Federalists would have been appalled by the mere suggestion of amendments. In veering from their original position, the Federalists not only showed political expediency, but also recognized the sincere apprehensions of a great many delegates. Silas Lee of Biddeford listened to courthouse conversations in Lincoln County and assumed that "the Majority are decidedly against the Measure."[25] Delegate Nathaniel Barrell predicted that ratification, if it ever came, "entails wretchedness on my posterity—Slavery on my children." While the Federalists put in motion their plan to bring in amendments, King was still perplexed by the Antifederalist attitude. "The opposition complains that the Lawyers, Judges, Clergymen, Merchants and men of education are all in Favor of the constitution," he complained, "and that for that reason they appear to be able to make the worst, appear the better cause."[26]

Thus the Federalists took no chances. Acceptable amendments had to be offered to the Antifederalists on a silver platter borne by someone they trusted and admired. The perfect choice was obvious. The popular Hancock was easily flattered, courted popularity, and had higher aspirations than the governorship. If approached in a suitable manner, Hancock would assent, bringing with his support perhaps a dozen or more votes.

Despite the public esteem which Hancock enjoyed, Federalist associates regarded him as vain and quite susceptible to any aggrandizement of his reputation or fortune. A Boston newspaper reported

[25] Silas Lee to George Thatcher, January 23, 1788, Thatcher papers, BPL.
[26] Rufus King to Madison, January 27, 1788, Madison papers, *DLC*.

a rumor passing along the eastern seaboard—"MR. HANCOCK is talked of as Vice-President," provided the Constitution were adopted. Could the rumor have been planted to turn Hancock's head? Everybody knew that Washington was to be offered the Presidency, but those who knew Washington well also had heard him disavow political ambitions, which would leave the Presidential door open to a New Englander. Those who knew Hancock well had already discerned the Federalist strategy. "Hancock pretends to be sick, that he may not hazard himself 'till he is clear there is a majority for it," Arthur Lee wrote his brother, "which it is to be apprehended will be obtained by the intrigue in Boston, which Hancock, King & Gorham are pretty adept in managing."[27]

From the Federalist caucus held on January 30 came the tour de force. "We cannot gain the question without some recommendatory amendments," Gorham conceded, ". . . with them I presume we shall have a small majority." Theophilus Parsons wrote a series of recommended amendments meant to mollify the discontented Antifederalists. Hancock was not too ill to listen to the Federalists explain their ruse. The next day, King revealed what the governor wanted in exchange for his support. "Hancock will hereafter receive the universal support of Bowdoin's friends; and *we told him, if Virginia does not unite, which is problematical, he is considered as the only fair candidate for President.*"[28] The governor was to present the amendments as his own idea, a bit of play-acting he seemed to enjoy.

While the convention was momentarily becalmed, Antifederalists in the *American Herald* office also considered making some concessions. Steadfast James Winthrop beseeched the delegates to amend the Constitution before ratifying it. Then, as the Antifederalist opposition caved in, Winthrop begged them to insist upon a bill of rights. Talk about amendments augured well for the Federalists, King thought, because it proved that the opposition was "not so confident of their Numbers since hitherto they have reprobated the Suggestion

[27] Arthur Lee to Richard Henry Lee, February 19, 1788, Lee papers, Virginia University Library.
[28] Rufus King to General Knox, February 1, 1788, King, *Life of King*, I, 319.

of Amendments and insisted among their Party on a total Rejection of the Constitution."

The strategy of delay had worked wonders, for the initiative now rested with the Federalists, and the Antifederalists found themselves fighting a desperate rear-guard action. When Hancock made his appearance, looking properly peaked for a man a few hours out of the sickbed, even Federalist George R. Minot was disgusted by the governor's reception. Hancock was led to his place with such ceremony, Minot said, that it "seemed to approach to servility, and looked like the blind adoration paid to Kings."[29] As secretary to the convention, Minot was in a choice spot to observe the proceedings. The governor made it appear that the amendments represented his own ideas, "formed in the entervals [*sic*] of his pain," to be sent forward with the duly ratified Constitution. In this way the ratification process would not be impeded, and the necessary amendments would be added to the Constitution later—they could take Hancock's word for it. The whole procedure seemed a mockery to Minot, as he peeked over Hancock's shoulder. The amendments "were most certainly in the hand writing of a leading constitutionalist, (Mr. Parsons) a few words excepted, which were in the hand writing of Dr. Jarvis, & one article by Mr. King." Hancock's appearance with the amendments unquestionably surprised the Antifederalists.

Once Hancock finished his speech, Federalist managers sighed with relief. Only two days earlier, King had revealed some misgivings about Hancock. "If Mr. Hancock does not disappoint our present Expectations our wishes will be gratified," he observed. "But his character is not entirely free from a portion of caprice." Suddenly, all the capriciousness was gone. The nine proposed amendments were a distillation of all the Antifederalists' favored nostrums. Discerning Antifederalists soon complained that there was more sound than fury in the list, but at the moment their own lack of cohesion left them without counterproposals.

Although bewildered and dismayed, the Antifederalists were still able to stall. They requested time to think about the amendments; a

[29] George R. Minot, *Diary*, entry "1788 Jany & Febry," Minot papers, *MHS*.

final roll-call vote was postponed until February 6. A committee was chosen to study the Hancock amendments and report. "We have a Majority of Fedaralists [*sic*] on this Committee and flatter ourselves the result will be favorable,"[30] King noted with tongue-in-cheek. King and his friends began playing cat-and-mouse with the Antifederalists—many fence-straddlers used Hancock's amendments as an excuse to jump into the Federalists' ranks. Antifederalists, hamstrung by town-meeting instructions, were given a clerical blessing if they switched, and besides "they ought to *repent of their wicked promise*." By proposing amendments, the Federalists had indeed spread confusion among the Antifederalists.

Although the tide of debate was obviously ebbing, several Antifederalists shunned any move toward a compromise. Dr. John Taylor recalled that nothing in the Constitution made allowance for amendments from the state conventions, and to discuss them was "treading on unsafe ground." Since the convention was to "take the whole or reject the whole," adjournment seemed to be the only alternative. Widgery agreed that an adjournment was the most feasible course. General Thompson, adamant and surly, said the Hancock resolution would win over "some men—he did not say Judases."[31]

On February 5, the Antifederalists made their last stand. A motion to adjourn so that the towns might discuss the proposed amendments was crushed—only 115 out of 329 delegates present voted for the desperate bid.

Wondrously, men who a few days before had been chastizing Federalists as would-be aristocrats were now clamoring to join them. In January, for example, young William Symmes had denounced the Constitution as a scheme designed "to burden us with a standing army of ravenous [tax] collectors—harpies, perhaps from another State . . . never known to have bowels for any purpose but to fatten on the life-blood of the people." The swift federal reversal caught up Symmes, and with the other recanters Symmes declared he had never been entirely opposed to the Constitution; hence, he could now support it, "acquitted to my own conscience." The sturdy Maine dele-

[30] Rufus King to Madison, February 3, 1788, Madison papers, *DLC.*
[31] *Debates of the Massachusetts Convention,* 227, 243.

gation had been shaken, too. Nathaniel Barrell had been chosen a delegate after he tortuously described the Constitution as "so obscure and ambiguous that the most capacious mind cannot fully comprehend it." But then Barrell made his political swan song. Barrell said he favored the motion to adjourn, but if that were impossible, he was tempted to risk the displeasure of his constituents and "adopt it without their consent."[32]

Faced with desertion by men who had formerly made up their phalanx, the Antifederalists strove to maintain some discipline. "Old Thompson howls, whines & whiffles" a Federalist jibed, as Thompson's scathing glances helped hold dozens of Antifederalists in line.[33] "The Antis are affraid [*sic*] & very skittish, for fear they may be lead [*sic*] into a *trap* by the proposed amendments," Henry Jackson complained, ". . . indeed they are so damnable stupid & ignorant they cannot trust themselves." Some Antifederalists, who had expected a week's absence from their shops and farms, found that four weeks in Boston had left them penniless. If the amendments could not persuade them, perhaps other means might. "The whole race of the *Antis* are a Set of *poor devils*, without one farthing in their pockets, & it will be impossible for them to leave the Town, unless they receive their pay," Jackson reported. The state treasurer reported his coffers were empty. But, Jackson added that the Federalists were spreading the word, "If the Constitution is adopted, there will be no difficulty respecting Pay. If it is *not* they must look to the Treasurer for it."[34]

Even this kind of pressure would not budge a few stubborn Antifederalists. To them, General Lincoln conceded, concessions had to be made, even though they were offered to Shays-tainted men, "who were so lately intoxicated with large draughts of liberty, and who were thirsting for more." Eager for news from Boston, Postmaster-General Hazard was anxious over the outcome, for notwithstanding the Federalists' abilities "a nose of wax will be counted one [vote], as well as any other nose."[35]

32 *Ibid.*, 173, 243, 264–65, 277–78.
33 Winthrop Sargent to General Knox, February 3, 1788, Knox papers, *MHS*.
34 Henry Jackson to General Knox, February 3, 1788, Knox papers, *MHS*.
35 Hazard to Belknap, February 3, 1788, *MHS, Collections*, 5th Series, III, 14.

Despite wax noses, the Convention session on February 6 opened with promise—for Federalists. Sam Adams saw Hancock winning all the glory and could not resist a final effort to capture some himself. Advancing a list of amendments that amounted to a bill of rights, the jealous Adams "almost overset the apple-cart." Both factions were instantly in a dither. The Federalists feared that Adams' eleventh-hour bid for popularity would only fan the fires of their opponents' suspicions. The Antifederalists were perplexed by Adams' dramatic gesture. Did he see the need for safeguarding the rights of citizens after all the explanations on that point? "When A[dams]. perceived the mischief he had made, he withdrew the motion; but some of the Anti leaders revived it, and he was finally obliged to vote against it," Jeremy Belknap wrote.

After Adams had suffered humiliation, the roll was called. Delegates from the seaboard towns cast their votes for the Constitution. The western delegates and those from the Maine interior cast anti-federal votes. While the eastern Federalists kept their blocs intact, their opponents had defectors from the back country who joined the seaboard group. Were they following the advice of Federalist clergymen and putting their consciences over their towns' instructions? Were they financially embarrassed and in need of promised funds for the trip home? Did Hancock's support finally swing them over? Or was the report (later proved false) of North Carolina's ratification, "exultingly inserted in several Boston newspapers" and "busily circulated" on that very morning, the final nudge that pushed them alongside the Boston lawyers and ministers? "Unfortunately every Blockhead and Bankrupt in the State has as good a Vote as a better Man," one Federalist lamented, but in the final count fewer than a dozen such blockheads and bankrupts had joined the better men for a Federalist victory.[36] One important question was still to be answered. Would the Antifederalists accept defeat graciously or defiantly?

The answer soon came. One by one, Widgery, Taylor, and other leading Antifederalists promised that they would stand by democratic principles, bowing to the will of the majority. Widgery said he would

[36] Lewis Morris to Samuel Webb, February 7, 1788, Webb papers, Yale University Library.

return to Maine to "sow the seeds of union and peace." Nasson made
similar pledge, while Major Swain magnanimously declared "that
had not, to his knowledge, been any undue influence exercised
he opposition." However, three Hampshire County delegates
o later complained of intolerable treatment and "unfair methods"
. the convention now kept their silence.[37] The only discordant note
heard that day came when General Thompson refused to join in the
tributes. Thompson threatened to continue his fight against the Constitution in language which seemed so intemperate that Parsons "reminded him of the danger of being punished for treason." The warning, instead of squelching Thompson, elicited a half-humorous reply.
"He should not fear being hanged," the stubborn Maine man said,
if he could hire Parsons as his lawyer.

The convention then adjourned to the senate chamber, where casks
of the best wines were opened for conciliatory toasts. "All appeared
willing to bury the hatchet of animosity, and to smoke the calumet of
union and love," Russell's *Centinel* reported. Though Nasson shook
the Federalists' hands in a sportsman-like gesture, he was an Antifederalist still "and at Present I glory in beaing in the Monnirty.
I farly told them I fought Licke a Good Solider and have been
Congarred."[38]

On February 8 the celebration continued, aided by two hogsheads
of punch contributed by grateful Federalists. But among the Antifederalists there was little joy. Silas Lee managed a halfhearted smile
as he told how a young girl pitied him for being an Antifederalist,
"& I believe she even thought me guilty of a crime." John Quincy
Adams smarted under the jibes of friends who "have long-since
branded me with the name of an anti-federalist." The sullen young
law clerk, impressed by the Newburyport celebration, noted his conversion but not his conviction. As with many another Antifederalist,
Adams went along with the crowd because "I think it my duty to sub-

[37] *Debates of the Massachusetts Convention*, 280–82. "It is past dispute that the
opposers of the constitution were in sundry instances, treated in a manner utterly inconsistent with that respect which is due to every freeborn citizen," complained the
Conway and Deerfield delegates. Northampton *Hampshire Gazette*, April 16, 1788.

[38] Samuel Nasson to George Thatcher, January [February] 8, 1788, Thatcher
papers, *BPL*.

mit without mumuring against what is not to be helped." A few days later, scenes in Theophilus Parsons' law offices made Adams smolder. Parsons gave every caller full details on "all the manoeuvres which they used in and out of Convention . . . [and] speaks with pleasure of every little trifling intrigue which served to baffle the intentions of the antifederalists."[39] General Thompson withdrew from Boston, in no mood for a social drink with his archenemies. "When he left Boston, his last words were—*I will throw the State into Confusion.*" There was much of the vanquished braggart evident in Thompson, and a fellow Antifederalist wished that the general would temper his behavior, since he could "not believe Thompson to be a man of bad heart."[40]

Some Antifederalists who had jumped on their adversaries' bandwagon searched for ways to justify their conduct. Nathaniel Barrell, mindful of what the voters back in York might think, ascribed his political conversion to "a revealing moment when powerful reason flash'd conviction on my mind." Barrell then evaluated his Antifederalist associates as "a set of the most unprincipled men." Barrell was not alone in his belief that by switching sides he had rid himself of unhealthy company. Of the recalcitrant 168, said Christopher Gore, "more than *twenty* have this moment a *State Warrant* against them for being some of the foremost in the last Winters Rebellion." A fondness for paper-money issues was at the root of most antifederalism, Gore thought, and he gloried in the fact that Warren had been denied a convention seat. Still, Warren had been active and "*acts like a snake in the grass.*" For the moment, Gerry was all but forgotten. "Gerry is crestfallen, but acquieses [*sic*]," Belknap reported.[41]

And so the ratification struggle moved to another battleground, with the signs of a Federalist victory increasingly discernible to all but the most zealous Antifederalists. Many battle scars had been left in the ratification struggle at Boston, however, and the lines of demarcation for the two-party politics of Massachusetts had been staked

[39] Adams' "Diary," *MHS, Proceedings,* 2nd Series, XVI, 380–81.
[40] Thomas B. Wait to George Thatcher, February 29, 1788, Thatcher papers, *BPL.*
[41] C. Gibbs to Washington, February 9, 1788, *DHC,* IV, 490–92.

out. Some who favored the Constitution were doubtful that the victory had been fairly won. The convention secretary looked back on the drama and summarized the Federalist success as an instance of "*Bad* measures in a good cause." Pondering the events he had watched at close hand, Minot declared that "never was there a political system introduced by less worthy means, than the new constitution." The Philadelphia Convention had been too eager to give the federal government wide powers, and then Federalists had insisted that the Constitution was their last hope. "This language alarmed the yeomanry, and made it necessary for the Constitutionalists [Federalists] to *pack* a Convention whose sense should be different from that of the people. The elections were strictly attended to . . . If by chance an anticonstitutionalist was chosen, no stone was left unturned to bring him to a renunciation of his principles . . . But the great body of middling land holders were opposed to it." Therefore Minot concluded, "The contest was . . . extremely unequal."[42]

Even more incisive was the analysis of a man who did not even attend the convention—James Madison. The Federalists won because among the Antifederalists "there was not a single character capable of uniting their wills or directing their measures . . . They had no plan whatever. They looked no farther than to put a negative on the Constitution and return home."

The Antifederalists paid dearly for their lack of leadership. "The Antis here are dumb with Silence," a Maine Federalist observed, "I have scarce heard one of them speak except Colo Scammon who says he is determined to fulfil [*sic*] the Scriptures & rejoice with them that rejoice & weep with them that weep." Not every Antifederalist was mute or shamed into silence, however. For men of Thomas Wait's stamp, there was a middle way. The Falmouth printer, who had condemned the Constitution early in January for "a certain darkness, duplicity and studied ambiguity of expression running thro' the whole," changed heart a month later when a Federalist helped him secure a postrider's appointment that paid £60 per annum. With one stroke, Wait renounced antifederalism. "I have been at peace with the Constitution for almost a fortnight!!! . . . when I heard that our

¹⁰ Minot, Diary, Minot papers, MHS

113

Convention had assented to, and ratified it, I rejoiced most heartily," Wait told his benefactor.[43]

Another Maine Antifederalist, whose convictions ran somewhat deeper, had no intention of disavowing his antifederal allegiance. "Thompson is roaring about like the old Dragon [ready] to devour the *Child now it is born* and breathes forth fire, arrows, and Death," a neighbor reported, "but his Hosts are almost fled." Thompson and other die-hards looked north to Exeter where the New Hampshire convention was assembling. Far from the influence of Boston merchants, Exeter might be more receptive to Antifederalist appeals, if only a leader could be found there to give the inexperienced farmer-delegate some encouragement and countermoves against the assiduous Federalists. The Antifederalist cause in New England might be revived in New Hampshire and Rhode Island. The cause, however, was still in search of a leader.

[43] Jeremiah Hill to George Thatcher, February 4, 1788; Thomas B. Wait to George Thatcher, February 14, 1788, Thatcher papers, *BPL.*

☆ VII ☆

A Federalist Ultimatum

IN RETROSPECT, Federalists looked upon the recommended amendments from Boston as a master stroke. "The plan of Massts. is unquestionably the Ultimatum of the foederalists," Madison declared. "Conditional amendments or a second general convention will be fatal."[1] The meandering course of ratification was having one effect. The involved factions vaguely perceived that the period of political drift in national affairs was terminating. What Jefferson later called the natural division of men into two parties was taking shape. Whether the avenue of approach was one of self-interest or idealism, the result was nearly always the same. Some citizens identified themselves with the corps of merchants and professional men who nourished seedling federalism, while others joined the Antifederalists—the men who lived on the land—in their tenuous coalition with entrenched state politicians. "The most certain Test of truth, that I can conceive, is consistency amongst Numbers [of Federalists] who affect to the same ground," a Virginian wrote General Knox, ". . . on the other hand discordency [*sic*] is as certain a Test of error, and I never knew so much of this as now exists amongst the opponents of the Constitution." This rag, tag, and bobtail band of Antifederalists retreated on most fronts as the winter of 1787–88 sent its last icy blasts along the Atlantic seaboard.

In Philadelphia the Antifederalists preferred to whistle in the dark, hoping somehow that the "recommended amendments" scheme from Boston would be discredited before it took hold elsewhere. "Philadelphiensis" thundered at Hancock's amendments, ". . . the people cannot be so ignorant as to be deceived by so pitiful a manoeuvre." "Philadelphiensis" then slashed at Hancock, who hoped to become "the *little king* if not the *big one* . . . and his amendments are introduced as a blind." Another scorching blast came from "Mer-

[1] Madison to George Nicholas, April 8, 1788, Madison papers, *DLC*.

115

lin," who in New York unleashed a bitter tirade against the exulting Federalists. "TRIUMPH ye speculators, who have purchased the fruit of the soldiers blood and toil, at two shillings and sixpence on the pound!" After a sober second look at the outcome in Boston, "Centinel" concluded that "every artifice was practiced" in overwhelming simple, untutored Antifederalists. Working in the shadows, he wrote, were "lawyers, doctors and divines, who were capable and seemed disposed to delude by deceptive glosses and specious reasoning."[2] These disclosures were a warning to other state conventions that they should discount the Massachusetts ratification.

Still apparently straddling the fence, Governor Randolph of Virginia read the Massachusetts amendments with apparent disgust. Realizing that the Massachusetts ratification probably "fixes the event" (although he was careful to hedge a bit), Randolph saw hardly an iota of real good in the proposals. Some of the amendments were "inadmissible, others pointed against the Negro States, and others milk & water." The young governor sent his detailed criticism to Madison, concluding that Hancock had introduced them simply "*to remove fears.*" Shifting uneasily, Randolph then began to backtrack. He was satisfied by the Massachusetts action, because "the men of talents and property" supported the Constitution against "the Shayites, and the gentlemen of bad fame with whom we recusants have been classed." In a moment of exhilaration, another Virginian with Federalist leanings saw things turning out better than the facts warranted. "Colonel R. H. Lee and Mr. John Page . . . are relinquishing their opposition," the president of the Continental Congress wrote, "but what to us is very extraordinary and unexpected, we are told that Mr. George Mason had declared himself so great an enemy to the constitution that he will heartily join Mr. Henry and others in promoting a Southern Confederacy." Correspondent Cyrus Griffin was as wrong in these predictions as he was in another, when he stated that he believed the Massachusetts ratification meant that "N. Hamp. will presently adopt it."[3]

[2] "Merlin," *New-York Journal*, February 14, 1788; "Centinel XV," Philadelphia *Independent Gazetteer*, February 22, 1788.

[3] Cyrus Griffin to Thomas Fitzsimons, February 18, 1788, *LCC*, VIII, 700.

Although Griffin was only relaying the sort of information that Federalists everywhere wanted to believe, the actual situation in New Hampshire lifted the spirits of the Antifederalists. Unable to make much headway along the New Hampshire seaboard, the Antifederalists had gained tremendous support in the back-country town meetings. For the first time, Federalists underestimated the strength of their opponents, fostering that classic road to defeat. Unlike the situations in Pennsylvania or Massachusetts, the Antifederalists had in Joshua Atherton a well-known, hard-working leader. At Amherst, Atherton was elected a convention delegate and was instructed to oppose the Constitution. Moreover, by 1788, Atherton had outlived the chants of 1777, when he had been arrested by patriots and temporarily detained as a "disaffected person." Learned in the law, devoted to the idea of state sovereignty, and by no means a political newcomer, Atherton quickly assumed command of the Antifederalists in New Hampshire.

Perhaps deluded by the overwhelming newspaper support, the New Hampshire Federalists warmed to their work but slowly. On January 4, 1788, the Warner town meeting voted against ratification. Captain Charles Barrett, who like Atherton had to live down the stigma of wartime loyalist suspicions, was chosen by New Ipswich as an anti-Constitution delegate after a heated election. Barrett assailed the Constitution as the foundation for a monarchy, declaring the "presidents would prove nothing less than four-year-old kings, and finally kings for life." At Dunstable, the town meeting elected an Antifederalist and instructed a committee to draft a list of objections for scrutiny at the Exeter convention. At Salisbury an advisory committee urged the town meeting to oppose ratification on the grounds, already heard in some Massachusetts meetings, that the Constitution "sanctioned or tolerated human slavery." When the Federalists finally awoke to what was taking place, they found that Antifederalists had "been indefatigable in disseminating their opinions personally among the interior inhabitants of this State."[4]

Besides the efforts of local Antifederalists, partisans in Massachusetts sent aid to their beleaguered brethren through Dr. James Kil-

[4] Tobias Lear to Washington, June 2, 1788, *DHC*, IV, 676.

ham of Newburyport, who took his young friend John Quincy Adams along as an observer. Kilham brought a bundle of pamphlets, which he turned over to Atherton. The presence of anti-Constitution professionals infuriated the Federalists. If Kilham's proselyting in Exeter "was not base conduct," asked a petulant adversary, "what is?"[5] Another Federalist, who apparently took affront, caused some public disturbance, for Adams noted that his companion "was troubled with the impertinence of one Hopkinson, a distracted fellow, who came and pretended to call him to an account for coming and intermeddling with concerns in which he was not interested." In the circumstances, the interference of an outsider was superfluous, for the lines were already drawn before the convention opened. A Maine man viewed the New Hampshire proceedings and reported that "it is with them as it was with us the Country Members Mostly against the Traiding Towns for it." Jeremy Belknap was still buoyant about the Massachusetts results until he heard "that 40 towns in New Hampshire have instructed their delegates in Convention to vote against the Constitution." The rumor took omnious undertones for "that number will be near one-half the Convention."

Although the printed debates give only the scantiest report of what went on, it is evident that the Antifederalists were anxious to press for an early vote. Atherton censured the Constitution for its implicit approval of slavery—a tactic sure to gain delegates or hold committed ones steadfast. Another Antifederalist decried the lack of a religious test, which "would leave the Bible . . . without any support" so that Catholics "or men of no religion would get into office, and that the blood of the martyrs would rise up against us." At least the President ought to take an oath, said one Antifederalist, for otherwise "A Turk, a Jew, or Rom[an] Catholic, and what is worse than all, a Universal[ist], may be President of the United States."[6]

Although Federalists soon saw all the signs of defeat, they did not forfeit. Most of the Antifederalists, an opponent noted, lacked speaking ability and appeared "dumb & obstinate as ———." Except for

[5] Jeremiah Libbey to Jeremy Belknap, February 26, 1788, *MHS, Collections*, 6th Series, IV, 396.

[6] John Sullivan to Jeremy Belknap, February 26, 1788, *ibid.*, 393–94.

Atherton and a few others, the Antifederalists "will not say a word on the subject, even in private conversation, being determin'd [to] put the issue on the important sign of [li]fting their hands, and I suppose every one of them has capacity to do that." In the corridors there were the visitors from Massachusetts alongside General Nathaniel Peabody, who was busy buttonholing delegates and thus did "more mischief than he could do had he a seat," a discouraged Federalist complained.[7]

In order to salvage the convention before the Antifederalists could hustle an outright rejection of the Constitution through, the Federalists decided to suspend the meeting temporarily. At their informal caucus they agreed that "the only thing that can be done to prevent its rejection is to have an adjournment," a saddened partisan reported.[8] Newspaper reports conceded that Antifederalists held as much as a fourteen-vote majority, but a powerful Federalist delegation headed by John Sullivan found that they could not persuade many to disregard the instructions of their town meetings. Accordingly, astute John Langdon acted as a go-between for a few wavering delegates who feared the consequences of voting contrary to the wishes of the folks back home. Langdon insisted that a lengthy interval would provide lukewarm Antifederalists with a good excuse for side-stepping the main issue. Otherwise, they would vote "against the Constitution, which they (however absurd) must do in case the question was called for."

There is some evidence that the Exeter convention actually rejected the Constitution by a fifty-four to fifty-one vote early in the last session—at least that is what newspaper readers in Boston and Providence soon learned.[9] But apparently this vote was not officially recorded, for the Federalists maneuvered an adjournment before the house as a substitute. Upset at seeing a certain antifederal victory frittered away, Atherton harangued the opposition for more than an hour. Spectator John Quincy Adams viewed the performance,

[7] Tobias Lear to Washington, June 2, 1788, *DHC*, IV, 676.

[8] Jeremiah Libbey to Jeremy Belknap, February 19, 1788, *MHS, Collections*, 6th Series, IV, 388.

[9] Boston *American Herald*, February 28, 1788; Providence *United States Chronicle*, February 28, 1788.

then pronounced Atherton "a miserable speaker, and a worse reasoner." Adams thought most of the Antifederalists gave only half-hearted opposition. Perhaps, too, Atherton had been made over-confident by that first vote, for he obviously injured the Antifederalist cause with his bluster. A Federalist who had been gloomy three days earlier began to take heart. "I am in great hopes that Mr. Atherton . . . will destroy what he aims to establish by his overmuch talking," he confided.

When the Antifederalists had nothing more to say, the roll call began. Landon's motion barely squeezed by the Antifederalists, with fifty-six favoring an adjournment until June 18, and fifty-one opposed to the ruse. The idea of adopting recommendatory amendments seems to have had little consideration because Atherton was stubbornly opposed to the scheme. "To ratify, and then propose Amendments is to surrender our all," he later observed, "and then ask our new Masters if they will be so gracious as to return to us . . . our most important Rights and Privileges."[10] Neither side was joyous over the outcome.

Apologizing for their failure, New Hampshire Federalists promised that by June "the Illiberal and Ignorant will be brought in to do what is right and Just." The Antifederalists, a Biddeford Federalist lamented, were intolerable desperadoes. "However, we must like the industrious bee suck honey from every obnoxious weed." Federalists agreed with the Portsmouth newspaper report that "impudence and illiberality . . . wrinkles the brow of antifederalism."[11] More than likely, that antifederal brow was also moistened from labor on the hayrack or behind the plow.

In confidence the Federalists admitted that things might have been much worse. Sullivan assured Belknap that Antifederalists had held a forty-vote advantage at the outset, including some "good men that were short-sighted; some few who longed for the onions of Egypt . . . some who were blinded through excess of zeal for the

[10] Atherton to John Lamb, June 11, 1788, Lamp papers, *NYHS*.

[11] C. Gibbs to Washington, February 24, 1788, *DHC*, IV, 520; Jeremiah Hill to George Thatcher, February 28, 1788, Thatcher papers, *BPL*; Portsmouth *New-Hampshire Gazette*, January 23, 1788.

cause of religion, and others who by putting on the masque of sanctity thought to win proselites." Among themselves, they admitted that a few Antifederalists had been prevented from attending the voting session by a well-timed dinner party, which Timothy Walker gave for select delegates so that they might be *"detained* at *his* house."[12] Apparently Walker served more than strong tea at his table.

Citizens to the southward heard the news with joy or sorrow, depending upon their political leanings. "O New Hampshire you have . . . done us much injury," wailed General Samuel Webb in New York, "Antifoederalists lift their heads." In their disappointment the New Yorkers held no celebration like the one touched off by news of the Massachusetts ratification, but a rousing party in the famous Coffee House on Manhattan left Webb nursing a happy heart but a throbbing head, "oweing to drinking & eating in a good cause." The close brush with disaster was a warning for Federalists, however. "We are busy—so are the Antis," Webb reported.[13]

Federalists were chagrined not only by the temporary loss of New Hampshire, but also by the lift that Antifederalist morale received from this first minor victory. Congressman Brown of Kentucky had little doubt that New Hampshire would eventually ratify, but he feared that "the present failure will be productive of bad consequences as it will give fresh spirits & Confidence to the Malcontents who were begining [*sic*] to despair & relax in their opposition."[14] Before the reversal in New Hampshire there was hope of ratification without a single dissenting state, another Federalist reported, but "there is now some danger that the whole plan will miscarry." Although assured that the next convention would have better Federalist management, Madison conceded that the postponement was "no small check to the progress of the business." Governor

[12] John Sullivan to Jeremy Belknap, February 26, 1788, *MHS, Collections,* 6th Series, IV, 393–94; the notation was written on the wrapper of a letter from Paine Wingate to President John Sullivan, April 23, 1788, *Early State Papers of New Hampshire* (ed. by Albert S. Batchellor), XXI, 851.

[13] Samuel Webb to Joseph Barrell, February 17, March 9, 1788, Webb family papers, Yale University Library.

[14] John Brown to James Breckenridge, March 17, 1788, Breckenridge papers, University of Virginia Library.

Clinton's friends who were trying to make New York a hotbed of antifederalism "will take new spirits. 'The events in Massts. had almost extinguished their hopes." "The conduct of New Hampshire has surprised us all this way," Simeon Baldwin wrote from New Haven. "We . . . had ever calculated upon that State as sure—our fears were centered upon New York."[15]

New York politicians on both sides of the fence had indeed kept their thoughts centered on New England. Shortly before the Massachusetts convention had ratified, Melancton Smith cautioned his Antifederalist friends against optimism there, despite reported anti-Constitution trends. "The *better* sort, have means of *convincing* those who differ from them," Smith counseled, "and how prevalent these kind of means may be, I Cannot pretend to say. I confess I fear their power."[16] Smith's worries were soon confirmed, but not until Federalists in the New York legislature had barely mustered enough support to call a state convention. With Clinton working behind the scene, a convention was scheduled for as distant a day as decency would permit. The antifederal foot-dragging made Clinton's foes furious. "I hate those that do a good thing with a bad grace," a Federalist commented, "—if the Devil had all Selfish men, I'm sure there would not be so [many] opposers to this Constitution."[17]

That which left gloom on Manhattan brought cheer to Philadelphia Antifederalists. The flagging spirit of antifederalism there was rejuvenated as the Exeter results became known. The opposition had made gains by keeping the people ignorant and the press silenced, an Antifederalist claimed, but a change was in prospect. "The system of deception practised by its advocates, is pretty generally found out by the people." Federalists could no longer make citizens in "each place on the continent believe that every other part but their own was in favor" of the Constitution. "Their *runners* and story carriers will no longer be attended to," he concluded hopefully.

---

[15] Simeon Baldwin to James Kent, March 8, 1788, Baldwin papers, Yale University Library.

[16] Melancton Smith to Robert Yates, January 28, 1788, Yates papers, *NYPL*.

[17] Joseph Barrell to General Samuel Webb, February 20, 1788, *Correspondence and Journals of Samuel B. Webb*, (ed. by Worthington C. Ford), III, 95n.

To others, the postponement in New Hampshire had brought confusion into a ratification process which had seemed orderly, almost running on a Federalist timetable. The conflicting reports contributed to the confusion. In Maryland and Virginia, it was announced that the Exeter convention had first ratified the Constitution, then adjourned to a later day. A Baltimore editor confessed this unique approach to ratification "appears to be an original one, for the motives of which we are left in the dark." Among certain quarters in Boston, the reaction was not one of confusion but of disgust. When "*A Federalist*" charged that Atherton was author of the anti-Constitution schemes in Exeter, a fitting exercise for one who was a contemptible Tory, the Antifederalists came back with a rejoinder. True, Atherton had been a wartime loyalist, but so had many of the leading Boston Federalists. Atherton was probably the only Tory opposed "to the New System from Georgia to New-Hampshire; while on the other hand, it is well known, every Tory, particularly those in a certain great town, are warm advocates for this System."[18]

What upset the Federalists most about the New Hampshire postponement was the fear that Antifederalist political ideas were taking hold. After scolding New Hampshire citizens for supposing that their interests differed from those of Connecticut or Massachusetts, Ellsworth went to the heart of the controversy. The Antifederalists seemed to believe that good government consisted merely in a system "which imposes the least restraints on its subjects" and is operated frugally. To this naïve approach, Ellsworth answered with Federalist dogma: "The cheapest form of government is not always best, for parsimony, thought it spends little, generally gains nothing. That is the best form of government which returns the greatest number of advantages in proportion to the disadvantages with which it is attended."[19] The Constitution was going to cost the people, but it would give them advantages in return. Ellsworth's political instincts told him that merchants understood this reasoning far better than farmers.

[18] *Massachusetts Centinel*, March 5, 1788; Boston *American Herald*, March 10, 1788.
[19] "Landholder XI," *Connecticut Courant*, March 10, 1788.

In high Federalist circles it was clear that the mistakes of the first convention could not be repeated at the second. "A man possessing all the virtues of an angel, may not have the majority of votes in States where the choice very frequently may depend on mere trifles," Henry Knox cautioned. While great stakes were involved, a contest might be won or lost on something "not more important than the color of a man's hair, eyes, his size, or carriage." Knox fretted, but so did scores of other Federalists as the political winds that were so favorable in early February seemed to be shifting. Enveloped in gloom, Cyrus Griffin began to voice doubts that the Constitution would ever be ratified. "The adjournment of N. Hampshire, the small majority of Massachusets [*sic*], a certainty of rejection in Rhodes Island," bickering in New York and Pennsylvania, and the reports of antipathy toward the Constitution in his own Virginia appeared overwhelming to the president of the Continental Congress.

As Griffin wrote these lines, his worst fears were being realized in Rhode Island. For Rhode Island legislators, pursuing the independent course that had kept them from sending a delegate to the Federal Convention, had ignored its ratifying instructions. Instead, the legislature sent the Constitution directly to the people. With no Federalist leader of consequence, the pressure for action on the Constitution in Rhode Island had come from merchants rather than from public men. Reports in December indicated the casual—if not cautious— approach of Rhode Island lawmakers to the Constitution. Rather than call a convention, the leading politicians asserted that the people had seen the Constitution in the newspapers "and that the people might consider it as they thought best—and if they pleased to, might adopt it." This seeming indifference to a great national question delighted outspoken Antifederalists, but their opponents failed to hail the example as one worth following elsewhere.

The Rhode Island brand of antifederalism was indeed a matter of some embarrassment to such leaders as Mason and Lee. The purely local circumstances that made antifederalism popular in Rhode Island contributed to its unpopularity elsewhere. In April, 1787, Randolph had complained that "Rhode Island is system[atical] in all her antifoederalism."[20] By its paper-money effusions, merchants everywhere had taken alarm. Well knowing that Rhode Island would oppose the Constitution, extreme Federalists were prepared to read her out of the Union.

Not totally insensitive to public opinion elsewhere, the Rhode Island country party answered Federalist charges of wilful indifference. Governor John Collins explained in September of 1787 that his state sent no delegates to the Federal Convention because it was violating the Articles of Confederation. He went on to say that Rhode Island would still join her sister states for any plan "advantageous to the Union."[21] In nearby Poughkeepsie, "Blackbeard" advised newspaper readers that since Rhode Island was practicing a kind of piracy through her peculiar paper-money acts, the twelve other states should join in "treaties of mutual defence against Rhode Island and Algiers." Oliver Ellsworth, in a truculent mood, seemed ashamed that Rhode Island was part of New England. "The little state of Rhode Island was purposely left by Heaven to its present madness," he warned, as a bad example that would frighten others into ratification.

Federalist delegates in the Rhode Island Assembly from the seaboard towns were powerless in their efforts to have a ratifying convention called. The false rumor that a convention had been approved was hailed in neighboring Massachusetts as the signal for "a very pleasurable event—for, saith the Scripture, *There is more joy over one sinner that repenteth, than, &c.*"[22] But the facts were soon out, showing that Rhode Island was unrepentant in her antifederal heresy. Antifederalists in the state legislature pushed through a proposal to send the Constitution directly to the voters. Although Federalists drew back from this unique approach in horror, the Rhode Island Assembly held that "*the business was reduced simply to this question*—Will this State agree to this Constitution or not?" Citizens would be able to demonstrate their feelings better in town halls than in "a Convention, who possibly might act contrary to the sentiments

[20] Edmund Randolph to Edward Carrington, April 11, 1787, Emmet collection, *NYPL*.

[21] *Records of the Colony and State of Rhode Island* (ed. by J. R. Bartlett), X, 258.

[22] Springfield *Hampshire Chronicle*, February 27, 1788.

and wishes of their constituents." Perhaps the reports of defection by some instructed delegates in Massachusetts had reached the Rhode Island Antifederalists. Despite an appeal from Federalists for a compromise (they wanted to have towns vote on the necessity for calling a convention), the measure won, forty-two to twelve.

Before the election, perceptive Federalists knew what the results would be, so they called a boycott of the polls. Antifederalists claimed that calling a ratifying session would have been a confession of error by Rhode Island for not participating in the Federal Convention. Rhode Island Antifederalists preferred to let the people decide rather than call a convention where "certain learned men (called lawyers and divines) might deceive them, by sophistry and fair speeches, even to believe a lie."[23] They also answered Ellsworth's vitriolic attack. "All his venom pointed at this State," declared "a real Federalist," rose from Ellsworth's indignation because Rhode Island appeared so firmly antifederal. Ellsworth himself was not only a public defaulter who stood to gain by ratification, the writer charged, but "Landholder" well knew the Constitution was "happily framed to cover the villanies of those harpies, who during the late war rioted upon the spoils of the distressed inhabitants" of Rhode Island.[24]

On the appointed day, Federalists boycotted the town meetings at Newport and Providence so effectively that the voting returns were a joke—only 12 pro-Constitution votes were cast in both cities. However, Federalists in Little Compton and Bristol ignored the boycott, and those towns favored the Constitution by votes of 63 to 57 and 26 to 23 respectively. Elsewhere, Antifederalists had things their way. In the town of Cranston, 101 antifederal votes were recorded against none for the opposition; Foster had no Federalist votes and 177 against ratification; Gloucester recorded an overwhelming 228 to 9 against the Constitution. Over the entire state there were 237 votes for the Constitution and 2,708 against it. The total vote was about 1,200 less than that cast in the preceding general election, which brought Federalist claims that at least that number of voters had

---

[23] "A Friend to Rule and Order," Providence *United States Chronicle*, March 15, 1788.

[24] "A real Federalist," *ibid.*, March 27, 1788.

ignored the balloting. In March, October, and December of 1788 the assembly Antifederalists rejected calls for a regular convention with the comfortable feeling that they reflected the will of the majority.

While Federalists at home and beyond her borders wailed over the perversity of Rhode Island, Governor Collins claimed that the township voting "was not done with the least design to give any offence . . . but upon pure republican principles." The majority who voted against the Constitution nevertheless thought it contained some good points that might "be added and adapted to the present Confederation." A disgusted Providence Federalist urged citizens to study "the principles of the Antifederalists in this State," written large in recent domestic policies, "the opposers of the new Constitution being uniform supporters of an iniquitous tender of a depreciated paper money at par."[25]

Rhode Island Antifederalists may not have been impressed by their opponents' alarms, but some Americans who were initially lukewarm to the Constitution found their resistance ebbing. After Jefferson read the Massachusetts amendments, he decided that his first reaction (that three states should hold out until changes were made) was no longer sound. Jefferson said he would settle for a bill of rights and explicit ineligibility of the Senate and President for second terms. "But the plan of Massachusetts is far preferable, and will I hope be followed by those who are yet to decide," Jefferson wrote.[26] While Jefferson's thoughts came too late to affect the course of ratification, his mental processes nevertheless showed how the Massachusetts amendments had weakened the Antifederalist position. Madison was pleased by the public reaction to recommendatory amendments, and he denied Randolph's charge that they were all "milk & water." Back in Virginia to mend his political fences, Madison soon perceived that the temper of the times demanded something in the nature of a bill of rights. Federalists had been shaken by the Virginia General Baptist Committee's unanimous recommendation against ratification in March, which reflected that growing sect's fear that if "Religious

[25] *Ibid.*, April 10, 1788.
[26] Jefferson to Edward Carrington, May 27, 1788, 13 *Jefferson Papers* 208–209.

liberty is not suffisiently secur'd thay pretend to other objections but that I think is the principle objection."[27] Madison realized that the Massachusetts amendments furnished a tool for converting Virginia Antifederalists, if they could be convinced that an amendment on religious freedom was only a matter of time.

Although the Boston recommendations had fractured some hitherto staunch Antifederalist walls, the fortress at the Philadelphia *Independent Gazetter* remained intact. Political partisans, however, needed public reassurance that their cause not only had merit, but chances of success. From Philadelphia—still the communications center of the Republic—the *Independent Gazetter* was sending forth messages of hope and encouragement to Antifederalists in every state. The more improbable a story, the faster it spread. Editor Oswald printed a report that Washington had cooled his ardor for the Constitution. "He cannot help feeling that he has been deceived, and has refused to have any thing to do with it farther, so that he will not be in the Virginia convention." Washington's refusal to take a convention seat was a fact, but the rest of the story was antifederal humbug. Even Federalists must have marveled at Oswald's ingenuity in supplying a silver lining for every dark cloud. With an eye toward the Maryland convention, where all signs pointed to an easy Federalist victory, Oswald took heart from the few scraps of good news. The worst was over for the Antifederalists, he announced in early April, as men everywhere saw the "shade of mystery" that covered the Constitution and discovered "the delusions with which it is replete." Antifederalists took heart despite the fact that postriders "are prevented from carrying intelligence, whilst newspapers are made the vehicles of deception, and dark intrigue employs the avaricious office-hunters, who long to riot on the spoils of their country."

Oswald's newspaper was never at a loss for philippics aimed at the Federalists, but during the breathing spell between the New England ratification battles and the Maryland convention he found a new target. Every age has found fault with postal carriers; thus when the Antifederalists, taking a cue from Oswald, began what seemed to be merited attacks on the post office, they chose a subject which had

[27] Joseph Spencer to Madison, February 28, 1788, *DHC*, IV, 525.

been at all times a favored whipping boy. According to customs of the day, postriders made private arrangements for carrying newspapers. Postmasters relayed them in return for a free copy. Officially, then, the post office had nothing to do with the sending of newspapers, although the exchange system whereby editors traded news freely was vital to eighteenth-century journalism because it supplied all reports save those of local origin. Besides postriders, ship captains and private travelers were sometimes importuned to carry newspapers. In this cumbersome manner, vital information eventually reached the farthest nooks of the Republic. The first inkling of mail trouble came during the Pennsylvania convention in December, when some Antifederalists complained that the flow of news from the outside world had been strangely interrupted.

A particular sore spot was the suppression of the "Address of the Minority." So convinced were the Philadelphia Antifederalists of its merit that they decided to broadcast copies throughout the country. The pamphlets apparently were ready about Christmas, but the bundles delivered to the Philadelphia post office mysteriously miscarried and were either delayed some months or never delivered at all. The Antifederalists apparently expected the "Address" to descend as a bombshell in Boston on the eve of the convention. Instead, the pamphlets were withheld either through the postmaster's ineptitude or design. Aware of the efficient Federalist avenues of communication, "Centinel" harangued the opposition, charging them with systematically stopping the mails addressed to Antifederalists. To halt the spread of information which would "prove fatal to the new constitution, all intercourse between the partriots of America is as far as possible cut off; whilst on the other hand, the conspirators have the most exact information." The Boston line was vital to both parties, but the post offices continued their sporadic service for Antifederalist newspapers, "whilst on the contrary, we find the devoted vehicles of despotism pass uninterrupted." The people knew how momentous the times were and would not permit "insidious and base stratagems . . . to hoodwink them out of their liberties."[28]

By mid-January, printers along the eastern seaboard were aware of

[28] "Centinel IX," Philadelphia *Independent Gazetteer*, January 8, 1788.

some bottleneck that was preventing the exchange of newspapers. The Philadelphia *Freeman's Journal* laid the blame at the doorstep of Postmaster-General Hazard, charging that his minions were making "a stretch of arbitrary power, that even Britain never attempted before the Revolution." If only Antifederalist newspaper editors had complained, the charges of conspiracy would take on more plausibility. But Federalist printers were soon in the chorus, ready to accuse Hazard of malignant designs. A Federalist editor in New Jersey declared the mail stoppage was "an harbinger of slavery" caused by erring "post-masters, or their jackalls," who held up the exchange of newspapers. Equally incensed was the Federalist-inclined Boston *Independent Chronicle*, which declared that since 1788 began, "Printers in the northern States have received scarce a single paper, printed beyond the Hudson."[29] No wonder the Antifederalists were suspicious, for the important exchanges stopped at the crucial time when the Massachusetts debates were at their height. Edward Powars, the forlorn hope of Boston antifederalism, added his voice to those of other dismayed printers, who lamented the news vacuum came when "the public are exceedingly anxious . . . to be acquainted with the progress of political affairs."[30]

The Antifederalist newspapers decided to turn the mail stoppage into a campaign boomerang. A purported letter from the eastern shore of Maryland, printed by Oswald, declared that New York newspapers were denied delivery to Baltimore, while "the papers of the Southward proceed [not] an inch farther than the office they are put in at," unless they contained Federalist screeds. Another letter from Worcester, Massachusetts, claimed the post office did not permit any newspapers to reach there "that contain any thing unfavourable to the New Constitution." If these letters were of questionable origin, there is no doubt about the spurious character of a note allegedly sent from Dr. Benjamin Rush to Hamilton. Printed in the *Freeman's Journal*, the fictitious letter had Rush reporting that "our scheme

[29] *New-Jersey Journal*, January 30, 1788; Boston *Independent Chronicle*, February 21, 1788.
[30] Boston *American Herald*, February 18, 1788.

of stopping the newspapers containing the anti-federal pieces, has succeeded; let Mr. ——— know, that 200 dollars will be forthwith transmitted as a small gratuity for his service."[31] The ordinary citizen must have easily supplied that blank with the intended name: Postmaster-General Ebenezer Hazard.

Unaware that he was being charged that very day with accepting bribes, the Postmaster General expressed astonishment that the "Address" of the Pennsylvania Antifederalists had only recently reached Boston. "This surprises me," he confessed, since the pamphlet had been published "long before any hints were thrown about *delays*."[32] The Postmaster General explained that his office had "nothing to do with newspapers; it is a matter merely between the printers and the riders." Yet Oswald, Bailey, and "the brainless Greenleaf" kept up their tirades against him. "In short, the whole noise appears to me to be an Anti-federal manoeuvre, like the 'bribery and corruption' at Boston," Hazard observed.

Although Hazard regarded the Antifederalist charges as too reckless to merit consideration, he soon found himself in a political hornet's nest. Oswald stepped up his attacks on Hazard, having satisfied himself that the local postmaster was not at fault for the postal bottleneck. The few newspapers trickling into Philadelphia, Oswald charged, were "by way of *grace* and *favor*" doubtlessly the result of "the vile *edicts* of a despotic post-master."[33] Hazard was probably unaware that the Philadelphia postmaster was indeed trying to undermine his superior by informing the post-office committee in the languid Continental Congress that Hazard was derelict in his duty. For such information, the Philadelphian expected his natural reward "if any new Arangement [*sic*] in the Department should take place . . . ."[34] Infuriated by Oswald's scathing comments, Hazard finally wrote a public letter deploring the personal "indecent attacks, replete with illliberality and rancour." The postriders and printers were

---

[31] Philadelphia *Freeman's Journal*, February 27, March 5, 1788.
[32] Hazard to Belknap, March 5, 1788, *MHS, Collections*, 5th Series, III, 24–25.
[33] Philadelphia *Independent Gazetteer*, March 12, 1788.
[34] James Bryson to Madison, March 12, 1788, Madison papers, *DLC*.

alone responsible for carrying newspapers, and Hazard vowed that he had done nothing to alter an arrangement that antedated the Revolution.[35]

The Postmaster General was learning how perilous political life could be during stormy campaigns. The thin-veiled antifederal charges of bribery in the post office continued, and even Federalist printers in Philadelphia joined their political adversaries in a chorus of complaints. Together they petitioned the state assembly for relief from the mail stoppage. The mail jam went beyond the newspapers, for at about the same time Elbridge Gerry wrote Hazard of his personal troubles with the post office. Gerry declared that his private correspondence to friends in other states was not being delivered and that he had reason to believe letters from them met a similar fate. This was "a species of robbery nearly allied to highway robbery," Gerry warned, and he advised Hazard to investigate the cause, "as Culprits are doing a more essential injury to you than they possibly can do to me."[36]

However good Hazard's intentions, he became a distinct liability to the Federalists. A Virginia editor asked whether the mail stoppage was a sample of the kind of service that people could expect under the Constitution. If so, the citizens must say "from *such a government*, '*Good Lord, deliver us!*' " The interception and publication of two private letters written by a leading Pennsylvania Antifederalist confirmed the suspicions of Oswald and his friends that a Federalist conspiracy was involved. Why, railed the *Independent Gazetteer*, had Hazard decided to choke off the newspaper exchanges "at this *peculiarly interesting crisis?*"[37]

"Have you seen any of the attacks upon me about newspapers?" Hazard asked an old friend. The Antifederalists, Hazard continued, "have been pelting me at a most unmerciful rate." The attacks were

[35] Hazard's letter of March 19 appeared in the Philadelphia *Independent Gazetteer*, March 24, 1788.

[36] Gerry to Hazard, March 25, 1788, Gerry papers, *DLC*.

[37] Winchester *Virginia Gazette*, quoted in the Philadelphia *Independent Gazetteer*, April 8, 1788, and in the Philadelphia *Freeman's Journal*, April 9, 1788. The letters had been published in the *Pennsylvania Gazette*, March 16, 1788, and in "Algernon," Philadelphia *Independent Gazetteer*, April 10, 1788.

part of an Antifederalist scheme to prevent ratification of the Constitution in the states still to hold conventions.[38] But Hazard grew more cautious, and he charged Belknap not to "let it be known that you have any thing upon the subject *from me*." "I think Hazard is in a bad box," a Massachusetts congressman ventured. "The fœderalists frown upon him for being anti. The opposers of fœderalism charge him hard with stoping [*sic*] the papers, and 'muzzling the press.' " The sympathetic congressman opposed Hazard's dismissal, "but a little shaking will put him right."[39]

Beset by critics, Hazard still managed a forced smile. When Jeremy Belknap asked Hazard whether a certain piece of information had reached New York, the Postmaster General said it had not, adding "it is very seldom that I see a Boston paper. If the Postmaster General prevents the circulation of newspapers, he does it *very effectually*." Continued attacks piqued Hazard, however, and he finally considered a libel action against Oswald as the chief Antifederalist agitator. Friends, Hazard added, "dissuaded me from it, alleging that he was going down hill very fast, and that a prosecution would support him." Federalist editor Benjamin Russell of Boston rose to Hazard's defense, claiming that he had investigated the delay in newspaper exchanges and found that some postriders between New York and Hartford were breaking open bundles of newspapers addressed to printers, selling them, and pocketing the proceeds. But at nearby Salem, the *Mercury* editor who looked at his empty mail box concluded that the whole affair had "so dark a complexion as may well give birth to alarming apprehensions."[40]

Although Hazard tried to perform his duties in a nonpartisan manner, his days as Postmaster General were indeed numbered. Already scorned by the Antifederalists, Hazard's Federalist friends were also making harsh judgments upon his beleaguered reputation. "Hazard has acted the part of a decided rascal," a friend told Alexander Hamilton. What condemned Hazard in the eyes of the Fed-

[38] Hazard to Belknap, April 12, 1788, MHS, *Collections*, 5th Series, III, 29–30.

[39] Samuel H. Otis to George Thatcher, April 13, 1788, *LCC*, VIII, 716.

[40] Philadelphia *Freeman's Journal*, May 28, 1788; *Salem Mercury*, May 29, 1788.

eralists was his apparent ineptitude at a critical moment in the ratification campaign. From the heights of Mount Vernon, Washington, no less a Federalist than Hazard himself, pronounced what was to be Hazard's political death warrant. By allowing the stoppage of newspapers, the post office had hampered the Federalists' propaganda efforts and given their "enemies very plausible pretexts for dealing out their scandals, and exciting jealousies by inducing a belief that the suppression of intelligence, at that critical juncture, was a wicked trick of policy, contrived by an Aristocratic Junto."[41] Thus Hazard had been indirectly responsible for "the aspersion he has incautiously brought upon a good cause," and one remedy for the error would come "through the medium of a better appointment," Washington counseled. In time, Hazard knew that he had somehow badly bungled the newspaper exchanges as rumors of his imminent replacement reached him. Not the first public figure to be worsted in a quarrel with the newspapers, Hazard believed that he had been victimized by his own desire to save public funds through various economies in the post office. Resigned to the fate that soon befell him, Hazard concluded that he was "too much of a Christian to be a *politician.*"[42]

[41] Washington to John Jay, July 18, 1788, Fitzpatrick, *The Writings of George Washington*, XXX, 17.

[42] Hazard to Belknap, October 2, 1788, *MHS, Collections*, 5th Series, III, 68–69.

☆ VIII ☆

The Rout at Annapolis

ANTIFEDERALIST TROUBLES with the mails were partly real, partly imaginary. But one obstacle had its basis in hard political realities, and the Antifederalists found it difficult, if not impossible, to surmount. The fact that only a dozen newspapers in the whole nation, hardly one-tenth of all those printed, had decided to support the Antifederalists was in itself a revealing statistic. That the printers were mainly located in the commercial centers, where Federalists furnished financial support for their friends, made the disparity understandable. But when Federalists decided to execute a *coup de grâce* on the hard-pressed opposition newspapers, then the Antifederalist press sent forth a plaintive cry.

The first victim was Philadelphian William Spotswood. As editor of the *Pennsylvania Evening Herald*, Spotswood's antifederalism was lavender if compared with Colonel Oswald's purple variety. As Federalists withdrew support, the *Herald* faltered, and as his financial woes increased, Spotswood practiced Quaker-like forbearance and refused to ascribe his troubles to vindictive Federalists. Not one to suffer silently, Oswald moaned as he too began receiving Federalist cancellations at a suspicious rate. Should financial pressure work its censorship, Oswald warned, the Federalists "will soon become as despotic as the *Ali-Agas of Turkey*."[1] After the *Herald* expired early in 1788, Federalists showed little sympathy for Spotswood. "There cannot be a greater proof that the body of the people are federal, that the antifederal editors and printers fail of support," one Federalist noted.[2]

The relentless Federalist pressure on newspaper editors brought varying reactions. Boston and Philadelphia readers read that Con-

---

[1] "Contemplator," Philadelphia *Independent Gazetteer*, January 12, 1788.
[2] Philadelphia *Pennsylvania Mercury*, quoted in Philadelphia *Freeman's Journal*, January 30, 1788.

necticut citizens had been ill-informed about the Constitution and were black-listed if they refused to sign endorsements for it. "All their newspapers were muffled; nothing but sophistical, abusive and fallacious performances in favour of it, could be published." It was rumored that John Hayes, printer of the Baltimore *Maryland Gazette*, incurred much Federalist wrath for printing Luther Martin's "Genuine Information." Federalists had "the advantage of every press, from New-Hampshire to Georgia, to circulate their calumnies," wailed an Antifederalist, while those against ratification "can resort to two or three, at most, who have spirit and independence enough to publish in vindication of these devoted victims to power and tyranny." This near-unanimous voice among the newspapers, he went on, accounted for the appearance of Federalist unanimity "that prevails throughout the whole continent . . . for wherever there is a printing-press, there you will find some federal hacks, or company of hacks, who claim an absolute dominion over *Mr. Type*." In Baltimore, the *Maryland Journal* under William Goddard (a former partner of Colonel Oswald) was nudged off the fence and became "highly and truly federal," to the discomfort of Antifederalists looking ahead to the Maryland convention scheduled for April. Ever ready to ascribe the politics of others to sordid motives, Antifederalists in Rhode Island complained because a Providence printer openly supported the Constitution. One correspondent said that he could not "account for it any other way than that you expect to be promoted (under it) to a place of profit or honour—which [motive] generally governs the principles of men."[3]

Nothing in the Antifederalist newspapers ever approached the *Federalist* essays of "Publius" in continuity or length, but antifederal essayists occasionally noted the voluminous "Publius" with an attitude not characterized by awe. A Philadelphia Antifederalist compared "Publius" to a Scottish preacher, famous for the length of his sermons. "*Publius* has already written, 26 numbers, as much as would jade the brains of any poor sinner . . . so that in decency he should now rest on his arms, and let the people draw their breath for a

[3] "Z," Providence *United States Chronicle*, March 27, 1788.

little."[4] The *Independent Gazetteer* told of a country bumpkin who went to visit his relative "Publius," and was asked how people in the back country received the Federalist's essays. The crude farmer replied that he had not heard much about them *"as the attention of the people was so much occupied on the subject of the* New Constitution, *they had not time or inclination to read any essay on* Foreign Affairs." No Antifederalist was a harsher judge of "Publius" than the French diplomat Monsieur Otto, who read the work with a certain aloofness. "Cet ouvrage n'est d'aucune utilité aux gens instruits, et il est trop savant et trop long pour les ignorans."[5] One hardly needs a knowledge of French to discern Otto's feelings about the eighty-five essays —they were too learned for the average man.

Not a real match for "Publius" in terms of volume or lucidity, but still a gadfly because of his abrasive style, was the "Centinel" of Philadelphia. The "Centinel" was Samuel Bryan, who never tired of calling the Federalists conspirators. Bryan assaulted Hazard's reputation constantly, asserting that there was some sinister connection between the Postmaster General and prominent Federalists. Nothing made Bryan unhappier than the small force of antifederal printers being thwarted by the post-office snarl. "The feigned unanimity of one part of America, has been represented to produce the acquiescence of another," he insisted, and the Postmaster General deserved much of the blame. Generally, the Antifederalists figured that "Centinel" must be valuable because he had so thoroughly angered the opposition. "If you would support the *majesty* of your *new* government," taunted one of Bryan's defenders, "shut his mouth—strangle him— thwattle him—thwack him—and roast him alive . . . ."[6]

Though "Centinel" drew special abuse from the Federalists, the whole fraternity of Antifederalist writers were charged with mercenary motives. Greenleaf, at his lonesome outpost in New York, heard readers harp on his partiality until he reminded them that "a *printer*, as a *printer*, has no choice so long as parties are not decided; he admits every good essay." If his *Journal* appeared too partial, he

[4] "Bob Short," Philadelphia *Freeman's Journal*, December 12, 1787.
[5] M. Otto to Montmorin [1788], 3 Farrand 234.
[6] Boston *American Herald*, April 10, 1788.

suggested that offended readers might "take one paper of each sort." By mid-March the suspicious Oswald was sending his copies of the *Independent Gazetteer* to New York by private hands, so that Greenleaf would have the latest Antifederalist doctrine from Philadelphia ready for local distribution despite any post-office difficulties. Greenleaf had support from Governor Clinton's backers on Manhattan, but the business community shied away from him because of his politics. New York Federalists looked upon Greenleaf as the cross they had to bear. He was "a poor, thick-sculled creature . . . so much in debt to Oswald for his printing-office as not to dare to offend him," was the way Hazard summed up Greenleaf's plight.[7]

Printing an Antifederalist newspaper in Boston was proving to be anything but a quick road to riches. Continued criticism of his columns put Powars on the defensive, and he countered by stressing the obligations of the printer in a free society. "He does not PRETEND to determine on publick ground what is right and wrong as it respects the community, and he will never refuse any DECENT speculation a place, though he should even lose SOME MORE of his customers."[8] A free discussion of merits in the proposed Constitution was thwarted by "attempts . . . to fetter and suppress such discussions, by THREATNING [*sic*] the Printer and DROPPING the papers that contain them." Powars, either because of pressure from subscribers or out of a sense of duty, published "Publius" as regularly as "Centinel." When Tench Coxe lampooned "Centinel," Powars even printed that Federalist attack. But his financial burdens increased, so that in mid-January he briefly changed the name of his publication and lowered the price from six to three cents.

Although the anemic support of the Antifederalist press can be overemphasized, their difficulties did contrast with the backing offered Federalist newspapers by the commercial community. Perhaps too, most of the invectives appearing in the press were thoroughly discounted, as Federalist Timothy Pickering heard. "The newspapers are so filled with lies that no dependence can be put on

[7] Hazard to Belknap, May 10, 1788, MHS, *Collections*, 5th Series, III, 37.
[8] Boston *American Herald*, December 17, 1787.

138

any account you receive in them respecting the Constitution," his correspondent maintained.[9] Neither side had a monopoly on inaccuracies. Federalists newspapers printed a running tally of the convention votes of seven states that gave them 242 more votes than they had actually received, while their low Antifederalist total was strangely accurate.

The frequent jostlings between antifederal newspapers and their rivals doubtlessly provided some amusement for the reading public, if not enlightenment. Nevertheless, Antifederalists in upstate New York believed that they were greatly handicapped because their adversaries appeared to control the press. A committee of affluent Antifederalists pledged their support for two hundred subscriptions if a printer could be induced to establish an anti-Constitution newspaper in Albany. Unhappy with the brand of journalism meted out by the Webster brothers—George and Charles—the Albany Antifederalists thought their cause would suffer without the support of a printer who would "disconcert these White Livers by publishing an impartial paper."[10]

The increasing tempo of the ratification struggle in New York and Virginia, as well as continued exertions in Pennsylvania during the early months of 1788, prevented any hiatus of antifederalism before the Maryland convention sat in Annapolis. Yates and Lansing, the New York delegates at the Federal Convention who had walked out on Hamilton, found in Governor Clinton a bulwark for their antifederalism. A joint letter giving reasons for their Philadelphia walkout reached the state legislature during debate on calling a ratifying convention. Their warning that the Constitution was engineered to compress all the states into a unitary system was an echo of Clinton's own feeling; and as noted earlier, the ratifying convention was finally agreed upon with scarcely a vote to spare. With one eye on Massachusetts and the other on Virginia, the New York Antifederalists tried to be realistic. Clinton's lieutenant, Melancton Smith, had

[9] Paine Wingate to Timothy Pickering, March 29, 1788, Wingate, *Life of Wingate*, I, 223.

[10] Abraham G. Lansing to Robert Yates, January 31, 1788, Yates papers, *NYPL*.

already discounted reports of antifederal strength in Boston. "I think it best always to reckon the strength of your adversaries as much as it is," he cautioned.[11]

Though the Massachusetts ratification was a bitter disappointment, the bad news from Boston prodded the Antifederalists in upstate New York. In the city of "New York they are all in a panic with the Adoption of Massachusets [sic]," Robert Yates reported, but in Ulster, Orange, and Westchester counties the Antifederalists were undaunted. A social butterfly in Manhattan later complained that she had never seen so "little disposition towards Gaiety [as] at present in this City." Everybody appeared to be more interested in the Constitution than in the theater. "All the Men are immers'd in Politicks," she sighed, "and the Women say 'Life, is not Life without them.'"[12]

Those Federalists who disliked Clinton about as much as they liked the Constitution saw in a Federalist victory their chance to humble the governor, and could scarcely conceal their desire for a dual victory. "If the tide turns here in favor of the new Constitution down goes the Ideal of the People," an anti-Clintonian gloated, "that tool of Popularity of which you have often heard me speak, our Governor, I mean."[13]

Excitement over the constitutional question was as keen north of the Harlem river channel as it was at the corner of Church and Wall streets. "I do beleive [sic] since the sentlement [sic] of America such Exertions have not been made upon a Question of any Kind as the present upon the New Constitution," an Albany Antifederalist declared. He found the opposition working "both night and Day to prosolyte [sic] the unbelieving Antifederals," while his party endeavored "to Dell [sic] in plain Simple Truth."[14] Methodically, the Antifederalists began searching for well-known candidates to stand as delegates for the ratifying convention. They also planned a complete

[11] Melancton Smith to Robert Yates, January 28, 1788, Yates papers, *NYPL*.

[12] Henrietta Maria Colden to Fanny Tucker, December 28, 1788, Tucker-Coleman papers, Colonial Williamsburg.

[13] Hector St. J. Crevecour to William Short, February 20, 1788, Short papers, *DLC*.

[14] Henry Oouthoudt to John McKesson, April 3, 1788, McKesson papers, *NYHS*.

canvass of the voters, for every free male citizen who had reached his twenty-first birthday was eligible to vote under the democratic resolution forced through by the Clintonians. The badgered printer Greenleaf in New York took heart from the upstate reports of antifederal activity. While city-bred Federalists were still flushed with the Boston triumph, Greenleaf reported an Ulster County mass meeting where the crowd huzzaed as the Constitution was burned "in the most public place of the town, with the usual circumstances of disrespect and contempt." Clinton's personal following along the Hudson and in the rural districts seemed vigorous and loyal. "We have Good Accounts from Many parts of the County," an Albany Clintonian observed. "The Anties Do not Dispair of Success."

An alliance between Clinton and Antifederalists in Virginia might have been consummated during this period, except that mail service between the two executives was suspiciously snarled. Governor Randolph, following the mandate of the legislature, had invited the states to consider a second federal convention. Randolph did his task with no alacrity, and consequently, the one governor who might have responded with delight—Clinton—received the invitation too late for concerted action. Randolph might have been relieved, but Antifederalists found in the long-delayed dispatch further proof that the post office was conspiring to thwart all their efforts.

The Virginia executive, once so certain of his antifederalism, became more and more irresolute. His letter of October 10, setting forth his reasons for not signing the Constitution, had been shown to a few legislators but was withheld from the public until January. Four Virginia Antifederalists applied some pressure, and Randolph hesitantly gave them permission to print it.[15] The rambling letter, filling nearly six columns of a Richmond newspaper, dwelt upon the tottering Articles of Confederation and "the miscarriage of the impost [which] almost rivets our despondency." Randolph explained his refusal to sign the Constitution forthrightly. Had he signed it, the governor would have bound himself "to be silent as to amendments." The needed amendments, Randolph explained at length, ranged from a southern check on unfavorable shipping laws to some

[15] Richmond, Virginia, *Independent Chronicle*, January 2, 1788.

141

limits on the presidential tenure. The equality of small and large states in the Senate annoyed Randolph, and he saw dangerous tendencies in the overlapping jurisdictions of the state and federal legislatures.

To this point, Antifederalists could read the letter with satisfaction. But in his concluding sentences, Randolph minimized his criticism by declaring that above all things, the most important consideration was preservation of the Union. Randolph said he would cling to the Union as the "rock of our salvation, and urge Virginia to finish the salutary work, which she has begun." More Federalists than Antifederalists found hopeful signs in Randolph's phrases, and Madison was told that the Constitution had gained much ground as a result of Randolph's blowing hot-and-cold.[16] The governor's letter helped convince some Antifederalists that a change was needed "& has pointed out not a single objection to the new plan in which they will coincide with him." Spencer Roane, a Virginian who shared none of Randolph's doubts, tore into Randolph. "Good God! how can the first Magistrate . . . after a feeble parade of opposition," say "that he will accept a Constitution which is to beget a monarchy or an aristocracy?" Any chance for amendments had been weakened by Randolph's "very candid declaration at the end of his letter."[17] To counteract the designs of ambitious men who mocked republican institutions, Randolph ought to have displayed "the utmost caution, secrecy, and political sagacity." Why, then, had Randolph laid all his cards on the table?

While Randolph appeared beset by doubts, Richard Henry Lee published a letter which probably was meant to counterbalance some of the damage. Lee's letter, like the governor's, bore an October date and was a stern lecture for Randolph on republicanism. It was published in midwinter, on the heels of the last letters of the "Federal Farmer," when Lee's authorship of those Antifederalist harpoons was well known. Lee's range of constitutional objections had already been covered in the "Letters," but here they were again presented in concise, hard-hitting form, concluding with the familiar exhortation

---

[16] George Turberville to Madison, January 8, 1788, Madison papers, *NYPL*.
[17] "Plain Dealer," *Virginia Independent Chronicle*, February 13, 1788.

for another federal convention.[18] Federalists acknowledged that Lee's latest letter "was doing mischief in Virginia," and it had also stirred the embers of antifederalism in Pennsylvania.

Lee's insistence upon a second convention was indeed finding fertile ground in Pennsylvania. Federalists were disturbed by the incessant attacks coming from rural areas, for the issue was supposed to have been settled weeks before at their convention. Madison ascribed the continued antifederal activity to a long-standing "habitual & factious opposition, to their rivals," and to a manifest desire to deny the national government "some essential ingredients"—such as sustaining revenues. Madison's judgment was confirmed by Tench Coxe, who reported that the western counties were circulating anti-Constitutional petitions, "but the Assembly will certainly dismiss them by a Majority of two thirds."[19]

The prime mover in Pennsylvania for another convention seems to have been the controller general, John Nicholson. After his anti-Constitution pamphlet gained him more brickbats than bouquets in Philadelphia, Nicholson tried to stay in the shadows as much as possible, so that his prodigious Antifederalist labors were known mainly among close friends and associates. Nicholson turned his attention toward the middle and western counties, where the climate for antifederalism seemed friendlier. Nicholson wrote a petition to the state legislature which condemned the Constitution as "burthensome, expensive and oppressive." This petition asserted that the Constitution had been ratified illegally, and asked that the December ratification-convention proceedings be annulled. Instead, ratification ought to be confirmed only if each state followed the procedure prescribed in the existing Articles of Confederation—that is, unanimous approval by the thirteen state legislatures.

Nicholson broadcast copies of the petition in January and awaited a reaction. The answers showed mingled feelings. A resident at the far-western end of the state was confused by the petition and did not

---

[18] R. H. Lee to Randolph, October 1, 1787, quoted in Philadelphia *Independent Gazetteer*, December 28, 1787.

[19] Madison to Randolph, January 10, 1788; Tench Coxe to Madison, January 27, 1788, Madison papers, *DLC*.

want to circulate it. "The truth is the people at large do not understand the subject and an appeal to them is certainly dangerous," the candid correspondent wrote, ". . . for I neither think the proposed goverment [*sic*] so diabolical as some of the Opposition seem to hold forth nor so good as its advocates represent." At Lancaster, the report was no more encouraging. A confidential survey among ardent Antifederalists there revealed no disposition toward a fight. "It was adjudged best," Nicholson's confidant wrote, "not to attempt any thing at this place, as there are a large Majority in the other side of the question." But at Northumberland, seven copies of the petition were quickly filled with names. "I'm sure four fifths of the people here are against it," the local Antifederalist bigwig reported. Many Carlisle Antifederalists signed the petition and favored unified action by citizens of York, Dauphin, Cumberland and Franklin counties to oppose "this detastable [*sic*] Foederal conspiracy."[20]

While Nicholson's petitions were being circulated, a collection of militia weapons was ordered, which Philadelphia Antifederalists twisted into a nefarious plot. The militia command, coming after the state convention and the Carlisle riot, was pounced upon by "Centinel." "Does not the timing of the measure determine the intention?" Bryan asked.[21] Federalists insisted that the weapons were being collected from militiamen as a routine matter, merely to determine which guns were no longer serviceable. But no effort was spared to instill in readers' minds the notion that Federalists actually feared an armed outbreak by their adversaries. An unnamed Federalist was quoted as declaring that five thousand lives would be "a small sacrifice, a cheap purchase for the establishment of the new constitution." Federalists quickly denied the implications and called the printed quotation a "base perversion." Before the rumors waned, however, Antifederalists began insisting that unless a second federal convention were called the nation would soon witness "all the horrors of a civil war."[22] This sounded like bluster, but Nicholson knew that around Carlisle a few Antifederalist hotheads were itching for a fight.

[20] William Petriken to John Nicholson, February 24, 1788, Nicholson papers, Pennsylvania Archives.
[21] "Centinel IX," Philadelphia *Independent Gazetteer*, January 8, 1788.

Obviously, the Pennsylvania Antifederalists found that an ounce of emotion was worth a pound of logic in their political struggle. Rumors of large orders for shot and powder imports from Europe were reported in Philadelphia. "What is the object of these extra orders for ammunition?" the writer asked. "He hopes the high-flying monarchy-men, and the rest of the aristocratics, have no thought of letting loose the dogs of war among such of their fellow citizens as intend to oppose the new constitution." Interspersed with these dire reports were calls for another convention that would make the Constitution more palatable to republican tastes. If Federalists insisted on "attempting to force it on the people," without drastic amendments, "the peace of the country must inevitably be destroyed."[23]

This propaganda barrage had its effect. In Cumberland County, a mass meeting sent its thanks to Antifederalist delegates in the recent state convention. Belligerently, the signers alluded to "the impending ruin ... should this engine of slavery ever be established ... [which] we flatter ourselves it never will." A short time later, a Cumberland County group complained that most of the newspapers received in Carlisle were full of Federalist lies. Denouncing writers "who thus sell their birthright for a mess of pottage," the committee charged that the state legislature had tried to play the midwife to "the birth of this 13 horned monster"—the Constitution.[24] A Montgomery County correspondent reported that committees were being recruited to fight against ratification unless amendments were added forthwith. Federalists at the state convention had practiced "cunning, *deception*, and *address*," the writer claimed, but in many counties it was difficult to find a single supporter of the Constitution. A small riot broke out at Standing Stone when Antifederalists circulated petitions denouncing the Constitution and held a parade with effigies of local Federalists mounted "upon the backs of *old scabby* ponies." One of the offended parties happened to be a judge, who promptly ordered the ringleaders arrested for contempt. A crowd assembled, in the ensuing

[22] James Pettigrew to John Nicholson, March 12, 1788, Nicholson papers, Pennsylvania Archives.
[23] Philadelphia *Freeman's Journal*, January 23, 1788; Philadelphia *Independent Gazetteer*, January 16, 1788.
[24] *Carlisle Gazette*, March 5, 1788.

melee the jailed Antifederalists were freed, and threats flew thick as the crowd declared "their intention to duck the [Federalist] junto if they repeated the insults."[25]

A purported letter from Franklin County asserted that the few Federalists west of the Susquehanna had been promised offices if the Constitution were ratified. "I am told that the 33 friends of the well-born in the county of Westmoreland consist of shopkeepers, packhorsemen, half pay officers, Cincinnati, attorneys at law, public defaulters, and Jews," the correspondent maintained. Scarcely a farmer in Franklin County could be found who was "in favor of this system of military power." The severe winter and deep snows had held political activity to a minimum, the writer concluded, but better weather would bring regular meetings of Antifederalists when work could proceed toward calling another state convention. Nor were these idle boasts, for warmer weather did indeed bring a political thaw in these western counties. By late July, thirteen counties were committed to send delegates to a convention of their own calling (since the state legislature pretty much ignored them) at Harrisburg.

Meanwhile, a steady barrage of propaganda, meant to foster enmity between farmers and bankers, appeared in Antifederalist newspapers. It was the old story of *city men* vs. *farmers*, as a Franklin County correspondent indicated. Federalists in Pennsylvania were concentrated along the Delaware banks, the writer ventured, and were "confined chiefly within the city, the majority of whom are under the influence and direction of the bank." The "bank" in this case being the Bank of North America—Robert Morris' House of Mammon in Philadelphia (so Antifederalists inferred), where the Constitution had already been erected on a pedestal.

Gradually, the Antifederalists concentrated their fire on the Bank of North America and its founder, hoping, no doubt, that in Morris' embarrassment all Federalists would squirm a little. "The Countryman" declared that "had it not been for the pernicious influence of that bank," Pennsylvanians would not have been stampeded into hasty ratification. Oswald eagerly took up the attack, hinting that Morris was having financial woes that he hoped to solve speedily

[25] Boston *American Herald*, April 10, 1788.

under the new Constitution. "Centinel" accused Morris—the war-time superintendent of finance—of owing the government large sums of money. Accordingly, Morris was an avid Federalist since public defaulters were banking on the Constitution for their financial salvation.[26]

The Antifederalist attack on Morris was intended to link support of the Constitution with the bank and also with squandered public money. "A Friend of the People" pointed to the ex post facto clause in the Constitution as a special refuge designed to square all public accounts. The offending passage "skreens [*sic*] public defaulters, and cancels all debts due to the United States." It was not surprising therefore that Morris had used all of his influence with the Congress to hold back a full disclosure of the facts. This would explain why some Federalists were indefatigable campaigners, for when a man found "his *pocket* and his *bacon* may be saved thereby . . . the public may go whistle for their money." Benjamin Workman warned frugal taxpayers that the Constitution was arranging for them a means to pay public debts twice. Pennsylvania had already retired a large portion of her public debt, but under the Constitution these efforts would be wasted. Pennsylvania "will be placed on a footing with the most delinquent state in the union," and all her previous expenditures "in support of public faith . . . terminate in a two-fold loss to our citizens."[27]

The fact that Morris was out of town, leaving the charges unanswered, gave Federalists little consolation. Perhaps with some justification, the Antifederalists in Philadelphia began to believe that in pouncing on Morris and the bank they had struck a vulnerable spot. "Our new government junto are greatly in the dumps, on account of the New Hampshire convention, and affairs with you," a letter to Carlisle observed. Stock in the Bank of North America was falling, while "the opposition to the new constitution seem on the growing hand here."[28]

[26] "Centinel XVI," Philadelphia *Independent Gazetteer*, February 26, 1788.

[27] "Philadelphiensis XI," *ibid.*, March 8, 1788.

[28] The letter with a Philadelphia dateline appeared in the *Carlisle Gazette*, April 9, 1788.

In time these reports reached Morris, who was mending his private affairs while participating in the politics of Richmond. From the Virginia capital, Morris branded the Antifederalist charges as oblique attacks on the Constitution. During the Revolution when he was in charge of public finances, Morris declared, he never touched *"one shilling of the public money."* Morris said that he had not kept silent because the charges, "if not controverted, might have influenced weak minds to oppose the Constitution." Morris' public letter dampened Antifederalist enthusiasm for attacks on the "money crowd," and Federalist newspapers put a lid on the affair when they printed George Bryan's confidential letter to a friend. Mysteriously, the letter came to Federalist hands and was used to put Judge Bryan, whom many presumed was author of the "Centinel" pieces, in a bad light. Bryan's letter gave as reasons for the Federalist strength in Philadelphia "the supreme influence of the Bank, the weight of Mr. Morris, the bankrupt and dependent state of the traders generally."[29] Federalists gave the letter a negative twist, so that Bryan seemed to be pleased by any misfortunes that befell the people—so long as the Antifederalists could make gains. Antifederalists raved at the opposition for tampering with the mails, but Federalists believed that they had unmasked "Centinel" and held him up to public contempt.

At the same time, Francis Hopkinson did some detective work. The Federalist sleuth learned that "Philadelphiensis" was Benjamin Workman. Once Workman's authorship of "Philadelphiensis" was known, his teaching position at the University of Pennsylvania became tenuous. Since the concept of academic freedom was too far in the future to save Workman from suffering for his antifederalism, he lost his job as a result of Hopkinson's investigation. Even so, Workman was not silenced; he loosed defamatory charges at Hopkinson that brought the newspaper warfare to the lowest grade of journalism. Although Hopkinson complained that his exposure of Workman simply meant that "scarce a Day passes without my Appearance in the News Paper in every scandalous Garb that scribling

[29] George Bryan to John Ralston, March 7, 1788, quoted in *Pennsylvania Gazette*, March 26, 1788.

148

Vengeance can furnish," a leading Antifederalist penman had in fact been put on a leash.[30]

These disclosures helped curb the antifederal spirit in Philadelphia, but it seemed that as one fire was put out another smoldering trouble spot burst into flame. When Oswald and his coterie found more friends west of the Susquehanna than perhaps they had expected, the Federalists made overtures for allies. Benjamin Rush appealed to Bishop Muhlenburg, one of the most powerful of all the Pennsylvania Germans, for aid against the Antifederalists. "I rejoice in the part a *great majority* of them have taken in the great contest," Rush wrote. "On them I rely chiefly to *outvote*, to *outwork*, and to *outpray* the Antifederalists in our state."[31] A troubled Carlisle Federalist advised his noisy opponents to forget politics, since their duty was to till the soil, pray, and leave "state affairs to able heads." The pretensions of some back-country politicians were bothersome to the Federalists. "If Common people all must mix,/To bear a part in politicks,/Confusion will ensue," a Federalist warned. The Pennsylvania Federalists also ridiculed the proposal for another federal convention. Noting that Antifederalists in the northern, central, and southern states took different grounds for their opposition, a Federalist said this proved discord as well as the "utter impossibility of another general convention."[32]

With a hopeful look toward Maryland, where reports of some antifederal strength lifted their spirits, the Philadelphia "Antis" hailed Luther Martin's "Genuine Information" as an unassailable argument against ratification. Printing the lengthy discourse was editor Spotswood's swan song, but the *Independent Gazetteer* picked up the refrain where the lamented *Herald* left off. "I am not sur-

---

[30] See the Philadelphia *Independent Gazetteer*, March 11, 14, 26, April 1, 3, 15, 29, 1788. Seeking a presidential appointment some years later, Bryan said he wrote both "Centinel" and "the Reasons of dissent of minority" at the Pennsylvania convention (Samuel Bryan to Jefferson, July 27, 1801, and July 24, 1807, "Applications, Jefferson Administration, 1801–1809," National Archives).

[31] Benjamin Rush to G. Muhlenberg, February 1788, *The Letters of Benjamin Rush* (ed. by Lyman Butterfield), I, 452.

[32] *Pennsylvania Gazette*, February 13, 1788.

prised that a convention was to be called at ten days notice, in this state," wrote "Candour." "My eyes are now opened—and I am determined henceforth to . . . procure amendments, and have a bill of rights affixed to it."[33] Martin's parallels between the Constitution and its British model gave Antifederalists a chance to renew their seige. One critic of the Constitution turned poet to charge that "Tho' British armies could not here prevail, Yet British politics shall turn the scale . . . *Congress* and *president* full proof shall bring, A mere disguise for parliament and King . . . ." When the Annapolis convention was only weeks away, one of the last "Centinel" papers appeared. As a warning for the state conventions still to meet, Bryan declared that future generations would view with wonderment the "audacity and villainy of the conspirators on the one hand, and the frantic enthusiasm, and easy credulity of the people" in some states on the other.

By indulging in unwarranted wishful thinking, the Philadelphia Antifederalists believed that any rumor would make Maryland into a stronghold for their cause. In late February, "a letter from Queen Anne's county" was hailed as proof of rising antifederal strength in Maryland. Newspaper reports from the North hinting that Maryland would have a two-to-one Federalist majority in its state convention were denounced as false. "It will be quite the reverse;" the letter read, "above three-fourths of the Western, and at least one-third of the Eastern Shores are warmly opposed to it." Martin's harangues before the state legislature *let the cat out of the bag*; and none of his [Federal Convention] *colleagues* have dared to contradict any thing he has said."[34]

The main difference between the contests in Maryland and those in Pennsylvania and Massachusetts was that some foremost members of the bar were Antifederalists. Where there had been complaints in Philadelphia and Boston that lawyers were all on the other side of the question, ready to browbeat their adversaries who were unlearned in law, in Maryland such a grievance was not valid. In Martin and

[33] Martin's speech was printed in the *Pennsylvania Evening Herald*, January 16, 19, 23, 26, 1788; Philadelphia *Independent Gazetteer*, February 12, 1788.
[34] Philadelphia *Independent Gazetteer*, February 26, 1788.

the Chases, Maryland Antifederalists boasted a triumvirate of legal talents that could hardly be matched in the state. Conspicuously absent from the Antifederalist delegation, as a matter of fact, were the elements that had been the warp and woof of the movement to the North—the yeoman farmer. Among the Antifederalist candidates for delegate posts there must have been some plain men of the soil, but by and large they were lawyers with long experience in practical politics who tried to derail the Constitution in Maryland.

Both factions had charted their courses before the drafting of the Constitution had been completed. At Philadelphia, the Maryland delegation at the Federal Convention had caucused to discuss the plan as it evolved. There Martin warned that the people of Maryland would not support any consolidated system. Doctor McHenry noticed that Mercer was making a list of the delegates, writing *for* or *against* by each name. McHenry asked what the words signified, and Mercer replied "laughing that it was no question but that those marked with a *for* were for a king."[35] In the convention Martin made much of the people's attachment to the states—"to these they look up for the security of their lives, liberties & properties" he chanted.[36] In terms of property, Martin himself had done well under Maryland laws, for he had made extensive purchases of land confiscated from British owners, using depreciated money to pay for it. Mercer, Jeremiah Chase, and the Ridgelys had also bought confiscated lands or paid old debts with the discounted state currency. The Constitution carried direct threats to their economic well-being, and the fear of lawsuits over confiscated lands may have strengthened their strong Antifederalist position.

Samuel Chase and Martin did not long conceal their antipathy toward the Constitution. Martin unleashed an attack in November, declaring that the Constitution was the result of a compromise between the "Monarchial party" and delegates from large states. Not only would large states continue their domineering course, but the federal courts would hold immense powers that they would certainly abuse. "Should any Individual dare to dispute the conduct of an

[35] 2 Farrand 190.
[36] 1 Farrand 340.

Excise Man, [after] ransacking his Cellars he may be hoisted into the Federal Court from Georgia to vindicate his just rights, or to be punished for his impertinence," Martin thundered.[37] Perhaps Martin genuinely believed what he said, although his future actions and his past financial dealings made him appear as an opportunistic demagogue. "So far did Mr. Martin proceed in his avowed hostility," a Federalist noted, "as even to detail in the face of decency . . . the petty dialogues and paltry anecdotes" of the Federal Convention. "I blush'd in my own bed-chamber when I read his speech."[38]

Nonetheless, the leather-lunged, thick-skinned Martin courted the popular cause. Moreover, at the outset newspapers in Baltimore and Annapolis treaded the political ground lightly. Unlike printers in Boston, New York, and Philadelphia, the political leanings of the Maryland newspapers were not evident at a glance. The quiet strength of the Federalists was misleading.

Martin's bombast and Chase's energy—the power of their names and past influence—almost convinced the Federalists themselves that ratification would find no easy course in Maryland. Several circumstances put the Federalists in a bad light—"bad" in the sense that the conservatives seemed bent on stacking the convention in their favor. The state senate had powerful forces that were determined to keep the property qualifications for voting high (£500) and to limit the convention to the power to "assent & ratify" the Constitution. These maneuvers were defeated, but they left an impression of highhandedness. The facts in themselves gave the Antifederalists some ammunition, but in their zeal they doctored the truth. "The present conduct of the well-born in Maryland . . . is something like what we might expect from them, in case their scheme of power and office-making was adopted," an Antifederalist taunted. Then he claimed that some of the Federalist "lordlings are selling to one another at public sale, for a song, all the mortgaged freeholds of the people who have been reduced by the distress of the times, heavy taxes, &c." The scheme was used to keep farmers from voting for convention delegates, "as

[37] 3 Farrand 151–159.
[38] John Brown Cutting to Jefferson, July 11, 1788, 13 *Jefferson Papers* 333.

none but freeholders are entitled to vote in that state."[39] He intimated that one of "the well-born . . . took out three thousand writs at one time, and had them executed in the most rigorous manner." Such clumsy propaganda made few converts.

During the winter, Maryland Federalists discerned the plan pursued by their adversaries. Some correspondence between the Maryland Antifederalists and the leading anti-Constitution men in Virginia called for concerted action on a southern program of amendments. A coalition between the slaveholding tobacco-exporting states seemed logical. The Virginia Antifederalists, calculating that their chances for maintaining a southern bloc would be strengthened by Maryland support, looked across the Potomac for aid in prying important concessions from the Federalists. A kind of antifederal manifesto, written by George Mason, was to be shown to friendly Maryland deputies at the Federal Convention, with a request for "concurrence & assistance." Maryland politicians were told that with these amendments the Constitution "would be unexceptionable."[40] The eleven proposals ranged from Mason's pet amendment—requiring a two-thirds majority in Congress before laws affecting shipping might be passed—to a one-term limit on the presidency. Obviously, the point was to arouse in the Maryland Antifederalists a fear of their northern bretheren, and thus promote a southern alliance.

Privately acknowledging their probable weakness in the forthcoming state convention, the Maryland "antis" apparently decided that their best hope of gaining amendments would lie in dilatory tactics. First, they would try to ward off a final ratification vote by seeking a temporary adjournment. If that succeeded, they could reconvene after Virginia Antifederalists had extracted concessions that would strengthen their hand.

Martin and his friends probably tried to keep their plans veiled, but as it developed, the Antifederalist strategy retained all the secrecy of a public hanging. "Their force will probably be exerted to adjourn untill [*sic*] the Convention of Virginia has decided," Daniel Carroll reported to Madison. Carroll thought the Antifederalists would lack

[39] Bennington *Vermont Gazette*, April 7, 1788.
[40] 4 Farrand 56–57.

the votes needed to effect their scheme. "If [the] New York Assembly appoint a Convention, and Massachusetts have adopted the Constitution there will be less doubt." After those two queries had been resolved favorably, Madison was still concerned that somehow Carroll was underestimating the Maryland Antifederalist strength. "The difference between even a postponement and adoption in Maryland, may in the nice balance of parties here, possibly give a fatal advantage to that which opposes the constitution," the Virginian observed after studying the tense situation in his home county. Washington's prestige was also thrown into the Maryland fight. He wrote Governor Johnson, warning that a postponement until the Virginia convention had acted would be regarded as "tantamount to a rejection of the Constitution."[41] The Federalists wanted no more adjournments of the New Hampshire variety. One case could be isolated, but two might initiate an epidemic. Meanwhile Martin, in full agreement with other Antifederalist leaders regarding a second convention, denounced the "political quacks" who prescribed dangerous remedies. Citizens were urged by Federalists "rashly to gulp down a constitution, which in its present form, unaltered and unamended, would be as certain death to your liberty, as arsenic could be to your bodies."

Federalists viewed the antics of their Maryland adversaries and ascribed their ardor to sordid human motives rather than to political idealism. Mercer's behavior was reportedly caused—but not excused— by his anger at Washington over pressure to pay an old debt. In his zeal, which he was later to regret, Mercer wrote letters that exceeded the bounds of decorum. Governor Johnson told Washington that the Antifederalists in his state "seem to me to be really more afraid of being restrained from doing what they ought not to do and being compelled to do what they ought to do than of being obliged to do what there is no moral Obligation on them to do."[42] The syntax was confusing, but Washington knew what Johnson meant and agreed

[41] Madison to Washington, April 10, 1788, Madison papers, *DLC*; Washington to Thomas Johnson, April 20, 1788, Fitzpatrick, *The Writings of George Washington*, XXIX, 463.

[42] Thomas Johnson to Washington, December 11, 1787, Edwin S. Delaplaine, *Life of Thomas Johnson*, 132–33.

with his conclusion: "Man unhappily needs more Government than he imagined." The alternative to energetic government seemed to be further domination by the radical crowd that had held the whip hand since the Revolution.

By a steady parade of newspaper essays, plus some entertaining tavern speeches on court days, the Antifederalist leaders maintained the appearance of vigorous opposition in Maryland. But as the election for convention delegates neared, their ineptness became obvious. In Hartford County, Paca and Martin were formidable candidates, but Samuel Chase's law clerk was brought around to fill out the ticket. In Baltimore, the Antifederalists offered only token opposition. Washington and Montgomery counties were written off as total losses. The bleak antifederal slate was in sharp contrast to the campaign noise.

The results proved that the Antifederalists had strength only where they offered well-known candidates who aroused voter interest with speeches full of verbal fireworks. Thus, Anne Arundel, Baltimore, and Hartford counties were opposed to the Constitution because the Antifederalists really exerted themselves there. "You can have no conception of the low arts made use of in those three Counties to poison the community," a Federalist told a Pennsylvania friend.[43] "Standing armies, whipping the militia, and all the other Inflammatory reasons so copiously held up to the public view in the dissent of your turbulent Minority." At Annapolis the Antifederalists surprised their adversaries by not offering a ticket until four days before the polling began. Then the Chases, Mercer, and Benjamin Harrison came forth with a flurry of activity. Mercer and Jeremiah Chase signed inflammatory handbills which they broadcast through Anne Arundel County. "The people were alarm'd at their positive assertions, and I am afraid when they attended the Polls, a wildness appeared in many which show'd they were realy [*sic*] frightened by what they had just heard," defeated candidate Daniel Carroll reported with rancor.[44] Carroll indicated the Antifederalists had assiduously spread fantastic rumors. The Federalists were secretly sup-

---

[43] "A Letter from Baltimore," *Pennsylvania Gazette*, April 30, 1788.
[44] Daniel Carroll to Madison, May 28, 1788, Madison papers, *DLC*.

ported by the French government—Robert Morris' plans of economic coercion on the states would be revived—a New Hampshire man preferred Washington as king—all these charges were hurled at dumbfounded Federalists.

Although their opponents insisted that the campaign had been conducted at gutter level, the Antifederalist ticket won Anne Arundel County with over fifty votes to spare. In Hartford County, Paca and Martin carried along two weaker candidates, while the strongest Federalist received fewer than one hundred votes. The six-to-one margin of victory was recorded, the Antifederalists said, despite the fact that Federalists had kept the polls open for four days while combing the county for like-minded voters. The two Charles Ridgelys in Baltimore County swamped their opponents, joined by two nondescripts who also far outdistanced their Federalist rivals. However, this three-county sweep marked the high tide of antifederalism in Maryland. Arrayed against the even dozen anti-Constitution delegates thus elected were more than sixty Federalists. In Washington County, the four Federalists each had 657 votes, while strongest Antifederalist received 25.

Although thoroughly crushed in the state-wide campaign, the Antifederalists bolstered their staggering morale with cries of fraud. They charged that in Baltimore numerous irregularities occurred at the polls, which were illegally kept open for several days. A number of foreign seamen, many armed with clubs, had intimidated peaceful citizens—"chiefly Germans"— and kept them from voting. Federalists had won Baltimore (they charged) by permitting nonresidents to vote, denying votes to some bona fide residents, and finally by stuffing the boxes with twice the number of possible ballots.[45]

Antifederalist plans in Maryland had miscarried so badly that when the convention first assembled in Annapolis the three leaders—Martin, Samuel Chase, and Paca—failed to take their seats. Pleased Federalists saw that ratification would be an easy matter. They voted to consider the Constitution as a single item, by a fifty-eight to five vote. All the oratory that followed was superfluous, but the Federalists knew appearances were important. If the three tardy Antifederal-

[45] Philadelphia *Independent Gazetteer*, April 24, 1788.

ists thought ratification and adjournment would be hurried to take advantage of their absence—and give them a future claim of "undue haste"—they were mistaken. Debates were limited to two half-hour speeches upon any single subject. These measures were simply adopted "to avoid the endless garrulity of Martin and the inflammatory eloquence of Chase and Paca, neither of whom took their seats until today, being disheartened at the weakness of their party," a Federalist observed.[46]

Despite their plans to throttle Antifederalist orators, the Federalists had such complete control that they became lenient with the recalcitrant handful in their midst. When Samuel Chase disregarded the time limit on debate and harangued them for over two hours, the Federalists let him rant on. "When he sat down a profound silence ensued for Some time, when T. J. [Governor Johnson] arose & observed, as there was nothing before the house, he moved they should adjourn for dinner." In this one-sided political game Martin was more ill-humored than usual because of a throat ailment, which, a spectator noted, shortened the session "& saved a great deal of time & money to the state."[47]

Accordingly, shorthand reporter Thomas Lloyd found that he had little to do, for a federal caucus had agreed to "hear the minority patiently" without even making a reply. When Chase spoke of the loss of state rights or alluded to Congress as a potential club for rich and ambitious politicians, his words fell upon a bored Federalist audience. Mercer, who had made too much noise in the hustings to be silent now, also took his turn. "But no converts were made—no, not one," Washington rejoiced when he heard how things had gone.

In desperation the Maryland Antifederalists tried to dilute the final vote with some recommendatory amendments. Paca had a proposition tucked under his arm, which he hoped could be the basis for compromise. Paca was a Whig from pre-Revolutionary days, and apparently his antifederalism was on principle rather than—as some intimated of his colleagues— on personal interest. Paca's three con-

[46] Providence *United States Chronicle*, May 15, 1788.
[47] William Smith to O. H. Williams, April 28, 1788, O. H. Williams papers, Maryland Historical Society.

secutive terms as governor were a testimony to his popularity among the men who were now ranged against him. If any Antifederalist delegate could have won over some of the opposition, either by logic or personal charm, Paca was that man. But, when he had launched a discussion on the subject of amendments, ready to offer a list of twenty-eight proposals for the delegates' consideration, their forebearance was at an end. The Antifederalists were powerless as Paca's list was shunted aside for a vote on ratification, which found eleven "nays" overwhelmed by sixty-three "ayes"—including Paca's own vote. The former governor explained that he was joining the opposition because he was persuaded that the desired amendments "would be peacably obtained." The phrase had an ominous ring. Governor Johnson thought the convention majority was taking an overbearing tone, and he gave the Antifederalists an opening.[48] Following Johnson's lead, the Federalists submitted to a request that a committee be formed to propose recommended amendments.

Dominated by Federalists, the committee on amendments took a more solemn view of the idea after a night's rest. Paca's original list was ripped apart, with only thirteen proposals surviving the impatient committee's scrutiny. Still, the tattered remnants had a framework which the more perceptive Federalists believed ladened with danger—far more so than the watered-down Boston amendments. Impatiently, the committee majority finally tossed the whole lot onto the table, refusing to permit the group to issue any report whatever. Although the Antifederalists claimed this was a highhanded way of stifling a call for needed alterations, the entire convention then voted to squelch the report.

Politicians are not always magnanimous in victory, and the Maryland Federalists had no inclination to allow the Paca-Chase-Martin faction any solace. With an eye cocked at the tabled report, they drank one of thirteen toasts to "speedy ratification by the remaining six [states], without amendments."[49] Mason's plan to create a southern antifederal wedge was stillborn. "A thorn this in the sides of the leaders of the opposition in this State," Washington wrote Madison.

[48] Daniel Carroll to Madison, May 28, 1788, Madison papers, *DLC*.
[49] *Pennsylvania Gazette*, May 14, 1788.

The Maryland decision "will if I mistake not" make the Virginia session "less tiresome."

Although the main business had been concluded after a short performance, there was an epilogue. With no reason for toasting or huzzaing, the Antifederalists in Annapolis had instead spent their time discussing ways of placing Paca's list before the people. Taking their lead from the minority at Philadelphia, the Maryland Antifederalists decided to issue their proposals in pamphlet form, as a discordant note that might drift southward. It is also possible that the Maryland Antifederalists, after their failure at the convention, needed a poultice for their wounds. The pamphlet certainly was more balm for them than for Virginia Antifederalists. One Maryland Federalist, whose ear was attuned to political refrains, "thought the address will be of little consequence in this State." Another reason which may have prompted the minority report was cancellation of Lloyd's plan to publish the convention debates. Since Federalists had "inflexibly preserved an obstinate and contemptuous silence," the record consisted mainly of antifederal remarks. Discreet Federalists reportedly met with Lloyd after the adjournment, took up a collection "*to defray his expences,* and he declared his intention *not to publish* what he had taken down."[50] Whatever the cause, Lloyd's promised volume never appeared. Glum Antifederalists had their own biased explanation.

Downcast by their defeat, Martin and his friends sulked for a time. Antifederalists elsewhere were assured by Samuel Chase, however, that the majority of Maryland citizens really wanted amendments, "but they are depressed and inactive."[51] The people "have lost all their former Spirit," Chase complained wearily, "and seem ready to submit to any Master." The loss of Maryland was indeed demoralizing. Only the hope of reversals in Virginia and New York kept the ill-organized Antifederalist effort from total collapse.

[50] Daniel Carroll to Madison, May 28, 1788, Madison papers, *DLC;* Annapolis *Maryland Gazette,* May 22, 1788; Baltimore *Maryland Gazette,* June 27, 1788.
[51] Samuel Chase to General John Lamb, June 13, 1788, Lamb papers, *NYHS.*

☆ IX ☆

Rumblings in the Back Country

ANTIFEDERALISTS disliked the aristocratic tone of John Adams' *Defence of the Constitutions*, but they could agree with his estimate of popular elections.

> Every flattery and menace, every passion and prejudice of every voter will be applied to; every trick and bribe that can be bestowed, and will be accepted, will be used; and, what is horrible to think of, that candidate . . . who has fewest scruples; who will propagate lies and slanders with most confidence and secrecy; who will wheedle, flatter, and cajole; who will debauch the people by treats, feasts, and diversions, with the least hesitation; and bribe with the most impudent front . . . will draw in tools and worm out enemies the fastest.[1]

Adams was wrong about the "rich and the well-born" Antifederalists could moan, but he was not wrong about the foibles of electioneering. "Unsullied honor, sterling integrity, real virtue, will stand a very unequal chance," Adams adjudged. The truth of Adams' remarks hit Antifederalists hard in the spring of 1788. They had received little good news from the election fronts, but of bad tidings they had received plenty. Opponents who, by their lights, had the fewest scruples had charged ahead of the honest and virtuous Antifederalists.

Only the Rhode Island referendum and New Hampshire adjournment prevented the ratification process from becoming a landslide. "The poor Anti-feds. seem to have got almost 'to the length of their tether,'" Postmaster-General Hazard observed with pleasure. "The Maryland majority has staggered them very much . . . and I think Virginia will give them the *coup de grace*." Colonel Oswald apparently regarded the Maryland vote as the deathblow. The scathing criticisms of "Centinel" were heard no more, and the *Independent Gazetteer* suddenly took a decidedly impartial tone.

[1] *Works of John Adams* (ed. by Charles F. Adams), VI, 51–52.

"Centinel's" bitter foe, Dr. Rush, surveyed the scene with immense satisfaction. "Mr. Bryan like his brother Shays will now be left a solitary example of political insanity and wickedness. All will end well."[2]

On a broad front, Federalists poked fun at their reeling adversaries. Going down the list of ratifying conventions, it was obvious that "the opposition, comparatively speaking, is almost nothing." The antifederal clamor for amendments was discounted as an extremely impractical and typical "wronghead" proposal. "To amend *before* the adoption will require that *all* the states, who are to become members of the new confederacy, should adopt *all* the amendments that shall be adopted by *any one* [state]," a Federalist argued. If the Antifederalists could be patient, amendments after ratification would require approval of only ten out of the thirteen states.[3] Pity the poor creatures, that they could not discern their true interests lay in a speedy ratification.

Much discussion was focused on the question of amendments, because it was obvious to even the most hard-bitten Antifederalist that the Constitution would be ratified. The only question in the minds of the opponents of the Constitution was whether they could muster sufficient strength in Virginia and New York for ratification conditioned upon the acceptance of certain amendments. Could ratification be valid if it would in effect be an ultimatum? Probably not, since it would demand explicit changes in the Constitution, which, if not made, would make ratification null and void. Without doubt, this was the last-ditch defense being prepared in the two great states which were still uncommitted. Clinton's henchman, Melancton Smith, ridiculed the Federalists' suggestion that amendments must come *after* ratification. Smith compared this argument with the tale of Agrippa, who told St. Paul that he was *almost* persuaded to become a Christian. If the Constitution were unconditionally ratified, Smith claimed, in later days they would hear no more about amend-

[2] Benjamin Rush to Jeremy Belknap, May 6, 1788, Butterfield, *Rush Letters,* I, 460.

[3] Quoted in the *Carlisle Gazette,* May 21, 1788, and in the *Pennsylvania Gazette,* June 4, 1788.

ments than St. Paul heard of Agrippa's conversion. "When the government is once organized, and all the offices under it filled, the inducements which our great men will have to support it, will be much stronger than they are now to urge its reception," Smith declared.[4] The needed alterations would "limit and abridge" many federal powers, "and is it probable that those who enjoy these powers will be so likely to surrender them? . . . Common sense says —— they will not."

Because the leaders of the Antifederalist movement were in the key states of Virginia and New York, their opponents regarded a second convention or conditional amendments as threats no less grave than outright rejection of the Constitution. Answering Smith's argument, Noah Webster insisted that concessions held out to Antifederalists were made simply in the interests of national unity, not because there were fundamental weaknesses in the Constitution. The recommendatory amendments of Massachusetts had been accepted by Federalists "not so much because they think the constitution will be *better* for them; but because they think these additions will reconcile the opposition . . . without making the constitution *worse*."[5] The amount of public discussion on conditional ratification in the Virginia and New York campaigns then in full swing is uncertain, but among leading Antifederalists there was much talk and little doubt. If their strength could be mustered at Richmond and Poughkeepsie, conditional ratification would be the political salvation of the Antifederalists, even though nine states might have already ratified.

Grudgingly, the Antifederalists conceded that the South Carolina convention scheduled for May was a lost cause. When the state legislature had first debated the call for a ratifying convention in January, Rawlins Lowndes had fought almost singlehandedly against the Constitution. Again, the spectacle of a lone public man trying to thwart the Federalists was repeated. Long-experienced in Carolina politics, Lowndes knew it was risky to quarrel with his fellow delegates from Charleston, but Lowndes had the reputation of following

[4] Melancton Smith, "An Address to the People . . . of New York," Ford, *Pamphlets on the Constitution*, 91–92.

[5] *American Magazine*, April, 1788, quoted in Ford, *Pamphlets*, 87.

principles rather than popular causes. After the first Federalist barrage on behalf of a ratifying convention had sent most of the Antifederalists scurrying for cover, Lowndes showed his mettle. Lowndes acknowledged that he was outnumbered by articulate Federalists who were "mostly gentlemen of the law . . . capable of giving ingenious explanations to such points as they wished to have adopted." What these gentlemen favored was an unnecessary experiment, Lowndes said, for with a little mending the Confederation could continue indefinitely. "What, risk the loss of political existence on experiment!" If the Federalists succeeded, Lowndes predicted that "the sun of the Southern States would set, never to rise again."[6]

Lowndes knew where the Achilles' heel of the Carolina gentry was, and he aimed at the mark. "Our kind friends in the north," he asserted, had carefully protected their shipping interests at the Federal Convention but had placed checks on slavery—"our only natural resource. Why, then, call this a reciprocal bargain, which took all from one party, to bestow it on the other?" No political parvenu, Lowndes knew that he was treading on ground held sacred by many of his Charleston friends. After Charles Pinckney chided him for being the lone Antifederalist orator, Lowndes answered that he had been pushed into his role by "a number of respectable members, men of good sense, though not in the habit of speaking in public." Aedanus Burke sat tight-lipped, never raising a whisper in Lowndes's support. But for the help of General Sumter and a few other delegates from the Ninety-Six district, Lowndes would have been the solitary opponent of the Federalist phalanx.

Lowndes harangued the Federalists for three days, exploiting the southerner's prejudice against the North. Ratification would mean, he predicted, that South Carolina would "dwindle into a mere skeleton of what it was," stripped of power until "he should value the honor of a seat in the legislature in no higher estimation than a seat in the city council." Not only was the taxing power surrendered, but the state's right to issue paper money would be swept away regardless of how great "our distress may be." Then Lowndes struck the note that chilled Federalists. Call another convention, he promised, and

[6] Elliot, *Debates*, IV, 272.

"every objection could be met on fair grounds, and adequate remedies applied where necessary."[7] If cries for amendments were ignored, the Constitution might be ratified, but it "perhaps might require the bayonet to enforce it." Shocked Federalists answered Lowndes with an impassioned plea for the Union and reminded the opposition that during the Revolution "the shackles of the south were broken asunder by the arms of the north."

Whatever interest Lowndes had in the Union was subordinate to his love for South Carolina. If the Federalists eager to build a navy would calculate "where this navy, so necessary, was to come from,—not from the Southern States, but the Northern ones,—they would easily perceive to whom this country would belong." However, the Federalists had made the Constitution into their golden calf, and everybody was supposed to bow down before it. Lowndes concluded with a declaration of conscience. He would not court popularity by supporting a bad cause. For his epitaph, Lowndes asked that the inscription read: "Here lies the man that opposed the Constitution, because it was ruinous to the liberty of America."

Startled Federalists tried to turn the discussion of another convention into a joke. Why talk so much now if "the ultimate decision depended on another body?" Lowndes' energetic performance had given the inarticulate Antifederalists a glimmer of hope. Thus emboldened, James Lincoln of Ninety-Six apologized for a lack of forensic ability as he seconded Lowndes' warning. The Constitution would create an aristocracy that would transfer power from the people to "a set of men who live one thousand miles distant from you." Lincoln wondered aloud why the President might hold office "for fourteen times four years" but yet "You do not put the same check on him that you do on your own state governor."[8] And for a clinching argument, Lincoln added the embarrassing refrain—why no bill of rights?

General Pinckney assured Lowndes and Lincoln that their hypothetical fears had all been discussed at the Federal Convention and dismissed one by one. Silence had been deemed prudent in many cases,

[7] *Ibid.*, 287–90.
[8] *Ibid.*, 314.

as in the presidential term, so that in an emergency citizens might exercise their own unfettered judgment. The same was true of freedom of the press and a bill of rights, Pinckney added. A bill of rights was usually prefaced with remarks about the freedom and equality of mankind. Could South Carolinians join in this kind of business, Pinckney asked, "when a large part of our property consists in men who are actually born slaves?"[9]

A few minutes earlier Lowndes had been thanked for serving as an antifederal spokesman, but at a crucial moment he cast the ballot that assured the calling of a ratifying convention. Lowndes and Burke, who also, but reluctantly, voted "aye," must have known that an Antifederalist victory would have been short-lived—too many prominent men in the tidewater commercial and planting communities supported the Constitution. The voting record told the story. The twenty-five man Charleston delegation unanimously favored the convention call. But in the parishes of St. Peter's, St. Stephen's, St. Matthew's, St. David's, and seven western districts there was not one vote supporting the Federalists. The final tally was seventy-six ayes, seventy-five nays.

Luckily for the Federalists, Lowndes thought as Patrick Henry did but lacked the latter's personal magnetism and determination. Thus, after that last gasp in the legislature, the Antifederalist cause in South Carolina went down to ignoble defeat.

The rapid decline in antifederal fortunes in South Carolina was hastened by the loss of Lowndes' leadership. Lowndes' anti-Constitution speeches in the assembly became the basis for attacks on him unlike any in his previous political experience. The few tidewater Antifederalists suffered these attacks in bewilderment. As Aedanus Burke later complained, "We had no principle of concert or union," while friends of the Constitution "left no expedient untried to push it forward." Newspaper editors clamped their columns shut to Antifederalist essays, "afraid to offend the great men, or Merchants, who could work their ruin." Thus "the whole weight and influence of the Press" was thrown on the Federalist side, aided by "All the rich, leading men, along the sea coast, and rice settlements; [and] with

[9] *Ibid.*, 316.

165

few exceptions, Lawyers, Pysicians [*sic*] and Divines, the Merchants, Mechanicks, the Populace, and mob of Charleston."[10] Either because of illness or because he had grown tired of battling his neighbors, Lowndes withdrew from the struggle when he was most sorely needed. Although Lowndes was apparently rejected by Charleston citizens in the contest for convention seats, St. Bartholomew's parish elected him to their delegation. Nevertheless, Lowndes refused to serve, abruptly ending his distinguished political career.[11]

Deprived of strong leadership, the South Carolina Antifederalists were caught in the same predicament that had plagued their political brethren in Philadelphia and Boston. Burke was elected as a lower-district delegate, but appears to have been struck dumb. Burke berated the Federalists and dissected the Constitution on foolscap, but, when it came time to speak, he was a mere cipher. "The country interest prevails over the mercantile in this State," a Charleston Federalist discerned, which would hurt the constitutional cause since "the farmers (who are rather contracted) entertain jealousies that it is a scheme to favor the mercantile interest." But he was not too discouraged, for he added, "we will have most of the orators with us, and the influence of the town." Antifederalists looked at the same facts and figures but drew other conclusions. One optimist reported that the tidewater region was divided over the Constitution, and that half of its citizens would join with the back-country delegates as Antifederalists. "The aristocrats feed themselves with the hopes that the back [country] members will not come down, as it is about harvest time when the convention meets; and so they seem to hold their heads high on the subject."[12]

If Federalists in Charleston held up their heads, it was with good reason. After the election returns for delegates had been tallied, the sea coast had gone to the Federalists almost without exception, while the western counties were Antifederalist—and this meant that friends of the Constitution had a clear-cut two-to-one majority before the convention opened. Confident of success, the Charleston Federalists

[10] Aedanus Burke to John Lamb, June 23, 1788, Lamb papers, *NYHS*.
[11] Journal of the Convention, entry of May 14, 1788, South Carolina Archives.
[12] Quoted in Philadelphia *Independent Gazetteer*, April 19, 1788.

could dismiss with annoyance the Antifederalist poem that warned against monarchy and worse.

> In Five short years of Freedom weary grown
> We quit our plain republics for a throne;
> Congress and President full proof shall bring
> A mere disguise for Parliament and King . . . .[13]

Delegates, not bad poetry, would make the difference between rejection or ratification.

By holding the convention in Charleston, Federalists made certain that debate would be conducted before the warmest friends of the Constitution. As delegates from the West arrived in the bustling seaport, they were courted by Federalists at private gatherings where the best sherry and Madeira were offered to men, whose palates rarely sampled anything but harsh, homemade liquors. At the convention, one of the first orders of business was the appointment of a barkeeper. In this elegant atmosphere, General Sumter, Burke, and a handful of their friends gave their fellow Antifederalists little guidance. Sumter's feeble effort at the outset to bring an adjournment until October gave the Federalists a chance to demonstrate their power. The postponement was necessary, Antifederalists argued, because "people in the back counties were not sufficiently informed" about the Constitution. They needed more time to ponder its provisions before making a decision. Restless Federalists squelched the motion by a 135-to-89 vote. Thus they crushed Sumter along with his back-country supporters, many of whom had already lost heart when ships arrived with news from Annapolis. Burke conceded that the final blow "came when Maryland's ratification was announced . . . further opposition was useless."

Patrick Dollard of Prince Frederick Parish was not inclined to capitulate to the Federalists, however; he reproached the opposition for supporting a Constitution that was "pregnant with a great variety of impending woes to the good people of *the southern States,* espe-

---

[13] Charleston *State Gazette of South Carolina,* January 28, 1788, quoted in Miner, *Our Rude Forefathers,* 204.

cially South Carolina."[14] Dollard was Lowndes' disciple when the inevitable *North* vs. *South* argument arose. Far less temperate than Lowndes, however, Dollard declared that ratification of the Constitution would unleash upon the South more woes "than all the plagues supposed to have issued from the poisonous box of Pandora." His constituents were determined not to accept the Constitution "unless by force of arms," which it "plainly threatens." Dollard—a forerunner of the Carolina fire-eaters of another day—then hurled defiance at the Federalists. Let them force through the Constitution, but then they would have to dispatch troops to his district to "ram it down their throats with the points of bayonets."

The pleas of Sumter, Dollard, and a few less formidable delegates had some effect on the Federalists. "We had a tedious but trifling opposition," Rutledge admitted. "We had prejudices to contend with and sacrifices to make," but such as were made proved to be harmless to Federalist objectives. Concessions were offered the Antifederalists, which would make it easier for the western delegates to return home. These were a set of recommendatory amendments, carrying forward the spirit of the Boston resolves without providing anything disturbing for friends of the Constitution. Outvoted by the Federalists on the ratification question 149-to-73, the disheartened Antifederalists were probably grateful to save a few crumbs, albeit stale ones, for home distribution.

The South Carolina Antifederalists publicly announced themselves ready "to induce the people quietly to receive, and peaceably to live under the new government." Privately, however, Burke let it be known that "4/5 of the people do, from their Souls detest it." "I am convinced, from my Knowledge of the Country," Burke declared, "that I am rather under, than over [estimating], that proportion." Charleston Federalists had held a grand procession, but in the back country "all is disgust, sorrow, and vindictive reproaches against the System, and those who voted for it." Reports from the western districts confirmed his analysis, Burke added, for he had heard "that in some places the people had a Coffin painted black, which, borne in funeral procession, was solemnly buried, as an emblem of the dissolu-

[14] Providence *United States Chronicle*, July 3, 1788.

tion and internment of publick Liberty." The back-country Anti-federalists, made of hardier timber than Burke, vowed "they will join heart and hand to bring Ruin on the new Plan unless it be materially altered."[15] If Burke could be believed, there was still plenty of fight left in the South Carolina hinterlands.

In the wake of the Charleston defeat, Lowndes had a long-delayed message from the New York Antifederalists. General Lamb's call for concerted efforts to bring about specific amendments impressed Lowndes, but in the case of South Carolina it was far too late to be of value. "Had your Plan been proposed in time I doubt not it might have produced a very good Effect in this Country," Lowndes replied. "A Strong Systematic Opposition," which could be "directed to the same specific Objects, would have had a Weight, which the Advocates for the Constitution must have submitted to," Lowndes added.[16] Since the Antifederalists in Charleston barely fitted that description, Lamb must have concluded that again it was a case of no program, no leadership, and no success. The story was painfully familiar.

At a Federal observation post in Philadelphia, the enemy seemed routed on all fronts. "Our opposition has been done for some days," Tench Coxe reported. Their spirits had been dampened by the large majority in Maryland, he wrote, and "South Carolina completed the matter." Jefferson's aide in Paris heard a novel version of the South Carolina affair. The friends of the Constitution had triumphed over "numerous Ennemys" there, despite the unusual efforts made "by the partisance [*sic*] of your nefarious & highly Criminal P. Henry, to Form a Confederation of the Southern States."[17]

Patrick Henry may have been with the South Carolina Antifederalists in spirit, but the flesh-and-blood Henry had no inclination to fight the Constitution on unfamiliar ground. Henry was content to let Federalists speculate on what strategy he was brewing, without writing pamphlets or carrying on a voluminous correspondence with other Antifederalists. Next to Washington, he was the best-known Virginian in America. Hence, anxious Federalists had been on their

[15] Aedanus Burke to Lamb, June 21, 1788, Lamb papers, *NYHS*.
[16] Rawlins Lowndes to Lamb, June 21, 1788, Lamb papers, *NYHS*.
[17] Edward Carrington to William Short, October 21, 1787, Short papers, *DLC*.

guard since Henry had joined Richard Henry Lee in declining a seat at the Federal Convention. As early as March, 1787, there had been suspicions that Henry would avoid the Federal Convention because of sinister motives. While the Convention was in progress, Jefferson was told that signs pointed to Henry's hostility toward a federal government. According to rumors, Henry "wishes either a partition or total dissolution of the confederacy."

When the Constitution had first gone to the states, both factions looked anxiously in Henry's direction. His approval meant Virginia would ratify without a prolonged struggle, but Henry's opposition would give Antifederalists what they lacked elsewhere—an acknowledged, first-rate political leader with an immense personal following among all ranks of voters. A Virginia delegate in Congress who favored the Constitution curbed his enthusiasm, waiting to hear "what part Mr. Henry will take—much will depend on him."

No wonder, then, that Federalists sighed and girded themselves for a stiffer battle when the rumors were confirmed. Using the legislative hall for his forum, Henry "upon all Occasions however foreign in subject attempted to give the Constitution a side blow," Madison was told. From the moment that Henry first expressed his opposition, ratification by Virginia became an uncertainty. Particularly distressing was the persistent rumor that Henry was ready to pursue his Antifederalist course to its extremity—the breakup of the Union into three confederations bound only by geographic and economic interests. Washington heard these rumors and declared that since he had long ago shaken off his "local views," he had little use for men unable to grasp the spirit of union. Madison's view was essentially the same; if Madison secretly admired the power of Henry's personality, he still loathed his principles. Jefferson, with all his reservations about the Constitution, shared the same vision of union. Frankly disappointed that the President was not limited to a single term, Jefferson insisted that care be exercised so "that neither this nor any other objection to the new form [shall] produce a schism to our union."[18] The Constitution was a great political gamble, but the Virginia Federalists believed that the survival of the Union was at stake,

[18] Jefferson to Alexander Donald, February 7, 1788, 12 *Jefferson Papers* 571.

and were ready to take a chance. Radical Antifederalists were not certain that the risk was necessary.

Through the fall and winter months, political opponents kept one eye cocked on the Virginia scene. "I think the fate of the Constitution and the political Salvation of the united states depend chiefly on the part that Virginia & this State take in the Matter," a Massachusetts Federalist noted on New Year's Day, 1788.[19] Antifederalists could have raised their glasses to such a toast. Whatever weakness in leadership they suffered from in New England, the picture in Virginia was happier to contemplate. The formidable names among the Virginia Antifederalists were enough to depress any adversary. While not the equals of Henry in terms of popular appeal, both Governor Randolph and George Mason commanded respect in any political assembly. Only a pace behind them were Richard Henry Lee, William Grayson, Thomas Nelson, Benjamin Harrison, and dozens of lesser figures. Thus Virginia Antifederalists could match their Federalist brethren with an impressive list—save alone for Washington's name. "The weight of Genl. Washington as you justly observe is very great in America," Grayson admitted, "but I hardly think it is sufficient to induce the people to pay money or part with power."[20]

What prompted such distinguished political leaders to embark on the hazardous Antifederalist enterprise? The most familiar answer of their opponents was "local views." With this catchall phrase the Federalists intended to leave the impression that the opposition was motivated by fears that their political power would be vastly diminished in a federal government. The national government would be aggrandized at the expense of the states, so that state officials would slip into secondary importance, while the right to tax and spend public money would mainly reside in federal hands. *That* was the real point of contention, Federalists maintained, and all the noise about northern rights or southern rights was a façade for the sordid motives of these local politicians. No matter what reasons Antifederalists publicly gave for their opposition, Washington said, "the real ones are concealed behind the Curtains, because they are not of a

---

[19] Jeremiah Hill to George Thatcher, January 1, 1788, Thatcher papers, *BPL*.
[20] William Grayson to Monroe, May 29, 1787, *DHC*, IV, 170.

nature to appear in open day." Few Federalists would have disagreed. "The conspiracy agst. direct taxes is more extensive & formidable than some gentlemen suspect," Madison declared. "It is clearly seen by the enemies of the Constitution that an abolition of that power will re-establish the supremacy of the State Legislatures, the real object of all their zeal in opposing the system."[21]

This harsh judgment contained enough foundation in certain specific instances to make it seem valid. Undoubtedly, some of the Pennsylvania state officials were anxious about their positions. The zeal of paper-money advocates in Massachusetts, Maryland, and Rhode Island made their protests of principle sound strained if not desperate. But in Virginia, Antifederalist principles were not a façade for state officials or paper-currency advocates. Only Henry continued to push a state legislative program that would be incompatible with the Constitution—and though powerful in state politics, his popularity was such that he might also have aspired to any office under the federal government with a fair chance of success. Mason, who had been offered more public honors from Virginia than he cared to accept, was a bitter foe of paper-money issues. Richard Henry Lee was among the first to admit the financial inadequacies of the Confederation. In examining the views of other prominent Virginia Antifederalists, it is discernible that their political opinions crisscrossed on paper money, on the British debt question, and on other so-called antifederal tenets. But among all Antifederalists there was one area of common agreement—the necessity to keep Virginia interests dominant in any league of the thirteen states. Whatever fetters were placed upon Virginia were, in effect, chains around the South. And to whom would the powers pass? Let pensive Benjamin Harrison give their answer. "If the Constitution is carried into effect, the States south of potowmac, will be little more than appendages to those to the northward of it."[22]

The fear of northern domination as a motive for antifederalism sprang from the same sources as that fear in New England of south-

---

[21] Washington to Bushrod Washington, November 10, 1787, *DHC*, IV, 371–74; Madison to Tench Coxe, July 30, 1788, Madison papers, *DLC*.

[22] Benjamin Harrison to Washington, October 4, 1787, *DHC*, IV, 313.

ern domination, which was noted earlier. But the southerner's fear of an overbearing North was much more intense and, in the final analysis, was based on considerable evidence. Slavery was never a threat to Massachusetts, where it had been easy to arouse passions there by calling Virginia slaveholders "the Southern Nabobs." Since almost her entire economy was agriculturally oriented, the South had to depend on outsiders—northern men or Europeans—to carry her products to world markets. Virginia (and the South) suffered from the age-old curse of agrarian societies, in that she was totally dependent upon others with conflicting interests. Under the Articles of Confederation, Virginia had been the caretaker of southern interests in the Continental Congress. No northern proposition, ranging from a commercial law favoring northern shipping to a treaty giving up Mississippi navigation, had the least chance of success while Virginia delegates breathed. The Constitution removed this veto power from the South, throwing supreme legislative and treaty powers into a new political arena where a majority would be all-powerful. It was too much to ask of the Virginia Antifederalists. Unless some amendments gave Virginia more control over her own destiny, the Constitution was unacceptable to them. The South should not risk its future on a simple majority vote in Congress.

The pre-Revolutionary jealousies between the North and South, temporarily stilled during the war years, had been fanned with vengeance. Too often, spokesmen from one region found their suspicions immediately aroused if the other region appeared to favor an idea or proposal. In New England, William Grayson observed that in the fall of 1787, the Constitution was given a warm reception, but Antifederalists "say that this is no wonder, as they have overreached the Southern people so much in its formation."[23]

Virginians were particularly suspicious of northern domination on the delicate Mississippi navigation question. As early as 1779, while speculating on some peace proposals, Richard Henry Lee had asked Mason if surrender of rights to travel on the Mississippi would not cause havoc in the back country. When John Jay began his long, fruitless negotiations in Madrid over the Mississippi, New England-

---

[23] William Grayson to William Short, November 10, 1787, Short papers, *DLC*.

ers readily supported plans to surrender river rights if their own maritime products could be sold in Spanish ports. With one eye constantly on the western territories, Virginians put themselves on guard against any northern scheme to barter away southern interests. "The navigation of the Mississippi is of the first consequence to all the southern states, Virginia inclusive," a southern congressman declared in 1781, "and will be more so to those new states congress may hereafter carve out of the lands proposed to be ceded" by Virginia and her neighbors to national jurisdiction.[24]

All the worst fears of southern leaders seemed confirmed in 1786 when Jay sent a report to the Continental Congress recommending sacrifice of Mississippi navigation in return for Spanish trade concessions. Apparently the North was oblivious of the great river's importance as a channel for western produce, and, in the uproar that followed, seven northern states combined to approve the proposition over the protests of solid southern delegations.

The willingness of northerners to bargain away southern interests in the Spanish negotiations gave rise to fears that greedy New Englanders were willing to split the Union into separate confederacies. Congressman Monroe believed this was their motive as he reported in 1786 to Governor Patrick Henry. Monroe lamented "a long train of intrigue" by northerners who wanted to prevent western settlements in order that the stream of migration could be diverted into vacant lands in New York and Massachusetts. Grayson warned the North that a blockade of Mississippi navigation "would destroy the hopes of the principal men in the S. States in establishing the future fortunes of their families," and reduce the value of western lands to a trifle. Most Virginians of any means had speculated in western lands, and few were willing to surrender chances for profits or estates for a numerous progeny. If the North persisted in its conduct, Grayson warned, the Union would be weakened, if not destroyed, "by disaffecting the S. States when they saw their dearest interests sacrificed and given up to obtain a trivial commercial advantage for their brethren in the East."[25]

[24] Joseph Jones to Theodorick Bland, January 2, 1781, *The Bland Papers* (ed. by Charles Campbell), II, 43–44.

Henry's worst suspicions had been aroused. Perhaps reports of this acrimonious debate caused the retiring governor to believe that the forthcoming Federal Convention was really a ruse for fixing northern supremacy in a federal union. At any rate, Henry refused to accept a place on the Virginia delegation, explaining his conduct later by declaring that from the outset he had "smelt a rat."[26]

Whatever public reasons Henry gave for not coming to Philadelphia, his "disgust exceeded all measure," and Madison believed his refusal to attend the Convention was undeniably due to the Mississippi business. John Marshall, with his law shingle hanging in Richmond, was struck by the tremendous amount of local interest in the Mississippi affair. "Mr. Henry, whose opinions have their usual influence, has been heard to say that he would rather part with the confederation than relinquish the navigation of the Mississippi." A slight bit of Federalist relief came from the opposing positions of Richard Henry Lee and Henry. While Henry denounced the northern barter of southern rights, Lee held that free access to the great river "must in its consequences depopulate and ruin the old States." Occasionally, a westerner agreed that the Mississippi fracas was blown out of proportion by prevailing sentiment. "I shou'd be more happy if our people were less anxious for this priviledge and more affected with the importance of manufacturing for themselves," one even-tempered Virginian in Kentucky observed.[27]

The Mississippi issue promised great advantages for the Antifederalists because its jingoism appealed to most southerners. At Henry's insistence the Virginia House of Delegates passed in November, 1787, a resolution that was an indirect blow at the Constitution. A committee that included Henry, Mason, and Monroe was instructed to remind delegates in the Continental Congress that the national body had no power to cede or suspend American rights on western waters. The Virginia assembly deplored the efforts of some members

[25] "Minutes of Proceedings," August 16, 1786, *LCC*, VIII, 427.

[26] Randolph to Madison, March 1, 1787, Moncure D. Conway, *Forgotten Chapters in the Life of Edmund Randolph*, 65.

[27] John Marshall to Arthur Lee, March 5, 1787, Richard H. Lee, *Life of Arthur Lee*, II, 321; Caleb Wallace to Madison, November 12, 1787, Madison papers, *DLC*.

of Congress to surrender a state's rights in the treaty negotiations, and held that such schemes were "strongly repugnant to all confidence in the federal government." It takes little discernment to see that this language was calculated to throw the onus of a blockaded Mississippi upon a national government which was much weaker than that promised by the Constitution. The back-country settler or the seaboard land speculator who did not see the risks inherent in a stronger national government, by such logic, was dense indeed.

Understandably, southern Antifederalists found only slight concern in the North for their cry of alarm over the Mississippi passage. It was the kind of issue that Gerry and the Massachusetts "Antis" would hardly have dared drag before voters, and Governor Clinton could not have aroused many Manhattan citizens by dwelling on the topic. For Oswald in Philadelphia, the issue was not pressing locally but still worth mentioning because of his newspaper's southern circulation. Hence the *Independent Gazetteer* once declared that if "the sole navigation of the Missississippi [*sic*] should be yielded to the Spaniards for a certain time . . . the chains of slavery will be so riveted upon us, that it will be very difficult to cast them off."

Southern Federalists certainly would have preferred to ignore the river question, if circumstances might have allowed it. Washington was disturbed by the way Henry and his lieutenant kept dangling the Mississippi bauble before the public eye, playing on self-interest and western emotions to the detriment of the Constitution. Washington wished that "the discussion of the Mississippi *could* have remained as silent, and glided as gently down the Stream of time for a few years, as the waters do, that are contained with the banks of that river." But northern indifference, or something worse, was well advertised by the southern Antifederalists who proceeded to make political capital out of the murky issue. General James Wilkinson, a man well-versed in the art of intrigue, visited Virginia and speculated that one of the first acts of the proposed Congress would be to surrender Mississippi navigation rights. Wilkinson "is not to be appeased in his violence against the constitution," Governor Randolph noted, "and it is presumed that thro his means the vote of Kentucky will have the same

176

direction."[28] An upsurge of antifederal strength in the western country caused Madison to revise his estimate of Kentucky politics. The Constitution had many friends there at first, he believed, "but, as elsewhere, the torch of discord has been thrown in and has found the materials but too inflammable." Northern members of the Continental Congress did little to pour oil on the troubled waters, either. As Kentuckians made overtures for admission as a separate state and also elected delegates to the Virginia ratifying convention, New England delegates remained cool toward the statehood application.

Other matters which lacked the emotional overtones of the Mississippi problem, but were nonetheless vexing to southerners, included the power of northern shippers and the Federalists' insistence that the country was fast headed toward ruin. Mason kept pounding on the need to curb a discriminatory shipping act as Yankee shipowners complained that their ships rotted in harbors while southern products went to Europe and the West Indies in foreign holds. William Nelson thought the ills of the Confederation had been greatly magnified. The Republic had been manhandled by the diagnosticians so "that every touch will make it worse, and . . . finally, it will die of the doctor." Venerable Benjamin Harrison took exception to the unlimited taxing powers and the federal right to regulate trade. "If our condition is not very desperate," Harrison explained, "I have my fears that the remedy will prove worse than the disease."[29]

Southerners with Antifederalist propensities suspected that any shift of power from state capitals toward a federal one would somehow benefit the North. Richard Henry Lee had certainly played on this point in his public letter to Randolph. By allowing Congress to pass laws regulating trade by a bare majority, Lee warned, the northern delegates would surely "create the most oppressive monopolies upon the five southern states, whose circumstances and productions are essentially different from theirs." This would make a mockery

[28] Randolph to Madison, December 27, 1787, Madison papers, *DLC*.

[29] William Nelson to William Short, January 11, 1787, Short papers, *DLC*. Ralph Wormeley to [Arthur Lee?], February 8, 1787, Lee papers, Harvard University Library; Benjamin Harrison to Washington, October 4, 1787, *DHC*, IV, 313; R. H. Lee to Randolph, October 16, 1787, Ballagh, *Letters of Lee*, II, 454–55.

of the Union, for the South would be treated like a poor relative. "It is supposed that the policy of the northern states will prevent such abuses! but how feeble, sir, is *policy* when opposed to interest among trading people, and what is the restraint arising from policy?" Of course, their opponents ridiculed such views as niggardly and short-sighted. "A Navigation Act ought doubtless to be passed for giving exclusive benefits to American Ships . . . ," a Virginia Federalist countered, "indeed, it is important to the interests of the southern States, that the growth of a Navy be promoted, for the security of that wealth which is to be derived from their agriculture."[30] Though nationalist-minded Federalists could agree wholeheartedly, Mason or Lee would have gagged at the mere suggestion of a northern navy, built at southern expense.

As honored in the North as in the South, Washington shared few of his fellow Virginians' apprehensions about a Union dominated by New Englanders. Rejecting the logic of Richard Henry Lee and Mason as so much gall and wormwood, the general all but terminated a lifelong friendship with Mason, whose plantation was only a short ride from Mount Vernon. As for Mason's "Objections," Washington grumbled, "To alarm the people seems to be the ground work of his plan." Mason's main point about shipping laws was that under the Constitution their threat hung over the South like Damocles' sword, "for such rigid & premature Regulations may be made, as will enable the Merchants of the Nothern [*sic*] & Eastern States not only to demand an exorbitant Freight, but to monopolize the Purchase of the Commodities at their own Price, for many Years." Mason reasoned that in terms of a simple majority, the five southern states would continually be pitted against "eight Northern & Eastern States" and would be overwhelmed.

Always short-tempered with those who opposed him, Washington regarded the 1787–88 proponents of state rights as disaffected scoundrels. Adamantly refusing to consider service in the state ratifying convention, Washington took few pains to conceal his contempt for fellow Virginians whose political company he had kept since the

[30] Edward Carrington to Jefferson, October 23, 1787, 12 *Jefferson Papers* 255; see also Pierce Butler to Weedon Butler, May 5, 1788, 3 Farrand 303.

Stamp Act crisis, but who now differed with him. Not all Virginians were as polarized in their political thinking, however, and to them the Antifederalists made numerous overtures. They beckoned converts by alluding to the recent past as undeniable proof of northern domination in national affairs. "I perceive that in almost all things the eastern states outwit and outhinges us," a Virginia legislator was informed, and it was likely "that under the proposed constitution, their interests would be always paramount to ours."[31] Virginians were reminded that not one of their sons had been appointed to office by Congress in the Northwest Territory, a good portion of which their state had ceded to the Union. Thus, not a single "place of honor, influence, or profit" fell their way in a country "which they owe to the bounty of Virginia." Moreover, current events emphasized the sectional differences. Passage of an antislavery law by Massachusetts in the spring of 1788 pleased New England idealists but alarmed the political realists. The latter group thought it was hardly the time to tread on southern toes as elections and ratifying conventions were being held below Mason and Dixon's line.

Apart from the sectional differences which Virginia Antifederalists exploited, other ill winds seemed to be blowing in their favor. A drought had shriveled the corn crop, tobacco prices were uncertain, mortgage payments were past-due, and taxes on many farms were far in arrears. It was a situation made-to-order for advocates of a state paper-money issue, who figured that this time-honored remedy for deflationary woes would be prohibited by the Constitution. Henry stood ready to champion a paper-money bill as debt-burdened small farmers began invading court houses, burning tax rolls, and doing in Virginia the same things that were classed as a rebellion in Massachusetts the previous year. "In several Counties the prisons and Court Houses and Clerks offices have been wilfully burnt," an alarmed Madison reported. "In Green Briar the course of Justice has been mutinously stopped, and associations entered into against the payment of taxes."[32] Several ringleaders were arrested, but there was no disposition in Virginia to create another Shays-like incident. So Ran-

[31] *Virginia Independent Chronicle*, November 14, 1787.
[32] Madison to Jefferson, September 6, 1787, 12 *Jefferson Papers* 103–104.

dolph did not call out the militia, local officials kept matters in hand, and the flare-ups in a few counties were quickly doused.

A second area of acute political sensitivity in Virginia which Henry exploited was the uncertain status of the old private British debts in Virginia. As in Maryland, this touchy issue had helped convert a few leading men to antifederalism. They had used wartime sequestration acts to rid themselves of heavy prewar indebtedness by using depreciated Virginia currency. Virginia courts were closed to British merchants who sought redress, but it seemed indeed likely that under the Constitution federal courts would make debtors pay their obligations in real rather than nominal terms. Henry expected imprudent planters who were sheltered by these state laws to find their way into the Antifederalist camp. As on the paper-money issue, Mason again parted company with Henry. The festering problem was reopened when the Virginia House of Delegates passed an anemic statute that vaguely promised British debtors redress. Henry used the debates concerning the debts to conjure up a whole host of evils which the Constitution would bring to Virginia. A disheartened Federalist reported that the spellbinder from Prince Edward County also had "endeavored to sow the seeds of Jealousy against the federal court, the new-england states and the spirit of Union itself." In Richmond taverns, over clerks' desks in law offices, and in the corridors of the house, the repeated objection made to the Constitution was "that the british debts must be paid if it is adopted" with Virginians hauled into federal courts with all the cards stacked against them. "The great opponents to the constitution say that a King Lords & Commons would be much more digest[ib]le."[33]

Federalists inveighed against Henry's demagoguery but showed some backhanded admiration of his political skill. "Henry is loud on the distresses of the People & makes us tremble with the Apprehension of a Rebellion if they are driven to dispair [*sic*]," Archibald Stuart reported, half in anger and half in salute to Henry's power. Always one to take advantage of any anti-British prejudices, Henry told the house that even if Virginia tried to reimburse British merchants for their losses "we or some other State shall fail in some tittle

[33] John Pierce to Knox, October 27, 1787, Knox papers, *MHS.*

& that will be a pre-text for the british to continue their Open Violation" of the Treaty of Paris. Henry asked "why we should go before the british in this Business," humbly with hat in hand? Were Britons more honest than Virginians? Nothing was more calculated to arouse local passions than to hint that the enemies of yesterday still held Virginia in bondage; Henry exploited this bias in his attacks on the Constitution by linking its supporters to Anglophilism. One Antifederalist writer hailed Henry as a prophet of Biblical stature who had warned the people that ratification meant the immediate payment of "all the debts due to the Britannites, yea, even the interest during the war." When Governor Randolph's antifederalism faltered to the vanishing point that winter, an encouraged Federalist lumped all of the remaining opponents of the Constitution together. "Most of those now opposed to it, are persons who estates are much involved, by owing large British debts, which they think must be paid when we have a federal head," a Richmond correspondent vowed. The accusation was too sweeping, but some of the staunchest Antifederalists rallying behind Henry feared personal ruin if the Constitution were ratified as it stood.

Henry's opportunism was manifest. He seemed ready to take every local issue and turn it into an attack on the Constitution, but some Antifederalists in Virginia were not. Mason still differed sharply with Henry over the British debts, and he also disagreed with him in the House of Delegates over the need for paper money and heavy port taxes. Federalists took obvious pleasure in the quarrels of their two leading opponents. When Henry bested Mason in a debate on repeal of the Port Bill, one observer thought Mason's remarks "were vague & inconclusive . . . & I fear the Effects of Age have sometimes been discoverable in him."[34] Mason, as an elder statesman, took his political bumps in stride. Moreover, it was apparent that Henry would assume leadership of the Antifederalists. "You know the force of this wonderful mans oratory upon a Virginia house of Delegates," a grudging admirer confessed. The great question was one of pure speculation—which would prove the more powerful endorsement—Washington's or Henry's?

[34] Archibald Stuart to Madison, November 2, 1787, Madison papers, *DLC*.

☆ X ☆

The Virginia Battleground

Aᴛ ᴛʜᴇ Fᴇᴅᴇʀᴀʟ Cᴏɴᴠᴇɴᴛɪᴏɴ, Madison had warned that jealous state legislators would be "disinclined" to cede local powers to the general government. "And if disinclined," he continued, "they could devise modes apparently promoting, but really thwarting the ratification." Still, the Virginia House of Delegates unanimously passed the bill calling for a ratifying convention the following summer. But careless drafters of the bill had omitted a provision for paying the delegates, and Antifederalists seized the oversight as an opportunity to promote a second convention. They insisted on a bill which not only provided for the Virginia convention expenses, but also promised to pay for delegates who might be chosen to a second federal convention. Federalists thought this device an undisguised effort to delay final action on the Constitution. "Mason on the subject was less candid that ever I knew him to be," a disgruntled Federalist remarked after the Antifederalists easily pushed the measure through. The unanimous vote on the convention call seemed a meaningless victory to Federalists in this new light, for the Antifederalists had flexed their muscles convincingly. "I fear since they have discovered their Strength they will adopt other Measures tending to prejudice people against the Constitution," a defeated Federalist admitted.[1]

Taken together, the two actions in the house proved that the Virginia Antifederalists could muster formidable opposition to ratification. This was Henry's way of creating a false façade for Virginia Antifederalists—on the surface it would appear that the Antifederalists had displayed good political sportsmanship by going along in the convention call, while their intention was to defeat, or at least delay, ratification by insisting that a second federal convention was virtually a necessity. During the debates Henry said "that if this

[1] Archibald Stuart to Madison, December 2, 1787, Madison papers, *DLC*.

Idea was not held forth our southern neighbours might be driven to despair seeing no door open to safety should they disapprove the new Constitution." Henry's admirer in North Carolina, Willie Jones, must have been listening, for he was soon pulling wires to schedule the North Carolina convention even later.

Doubtlessly the Virginia Antifederalists thought all delays would prove embarrassing for their opponents. By postponing action for many months, the course of ratification in other states could be carefully observed. If, perchance, any states "were agnst [*sic*] it our State might mediate between contending parties," Monroe wrote with naïve candor, "& lead the way to an union more palitable [*sic*] to all." Although reports of the unanimous convention call appeared favorable in the newspapers, seasoned Federalists were cautious. "It is not to be inferred from hence that its opponants [*sic*] are silenced," Washington warned Hamilton.

When Madison first heard reports of the convention call, he accepted them at face value, believing that citizens in other states probably would be impressed by the apparent unanimity. "The example of Virginia will have great weight," Madison erroneously surmised. "It would be truly mortifying if any thing should occur to prevent or retard the concurrence of a State which has generally taken the lead on great occasions."[2] Randolph helped promote the scheme of soliciting other states to agree upon amendments, but when he broached the idea to Madison, the latter's reply was short and to the point. Madison ridiculed the plan as impractical in one sense and dangerous in another. Ratification had to be without strings attached, or it was no ratification at all. Meanwhile, Randolph had second thoughts himself and agreed on "the impropriety of the Idea." As his antifederalism ebbed, Randolph finally found ways to procrastinate until any effort to work in league with other states for amendments would prove abortive.[3]

Since Virginians regarded political conversation among life's finest pleasures, it was natural that the Constitution would soon engross their

[2] Madison to Edmund Pendleton, October 28, 1787; Randolph to Madison, September 30, 1787, Madison papers, DLC.

[3] Randolph to Madison, October 23, 1787, Madison papers, *DLC*.

devoted attention. "The Topic of the day is the new Constitution," a Richmond visitor reported. At Fredericksburg, the Constitution was "the subject of general conversation in every part of town, and will soon be in every quarter of the state." Although Randolph tried to appear noncommittal, most public men were soon taking sides. Some waited anxiously to see where Henry stood. Monroe believed that no topic since the Revolution had excited more discussion, and predicted that "there will be a greater division among the people of character than then took place." Both Antifederalists and Federalists thought that Randolph was on their side. The governor himself, surprised by the "happy and politick resolution" calling for a convention, blew hot and cold. Confessing to Madison that he favored ratification to a splintering of the Union, he voiced suspicions that "the tide is turning against the Constitution." Randolph was a tortured man as he groped for a pathway leading out of this political maze. "The bar are generally against it; so are the judges of the general court. I have inquired about reports concerning myself, and if popularity had been my object, as some suppose, I should have overshot my mark."[4]

Randolph's vacillating course was in itself a strong indicator of the even balance between the two contending factions. Until that time, on the big issues of war or peace, Whigism or Toryism, stamp tax or no stamp tax, the great men of Virginia had for the most part stood on one side of the question. It is no surprise that Randolph was now confused, for the lines forming for and against the Constitution offered no easy choice for the opportunist. A favorite pastime of Virginia public men during the autumn dog days of 1787 was to count noses, assigning characters to one side or the other. The more Federalists speculated on their chances, the darker their prospects seemed. Early in November, Washington was told that all appearances indicated that Virginians were opposed to the Constitution, "particularly in the Southern and Western parts of the States [*sic*]." Most of the state legislators were said to be Antifederalists after Henry had finished with them, another Constitution supporter lamented, and upon their return home "they will influence the people

[4] *Ibid.*

184

generally against it—& it will fall." Jefferson was informed by a zealous Philadelphian that all the news from Virginia indicated that she would "not come in."[5]

One striking fact about the Virginia political situation was the slight influence of the *city* vs. *country* alignment noticed in other large states. The western farmers in Massachusetts and Pennsylvania took their cue for antifederalism from the stance of city merchants and bankers. In Virginia as in most of the South, however, there were few cities of note, no bankers or stockjobbers of prominence, and no mercantile houses with great influence. Most Virginia planters spread their credit as far as they could, which often meant from Annapolis to London. The great warehouses that still served them rested on the banks of the Thames. There was so little local commerce that some of the older mercantile posts, like Dumfries, were fast falling into disuse. Where merchants in other states found friendly voices in their legislatures, the phalanx of planters in Virginia held little sympathy for the group holding their promissory notes. When the Virginia legislature began to realize in 1787 that its Port Bill was ruining the few remaining merchants, it reluctantly repealed the measure.

The struggle for ratification of the Constitution in Virginia, then, was to be a battle between men whose interests were tied to agriculture, either totally or in part.

Probing for Antifederalist weaknesses that might be exploited, Henry Lee looked about and concluded that there was one group which was:

> opposed to any system, was it sent from heaven which tend to confirm the union of the states—Henry is leader of this band—another who would accept the new constitution from conviction of its own excellence, or any federal system, sooner than risk the dissolution of the confederacy, & a third who dislike the proposed government, wish it amended but if this is not practicable, would adopt it sooner

[5] Washington to Dr. Stuart, November 5, 1787, *DHC*, IV, 365; John Pierce to Knox, November 12, 1787, Knox papers, *MHS;* Francis Hopkinson to Jefferson, December 14, 1787, 12 *Jefferson Papers* 423.

than jeopardize the union—Mason may be considered as the head of this set.[6]

Madison, busily piecing together all such scraps of information from his Virginia correspondence, agreed with Lee's analysis. Madison believed that in a showdown over the Union, Randolph and Mason would be pitted against Henry. Moreover, Madison was beguiled by his correspondents' insistence that the great body of the people were not torn by doubts, but were heartily in favor of the Constitution. As Madison soon learned, this was not true. But in December, 1787, sitting before a warm fireplace in New York, Madison wanted to believe his friends. Deluded on one point, Madison was still sound on others.[7] "Mr. Henry is the great adversary who will render the event precarious."

Henry, for his part, was beginning to enjoy the fight. When Henry's attitude toward the Constitution had still been a mystery, Washington sent him a friendly, probing letter, which drew an equally gracious reply. "Perhaps mature Reflection may furnish me Reasons to change my present Sentiments," the wily Henry wrote, "into a conformity with the Opinions of those personages for whom I have the highest Reverence." Richard Henry Lee sent Washington a conciliatory letter, assuring the general that the proposed Constitution "abounds with useful regulations." But he alarmed Washington when he mentioned, in the same breath, the scheme for a second convention. "As there is so great a part of the business well done already, I think that such alterations as must give very general content, could not long employ another Convention." Mason also thought it necessary to genuflect before Mount Vernon. He sent Washington a copy of his objections, "which a little Moderation & Temper, in the latter End of the Convention, might have removed." Somewhat less than flattered by such attention from the principal Antifederalists, Washington gave credence to unflattering reports of neighbor Mason's conduct. The general believed that he discerned the genuine motives for the recusant trio's conduct. "Whilst many *ostensible* reasons are assigned" for their opposition, "the real

[6] Henry Lee to Madison, December 7, 1787, Madison papers, *DLC*.
[7] Madison to Jefferson, December 9, 1787, 12 *Jefferson Papers* 410.

ones are concealed behind the Curtains, because they are not of a nature to appear in open day."[8]

When Antifederalists in other states displayed their ineptness during the winter 1787–88, Henry moved ahead undaunted. Ardent Federalists admitted that they made few conversions south of the James River. "So many of the influential characters Unite there on the wrong Side, that the people must be misled for want of the necessary information," a bewildered Federalist observed. In confirmation of this report, a Northern Neck Federalist said that if the lower section persisted in its antifederalism, "a Division will take place & this part of the State [will] accede to the Confederacy." Federalists talked much about the Union, yet when their program appeared stalled—in New York, Rhode Island, and Virginia—they changed arguments and chanted "secede!" "The Federal Sistum is rufly Handled by sum vary Able Men in this State," Madison was warned, and there were rumors that Madison himself was "Actually Writing a Pece against it."[9]

In the crosscurrent of politics swirling around Richmond, Randolph thought he saw indications of the Antifederalists edging ahead. The "second convention" bill directing Randolph to communicate with other governors swept through the legislature, with accompanying praise from the Antifederalist side of the house. Increasingly embarrassed by the company that welcomed his stand in Philadelphia, Randolph purged himself of a tortured conscience in long letters to Madison. "I have no extreme ardor to acquire converts to my opinions," he confessed.[10] Much as he feared the calling of a second convention now, Randolph added, it seemed "that the only expedient which can save the federal government in any shape in Virginia, will be the adoption of some such plan as mine."

[8] Henry to Washington, October 19, 1787, *DHC*, IV, 338; Richard Henry Lee to Washington, October 11, 1787, *ibid.*, 323–24; Mason to Washington, October 7, 1787, *ibid.*, 315; Washington to Madison, October 10, 1787, *ibid.*, 321; Washington to Bushrod Washington, November 10, 1787, *ibid.*, 371–74.

[9] Edward Carrington to Knox, January 12, 1788, Knox papers, *MHS*; T. Hughes to Horatio Gates, November 20, 1787, Emmet Collection, *NYPL*; L. Taliferro to Madison, December 16, 1787, Madison papers, *DLC*.

[10] Randolph to Madison, December 27, 1787, Madison papers, *DLC*.

Still, Randolph took his time in forwarding the second-convention of proposals. The resolutions had passed the assembly in mid-November, but Randolph kept them in his desk for almost a month. When Randolph finally forwarded them to other governors, it was December 27—the same day he wrote Madison of all his misgivings. To make matters more suspicious—from the Antifederalists' viewpoint—Governor Clinton did not receive them until March 7, when it was too late for action in the friendly New York legislature.

Meanwhile, Virginians' interest in the Constitution ran so high that debating societies drew large audiences when its merits and faults were argued. After the Constitution had been debated a full evening before the fashionable Robin Hood Society in Richmond, an enthralled spectator declared the engrossing subject was "a means of Discovering more of the Welch Blood in our Citizens than I ever immagined they possessed." A second round of the debate was scheduled, with excitement on both sides high since the Morrises —Governeur and Robert—were in town and promised to be on hand.[11]

Virginians abroad were no less excited by the contest. Correctly assuming that Washington's reserve would keep him out of the active political arena, Jefferson thought Madison would have to carry the fight against the antifederal coalition. "Madison will be it's main pillar; but tho an immensly [*sic*] powerful one, it is questionable whether he can bear the weight of such a host." Hence, "the presumption is that Virginia will reject it." However, Jefferson saw this as no real tragedy, because he too believed another federal convention would have to be called "to adopt the improvements generally acceptable, and omit those found disagreeable." Omitting a bill of rights was "a degeneracy in the principles of liberty to which I had given four centuries instead of four years." The possibility of the President turning into a king was positively frightening, and the more so from his European experience with monarchs. Writing to the man who would undoubtedly first fill the office, Jefferson said "there is not a crowned head in Europe whose

[11] Land McCraw to James Breckenridge, November 28, 1787, Breckenridge papers, University of Virginia Library.

talents or merit would entitle him to be elected a vestryman by the people of any parish in America."[12]

Long before the March elections, both factions began lining up prominent candidates for seats in the May ratifying convention. Here the Federalists lacked the advantage that they held in all the northern states of placing prominent figures against relatively unknown, and often inexperienced, candidates. Antifederalists in Virginia could match their adversaries' list with names drawn from a cross section of the leading professional and political men. Mason ran into trouble with Constitution supporters in Fairfax County, but influential Antifederalists in nearby Stafford County assured him that he could have a place on their delegation. Henry's place on the Prince Edward County delegation was never questioned. His enemies admitted the folly of trying to defeat him, but in the same breath deplored Henry's tactics. "That gentleman has descended to lower artifice & management upon the occasion than I thought him capable of," a shocked Federalist divine noted.[13]

It appears that many candidates avoided a clear-cut statement of their predilections during the hustings, preferring to be elected simply on their past merits. Prestige won votes where principles were silent. Randolph seems to have been among this group. In dozens of cases, the leanings of the candidates were an outright mystery.

However, the list of known Antifederalists was long and imposing. Only the name of Richard Henry Lee was conspicuously absent. Lee's sudden withdrawal from the active campaign was attributed to a variety of causes. One report hinted that Lee had a hornet's nest under his own roof. "R. H. Lee has in great measure declined to act in the Opposition," a veteran politician observed, "finding that even his own family have separated from him." Lee's oldest son was called "one of the most zealous and active friends of the fœderal government in Virginia." Madison heard that there were

[12] Jefferson to William Carmichael, December 15, 1787, 12 *Jefferson Papers* 425–26; Jefferson to William S. Smith, February 2, 1788, *ibid.*, 558; Jefferson to Washington, May 2, 1788, 13 *Jefferson Papers* 128.

[13] Rev. John B. Smith to Madison, June 12, 1788, Madison papers, *DLC.*

"several things which promise a Change of Conduct, tho perhaps not of Opinion on the part of Mr. Lee." Washington, when told that Lee's resolution was weakening, figured Lee wanted to bow out of the Antifederalist camp because "he finds himself in such bad company."[14]

In all likelihood, Lee was inactive because of poor health. Some kind of physical setback apparently occurred during the winter, for by mid-February Lee's brother joined Mason in begging him to become a convention candidate. Mason sympathized with Lee's reasons for not wanting to campaign, but pointed out that his inactivity would make it appear that Lee had "deserted a cause in which you have published your persuasion of its being of the last moment to your Country." There were rumors that Lee had "given up all idea of opposing the Constitution because your friends think differently, & have recommended two violent Constitutionalists to the freeholders of Westmoreland." Lee's candidacy as an Antifederalist would quiet these reports, Mason insisted. Arthur Lee shared Mason's view, and the language of his entreaty was addressed to a sick man. "I confess I wish to see you elected whether you serve or not," Lee's brother wrote. He recommended a fairly safe Antifederalist seat in Fauquier County which could be won without a strenuous campaign. "I cannot but think you might board within a few miles of Richmond & by going there in the day only, avoid all risque of its unhealthyness."[15] It was some months before Lee shook off his languor sufficiently to write a few letters for the Antifederalist cause.

Lee's brother stayed in Gunston Hall almost a week, waiting for the icy Potomac to thaw. Although the weather was bitterly cold that February, the political campaign in Virginia was already beginning to warm up. "Virginia is the only State in which the parties pro & con seem to run very high," a shrewd foreign observer re-

[14] Edward Carrington to Knox, January 12, 1788, Knox papers, *MHS; Virginia Independent Chronicle*, January 16, 1788; Tench Coxe to Madison, January 23, 1788, Madison papers, *DLC*; Washington to Jefferson, January 10, 1788, *DHC*, IV, 439–40.

[15] Arthur Lee to Richard Henry Lee, February 19, 1788, Lee papers, University of Virginia Library.

ported.[16] Smug over the result of the Massachusetts' convention in Boston, northern Federalists thought the decision to hold the Virginia convention in the spring would be no hindrance as state after state ratified so that "the general example will carry everything before it." The real architect of the Antifederalist program in Virginia took his share of hard knocks *in absentia*. "Henry is in my eyes a very Guilty man," Crevecour observed, "for I abhor all Antifederalists & cannot help considering them as people who want to Sacrifice the Glory, the Prosperty of this Country, to their Selfish, or rather hellish views; Such is I believe Messrs Lee, Henry & Co." A New Hampshire Federalist cast his glance southward and came to a similar conclusion. If Providence could have spirited Henry and Mason "to the regions of darkness," the whole course of ratification would have been smooth.[17]

Nothing worried the Federalists so much that winter as Henry's renowned political skill. Madison sought to offset the force of Henry's blows in every possible way and, seeing in Randolph the weakest of all the Antifederalist links, worked for an outright conversion of the governor. Randolph was complimented for following his conscience into the opposition, however, what if he had been with the Federalists from the start? Ratification by Virginia would then have been a cut-and-dried matter. Then "Mr. Henry would either have suppressed his enmity, or been baffled" in his policy of opposition. Madison then told Randolph his great fear: that Henry's game was to set up a separate southern confederacy, and he only wished the Constitution amended "to render it subservient to his real designs." Thus the friends of the Union who worked for amendments "would not only find themselves not a little differing from each other as to the proper amendments, but perplexed & frustrated by men who had objects totally different." By the same token, a second convention would upset all the good work of the first, and "give opportunities to designing men which it might be impossible to counteract."[18] The letter from Madison seems to have provided

[16] St. John Crevecour to William Short, February 20, 1788, Short papers, *DLC*.
[17] Nicholas Gilman to John Sullivan, March 23, 1788, *LCC*, VIII, 709.
[18] Madison to Edmund Randolph, January 10, 1788, Madison papers, *DLC*.

Randolph with the final nudge he needed to get off the fence. The inferences were plain. If Randolph stayed with the Antifederalists, perhaps he would unwittingly become a party to some dark scheme to destroy the Union. Madison wrote no more important letter during the campaign, and he must have known what stakes rode with his message as he signed and sealed it.

Other Antifederalists found that the battle was uphill and too rigorous. One fair-weather "Anti" reportedly said "that the game is up for George [Washington] has been undoing all that they have done!" Unexpected and welcome allies were found among the Baptist preachers, however, and this development gave back-country Antifederalists new heart. "The Baptists are now generally opposed to it," Madison learned. A neighbor who itched for office sounded out leaders of that sect, "& on his return, I hear, publickly declared himself a candidate" on the antifederal ticket. "The Prechers of that Society are much alarm'd fearing Relegious liberty is not Sufficiently secur'd," a Federalist warned, and so "thay pretend to other objections but that I think is the principle objection," and it had to be removed because in the hinterlands "that body of people has become Very formible in pint of Elictions."[19] The Reverend John Leland chilled his congregation with a manifesto that was distinctly antifederal in tone. Leland warned them that the Constitution offered no security for religious freedom because an established church might become a reality. Moreover, there was no religious test for federal officeholders.

Undoubtedly the Virginia dissenters were more sensitive than their northern brethren because the fight against the established Anglican Church had only recently been concluded. After decades of struggle, Jefferson's bill establishing religious freedom in Virginia had become law in 1786, strongly supported by back-country dissenters who had long fought against the remnants of a state-supported church. Only a few weeks before the March election for convention delegates, the Virginia General Baptist Committee met in

---

[19] Burgess Ball to Madison, December 8, 1788; James Madison, Senior, to Madison, January 30, 1788; William Moore to Madison, January 31, 1788; Joseph Spencer to Madison, February 26, 1788, Madison papers, *DLC*.

Goochland Country and agreed that as it stood, the Constitution provided insufficient guarantees "for the secure enjoyment of religious liberty."[20] A political realist of Madison's stripe soon perceived the damage caused by lack of a bill of rights, and was to make amends. The leading Antifederalists took the clamor for a bill of rights as a base for their opposition, but did not use it as a lever in bargaining for the other desired amendments. In effect they said, "Of course the bill of rights is important and we want it, but let's get on to more vital matters affecting relations between the states and the national government." The back-country convert to the Baptist faith did not see it that way. It was much easier for him to understand that an atheist might become President under this Constitution than to become aroused over six-year terms in the Senate.

Typically, the Virginia Antifederalists fought in desultory fashion with whatever weapons came to hand. At Abingdon an Antifederalist named Chichester "had his pockets full of Mason's objections; which he leaves wherever he calls." With an assistant, the Antifederalist was touring the country, drumming up anti-Constitution sentiment and seeking candidates for the Richmond meeting. Mason's industry in supplying copies of his pamphlet to these tireless campaigners drew Federalist wrath. "I think he might have been satisfied with the publication of his objections, without taking the pains to lodge them at every house," a friend told Washington. Whatever headway the opening sentence of Mason's pamphlet—"There is no Declaration of Rights"—made with the average citizen, it was his remark on commercial advantages for the North that held some planters and professional men at bay. One Federalist read the pamphlet and thought Mason had only one weighty argument—that which dealt with the regulation of commerce by a simple majority in Congress. But Mason assumed that the northern members would "from the first instant . . . abuse the power intrusted to them." If the worst happened, and a bill prohibiting the export of southern products in foreign ships became law, southerners could build their own ships, "for which they have at present all the materials. & Untill

[20] Robert B. Semple, *A History of the Rise and Progress of the Baptists in Virginia* (Richmond, 1810), 76–77.

that happens, is it not better, the People of the Eastern States, should be the Carriers, than, as is at present the case, the subjects of Great Britain?"[21]

Mason's arguments were aimed at the pocketbook. Henry's attacks on the Constitution, stepped up in the last month of campaigning, were mostly visceral. Although Randolph had once reported that public discussion on ratification had finally abated, "not from a want of zeal in either party, but from downright weariness," the tempo soon regained the pace of the preceding autumn. Contrasting the goals of the two opposition leaders, the Federalists gave Mason the benefit of the doubt. "His principles have not the pliancy of his gloves," a critic of his pamphlet admitted.[22] But Henry was another matter. While Henry's silver tongue carried all before it, "no one can foretell at what instant we may fall prey to his ambition." Late in February, Henry wrote Randolph declaring "his determination to oppose the const, even if only ½ a state should oppose. The baptist interests and the Counties on the So Side of the Ja[me]s river, from Isle of Wight, upwards, are highly incensed by H[enr]y's opinions, and public speeches, whensoever occasion has presented."[23]

Federalists who braved the spring rains, muddy roads, and vagaries of tavern accommodations in order to learn the temper of voters came home with conflicting reports. After traveling through Cumberland, Powhatan, Chesterfield, and Petersburg—areas where Henry's influence was strong—a Federalist conceded that citizens there were "much disposed to be his blind followers." Hopefully, some Antifederalists would part with Henry if he began tinkering with the Union. The great fear was that timid, weak men might have good intentions but do untold damage. "There is no accounting for the effects which Mr. Henries address and Rhetoric may have upon them afterwards." After all the noise generated by the exciting campaign, many voters were in a quandary. At Smithfield a dazed citizen observed that the Constitution was "the only subject in conversation

[21] T. Hughes to Horatio Gates, November 20, 1787, Emmet Collection, *NYPL*.
[22] "Civis Rusticus," *Virginia Independent Chronicle*, January 30, 1788.
[23] Randolph to Madison, February 29, 1788, Madison papers, *DLC*.

among all kinds of persons, & various are the opinions with respect to it, dreadfull [*sic*] are some of their prophesies & fatal their denunciations." Whether it was worth ratifying or not, he added, "I beleive [*sic*] God only knows."[24]

Rumblings from Kentucky augured well for the Antifederalists. The fledgling *Kentucke Gazette* at Lexington barely noticed the proposed Constitution until February, when it printed Richard Henry Lee's open letter to Randolph. This was soon followed by a direct local attack, wherein the author claimed the Senate would be "a body irregular, deformed, and disproportionate." The clause forbidding interference with slave importations until 1808 would be excellent "in an Algerine constitution: but not so well calculated (I hope) for the latitude of America." Nothing was printed about that burning topic which must have been on every tongue: navigation of the Mississippi. A foe reported the frequent dispatch of letters from Henry's office to Kentucky designed to alarm settlers "with an apprehension of their interests being about to be sacrificed by the Northern States."[25]

If Henry only reported the truth of that matter, it would have been damaging enough. Every member of the Virginia delegation in the Continental Congress knew how adamant northerners had been on the Mississippi question. Thus Congressman William Grayson never tired of listing among his objections to the proposed Constitution the likelihood that "the proposed method of making treaties, *ie,* by two thirds of the Senators *present* will be the means of losing the Mississippi forever." Delegate John Brown, the only Kentucky man in the Congress, was for the Constitution simply because he thought nothing could be worse than the *status quo.* Frustrated by the northern delegates' hostility toward Kentucky statehood, Brown thought the feeble national government was about to totter. "It cannot it will not drag on much longer, & should the new

[24] Edward Carrington to Madison, February 10, 1788, Madison papers, *DLC;* J. Preston to John Brown, February 10, 1788, Brown Family papers, Yale University Library.

[25] Rev. John B. Smith to Madison, June 12, 1788, Madison papers, *DLC.*

be rejected God only knows what will be the event." Disappointed over both the statehood matter and the Mississippi threat, Kentucky voters leaned heavily toward the Antifederalist candidates.

As the election returns drifted in slowly from scattered counties, no definite trend could be established. Every prominent Antifederalist who sought a convention seat had been elected, while no leading Federalists had been rejected by voters. Madison was congratulated for turning "The Sinners of Orange from their wicked ways." Mason campaigned successfully in Stafford County with an attack on the Federal Convention delegates. "You may have supposed that they were an assemblage of great men—There is nothing less true," Mason reportedly said. "From the Eastern [New England] States there were Knaves and Fools from the states southward of Virga: They were a parcel of Coxcombs and from the middle States Office Hunters not a few." Perhaps Mason said this, but it was more likely a Federalist's effort to discredit him.

Federalists did well in the Tidewater region, but beyond the James River, Antifederalists had things their own way. Admitting setbacks there, a Federalist reported the campaign there had been "made in Phrenzy, and terminated in deputations of weak & bad Men, who have bound themselves to vote in the negative, and will in all cases be the tools of Mr. H——."[26]

The sagging morale of Antifederalists in Philadelphia was bolstered when election news reached them indicating that their side had at least held its own, and perhaps even gained a majority of the seats. An optimistic report declared that Grayson, Henry, Mason, and Randolph had all won, which meant "that Virginia will, by a very decided majority, reject a measure which I am candid to own at first met with my approbation." Federalists in New York found little consolation from the back-country returns. Hot-and-cold Cyrus Griffin took heart from the list of Federalist winners, however, and touched on the antifederal weaknesses which still might give friends of the Constitution an edge. "Henry is mighty and powerful but too

[26] George Turberville to Madison, April 12, 1788; Edward Carrington to Madison, April 8, 1788, Madison papers, *DLC*.

interested—Mason too passionate—the Governor by nature timid and undecided—and Grayson too blustering."[27]

Randolph's victory was trumpeted as an endorsement of Antifederalist principles, but knowledgeable Federalists reasoned otherwise. Madison believed Randolph to be "so temperate in his opposition" that he could not be classed as an Antifederalist. Monroe was elected as an Antifederalist, but Madison thought he was "a friend though a cool one." Then there were a dozen top-ranking, dyed-in-the-wool Antifederalists, headed by the inimitable Henry. Probing for the great weakness in the Antifederalist position, Madison believed he had found it. "The adversaries take very different grounds of opposition. Some are opposed to the substance of the plan; others to particular modifications only. Mr. H——y is supposed to aim at disunion," Madison observed. Mason was turning "every day more bitter, and outrageous in his efforts to carry his point." Mason would probably "in the end be thrown by the violence of his passions into the politics of Mr. H——y." The Antifederalists had forced their adversaries into a hedging position on one important point, Madison conceded. No perceptive Federalist now closed the door on amendments. The great battle would be over the strings attached to the proposed alterations. Once certain of their strength, Madison speculated, the Antifederalists would either press for "a conditional ratification, or a proposal for a new convention will ensue."[28]

The nice balance of the two contending parties on the eastern side of the Alleghenies caused Antifederalists and Federalists alike to scan all reports from over the mountains for favorable signs. "Kentucky it is supposed will be divided," Madison wrote hopefully. Then in April the Kentucky returns reached Richmond. The political sins of the northern Federalists were visited upon their southern counterparts, for the Mississippi treaty and delayed statehood had been more than the Federalists could explain away. A dominantly Antifederalist delegation had been elected, as even the Federalists ad-

[27] Philadelphia *Independent Gazetteer*, April 16, 1788; Cyrus Griffin to Madison, April 14, 1788, Madison papers, *DLC*.

[28] Madison to Jefferson, April 22, 1788, 13 *Jefferson Papers* 98–99.

mitted. "The torch of discord has been thrown in [Kentucky] and has found the materials but too inflammable," Madison lamented.[29]

As the noise and strain of the spring elections faded, Virginia Antifederalists took heart. They had fought the Federalists to a standstill throughout the older parts of the state, and had won over the settlers in Kentucky. Henry's tactics in the West had paid off handsomely. The chances of forcing the Federalists to concede the calling of a second convention suddenly seemed much brighter.

[29] Madison to Washington, April 10, 1788, Madison papers, *DLC*.

☆ XI ☆

Mr. Jefferson's Blessing

A FTER A LONG, hard winter for the Antifederalists, spring brought renewed vigor to their efforts. The elections in Virginia had given them hope for success there, while the campaign in New York held even more promise. New Hampshire delegates reassembled in an atmosphere where no exertions were spared to keep alive the anti-Constitution sentiment predominant in February. North Carolina seemed completely dominated by Willie Jones and his Antifederalist clique, ready to follow Henry's lead. Rhode Island was in no mood to call a convention after rejecting the Constitution by popular referendum. Not only had there been a series of local successes, but something like a national organization for integrated effort was finally making headway.

With the blessing of Governor Clinton, General Lamb served as spokesman for the Federal Republican Society in New York, where bundles of pamphlets were forwarded to their allies throughout the winter months. Lamb and his son-in-law Charles Tillinghast accelerated the pace of their correspondence as New York citizens prepared to cast ballots in their own convention elections. Prodded by Lamb, the Antifederalists began to bestir themselves. Lamb peppered New England with his bundles, but except in New Hampshire the tracts arrived too late to help the cause. Closer to home, Antifederalists in New York nursed the old notion that their state was the life line of the Union, confident that the Constitution would be a dead letter without their assent.

After Antifederalists in the New York legislature had reluctantly called a ratifying convention, Governor Clinton exhorted his followers to line up attractive slates and work assiduously for their election. A dismayed Albany Federalist noted that Clinton "fills up every post with Vagabonds," but the gentlemen who complained about the governor's actions "will not form against him."[1] Contrasted with Federalist indifference or despair in upstate New York were the tireless Antifederalists. "They use every act, & strain every Nerve to gain their Points." They inundated the county with floods of reprints of the "Federal Farmer's Letters," the essays of "Centinel," and similar anti-Constitution screeds. Through the fall and winter months both factions had plunged into a battle of words that kept newspaper readers amused if not enlightened. New Yorkers were old hands at vehement party politics, and they now engaged in the ratification contest with all the lusty spirit that had marked former struggles.

Governor Clinton willingly risked his enormous popularity by siding with the Antifederalists. Gathered around him were veterans who smarted under losses incurred when forced to sell soldier's certificates at depreciated prices "to the Advantage of a few Harpies who prey upon the Vitals of the State, and leave the Soldiers unredressed and dissatisfied." Other Clintonians believed republican institutions could never spread over a far-flung territory, so that inevitably a federal Congress with extensive powers would "form a mighty continental legislature, in time (and God only knows how soon) to merge and swallow up the legislatures of the particular states."[2] Landowners who saw their tax burden shifted to duties on imports destined for, and eventually paid by, inhabitants in surrounding states saw few advantages in a shift of power from the banks of the Hudson.

Aided by kinsman DeWitt Clinton, Abraham Yates, Melancton Smith, and other favorites, Clinton lost little time in attacking the Constitution publicly. The Clintonians began firing salvos at the Constitution when it first appeared. For a public forum they turned to Thomas Greenleaf, publisher of the *New-York Journal and Patriotic Register*. For a time, the New York *Morning Post* also found room in its columns for Antifederalist screeds. But when the pale of polite argument was passed and the quarrel grew more heated,

[1] Major William North to Knox, February 13, 1787, Knox papers, *MHS*.
[2] John Holt to Lamb, [undated], Lamb papers, *NYHS;* "Rough Hewer" manuscript, 1784, Yates papers, *NYPL*.

Greenleaf's newspaper became the sole refuge for the Clintonians in the rising metropolis. The governor set the tone when he leaped into the fray with his "Cato" essays, a series of scathing jabs which (among other things) questioned the legality of the Constitution. Clinton flayed the Federal Convention for exceeding its authority by proposing "a new political fabric," which would destroy the states through "a consolidation of them into one government." Nor was Clinton above exploiting northern prejudice toward southerners, and more than once he contrasted the "luxury, dissipation, and a passion for aristocratic distinctions; where slavery is encouraged," with the spirit of equality and independence, "natural to the climate and soil" of New York.[3] Was it reasonable to assume that a Georgian or even a New Englander would have the same interests as a New Yorker or "preside over your lives, liberties, and property, with the same care and attachment?"

When Greenleaf eventually emerged as their one ally among the nine Manhattan newspaper publishers, Antifederalists sought to overwhelm the opposition with persistence rather than by numbers. Hence they crammed the columns of the *Journal* with a torrent of abuse against Federalists larded with dark hints about their real designs. "Politics run high here," a beseiged New Yorker observed, "It is a heavy tax on us to read the many pieces with which our papers abound." Antifederalists knew that voters were more often influenced by something other than reason and logic. After complaining that personal freedom was ignored in the Constitution, one writer forecast the return to general search warrants with:

> Excise laws established, by which our bed chambers will be subjected to be searched by brutal tools of power, under pretence, that they contain countraband or smuggled merchandize, and the most delicate part of our families, liable to every species of rude or indecent treatment . . . .

As if it were not bad enough to contemplate one's daughter being raped by these overbearing revenue agents, the writer predicted that northern militia men might have to help crush southern slave re-

[3] "Cato II," *New-York Journal,* October 11, 25, 1787.

volts.[4] With no bill of rights, what detestable tyranny might not be practiced under the Constitution?

Clinton's motives for supporting antifederalism were easily discernible to the opposition. An opponent of Clinton's recalled that every recent attempt to prop up the national government had brought out a few state-centered politicians who would "mount the political hobby-horse, and set the cry of——Liberty!" Antifederalist demagogues were trying to perpetuate an unwieldy system with "upwards of 2000 men" controlling the various state legislatures. A wise and frugal federal government would "lessen the expenses of our political house-keeping," collect taxes from import duties "without unequal and oppressive land taxes," and might "extinguish state parties, which are so detrimental to social happiness."[5]

Certainly Clinton saw little personal gain in ratification. As matters stood, he was the most powerful elected official in the Union, with a sizeable patronage army ready to do his bidding, and a fat state treasury. Clinton's popularity was greatest in the farming areas and poorest in the city precincts. "We are weak here," Melancton Smith once lamented from New York. The problem for New York Antifederalists was simply to keep the Constitutional "contagion" from spreading from Manhattan to the farming areas.

Although Clinton had stated his position on the Constitution by mid-December—no ratification without amendments—his opponents ridiculed a conditional ratification. Clinton attacked the idea of "adopt first, alter later," as a supplication unworthy of free men. Madison pondered this view and decided that Clinton and his friends "notoriously mediate either a dissolution of the Union, or protracting it by patching up the Articles of Confederation."[6] The evidence hardly supports Madison's sweeping assertion, which probably was a calculated overstatement meant to frighten Edmund Randolph. It is more likely that Clinton believed that the Union could not exist without New York and would have to take her in on his terms. It was the same attitude that marked Henry's antifederalism in Vir-

[4] "A Son of Liberty," *New-York Journal*, November 8, 1787.
[5] "Americanus," *Poughkeepsie Country Journal*, August 29, 1787.
[6] Madison to Randolph, January 10, 1788, Madison papers, *DLC*.

ginia, and hardly surprising when one considers the strength of the two large states in political councils of that day. If any of Clinton's followers wavered, he had only to throw up the bugaboo of federal land taxes to frighten them back in line. Assemblyman John Williams told his friends in Washington County what they could expect under the Constitution if it were adopted as it stood. "What has kept the taxes so low in this state—the reason is obvious, our impost duties." Williams called this "a privilege providence hath endowed us with," and Antifederalists saw no reason to mock divine intervention. Under the Constitution, Clinton's friends warned, not only would the tax load fall on farms, but excises "may be laid heavy on taverns and sphits [*sic*], so that the emoluments from taverns, which are now converted to the use of the poor, must go to Congress."[7] Bombarded with such arguments, it is not surprising that droves of New York farmers remained loyal to Clintonian antifederalism.

In the campaign for convention seats Antifederalists offered their choice candidates in safe districts rather than risk them in hostile Manhattan. Clinton himself was entered in Dutchess County as well as in the city, on the theory that he would probably lose in Hamilton's back yard. Meanwhile, Federalists did what they could to blacken Clinton's name. Newspaper readers were told that Clinton's antifederalism "has excited the curiosity as well as the indignation of America," and, if he carried New York with his schemes, "it will involve not only your State, but the whole continent in CIVIL WAR!" Angered by such attacks one indignant Antifederalist challenged the opposition to rise above gutter-level journalism.

It is an excellent method when you cannot bring reason for what you assert, to fall to ribaldry and satire. . . . instead of arguments, spit out a dozen mouthful of names, epithets, and interjections in a breath, cry Tory! Rebel! Tyranny! Centinel! Anarchy! Sidney! Monarchy! Misery! George the Third! Destruction! Arnold! Shays! Confusion! & c. & c.[8]

[7] *Poughkeepsie Country Journal*, January 19, 1788.
[8] *Poughkeepsie Country Journal*, April 22, 1788.

Editor Greenleaf, lonely but tireless, hurled a lesson in semantics at the opposition. "If the words, federal federalism &c. are to be taken in their general and common acceptation, as derived from feodus, a league or covenant, entered into for the mutual advantage of all; there cannot be found greater abuse of words than in this instance."[9] For the Federalists of 1788 wanted "nothing but the elevation and aggrandisement of a few over the many," and new fangled "federalism" amounted "to nothing more nor less . . . than a conspiracy of the well born few."

The Federal Republican Committee in New York dispatched 1,485 copies of Mercy Warren's "Columbian Patriot" and reprints of the "Centinel" essays to every county of the state. Some local workers may have shared the feeling of the Albany antifederal committee, who received the "Columbian Patriot" with less than enthusiasm. "A well composed piece," they reported, "but in a stile too sublime and florid for the common people in this Part of the Country." Old Abraham Yates enjoyed political fights and was ready to take the antifederal banner into Schoharie and Montgomery, but had anxious second thoughts. Since Federalists had repeatedly charged the Clintonian crowd with being "Anti" only "for fear of geting [*sic*] out of office," Yates asked, "will not my going round give new Springs to that argument?" In Columbia County, a Federalist reported, enemies of the Constitution were "daily going about to poison the Tenants" on the large estates, where they did "considerable mischief among the Ignorant."[10] Since thousands of tenant farmers still worked on estates that were holdovers from the patroon days, these voters were tempted by both sides. Tenants in Albany County were assured that their landlords might have interests directly opposed to their own, but fortunately the secret balloting meant there could be no reprisal for the tenant who followed his conscience. These yeomen were asked to support the Constitution if they wanted a national government that would "have the power,

9 "None of the Well-born Few," *New-York Journal*, April 30, 1788.
10 Committee of Albany to New York Committee, April 12, 1788, Lamb papers, *NYHS*.

by a capitation or poll-tax, to rate the poor equal to the rich," or double the costs of government.[11]

Clinton's partisans conceded that New Yorkers were indifferent souls on election day "when there is no great opposition," but when the political waters were turbulent the people responded in force. Every canvass of voters in upstate New York convinced Antifederalists that voters were far from indifferent in 1788. Upset by the way Antifederalists were building strength, Albany supporters of the Constitution sought to deprecate their activities. "In every part they are unceasing in their exertions.———Like the hags of Macbeth, they are continually dancing round the cauldron of sedition, each throwing in his proportion of spells—singing 'Come misrule—come toil—come trouble, /Anarchy reign, and discord bubble.' " A New England Federalist looked at the situation in New York and urged friends there to push the Constitution through "by fair means or foul." The "wilfully and wickedly Ignorant" Antifederalists were motivated by selfish views, he added, but "the time is at hand when the Mass of Humanity will have nothing but Pity for the wretched Antis, whose remorse & Shagreen, will be a sufficient punishment for all their Vilainy [*sic*]."[12]

All the newspaper bickering and arguments on courthouse steps finally came to a halt. At Kinderhook, where "Federal & Antifederal were both in good Earnest—No pains has [*sic*] been Spared in Collecting the Votes," the election was a seesaw affair. While the ballots were being counted, an Antifederalist feared the worst because of reports "That Compulsive Measure has been used to lead the Tennants" into the Federalist camp.[13] The final canvass removed his anxiety. Antifederalists overwhelmed the opposition at Schenectady so completely that a local Federalist tried to forget the humiliating experience. "At the time of Election it could be Easily perceived that those few of us that were in favour of the Constitution

---

[11] "A TENANT," Philadelphia *Freeman's Journal*, May 21, 1788.

[12] Providence *United States Chronicle*, April 10, 1788; *Poughkeepsie Country Journal*, April 22, 1788.

[13] C. Wynkoop to P. Van Gaasbeek, May 5, 1788, Roosevelt Library, Hyde Park, New York.

were Looked upon as belonging to the Tyrannicle [*sic*] party."[14] Antifederalist candidates in Dutchess County, including the man charged with "monarchical sentiments," swamped their rivals with a 900-vote plurality.

Columbia County politics ran high—too high to suit one candidate. Peter Van Schaack, banished to England as a tory in 1778 and only recently returned to his native ground, sought and lost a delegate's seat on the Federalist ticket. "You cannot conceive what agitation it has occasioned," he dolefully reported, "it was a war of tongues, but a few bloody noses have been the consequence."[15] The prodigious efforts of Albany County Antifederalists paid off with the election of six delegates and a 2,000 vote majority. Jubilant Antifederalists sped word of their victory to New York on a special sloop, informing friends there that they "had a Majority in every District except the City of Albany." The 7,449 ballots counted there indicated slight apathy toward the Constitution. James Duane learned that settlers west of Albany were distinctly antifederal in sentiment. A disgruntled associate, who claimed to "have had a good Dele of Trubel" in spreading Federalist doctrine, told Duane "A Number of our Setteers went to Scancantay to vote in the Last Election as I am informed and theam and the most that went to Schohare was Antifederal Electors."[16] So the Mohawk Valley and upper Hudson swung into the Antifederalist columns with ease. Beyond the city of New York, there were but few jarring reports. A couple of Federalists with personal followings had won seats in Kings County, and voters in Westchester County had been duped (so Antifederalists believed) into choosing six Federalists.

Convinced that Clinton's friends would try last-minute city shenanigans, Hamilton's forces warned voters to "Keep a good look-out. The enemies of Federalism know they can do nothing in this city by fair play." Chicanery at the polls was charged when spurious ballots "were dealt out as Federal Tickets with the Governor at

[14] Abraham Oothout to James Duane, May 19, 1788, Duane papers, *NYHS*.

[15] Peter Van Schaack to Henry Walton, June 3, 1788, Henry C. Van Schaack, *Life of Van Schaack* (New York, 1842), 425–26.

[16] John Myers to James Duane, June 23, 1788, Duane papers, *NYHS*.

the head, but so folded down as not to be perceived" by unsuspecting voters.[17] Federalists were determined to carry the city, by an impressive, lopsided vote. The unusual turnout was not deemed necessary "for the sake of carrying their Election (for of that they were perfectly secured by a vast Majority) but to make it appear, if possible, that a Majority of the Inhabitants of the State are Federal," a hostile observer noted.[18] He insisted that "this will make no Ado except in Appearances."

Appearances in politics are important, however, and were no less so in 1788. The Federalists on Manhattan proceeded to crush the opposition with well over a ten-to-one majority. "The Governors party of Antis shew[ed] themselves only the first day—and were so very weak that we only heard from them afterwards by hand-Bills," a Federalist gleefully reported. More returns from upstate areas diluted the sweetness of the Manhattan victory. Forty-six Antifederalists had been chosen, with the nine city Federalists joined by only ten others from the entire state. Hamilton brooded as the returns arrived on the Hudson packets, upsetting all his hopes. "The elections have gone wrong," he lamented. The blame was all Clinton's. "The whole flood of official influence, accelerated by a torrent of falsehood, easily gave the public opinion so violent a direction in a wrong channel," Hamilton explained, "that it was not possible suddenly to alter its course."[19]

Clinton's lieutenants had thoroughly outmaneuvered the Federalists in New York. In no state would the Antifederalist victory be so shattering, but as in other states the Antifederalists were not sure of what their victory meant. Abraham Lansing kept his ear to the ground in New York and reported that "among the federalists here they are in hopes that the Anties will not Dare Refuse adopting the Constitution, they may Indeed adjourn, and adjourn again but they

[17] "One and All," broadside dated April 29, 1788; "One of Yourselves," broadside dated April 30, 1788, *NYPL.*

[18] Thomas Tucker to St. George Tucker, May 2, 1788, Tucker-Coleman papers, Colonial Williamsburg.

[19] Samuel B. Webb to J. Barrell, May 11, 1788, Webb papers, Yale University Library; Hamilton to Gouverneur Morris, May 19, 1788, Hamilton papers, *DLC.*

will at Last adopt it."[20] However, the Antifederalists had talked so much about "previous amendments" that this seemed to be their game—not outright rejection of the Constitution. Hamilton, reviewing the Federalist defeat, considered the twenty-seven extra votes Clinton had in his pocket and thought the worst. Clinton planned to fight ratification even if twelve other states approved the Constitution.[21] "It is reduced to a certainty, that Clinton has, in several conversations, declared the *Union* unnecessary," the bitter Hamilton warned.

In his disappointment Hamilton magnified pebbles into boulders. Henry Knox, not so brilliant but still a better judge of character, looked at the same scene with a less jaundiced view. The Antifederalists were indeed "obstinate and artful," he admitted, but they probably lacked "the hardihood to openly reject the constitution [and] should Virginia adopt it . . . they will adjourn to a distant day."[22] Jay had similar impressions. He doubted if Clinton could keep all the delegates in line because some Antifederalists were really "Friends to Union and mean well." So, even if Clinton were indifferent to the fate of the Union, he would not be able to stampede the state convention into an outright rejection. Moreover, angry city Federalists were talking about playing a trump card. Since the election had proved that the sentiments of upstate New York were at such a variance from those held by citizens living in the environs of Manhattan, why not split the state asunder? Jay told Washington the "Idea has taken Air" and frightened some Antifederalists.[23] Then Jay went on to make a more revealing point about the Antifederalists. "I cannot find that they have as yet so looked forward to contingent Events, or even to those the most probable, as to have united in or formed any System."

Jay's shrewd observation touched on the great Antifederalist weakness. Although all their leaders paid lip service to the idea of a

[20] A. G. Lansing to Yates, June 1, 1788, Yates papers, *NYPL*.

[21] Hamilton to Gouverneur Morris, May 19, 1788, Hamilton papers, *DLC*.

[22] Knox to Otho Holland Williams, June 11, 1788, Williams papers, Maryland Historical Society.

[23] John Jay to Washington, May 29, 1788, *DHC*, IV, 643.

second convention, there was no harmonious effort to bring about such a gathering. Clinton looked to Randolph in Virginia for some assistance, while the latter's dilatory manner let precious time slip by. The milling throng of Massachusetts Antifederalists, the discontented groups in Pennsylvania and New Hampshire, the clearly hostile Rhode Island "Antis" sought a political Moses to lead them out of the wilderness. Instead of a powerful leader, however, a swarm of minor prophets appeared in each locality, and for the most part they fared rather badly. The problem thrust upon the Antifederalists was one of unity—unity of purpose and unity of program. Immensely powerful in their own back yard, the Antifederalists seemed unsteady when they ventured forth on national concerns.

Though Clinton was in some ways politically naïve, he realized that unity was important. It must have been at Clinton's bidding that Lamb and his Federal Republican Society tried to promote the antifederal cause. However, the Federalists appear to have had at least one man who was privy to the society's secrets, for their bundles of pamphlets were often mislaid or broken into. Federalist editors north of New York needled Lamb unmercifully as a sower of dissent until Oswald was provoked into a defense. A grateful nation would hail the name of Lamb "when those of his infamous political adversaries,—the *upstarts and mushroons* [*sic*] of the hour 'will stink in the very nostrils of posterity.' "[24]

After the New York elections assured Antifederalists a heavy majority in the convention, Lamb's committee redoubled its efforts to give antifederalism cohesion and direction. A call for joint action was dispatched to friends in New Hampshire, Rhode Island, Virginia, and the Carolinas. Lamb urged them to use their talents and influence "to procure amendments to the System previous to its adoption." He pleaded for industrious committees of correspondence so that "they should understand one another on the Subject, and unite in the Amendments they propose."[25] The plan might have wrought a different course of history had it been conceived and

[24] Philadelphia *Independent Gazetteer*, December 27, 1787.

[25] John Lamb to Nathaniel Peabody, May 18, 1788, *Historical Magazine*, II, 3rd series (1873), 280–81.

implemented eight months earlier. As matters stood, however, the plea came too late. Lowndes and Burke could only finger the pamphlets they received, note the fact of ratification, and still complain that most of the people were really Antifederalists at heart. "Should either Virginia or New York state reject it," Burke consoled Lamb, "the system will fall to pieces, tho the other nine States may agree to it." A similar appeal to Samuel Chase drew a discouraging response. Maryland citizens were demoralized by the way the Constitution had been pushed through the Annapolis convention, Chase avowed, but such Antifederalist spirit as remained would be mustered for the forthcoming local elections.[26]

Reviewing the February events at Exeter, Federalists concluded that the opposition came within a whisker of wrecking the Constitution. "Had they acted like good politicians," Washington's wartime secretary reported, all would have been lost. Only antifederal ineptness had prevented a Federal debacle. By June, Federalists assured themselves that matters were well in hand. Still the principal Antifederalists were hustling about, trying to keep committed opponents of the Constitution in line. The back country had been thoroughly canvassed, Washington learned, and the antifederal trend had been reversed by late May. Citizens formerly convinced that the Constitution spelled their ruin "now only appear to be mortified that New-Hampshire will not make the ninth State," his informant concluded.[27]

A few Federalists were nevertheless uneasy. Nicholas Gilman regretted "the delay of our backsliding State," which for a time made everything doubtful. During the adjournment Antifederalists had been more systematic in their campaigning—"the leaders are known to each other and are indefatigable in their exertions." If they succeeded at the reconvened session, the pessimistic Gilman feared, "the sword will soon be drawn."[28] Joshua Atherton, the mainspring

[26] Aedanus Burke to John Lamb, June 23, 1788; Samuel Chase to John Lamb, June 13, 1788, Lamb papers, *NYHS*.

[27] Tobias Lear to Washington, June 2, 1788, *DHC*, IV, 676.

[28] Nicholas Gilman to the President of New Hampshire [John Sullivan], March 23, 1788, *LCC*, VIII, 709.

Courtesy of the New-York Historical Society, New York City

GEORGE CLINTON

PATRICK HENRY

This portrait was painted by Thomas Sully in 1815 from a contemporary miniature now owned by Amherst College. The portrait is owned by Colonial Williamsburg, Incorporated, and hangs in the restored colonial capitol in Williamsburg, Virginia.

of antifederalism in New Hampshire, had indeed kept busy. He
agreed with Lamb that the recommendatory amendments, such as
Massachusetts proposed, carried little or no weight. Atherton
thumped for amendments prior to final ratification, and agreed with
Lamb that any other form of action would amount to total surrender
to the opposition.[29] For allies in their anti-Constitution attacks Atherton and Nathaniel Peabody counted on the support of delegates
known to favor state paper-money issues. Though the strength of
this faction was ebbing, the paper-money crowd had enough fight
left to make the issue seem doubtful when the convention was only
weeks away.

Atherton was singled out as a target for much abuse by the Federalists, who heavily underscored his wartime Toryism. Angered
by Federalist attacks, Atherton chaffed as he noted the many devices
used to discredit Antifederalists. "The presses are in a great measure secured to *their* side," and Antifederalists were denounced as
"enemies to their Country and they often make them say what they
never Thought." After being misquoted in the Exeter *Advertiser*,
Atherton tried to get a rebuttal printed to "brush off the mask of
Falsehood." Since the New Hampshire newspapers were cool toward
any Antifederalist efforts, Atherton impatiently awaited the bundles
of pamphlets from New York with their reinforcing arguments.
Prolonged delay of his mail made Atherton share the suspicions of
Antifederalists in other states. When the "Federal Farmer's Letters" arrived too late to be of any service, Atherton figured it was
hardly a coincidence. "Is it not surprising how these Pamphlets
have been kept back?" was his petulant query.

After Lamb's first overture Atherton had agreed that the New
York Antifederalists could render their cause invaluable aid. Hoping
that the New Hampshire convention could be delayed, Atherton
pleaded for battle plans. "Could our Convention receive your Resolution not to adopt, without the necessary Amendments, before they
have proceeded too far, together *with your Amendments,* I have
not the least Doubt but a great Majority would immediately close
with your views and wishes," he urged. But Atherton confessed that

[29] Joshua Atherton to John Lamb, June 11, 1788, Lamb papers, *NYHS.*

the New Hampshire Antifederalists had no particular plan in mind themselves. In fact, they had not even bothered to put down on paper the amendments they presumably thought so vital. "The Subject of Amendments shall not be forgot," Atherton assured Lamb, whereupon he appears to have put the topic out of mind.

With eight states supporting the Constitution, the burden of proof that it was not a panacea for all political ills now lay with the Antifederalists. Atherton had to strain every oratorical power he possessed as he tried to rekindle old doubts about the destruction of "thirteen Pillars" in favor of one Colossus. Without Atherton the Antifederalists would probably have been totally ineffective. With Atherton the Federalists had only to sit through a few days of uncomfortable haranguing before they clamped down on the obstreperous Amherst lawyer. Patiently they could listen to attacks on the proposed judiciary system or hear Antifederalists warn that the Constitution was a grand engine designed to "swallow up the Sovereignty of the several States." Desperately Atherton and his small band of followers tried to keep the debate going, hoping to delay a final vote until some word might reach them from Poughkeepsie. When the main question was called for, after only a few days of debate, the Federalists tested their strength. Vainly, the Antifederalists tried to pass conditional amendments. Atherton, perhaps hoping against hope that some breathless express rider from New York would arrive at any moment, favored another adjournment. When the vital question was put to the convention, fifty-seven Federalist votes were counted, while forty-seven Antifederalists said "nay."

As enthusiastic Federalists sent their express rider toward New York, downtrodden Antifederalists tried to soften the blow. In a conciliatory mood brought on by the "behavior of the minority (except a few)," the Federalists switched enough votes to appoint a committee that would frame recommendatory amendments. Despondent because "the gilded Pill was swallowed," Atherton offered his excuses. The Federalists had all the "Weight and Influence of the Men now in Office, together with all the Speakers in the State great and small." Even so, they had not carried the day by force of debate or discussion, "but by other Means, which were it not for the Depravity of the human Heart, would be viewed with the warmest Sentiments of Disapprobation."[30] The amendments were a slapdash affair, Atherton admitted, put together "in great Haste." Embarrassed by the Antifederalist debacle, and still convinced that great changes were needed, Atherton tossed further responsibility to the Clintonians in New York. "Be the Glory all yours," Atherton commented, "if the other States desert you!"

The New Hampshire convention results revealed that the Federalists had learned many lessons as the ratification campaign had progressed. The early cry of "this or nothing" had long since been abandoned, as the concession of a bill of rights had cut the ground from beneath the Antifederalists. By conceding the need for some alterations dealing with personal liberties, the need for a second federal convention would disappear. This concession mollified the rank-and-file Antifederalists but only frustrated the leaders. Again in New Hampshire the outcome showed that among the inner circle of Antifederalists, declamation over the lack of a bill of rights merely served as a springboard for other attacks on the Constitution. Easily aroused by appeals for safeguards on personal liberties, most citizens became restless when the talk turned to the sophistry of government. Disgusted by this "General Lethurgy," Atherton too had learned the hard lesson: it was virtually impossible to mobilize public opinion for any Antifederalist program that went beyond a bill of rights.

By the events on that first day of summer, 1788, ratification became an accomplished fact. Yet a remarkable feature of the Antifederalists' reaction to the New Hampshire news was the inclination to shrug it off. At Poughkeepsie, Governor Clinton tried to keep a tight rein on proceedings by assuring partisans in New York that the Portsmouth ratification "has had not the least effect on our Friends at this Place." Rhode Island Antifederalists reacted angrily when Providence citizens held a celebration June 24 honoring "the Ninth Pillar." Since Federalists were using the New Hampshire reports as a pretext to "insinuate that the opposition of this State to the Constitution was given up," the Antifederalists planned their own celebration honoring recalcitrants. The well-organized Antifederalists

[30] Joshua Atherton to John Lamb, June 23, 1788, Lamb papers, *NYHS*.

in North Carolina, as well as those in New Hampshire, seemed to have expected the worst from Virginia. Ratification by all other states except New York was discounted by headstrong Timothy Bloodworth, who welcomed a chance to join northern Antifederalists in a last-ditch stand.[31]

Die-hard opposition elsewhere did nothing to bolster antifederalism in New England. Indeed, it contracted rapidly as political realists who caught the scent of victory exhibited nimble convictions. One Maine delegate who had been elected to the Massachusetts convention as an Antifederalist voted for ratification, then returned to York and wrote a scathing denunciation of his recent associates. Some Antifederalists had been "ill treated as torrys and are now ready to sacrifice all for revenge," some were hopelessly in debt and wanted paper money "to cheat their creditors," and others were ignoramuses and dupes.[32] Such confessions of past errors, given to the right people, probably provided more than one political salvation. Samuel Adams, after extricating himself from the unfortunate predicament at the Boston convention, swung over to the Federalists because he wanted and needed a public office. Adams heard disturbing rumors from others whose newly adopted Federalism fitted uncomfortably. Nathan Dane assured Adams that the most zealous Federalists, who were "Artful and active, do not intend that any amendments Shall be adopted, even after the Constitution Shall be put into operation, if they can [in] any way prevent it—at least they will oppose all amendments which, I believe, the Republican and honest Part of the Community will contend for."[33] But perhaps Adams rationalized his alliance with Federalists as a holding operation. After all, had not Dane concluded that "time only can determine" whether honest men "or the friends of influence and corruption will succeed?" If Adams agreed, he might have decided that the best way to serve antifederal principles was to become a Federalist officeholder.

[31] George Clinton to John Lamb, June 28, 1788; Timothy Bloodworth to John Lamb, July 1, 1788, Lamb papers, *NYHS.*

[32] Nathaniel Barrell to George Thatcher, February 20, 1788, Thatcher papers, *BPL.*

[33] Nathan Dane to Samuel Adams, May 10, 1788, Adams papers, *NYPL.*

Gerry and Warren were made of sterner stuff. Gerry's friends urged him to oppose Hancock for the governorship in the spring elections. Still smarting from his thrashing in the convention race, Gerry made excuses. "I have been ungratefully used by many of my fellow citizens & want not to negotiate any more of their public concerns," he complained.[34] Like most politicians who have tasted the forbidden fruit, however, Gerry had no real desire for retirement. "I shall not shrink from my duty to the public in general, whether in or out of office," Gerry hedged. Any perceptive political observer knew of Hancock's immense popularity, but neither Gerry nor Warren conceded everything to the opposition.

Somewhat imprudently, Warren made no secret of his desire to become the next lieutenant governor. Gerry appears to have been more discreet and was hence a lesser threat. Accordingly, the Federalists levied their batteries on Warren. A few days before the polling, the leading Federalist newspaper charged that Warren's ambition was shamelessly unbounded. An unnamed listener claimed that Warren had said that he meant *"to make Shays's adherents, and the antifederalists, a stepping stone by which I may mount to the seat of government."*[35] This canard and other innuendoes infuriated Warren, and he denied the report categorically and held that the Federalists' "malignity was unaccountable." One observer thought Warren took his rebuffs too seriously. "His mind has been soured, and he became discontented and querulous," John Quincy Adams noted.[36]

Rashly, a few Boston Antifederalists continued to talk about pitting Gerry against Hancock in the governor's race. Gerry knew opposition to Hancock was futile and refused to campaign. Even so, high-riding Federalists spread stories that Gerry was in financial straits and might soon lose his handsome Cambridge town house. Taking the dismal election returns with more humor than the melancholy Warren, Gerry suggested a social visit "although the alarm of our being together might be such as to station sentries at Charles-

[34] Elbridge Gerry to Samuel Gerry, April 6, 1788, Gerry papers, *MHS*.
[35] *Massachusetts Centinel*, April 5, 1788.
[36] John Quincy Adams, "Diary," *MHS, Proceedings*, 2nd Series, XVI, 435–36.

town bridge" by Boston Federalists.[37] "Neither the stationing of
Sentries, or the malicious wishes & Obliquy of the federals, will ever
prevent my visiting my friend" was Warren's answer. "No man
was ever persecuted with such inveterate Malice as I am. It follows
me in every step." By this time Warren and his enemies were indulging in that "pleasure of hating" that Henry Adams believed
was a characteristically New England pastime.

Baiting Antifederalists became good sport for newspaper editors
as it became apparent that the Constitution had triumphed. The
earlier judgment of the *New-Hampshire Spy* "that none but *fools,
blockheads,* and *mad men* will dare to oppose it" seemed confirmed.
An advertisement in New Jersey proclaimed that on the Fourth of
July there "will be sold, *for the benefit of the Antifederalists,* the
OLD ARTICLES OF CONFEDERATION." A wartime patch-
work, the articles had been found "much the worse for the wear,"
and must be sold. To encourage the sale, "the State of RHODE-
ISLAND [will be] thrown into the bargain," the auctioneers announced. How ludicrous seemed that prediction, made six months
earlier by "Portius," that the four remaining states might take a
righteous stand while "Still adhering [*sic*] to the Articles of Confederation." Few citizens thought the nine errant sisters had committed "point-blank *national infidelity*" by "open REBELLION
against the National Constitution," but the Articles of Confederation called for unanimous action, hence allowing the Constitution
to operate after only nine ratifications was a barefaced violation of
public faith.[38] By June such reasoning appeared so specious and contrived that most northern Antifederalists were ready to concede the
point.

Even Jefferson, who had once been intrigued by the idea of nine
states ratifying while the other four held out for amendments, shifted

[37] Elbridge Gerry to James Warren, June 28, 1788, James T. Austin, *The Life
of Elbridge Gerry,* II, 84–88; James Warren to Elbridge Gerry, July 20, 1788,
Gerry papers, DLC.

[38] Portsmouth *New-Hampshire Spy,* October 27, 1787; Elizabethtown *New-
Jersey Journal,* June 25, 1788; Bennington *Vermont Gazette,* May 26, 1788;
Providence *United States Chronicle,* May 15, 1788; "Portius," Boston *American
Herald,* November 12, 1787.

to new ground. Still skittish about the Presidency, Jefferson thought long-standing American fears of a strong executive were "only put to sleep by the unlimited confidence we all repose in the person to whom we all look as our president"—Washington. "For the present however, the general adoption is to be prayed for," Jefferson added, and he hoped his home state would give the Constitution "the 9th vote of approbation. There could then be no doubt of N. Carolina, N. York., and New Hampshire."[39] Jefferson was not alone in believing that Virginia, even at that late hour, might either have fixed the certainty of ratification or kept events dangling by insisting upon a second convention with a hodgepodge of amendments.

Patrick Henry, for example, had never expressed the slightest doubt. A union without Virginia would be no union at all. It was a fact worth exploiting to the full.

[39] Jefferson to Edward Carrington, May 27, 1788, 13 *Jefferson Papers* 208–209.

☆ XII ☆

The "Ticklish Situation" at Richmond

As balm for their wounds, Antifederalist leaders in other parts of the Union pointed to Virginia and New York as the crucial citadels. Here the forces of republicanism would break Federalist lances, overturn the errors propagated so successfully elsewhere, and provide a rallying point for Antifederalists that would culminate in the calling of another federal convention. Henry's popularity in Virginia never seemed higher, nor Clinton's grip in New York any stronger. Federalists, a few extremists to the contrary, no longer argued about whether amendments were necessary. The only divergence of opinion among Antifederalists and their opponents was over the timing—should amendments be a condition of ratification— or could Antifederalists trust the new government to lay curbs on its own power? Clinton, Henry, and Mason were suspicious of Federalist intentions. They insisted that a second convention was needed to correct the errors of the first.

The goal of a second federal convention was simple to understand, easily promoted, and (considering all the discordant elements heard since the Philadelphia meeting had adjourned) seemed to make a good deal of sense. But after that, what? Let the discussion turn to amendments, and there was only the fuzziest kind of outline. Keen-sighted Madison diagnosed the Antifederalist malady all too clearly in *Federalist XXXVIII*. There he warned newspaper readers up and down the country that quarrelsome "Antis" were incapable of leadership. By a skillful jumble of Antifederalists' objections, Madison accented "the discord and ferment that would mark their own deliberation." This alone was proof that the Constitution as it stood was God-sent. Although Madison ridiculed the opposition in an almost lighthearted manner, he thinly disguised a barb aimed toward Mason. While one Antifederalist ranted against the threat of direct taxation, "The patriotic adversary in a State of great exports and imports, is not less dissatisfied that the whole burden of taxes may be thrown on consumption," Madison noted. "This politician discovers in the Constitution a direct and irresistible tendency to monarchy; that is equally sure it will end in aristocracy." The inference was plain. Antifederalists knew only how to carp or criticize but lacked constructive judgment.

Despite the fact that antifederal ideas on amendments were vague, many Virginians saw constitutional flaws that needed correcting. Undoubtedly, Mason and Lee believed the Virginia delegates could be persuaded to make conditional amendments. Mason had been stirring about with more energy than usual, hobbling on his gouty legs with an insistent message: without amendments the Constitution spells ruin for Virginia. Perturbed opponents thought Mason's zeal stemmed from personal irritation at attacks made upon him, as well as from "a vain opinion he entertains . . . that he has influence enough to dictate a constitution to Virginia, and through her to the rest of the Union." Madison heard that Mason was working overtime without his former moderation. Mason's methods, Madison declared, "will neither add to the dignity of his character; nor I should hope, to the Success of his cause."[1]

More concerned with success than dignity, Mason consulted Richard Henry Lee about the strategy they should employ to gain amendments. Lee's advice was to follow the example of the English Parliament set down exactly one hundred years earlier by ratifying the Constitution, but with amendments inserted and a two-year deadline for their passage. If the first Congress failed to act on the amendments in the specified time, Virginia would simply declare itself "disengaged from this ratification."[2] The amendments should "plainly and strongly" provide bulwarks for the states against the national government, particularly the southern states. Lee agreed with Mason about the need to check the congressional power to regulate commerce. Otherwise, the eight northern states would have the means of strangling the five southern ones. Lee would not venture to

[1] George Nicholas to Madison, April 5, 1788; Madison to Nicholas, April 8, 1788, Madison papers, *DLC.*

[2] Richard Henry Lee to Mason, May 7, 1788, Ballagh, *Letters of Lee,* II, 466–69.

Richmond, but he tried to serve the Antifederalists with his pen. Writing to influential Virginians that spring, Lee made conditional amendments a consistent theme.

For Federalists, as Madison had said, the Massachusetts plan was the first and last line of retreat. "Additional amendments or a second general Convention will be fatal," because at the least they would add further delay to the ratification process, which needed expedients rather than deterrents.[3] Washington, hearing of the pressure for amendments, admitted that some helpful alterations to the Constitution had been suggested. "But to make such amendments as may be proposed . . . the condition of its adoption would, in my opinion, amount to a compleat rejection of it," the General decided.[4]

More and more, citizens on both sides of the political fence compared the Constitution to some kind of a machine. The Federal Convention mechanics had put it together, and the tinkers were now at work. There was no certainty that the new device would work, but a majority agreed that the old one was falling apart. "Am sorry to find that the New Constitution is still in great Jeopardy in Virg[ini]a," Congressman John Brown noted in mid-May. "'Tis with great difficulty that we can keep the Old Machine in Motion [and] without the prospect of the adoption of the New it would be impossible."[5] Madison's fretful kinsman tried to down the constitutional pill, but could not discern how thirteen sovereign states would blend into a harmonious republic. "The Imperium in imperio will be the fruitful Source of a thousand jarring Principles," Madison was told, "which would make the new Machine, notwithstanding all the Oil you can give it, to go heavily along."[6]

As each swing of the pendulum brought the Richmond convention closer, the deeper fear of some Federalists was not the public clamor for amendments but rather the private plans of Patrick Henry. Convinced that he was holding something sinister up his sleeve, the opposition surmised that the old hero would play his popularity to

[3] Madison to George Nicholas, April 8, 1788, Madison papers, *DLC*.

[4] Washington to General John Armstrong, April 25, 1788, *DHC*, IV, 592.

[5] John Brown to James Breckenridge, May, 14, 1788, Breckenridge papers, University of Virginia Library.

[6] Rev. James Madison to Madison, February 9, 1788, Madison papers, *DLC*.

the hilt. Most alarming to the Federalists was a rumor that Henry favored splintering the Union into regional confederacies. Observers thought Henry's plans "formed a pabulum for eternal contention," a judgment echoed by Federalists who knew only too well Henry's spellbinding power.[7] Had a man of lesser stature spoken so glibly of separate confederacies, he might have been dismissed as an ineffectual eccentric. Henry, however, was persuasive to the point that it was hardly safe to leave any but the most zealous Federalists with him, for fear that another Henryite might be created. At Hampden-Sydney College a four-square Federalist believed the "idea of Virginia standing independent of the other States, or forming a partial confederacy or a foreign alliance is more openly avowed by some people in this quarter, than any where else."[8] The cause of this wild-eyed logic was evident. "I am certain the sentiment originated with the old Govr"—Henry.

Henry's energy confounded the opposition as he pressed his point on likely converts. Envious of Henry's tremendous popularity, Federalists flinched as he entered a public room and at once became the center of attention. While eager listeners downed draughts of cider between his phrases, Henry would thump the table at the proper moment, choose the right adjective, and then walk away while his charmed audience nodded their heads in agreement. Virginia was strong and could bend the Union to her will. Southern rights would be precariously held by a northern-dominated federal government. The Constitution needed drastic revamping before any Virginian with sound judgment could support it. When Henry said these things, they somehow made a good deal of sense. Thus Federalists conceded that Henry was busy looking for and finding Antifederalist support; but the inner circle of opposition was convinced that Henry's band of admirers would have quickly dissolved had his "real designs" been made public. "The opposition," shrewd George Nicholas predicted, "except from that quarter will be feeble."[9]

[7] George Gilmer to Jefferson, December 23, 1787, 12 *Jefferson Papers*, 453.

[8] Rev. John B. Smith to Madison, June 12, 1788, Madison papers, *DLC*.

[9] George Nicholas to Madison, April 5, 1788, Madison papers, *DLC;* Edward Carrington to Jefferson, April 24, 1788, 13 *Jefferson Papers* 100–103.

Henry's shoulders were broad enough to take a considerable burden of abuse, both public and private. Mason and Lee were the intellectual forces behind Virginia antifederalism, but Henry's brand of constitutional opposition was much more salable at the courthouse square. Planter Mason's knowledge of the law made those formally admitted to the bar respect him, while lawyer Henry's loose logic brought contempt from fellow barristers. But none denied that Henry won juries handily. At the Virginia convention the jury was expanded fifteenfold, and, if Henry's courtroom skills lost none of their effectiveness, the Antifederalists could indeed take heart. "All the Satires of Mr. Henry [will be] made use of to break & split the union," wrote a French observer, who believed that the triumph of antifederalism would be Henry's personal victory.[10] A French diplomat in New York reported that Henry was the chief Antifederalist in Virginia and "Son systeme seroit de detacher son Etat de la confederation." The French onlookers reflected prevailing Federalist opinion. To Federalists, Henry was cast as the chief villain in the Richmond drama.

Henry's role as the Antifederalist star was cast, with Mason certain to be a featured player. In point of influence and personal popularity, the two were a fair match for their rivals. Always sensitive, Mason could not have read with indifference the personal attacks from the "Landholder," which portrayed him as a mendacious southern politician, a man governed by "narrow views and local prejudices." Ellsworth made Mason into a whipping boy to promote his own exploitation of sectional jealousies. Then there was another Federalist blatantly false story circulating, but bound to have gained credence in some quarters. According to this report, Mason had never mentioned a bill of rights in the Federal Convention, and he had urged that property qualifications for one office "(and that not the highest) would be *sixteen thousand dollars.*"[11] Mason would have been less than human had these attacks not ruffled his composure. Not improbably, Washington's coolness and the decided Federalism of other lifelong friends in Fairfax County also injured

[10] St. John Crevecour to William Short, June 10, 1788, Short papers, *DLC.*
[11] *New-Jersey Journal,* January 16, 1788.

Mason's feelings, forcing him into a defensive position. Thus Mason worked all the harder to prove he was right and Federalists were wrong.

Joining Mason in the preconvention skirmishes at the levels of logic rather than emotion, Richard Henry Lee parried the charge that he was sulking in his tent while other Antifederalists gave battle. Agreeing with Mason that amendments were vital steps prior to ratification, Lee sent the message where it might do the most good. With his withered hand swaddled in a black silk bandage, Lee used the other to write Edmund Pendleton a persuasive statement of the Antifederalist position. Pendleton, universally respected for his knowledge of the law and his moderation in politics, must have read Lee's analysis with interest if not approbation. Every candid man admitted the Constitution needed amending, Lee wrote, but some —perhaps Pendleton himself—feared that a second convention might "risk the whole." By utilizing most of the Massachusetts amendments and adding safeguards for southern agriculture, frequent elections, freedom of the press, and trial by jury, the good parts of the constitutional fabric might be saved "without risking the convulsions of conventions." As an afterthought Lee—who like Mason was no lawyer but knew the law well—added his concern about the acts of Congress which would become part of the supreme law of the land. "To prevent suprizes, and [the] fixing of injurious laws," statutes should undergo a two-year probationary period. An amendment could establish this condition and save the United States many future headaches, for it was "much more easy to get a good law continued than a bad one repealed."[12] With a conditional ratification covering these matters, Lee urged, Virginians could safely support the Constitution.

Letters such as Lee's, though addressed to Pendleton, were doubtlessly passed from hand to hand. Persuading Pendleton to call for conditional ratification was unlikely, but if a seed of doubt could be planted in his mind, it might sprout elsewhere among the dozens of elected delegates, "who make the Union their great & first object,

[12] Richard Henry Lee to Edmund Pendleton, May 22, 1788, Ballagh, *Letters of Lee*, II, 469–74.

but are for carrying their efforts to amend the constitution as far as possible within that object."[13]

Somewhat tardily, New York Antifederalists sent Colonel Oswald southward to make certain that the leaders North and South understood each other. The decision to send Oswald was perhaps due to difficulties in the postal service. Convinced that their letters had not been accidentally misplaced, Antifederalists made certain that nothing would interrupt dispatches addressed to supporters in Richmond. Henry readily agreed to General Lamb's suggestion that a Federal Republican Society be formed in Virginia—and at a caucus of Antifederalists, Mason agreed to act as chairman of the group committed to a conditional ratification.[14] Oswald stayed in Richmond long enough to receive assurances of their determination to forestall an unqualified ratification, made arrangements to send letters to seemingly uncommitted merchants so that Federalists would not tamper with future correspondence, and then returned to report his success.

Poor Randolph, trying to be tight-lipped as the day approached when he would have to stand and be counted, was courted by Antifederalists who either had not read his equivocal letter or had not understood it. A load of fresh doubts entered his mind. On the threshold of decision, he was beset by a dozen fears. What would be the status of the old continental dollars if the Constitution were ratified? Were those who talked of previous amendments using that device so that a "higher game might be played"? Ratification by Maryland had helped clear the air, for Randolph regarded the events at Annapolis as a sledge-hammer blow against southern antifederalism. Yes, Randolph's mind was made up—almost.

Madison played the sage, assuring the sorely troubled governor that all his suspicions were groundless. The wily Federalist put as much between his lines as he put into them. The Antifederalists were becoming such a desperate lot that anyone who remained with them would have to be a conspirator himself. Randolph's spine must have

[13] Edward Carrington to Knox, March 13, 1788, Knox papers, *MHS*.
[14] Patrick Henry to John Lamb, June 9, 1788, Lamb papers, *NYHS*.

stiffened as he read Madison's insistence that those who talked about conditional ratification or a second convention "Secretly aim at disunion."[15] There was nothing subtle in Madison's final hint. Unless Randolph intended to abet Henry in some desperate maneuvers, he had better climb off the fence and join the Federalists.

While Randolph tortured himself with a case of acute indecision, Gouverneur Morris slipped into Richmond for a personal inspection of the situation. He was delighted to find that the Antifederalist fever of a few months earlier seemed to have subsided. "I am mistaken if some Leaders of the Opposition are not more solicitous in the present Moment how to make a good Retreat than how to fight the Battle," Morris reported. "It is you know a sad Thing for a great and deep Politician to make a great Blunder and fall in a deep Ditch," he told Washington, "and yet this may easily happen when Men walk on *bad Ground*."[16] The description fitted Randolph most aptly. Were Mason and Henry aware of the slippery doctrines gingerly held by a few presumed Antifederalists? Henry had passed a bon mot at a recent dinner party when he said, "I am too old not to read *books*; I must read *men*."[17] What did Henry see when he looked at Randolph or into the faces of the bone-weary delegates who rode into Richmond from the "dark and bloodie ground" of Kentucky?

Whatever secret plans the opposing factions had as they drifted into Richmond by twos and threes, both increasingly staked their hopes on a single issue. For Antifederalists, the watchword was "previous amendments." For Federalists, the expression meant to dissolve all doubt was "Union!" Henry and Mason, of course, considered a union without Virginia unthinkable—and assumed the twelve other states would pay whatever price they asked to keep the nation unified. Every delegate must have been aware of the high stakes. At the Swan and other bustling taverns, no one pretended to

[15] Randolph to Madison, February 29, April 17, 1788, Conway, *Life of Randolph*, 101–102; Madison to Randolph, April 10, 1788, Madison papers, *DLC*.

[16] Gouverneur Morris to Washington, April 29, 1788, *DHC*, IV, 603–604.

[17] Lee, *Life of Lee*, II, 351*n*.

know the outcome. Late arrivals found the quarters cramped, but with the weather warm and dry, it was a better time for drinking and thinking than for sleeping three in a bed.

Henry and Mason lost little time in making their plans. They wanted time to chat with the delegates—the undecided delegates—consequently they decided to drag out the sessions so that Henry's eloquence, Mason's persuasiveness, and whatever else they could piece together would work its magic. It was Mason's chore to draft an antifederal manifesto (Federalists charged that Mason longed to become the lawgiver to the nation, since he was puffed with pride over his Virginia Constitution of 1776), and Henry gave the long list of desired amendments his approval. Henry declared their immediate inclusion in the Constitution was "the only remaining Chance for securing a Remnant of those invaluable Rights which are yielded by the New Plan."[18] Then, there was the Kentucky delegation.

From all indications, what the Antifederalists needed to do with the Kentuckians was simply to hold them in line. Henry had warned friends in Kentucky that northerners were eager to sacrifice the right to Mississippi navigation for their own pet projects; and those who knew the truth of his assertions maintained a discreet silence. When told that the Kentucky delegates would probably hold the key votes on ratification, Congressman Cyrus Griffin assumed the federal cause in his home state was lost, because he knew how Kentucky petitions were manhandled by northern colleagues. In mid-May, Kentuckian John Brown's latest information (at his post in Congress) was that the Constitution "has few or no Supporters in that Country." Some personal acquaintances who were Federalists at first had switched sides, and at a Danville meeting called to consider the Constitution, Brown knew the outcome without hearing it confirmed—another boost for Antifederalists.[19] An almost solid antifederal delegation from the Kentucky country seemed assured.

Little more could have been expected, for the Federalists were on thin ice when the Kentucky statehood question arose. Madison

---

[18] Henry to John Lamb, June 9, 1788, Lamb papers, *NYHS*.
[19] John Brown to Madison, May 12, 1788, Madison papers, *DLC*.

Courtesy of the Library of Congress

GEORGE MASON

Courtesy of the North Carolina Department of Archives and History

WILLIE JONES

and Hamilton agreed on most matters but differed sharply over Kentucky, and Hamilton professed a northerner's prejudice against equal status for that region with its western as well as southern ties. Congressman Brown lost some of his Federalist fervor as he watched northern supporters of the Constitution shut the door on Kentucky. A colleague reported that Kentucky was full of "wrong heads" after "some antifed in Maryland . . . fastened on the Ear of Genl. Wilkinson who was accidentally there and persuaded him that in case of a new Govt. the Navigation of the Mississippi would infallibly be given up."[20] The fact that northern Federalists were hostile to Kentucky statehood was undeniable, and whatever headway Henry and his friends had made for antifederal ideas there was reinforced by the Federalists' dilatory policy.

What became increasingly evident to Federalist and Antifederalist alike as they assembled in New Academy Hall was that a handful of independent delegates would decide the issue. With these men, the Antifederalists laid down a barrage that was unquestionably the most skillful ever employed by opponents of the Constitution in 1787–88. Henry preached the gospel of particularism and of southern rights, while he played on fears of northern domination. Mason carried the theme a bit further by insisting that unconditional ratification was unconditional surrender, a capitulation "so utterly absurd, that I can not think any Man of Sense candid in proposing it." Grayson was given to ridicule. The Constitution was "a most ridiculous piece of business," he had once said, ". . . like the legs of Nebuchandnezar's image . . . formed by jumbling or compressing a number of ideas together, something like the manner in which poems were made in Swift's flying island."[21] Behind this trio of leaders stood a dozen Antifederalists with legislative experience— Theodorick Bland and James Monroe, for example—who lacked the fervor of the three Antifederalist directors. How many of these

[20] John Brown to Madison, June 7, 1788; Hugh Williamson to Madison, June 2, 1788, Madison papers, *DLC*.

[21] Mason to Jefferson, May 26, 1788, 13 *Jefferson Papers* 204–206; William Grayson to William Short, November 10, 1787, Short papers, *DLC*.

participated in the inner circle of Antifederalist strategy is not certain, but the lines of factional discipline were nowhere so rigid as they proved to be in the Richmond convention.

When the debates actually opened and after Pendleton had been chosen president of the convention, the Antifederalists made their first move. It was a calculated risk, based on the assumption that time worked in their favor. The Federalists were also working on the same premise, however, so that a rare display of unanimity followed. Mason moved that the Constitution be considered in that most tedious of all ways—clause by clause, paragraph by paragraph. As delegates on both sides approved the motion, there may have been a few raised eyebrows, but the accord was short-lived. Henry tried to revive charges that the Federal Convention had overstepped its powers by ignoring the original summons to revise the Articles of Confederation. But Pendleton squelched this maneuver by insisting that this was flaying a dead horse—"the people have sent us hither to determine whether this government be proper or not" —and, hence, the fact of their presence made Henry's innuendoes meaningless. Henry, quick to sense a tactical blunder, hurriedly retreated. "Two unlucky circumstances" shook the Antifederalists before the day was over.[22] Randolph came to the end of his meandering course, and news of the South Carolina ratification reached Richmond.

Whatever the Antifederalists thought of Randolph's act of atonement, it took some courage on his part to do what politicians seldom do—admit a past error. Randolph struck at Henry for harping on the beauties of the Confederation. The Confederation, Randolph said, was a farce falling into ruin. The question was simply one of union or no union, and on that basis he was willing to take the Constitution as it stood—without amendments—because "union is the anchor of our political salvation."[23] Eight states had ratified, so that this was no time for surly foot-dragging, but rather an opportunity to fix the cornerstone in place. "I am a friend to the union," Ran-

[22] William Grayson to Nathan Dane, June 4, 1788, Dane papers, *DLC.*
[23] *Debates and Other Proceedings of the Convention of Virginia* (comp. by David Robertson), 30–32.

dolph concluded amidst Federalist jubilation. Perhaps Madison's smile was contrasted by Mason's dour look and sourer view of Randolph's unexpected change of heart. Obviously, the Antifederalists were upset. "Henry & Mason made a lame figure and appeared to take different and awkward ground," was Madison's prejudiced judgment of the first day's proceedings.[24]

News of the South Carolina ratification also put more pressure on the Antifederalists, for with eight states already in line there was a strong psychological urge to join the parade. When the day's business was finished, the Antifederalists hurried into a caucus. "We are alarmed," Grayson confessed, but "we do not despond. The district of Kentucke is with us, & if we can get over the four Counties, which lye on the Ohio between the Pensylvy. line & Big Sandy Creek, the day is our own."[25] Thus Antifederalists looked to that huge northwest corner of Virginia as the pivot of their hopes.

As delegates jostled along the dusty Richmond thoroughfare the next morning, some brandished copies of a Richmond newspaper containing Tench Coxe's timely attack on the Antifederalist position. Previous amendments were impracticable, because those who proposed them had only jumbled ideas about what they wanted, and the cherished amendments "in some States, would meet with as much disapprobation by those [Antifederalists] in others."[26] Since under the Constitution, the *"landed interest* must ever possess a *commanding majority"* in Congress, what legitimate fears had Virginians of northern shipbuilders or bankers? But if Virginia rejects the Constitution, a whole Pandora's box of evils would be opened, with the breakup of the Union a certainty.

Henry was not the type of man daunted by newspaper barbs or yesterday's setbacks. He took his place again, adjusted a brown wig over his thinning hair, and waded into battle with a fresh approach. The Federalist cant was that amendments might be easily adopted, once the Constitution had been ratified, but Henry pointed to all the stumbling blocks the Constitution erected to discourage change.

[24] Madison to Washington, June 4, 1788, Madison papers, *DLC.*
[25] William Grayson to Nathan Dane, June 4, 1788, Dane papers, *DLC.*
[26] Richmond *Virginia Gazette,* June 5, 1788.

A bare majority in four small states might prove so stubborn "that one twentieth part of the American people, may prevent the removal of the most grievous inconveniences and oppression, by refusing to accede to amendments. Is this an easy mode of securing public liberty?" Turning to the urgent pleas for energetic government, Henry doubted whether the Constitution would muster "sufficient energy" to hold a far-flung consolidated government together. Henry was impatient with those who insisted that regional interests were protected by a system of checks and balances in the Constitution. A system lacking republican principles left no reins in local hands. "What avail your specious, imaginary balances, your rope-dancing, chain-rattling, ridiculous ideal checks and contrivances?" Henry charged that the Federalists had maneuvered the Constitution through other state conventions with unseeming haste even though "a great majority of the people even in the adopting states" were antifederal. "Pennsylvania has *perhaps* been tricked into it. If the other states who have adopted it, have not been tricked, still they were too much hurried into its adoption."[27] Thus the Constitution came to Virginia as the handiwork of a usurping body, stamped with the features of a monarchical, consolidated government, and handed to them after eight states had been cajoled into ratification.

It was a typical Henry performance, the kind he gave at intervals for almost three weeks. Randolph tried to check Henry's meandering course by observing that these daylong orations would prolong the convention until it would become an endurance contest. "If we go on in this irregular manner," Randolph chided, ". . . instead of three or six weeks, it will take us six months to decide this question." Mason seems to have had more energy than usual, too. "Every piece of address is going on privately to work on the local interests and prejudices" of the uncommitted delegates, Madison complained. Grayson said little in the convention but kept busy writing letters, bending ears, and caucusing with other Antifederalists. Before the first week was over, the Antifederalists had recovered from the shocks of Randolph's defection and the South Carolina ratification. The great question mark hung over the heads of "seven or eight

[27] Robertson, *Debates of the Virginia Convention*, 45–46, 49, 55–56.

dubious characters, whose opinions are not known," Grayson informed well-wishers in New York.[28]

So close did the contest seem that propositions which might have been termed ludicrous a few months earlier seemed to make sense. "Denatus" posed the dilemma before delegates by declaring that ratification without amendments would be ruinous, but outright rejection would end in disunion. The safest course was to adopt a set of amendments, hand them over to Washington, and let him choose the proper ones. Washington would certainly take "the natural rights of mankind" into account, and "whether his amendments would agree with speculative reasoning, or not, his name [would go far] to sanctify the whole."[29] Antifederalist leaders had no intention of relying on the goodness of Washington's heart or on the charity of any other Federalist. Gouverneur Morris, an able judge of men and political currents, granted that Henry's oratory could "stir Men's Blood," but believed eloquence was no match for Federalist truth. Thus Morris was hardly discouraged. "My Religion steps in where my Understanding falters," he vowed, "and I feel faith as I lose Confidence."[30]

Confident or not, both factions tried to put up bold fronts. Outside of Randolph, who was "reprobated by the honest of both sides," the delegates played at the game of tallying votes in high spirits. Staunch Antifederalist Theodorick Bland saw the convention evenly divided with "one half of her crew hoisting sail for the land of *energy,* and the other looking with a longing aspect on the shore of *liberty.*" His "one ray of hope" was that both Federalists and Antifederalists were "in perfectly good humour with each other." Bland was fairly certain that the Antifederalists had enough votes for pushing through previous amendments and had "drawn many doubtful minds to our side of the question." Every delegate who thought it imprudent "to mount a highblooded, fiery steed, without a bridle" was invited to join them. "The issue will depend greatly on the

[28] Madison to Washington, June 4, 1788, Madison papers, *DLC;* William Grayson to John Lamb, June 9, 1788, Lamb papers, *NYHS.*

[29] *Virginia Independent Chronicle,* June 11, 1788.

[30] Gouverneur Morris to Hamilton, June 13, 1788, Hamilton papers, *DLC.*

management on both sides, and mere fortuitous events, as in all cases where forces are nearly equal," Bland concluded.[31]

After the preliminary skirmishing for position, the Antifederalists opened an offensive barrage that was intended to breach resistance to previous amendments. Encouraged by reports from New York that Clinton's party was unalterably opposed to unconditional ratification, every Antifederalist resource was used to exploit fears of overbearing northern interests. Nothing brought the point home better than the Mississippi question. Henry kept goading the Federalists on the touchy issue, knowing that it was a major weakness in the appeals for union. For in Henry's mind union simply meant that the stronger northern states could outvote the South. When Monroe gave an accurate account of the whole torturous Jay-Gardoqui negotiations, as well as the reaction of Congress to Jay's report, it seemed clear that northern politicians had been quite willing to put up southern stakes in their gamble for Spanish trade. Monroe reminded the Richmond convention that the northern delegates had a positive dread of an expanding West that might ally itself politically with the South. "The northern states would not fail of availing themselves of the opportunity given them by the constitution, of relinquishing that river, in order to depress the western country, and prevent the southern interest from perponderating." The style was a little florid, but Kentuckians saw the point. If there were doubts, however, Grayson moved in to make Federalists squirm even more. Grayson went beyond Monroe in depicting the northern delegates as conniving men bent on exalting their seafaring economy at southern expense. "Their language has been———," said Grayson, " *'Let us prevent any new states from rising in the western world, or they will outvote us . . . we will lose our importance, and become as nothing . . . . If we do not prevent it, our countrymen will remove to those places, instead of going to sea, and we will have no particular tribute, or advantage from them.'* "[32] The Federalists had charged that Henry and his friends were "scuffling for Kentucky votes," so Henry put the question to his opponents. What proof

[31] Theodorick Bland to Arthur Lee, June 13, 1788, Lee, *Life of Lee*, II, 337–39.
[32] Robertson, *Debates of the Virginia Convention*, 238–49.

had they that the Mississippi would *not* be offered as bait by the North for a favorable treaty with Spain? None could be offered, Henry insisted, so the status of the West was left a cipher. As well might Virginians throw their Kentucky brethren "into the arms of Spain."

Mason or Grayson relieved Henry occasionally, but it was difficult to keep him off his feet. The Federalists spent far more time answering Henry's arguments than they cared to, but there was no way to hurry matters along. After more than a week of verbal jostling, Madison analyzed the course of the debate and concluded that the taxation power of Congress and the jurisdiction of federal courts were the festers which the Antifederalist surgeons probed with blunt instruments. The portion of seats allotted to Virginia in the first Congress nettled some delegates, while others backed Mason when he returned to that favored theme of a two-thirds majority in Congress for regulating trade. "Besides these," Madison added, "the Mississippi, the Indiana claim, with some other local matters were made a great handle of, particularly out of doors where the chief mischief is effected." The great Antifederalist hope, so Madison speculated, was to delay matters until word of a federal setback in the New York convention could arrive at a dramatic moment. Barring that kind of miracle, the Antifederalist strategy seemed to turn on "previous amendments which is preferable game." "If we have a majority at all," Madison confessed, "it does not exceed three or four." To watchful, waiting Rufus King, the Federalist factotum was candid—the outcome was as "ticklish as can be conceived."[33] If defeat came, "Kentucke will be the cause."

The Antifederalists were equally nervous and skittish about reaching anything with the appearance of a showdown vote. Grayson, looking at the "ticklish situation" (he was in agreement with Madison on the descriptive adjectives, if nothing else), thought the key vote still rested in the four upper counties. From the Kentucky delegation there had been a few defectors, but thirteen men from beyond

[33] Madison to Washington, June 13, 1788; Madison to Rufus King, June 13, 15, 1788, Madison papers, *DLC;* Madison to Hamilton, June 16, 1788, Hamilton papers, *DLC.*

the mountains seemed firm Antifederalists. "I believe it is absolutely certain that we have got 80 votes on our side which are inflexible, and that eight persons are still fluctuating & undecided," was Grayson's analysis on June 18.

Considering all the circumstances, Grayson's accuracy was uncanny. The pressure to end the convention was mounting—crops needed tending, the legislature was going to reconvene, and each day added to expenses that for some delegates were a considerable burden. With a week left, the Antifederalists knew what they must do—find five more votes. So the "scuffling" went on in Richmond while Henry and his friends speculated on affairs in Poughkeepsie, and perhaps envied Governor Clinton with his comfortable majority.

✫ XIII ✫
"The Union Is Preserved"

GOVERNOR CLINTON and his political cohorts were northern men who still spoke Patrick Henry's language. Events in the early summer raised some doubts, however, whether the Clinton crowd really understood each other. No political body had ever assembled in the United States with a more obvious caste of mind than the delegates who converged on Poughkeepsie. Yet the outcome has puzzled historians and confused observers of political behavior. About the only certainty arising from the New York convention of 1788 is the strengthened generalization that the Antifederalists were inept and disorganized. In New York, the state where the Antifederalists organization seemed the most promising, disunity was appallingly evident from the outset of the Poughkeepsie proceedings.

Federalists did all they could to make the roads from each county courthouse to Poughkeepsie as bumpy as possible. The political maneuver which held the greatest promise had been noisome attacks on the Clintonians as the party of disunion. Hamilton, trumpeting the warning in "Publius, No. 1," never tired of using antifederalism and disunion as synonyms. Considerable effort was made to place the New York Antifederalists on the defensive as entrenched local politicians who would willingly rip the Union asunder rather than give up their petty places of power. Clinton's known propensities toward local controls led an opponent to declare that the governor really wanted the United States cut into three parts with "three times the officers, and three times the expense of the proposed plan." "*If the union is preserved*" then Britain and Spain would offer the infant republic no threat, "*but if it should be divided into three parts*, European politics would soon play off *one* [section] against another."[1] Antifederalists apparently desired either a flabby confederation or no union at all. Despairing St. John Crevecour in New York was

[1] Portsmouth *New Hampshire Spy*. November 16, 1787.

certain that in Virginia "all the Satires of Mr. Henry" would be used "to break & split the union," and if "Mr. Henry Triumph[s] be assured that this highly antifederal States, will refuse it also."[2]

If the Antifederalists had such a scheme in contemplation, they discreetly kept it out of their correspondence. General Lamb's endeavors were on behalf of a unified demand for prior amendments to the Constitution. In his letters North and South, Lamb never went further than to propose the use of "our best endeavours to procure amendments to the System previous to its adoption." After New Hampshire had ratified, dejected Joshua Atherton tried to put props under New York Antifederalists by suggesting that they drag their feet as much as possible in forming the new government, but Atherton only wanted more concessions from the opposition. Assuming the worst, Atherton speculated on the possibility that Virginia might also ratify, and asked rhetorically if New York should not then "do the same, and throw her whole weight into the new Congress on the side of proper Amendments?" Atherton's own solution was for New York to do nothing, for "her wholy standing out will have the most Weight"; in short New York could play coy and wrest a compromise from the Federalists on some of the concessions Antifederalists desired. Indeed, cries of "Union!" had a hollow ring for Lamb's friends who saw in Federalist ranks "some of the most selfish avericious, [*sic*] Narrow contracted set of Mortals that now exist in these thirteen disunited States."[3]

During the interval between the elections and the convention, New York Antifederalists assumed that amendments would be offered as a condition for ratification. Abraham Lansing tempered his delight over the outcome at the polls with a word of caution about the amendments. Lansing asked Yates to send any proposed alterations "under Cover to me, by a Skipper who has the Character of an *Honest Man and is Anti*—Disappointed Federalists will do any thing." Yates' seat in the Continental Congress gave him a good observation post but also subjected him to pressures, since he was

2 St. John Crevecour to William Short, June 10, 1788, Short papers, *DLC*.
3 Joshua Atherton to John Lamb, June 23, 1788; Hugh Ledlie to John Lamb, January 15, 1788, Lamb papers, *NYHS*.

surrounded by Federalists who considered Manhattan their bastion. While the congressmen killed time, waiting for more delegations to appear so that business could proceed, Hamilton hinted to Yates that the Antifederalists ought to settle for recommendatory amendments. When Yates denounced an unqualified ratification as "an absurdity," Hamilton asserted that the alternative was a splintered Union. Yates seemed unimpressed. "I told him I would be exceeding sorry of that," the Antifederalist remarked, "but rather than to adopt the Constitution I would Risk a government of Jew, turk or Infidel." The stubborn attitude of the Antifederalists drew continual scorn from the opposition. "N York will accede with the worst possible grace," one of Yates' colleagues predicted, "I think she will be bullied into it."[4]

Clinton had the Federalists guessing, but unfortunately the governor and his friends were guessing, too. Weary Joshua Atherton looked longingly to the New York crowd as the last hope of antifederalism. "To you perhaps our America must owe the indelible Honor of chaining and reducing within proper Bounds this young Lion," Atherton pleaded.[5]

The basic weakness of the New York Antifederalists seems to have been their lack of alternatives. Clinton apparently had great faith in the scheme for an antifederal entente between Virginia and New Hampshire. Suddenly, the events in Concord revealed that his alliance there was a phantom. Reports from the South boded ill. No matter how much Clinton whistled in the dark, he found himself in a political quagmire because he and his friends had not expected this sudden collapse of the antifederal cause. Perplexed and confused, the Clintonians tried to plot their next move. The result was that they did very little. Even Federalists could see that the huge Antifederalist majority—good as it looked on paper—might be meaningless. "I cannot find that they have so looked forward to contingent Events, or even to those the most probable, as to have

---

[4] A. G. Lansing to Yates, June 1, 1788, Yates to Lansing, May 28, 1788, Yates papers, *NYPL*; Samuel A. Otis to George Thatcher, March 18, 1788, *Historical Magazine*, Vol. VI, 2nd Series, 346.

[5] Joshua Atherton to John Lamb, June 23, 1788, Lamb papers, *NYHS*.

united in or formed any System adapted to them," the analytical Jay reported.[6] Plainly, the Antifederalists trooped off toward Poughkeepsie more disorganized and more distressed than they cared to admit.

The public image of the Clintonians, however, was still one of great strength. No Federalist brow was more furrowed than Hamilton's, for he believed that despite a certain aimless drift amongst the opposition, there was a consistent thread in their hostility toward a federal union. Hamilton drew a picture in murky hues for Madison, well knowing that his friend would make good use of it in Richmond among the wavering. "For my own part the more I can penetrate the views of the Antifederal party in this State," Hamilton observed, "the more I dread the consequences of the non adoption of the Constitution by any of the other States, [and] the more I fear an eventual disunion and civil war. God grant that Virginia may accede. This example will have a safe influence on our politics." Increasingly, Hamilton insisted that the Virginia convention could either assure ratification or bring on delay and defeat.

While Hamilton cast anxious glances southward, his opponents showed equal concern over Virginia affairs. A confidential letter drafted by Lamb's committee early in June made it plain that the New York Antifederalists expected support from Richmond in their drive for amendments. The long-delayed message from the Virginia assembly had beckoned concerted action. There was nothing inflammatory in Lamb's message, which was rather a dispassionate plea for unity so that "the obnoxious and exceptionable parts in the new System would be so changed as to create Confidence in it." All the Antifederalists still deliberating the Constitution were asked to join "in some rational plan to procure such amendments as would preserve the strictest union with, and affection between, sister States." The alarms over disunion appear to have been only Federalist concoctions. The New York Antifederalists asked for nothing more than either moral support or concerted action in their efforts to call a second amending convention. As even Hamilton was privately forced to admit, the Clintonians were not as reckless with the Union

[6] John Jay to Washington, May 29, 1788, *DHC*, IV, 643.

as he sometimes made it appear. "The object of the [Antifederalist] party at present is undoubtedly conditional amendments," he told Madison in late June.[7]

The Federalists fretted privately while they publicly professed little alarm over the election results. General Knox considered the Antifederalists "obstinate and artful." "They will not probably have the hardihood to openly reject the constitution should Virginia adopt it," he added, "but they will adjourn to a distant day."[8] Someone close to Clinton had been indiscreet. It was common knowledge among Federalists that the opposition might try to shove through an adjournment to some indefinite date. To forestall this plan, Federalists decided to exploit the Union issue through such good news from Concord or Richmond as came to hand.

When the Poughkeepsie convention opened on June 17, Antifederalists hoped that friends in New Hampshire and Virginia would furnish them with levers to pry major concessions from the Federalists. At the end of the first day a jubilant Antifederalist surveyed the scene with delight. "The Numbers of the Anties astonish the Federalists and they look on their Case as desperate," he observed. A day later, all went well. "Unanimity and Harmony reigns among the Anties—the Promptitude with which they assembled—their Concurrence in Sentiment and their Determination to bend their Force to the same Point are the highest evidences thereof —and shut out the shadow of Hope, in the Federalists, of creating Divisions."[9] However, a Federalist observer wrote a conflicting account. He thought the Antifederalists were embarrassed by their predicament. "I believe they do not know what to do," Kent reported, although he had heard rumors that some of Clinton's friends promised not to vote against the Constitution.[10] Neither side was in a hurry. When the Federalists knew they had a majority, they

---

[7] Draft of letter from Federal Republican committee to friends in Virginia, June 6, 1788, Lamb papers, *NYHS;* Hamilton to Madison, June 21, 1788, Madison papers, *DLC.*

[8] Knox to O. H. Williams, June 11, 1788, Williams papers, Maryland Historical Society.

[9] James Hughes to John Lamb, June 17, 1788, Lamb papers, *NYHS.*

[10] James Kent to Robert Troup, June 20, 1788, Miscellaneous papers, *NYHS.*

would quickly press for a vote on ratification; and when they were uncertain of their chances or knew an outright majority was against them, they would inch along by requesting a clause-by-clause debate. This had been their strategy in Massachusetts, in Virginia, and now it was to be followed in New York. In the name of moderation, the Antifederalists had gone along with the proposal—usually because they had nothing better to offer themselves. Prolonged debate might not turn up any new ideas, but it would delay matters until results of the other conventions arrived.

While in debate, the Federalists built their case on the firmament of the Union, but truculent Antifederalists warned that they would not be bullied into ratification. Melancton Smith assured them that the Antifederalists were not afraid of "a war with our neighbors" if that was the alternative to unconditional ratification. In dismay, Hamilton followed and pictured the woe that would befall the state if it left the Union. Hamilton noted that the nation was a conglomerate of sectional interests and divergent groups, but despite the clashes of sections and states, compromises had taken place in the Federal Convention; and nothing better could be expected if another were called together. "Let a convention be called tomorrow; let them meet twenty times,—nay, twenty thousand times," Hamilton warned the proponents of a second convention, "they will have the same difficulties to encounter, the same clashing interests to reconcile." The whole point of the Constitution, Hamilton argued, was to preserve the rights of states and still "answer all the purposes of the Union."[11] Not always the best reader of the political barometer, Hamilton's judgment was improving. "Our arguments confound, but do not convince," he reported. "Some of the leaders, however, appear to be convinced by *circumstances*, and to be desirous of a retreat." The smugness of the Antifederalists was disappearing as Hamilton even detected "an air of moderation" pervading the convention. A bitter opponent confirmed Hamilton's opinion. "The Spirit of Moderation Prevails," Antifederalist Henry Oouthoudt noted, "how long uncertain."[12]

[11] Elliot, *Debates*, II, 236, 239.

Actually, the Antifederalists had persuaded themselves that in a clause-by-clause debate they could convince Federalists of the need for amendments. Robert Yates left the convention hall, confident of the Antifederalist majority, and sent George Mason an explanation of their strategy. A lengthy debate would do no harm, Mason was assured, because of "the Steadiness of our Friends," and would moreover "prevent the Opposition from charging us with Precipitation." The Clintonians had also taken a hard look at the situation in Virginia and decided that the Antifederalists there would probably fail. Otherwise, Yates told Mason, there might have been some point in opening a correspondence between the two conventions, but "the doubtful Chance of your obtaining a Majority" made this appear fruitless. Still the New York Antifederalists asserted that it was their "fixed Determination to not adopt the present Constitution without previous Amendments."[13]

The Antifederalists' complacency was a tonic for Hamilton and his friends. Their best work came after the convention adjourned each day, talking in friendly fashion to Antifederalists in the hallway or on the staircases "and pressing their point." Lamb's son-in-law shuffled through the Dutchess County courthouse with only a scowl for Hamilton. "You would be surprised, did you not know the Man, what an *amazing* Republican Hamilton wishes to make himself be considered—*But he is known.*" What bothered the Antifederalists was not Hamilton's chameleon-like qualities, but rather his successes. Clinton and his friends privately joked that Hamilton was giving them a warmed-over version of *Publius,* but the governor added that this "second Edition of Publius, [was] well delivered." While the Antifederalists were wary of Hamilton, they found John Jay more friendly and, one is tempted to say, less of a hypocrite. Jay's "manners and mode of address would probably do much mischief, were the members not as firm as they are," was the report

[12] Hamilton to Madison, June 19, 1788, *DHC,* IV, 713; Henry Oothoudt to A. Yates, June 21, 1788, Yates papers, *NYPL.*

[13] Robert Yates to George Mason, June 25, 1788, Emmet collection, *NYPL.*

Lamb heard.[14] An informal group headed by Yates also tried its hand at drafting amendments that might be used as the basis of their formal proposals. "We have had no Committee to draft Amendments," Yates admitted to Mason, but he sent the Virginian "a Copy of those which many of us have agreed to." It would seem that the Antifederalists hardly took the business seriously. Clinton sent a set of the reworked proposals to Lamb in New York, asking him to examine them with care since "there was not time to do it as the sloop is going." Federalists heard with delight that their opponents were tinkering with some amendment proposals, but "cannot agree amongst themselves. It is therefore possible that this Circumstance may create a Division in favor of the Foederalists."[15]

Antifederalists who were some distance from Poughkeepsie saw the political crisis with more clarity than those on the scene. Abraham Lansing had feared that the Clintonians would be ensnared by the Federalists in the clause-by-clause debate. Although too late with his warning, Lansing correctly foresaw that "the Federal Gentlemen will no doubt avail themselves" of this plan "and procrastinate the Business as long as they possibly can."[16] He pointed out that delegates from farms could hardly spare long weeks away from their crops and fields. Moreover, the Federalists had repeatedly proved that they were better manipulators than their adversaries. "The determination of Massachusetts has shewn us what Federal Chicanery can Effect." Prudent Antifederalists must have agreed that after a thumping victory at the polls, their leaders seemed disposed toward dilatory tactics rather than decisive action. Their misgivings about a prompt adjournment, which probably would have sent the Federalists into a panic, increased as each day passed.

Meanwhile Federalist newspapers kept up a propaganda barrage aimed at weakening the Clintonians' resolve. Federalist writers insisted that the alternative to ratification was political ostracism. "This question alone will be for them to decide upon—*Will New York*

14 C. Tillinghast to John Lamb, June 21, 1788, Lamb papers, *NYHS*.

15 Clinton to Lamb, June 21, 1788, Lamb papers, *NYHS*; Robert Yates to George Mason, June 25, 1788, Emmet collection, *NYPL*; William Duer to Madison, June 23, 1788, Madison papers, *DLC*.

16 A. G. Lansing to A. Yates, June 22, 1788, Yates papers, *NYPL*.

withdraw from the union?" If the Poughkeepsie delegates rashly voted against the Constitution, the future of New York would be indeed dismal. "She will in that case be surrounded by enemies— made such by herself." More blunt was "a gentleman of the first distinction," who told New Englanders that "although there is a majority of the mynheers against it at present, the *policy* of New-York will be an adjournment, until they see what other states do— and with the property, *landed* and *commercial*, of the State against them, the majority I think will be wrought upon."[17]

The temporary excitement caused by arrival of the New Hampshire report subsided, with the Antifederalists apparently unmoved. A congressman who was visiting Poughkeepsie told colleagues the news from Concord had "made no impression on the Convention at all." This dismayed the Federalists, who fell back on their old hope "that the anties will not agree among themselves." Pushing the idea that the convention was only empowered to adopt or reject the Constitution, several Federalists tried to rule out any possibility of amendments. Abraham Yates winced at such reasoning and noted that "the federal gentlemen had the most Extraordinary talents of swallowing Cammels [*sic*] themselves and Recomm[endin]g others to stick at nats [*sic*]."[18] Yates told Clinton even an adjournment would be risky, for delays might give Federalists "a farther opportunity to shew their dexterity at management" or wavering Antifederalists, and meanwhile keep the state "in one Continual Convulsion."

So the convention debates droned on, with both parties willing to postpone a decisive vote. Obviously, Hamilton and Clinton were trying to outwait rather than outwit each other. Though some of his closest friends conceded Virginia to the Federalists, Clinton banked on help from Henry in the form of a long list of conditional amendments. Clinton must have hoped that these amendments would arrive while he still held the whip hand, so that they could be pushed through the New York convention as proof of Antifed-

[17] Providence *United States Chronicle*, June 19, 26, 1788.

[18] A. Yates to G. Clinton, June 27, 1788; Henry Oothoudt to A. Yates, June 27, 1788, Yates papers, *NYPL*.

eralist solidarity and determination. Hamilton waited for news of another vein. Hamilton's entreaties to Madison showed that he regarded the Virginia vote as a decisive force in his own convention. Clinton was too firm. He would never budge, but his cronies were made of softer mettle. "Should Verginia adopt and wether they will or not is problematical then there will be New exclamations," shrewd Abraham Yates noted. "Can our State stand alone? Is our State wiser than all the Rest &ca. if that storm is wethered I suppose they will see that it will be in vain to throw any farther Obstecles in the way and they will soon finish."[19] For once, Yates and Hamilton were in agreement.

During this war of nerves, both sides showed signs of extreme exasperation. John Lansing engaged Hamilton in a bitter debate that went beyond the bounds of decorum. "They both got extremely warm," an eyewitness reported, "insomuch that Lansing was charged by the other with want of candor & indecency." Finally, Oouthoudt stopped the episode by ruling in favor of an adjournment. The incident was so disagreeable both sides soon wanted to forget it. Following that wild scene, General Samuel Webb had mournful news for his Federalist friends in New York. "We have not the most distant prospect that our Convention will adopt the New Constitution," he moaned.[20] After two weeks of debate the count still remained at forty-six to nineteen with the Clintonians and "their troops (a set of ignorant Dutchmen) under perfect command . . . they begin to grow abusive."

What seemed to be the Antifederalists' finest hour was, however, the last bit of glory left to them. They proposed amendments restricting a standing army, curbing the taxing powers of Congress, and checking other designated evils in the Constitution. The tone of the Hamilton-Lansing exchange was resumed after the Sabbath recess, with personal remarks crossing the room so frequently that Smith ironically observed that "in theatrical exhibitions, the farce succeeds the tragedy." That same afternoon the farce was indeed

19 A. Yates to A. G. Lansing, June 29, 1788, Yates papers, *NYPL.*

20 Samuel Webb to J. Barrell, June 1 [2], 1788, Webb Papers, Yale University Library; Christopher Yates to A. Yates, June 30, 1788, Yates papers, *NYPL.*

over, for the express rider galloped into Poughkeepsie with dispatches from Richmond. The Antifederalist tragedy was complete. "We hope it may have the desired affect," a pessimistic Federalist grumbled, "but *I doubt*." Although it seemed that a miracle would be needed to pull fifteen or twenty Antifederalists away from Clinton's coattails, a force more powerful than all of the governor's patronage was at work—political realism. More than a dozen men elected as Antifederalists began speculating about the political future when the news from Richmond was confirmed. Their consolation was that they had not budged until their allies elsewhere had collapsed.

Ratification by Virginia ended all serious resistance to the Constitution. Madison had hit upon a scheme that would pacify the opposition. On June 18 it appeared that the Richmond convention was to reach a climax, with the handful of wavering members ready to swing toward any conciliatory proposition. Although Henry disclaimed any desire to break up the Union, that notion had been implanted in too many minds to be easily disregarded. On the other hand, the Federalists themselves conceded that the Constitution was far from perfect. To guide these uncertain delegates between Scylla and Charybdis, Madison exercised a marvelous sense of timing. Working with key Federalists, Madison led them from the "all-or-nothing" position, which threatened to flounder their cause, by suggesting compromises. Madison and his friends moved among the delegations seeking support for their new approach. They expressed a willingness "to preface the ratification with some plain & general truths that can not affect the validity of the Act,"—in short, a bill of rights—and promised to recommend a few other alterations "as objects to be pursued in the constitutional mode." The spirit of compromise, Madison explained, was "rendered prudent by the nice balance of numbers, and the scruples entertained by some who are in general well affected."[21]

While Madison searched for a means to sugar-coat the pill, Henry and Mason spent their time trying to make the Constitution more

[21] Madison to Rufus King, June 22, 1788, King, *Life of King*, I, 336–37.

distasteful. Since their first loyalty was to Virginia, they directed their appeals to local passion, pride, and power. The threat of British debt collections, the precarious titles of western land claims, and a score of other problems that vexed Virginians were exploited by Antifederalists, who insisted that they could only be handled fairly by Virginia lawmakers and administrators. One "well-wisher of Government" called for an involved method that would allow state legislatures to invalidate federal laws, subject to the review of a "Supreme Censorial Court."[22] Madison was nudged closer to a conciliatory frame of mind by Antifederalist onslaughts on the proposed judiciary. The power to try cases between citizens of different states, along with jurisdiction over "cases antecedent to the Constitution, such as British debts, and an apprehended revival of the Fairfax-Indiana-Vandalia &c. claims are also brought into view in all the terrific colours which imagination can give them." The fourteen delegates from Kentucky were courted by both factions with charges and countercharges flying thick-and-fast. "These Gentlemen will determine the fate of America," Henry Knox decided. With a watchful eye cocked toward Richmond, Knox found only a glimmer of hope in every scrap of information. "The best fruit at present from that quarter is that Mason is angry," Knox observed.[23]

Mason had little reason to be happy. He had spent hours arguing that the federal courts would force litigants to travel hundreds of miles to distant trials. He had warned delegates that Englishmen would sue for old claims and have their judgments enforced "by the *ultima ratio regum*"—presumably a federal bayonet. Mason predicted that "all that of country between the Blue Ridge and the Alleghany mountains, will be claimed, and probably recovered in the federal court, from the present possessors," if the Constitution were ratified unaltered. But for all of Mason's oratory, which was in fact based on a lifelong study of the land statutes, Madison turned away wrath with a soft answer. Madison admitted that the

[22] "A well-wisher of Government," *Virginia Independent Chronicle*, June 18, 1788.

[23] Madison to Hamilton, June 20, 1788, Hamilton papers, *DLC*; Knox to Colonel Wadsworth, June 22, 1788, Knox papers, *MHS*; Knox to Rufus King, June 19, 1788, King, *Life of King*, I, 336.

judiciary clause "might be better expressed" and needed alterations. But, he added, all the dreaded predictions that Mason pictured were based on "ifs," which might dissolve in the air—"the dangers he has pointed out do not necessarily follow. . . . if we take a liberal construction."[24]

With the end of the weary convention in sight, Henry made the Antifederalist position clear. "If previous amendments are not obtained, the trial by jury is gone: British debtors will be ruined by being dragged to the federal court—and the liberty and happiness of our citizens gone—never again to be recovered." This brought a quick reply from the Federalists, who charged that Henry "means to frighten us by his bugbears and hobgoblings." Federalists also were shocked when Mason predicted that armed resistance would inevitably come unless amendments were agreed upon; unqualified adoption of the Constitution would lead to "awful consequences." Madison interpreted Mason's mood as one of utter hopelessness. "Col: Mason . . . talked in a style which no other sentiment could have produced."[25]

High-strung Henry Lee gained the floor and scolded the Antifederalists for their hints of civil discord. If civil war did ensue, Lee rejoined, who would be accountable? "Such speeches within these walls, from a character so venerable and estimable, easily progress into overt acts, among the less thinking and vicious," Lee cautioned.[26] Thus raw edges of personal feelings were exposed in the tense debates. Mason, disclaiming any personal desire for violence, mumbled his determination to go along with the majority vote, "whatever it might be." Henry made an effort to "gloss [over] what had fallen from his friend," and "declared his aversion to the Constitution to be such, that he could not take the oath; but that he would remain in peaceable submission to the result."[27] There was nothing to be gained by further debate. The course of speeches had meandered into the quicksand of rude insults.

[24] Robertson, *Debates of the Virginia Convention*, 372–77.
[25] *Ibid.*, 414, 418; Madison to Washington, June 23, 1788, Madison papers, *DLC*.
[26] Robertson, *Debates of the Virginia Convention*, 420–26.
[27] Madison to Washington, June 23, 1788, Madison papers, *DLC*.

Out of sheer exasperation and exhaustion, then, the Virginia convention came to a quick denouement. Madison's discernment of the situation was clinically correct. He thought the wild speech of Mason's, and Henry's follow-up, "seemed to betray despair." Antifederalist confidence had been drained away, to be replaced by doubts and anxiety. As their courage ebbed, the Federalists' mounted. The following morning found them ready with a plan to end the debate by an immediate vote on ratification. To bait the hook for undecided delegates, Chancellor Wythe explained that the Federalists would support a list of amendments, provided they were recommendatory rather than conditional. Henry quickly denounced the proposal and offered a counterproposal—a list of amendments which would be circulated among the states for their approval prior to a final ratification. Virginia had been a prime mover in the whole business, Henry contended, and any action she proposed would gain a wide acceptance. The language of free men was *"till you remove the defects we will not accede."*[28] A headlong rush to ratify now, he warned, would leave a restless opposition. Among other things, Virginians might consider how the Constitution would jeopardize their slave holdings. "The majority of congress is to the north, and the slaves are to the south." Federalists talked about preserving the Union. "I fear you will have no union, unless you remove the cause of opposition," Henry concluded.

The last day of debating was climaxed by Henry's lashing speech directed at Randolph, whose defection rankled the Antifederalists all the more because he insisted on being so active. Henry tried to make Randolph's arguments look threadbare. The wind outside began to howl while Henry spoke, taking alternate verbal jabs at Randolph and the Constitution. The skies darkened as Henry continued, and master showman that he was, Henry began to paint a word picture of "the awful immensity of the dangers" in the Constitution. Lightning crashed outside as Henry told the delegates that some unseen power was participating in their affairs, looking down anxiously upon them to learn whether they would bring "consequent happiness or misery" to mankind.[29] Then came more lightning, as

[28] Robertson, *Debates of Virginia Convention*, 420–26.

Henry furnished his own verbal storm. A bolt struck so near the Academy that the building shook, windows rattled, and "put the house in such disorder, that Mr. Henry was obliged to conclude." There could be no vote on the Constitution that day.

The next morning the weather was calm, even though the delegates on Shockoe Hill were not. Benjamin Harrison, James Monroe, John Tyler—the lesser lights among the Antifederalists—tried to keep the opposition at bay. Mason was sullen, while Henry bided his time. James Innes summed up the Federalist position with a stirring appeal to the delegates' memories. During the Revolution the localism which now seemed so rampant had been smothered by wartime expediency. Rather than hold that "the northern oppression will fetter, and manacle the hands of the southern people," Innes continued, he held a brotherly affection for other sections and above all for the Union. If Virginia insisted on previous amendments, other states would assume that the *"ancient dominion"* was trying to dictate terms to them.[30] Innes' speech brought the convention to a critical point. Henry, in a sportsmanlike gesture, praised Innes for his "great eloquence—eloquence splendid, magnificent and sufficient to shake the human mind!" Nevertheless, Henry said, his political faith was not shaken. Subsequent amendments secured no rights, because they left the dearest liberties of mankind to Federalist whims. Henry accused the Federalists of double talk. "Their view is to defeat every attempt to amend," he charged.

Suddenly, Henry's mood changed. He spoke as a man who fought without hope. If the Antifederalists lost, he said, he would not attempt to stir unrest among the people. "My head, my hand, and my heart shall be at liberty to retrieve the loss of liberty, and remove the defects of that system, in a constitutional way." Mason was gloomy and speechless.

The Antifederalists then moved Henry's motion for previous amendments ahead of Wythe's proposal for unqualified ratification. Grayson's diagnosis of the Antifederalists' problem proved painfully

[29] *Ibid.*, 445–46; William Wirt, *Sketches of the Life and Character of Patrick Henry*, 313.
[30] Robertson, *Debates of the Virginia Convention*, 451–55.

correct. The balance would be tipped by a few delegates from the Allegheny country. The southern tier and the Kentucky delegates sided with Henry, while the Tidewater and northern counties went Federalist. But the delegates from the region between the Shenandoah Valley and the upper Ohio voted as a Federalist bloc. Grayson had warned the Antifederalists, and yet they had been able to make few friends in this Allegheny delegation. Only five converts would have given them victory. The vote of eighty-eight nays to eighty ayes showed how close the Virginia Antifederalists came to a staggering upset. In an atmosphere of mingled relief and disappointment, Wythe's motion passed by a ten-vote margin.

For Henry, Mason, and the other Antifederalist leaders, the whole affair must have seemed like a bad dream. A few hours later, the Antifederalists were searching for an honorable avenue of retreat from their humiliating loss. Most Federalists saw no harm in granting concessions that had more form than meaning. Henry, Mason, Grayson, and a few other Antifederalists were named to a committee that had the perfunctory business of re-introducing the amendments Henry had brought in earlier. Their main job came in replacing "previous" with the harmless word "recommended." "The Decision has been distressing & awful to great Numbers," disappointed Spencer Roane reported.[31] In contrast with the celebrations in Philadelphia and Boston, where tavern rounds, the firing of muskets, and bonfires and merriment had been the order of the day, the Richmond streets were quiet. "There is no rejoicing on account of the Vote for ratification—it would not be prudent to do so," Roane explained, "and the federalists behave with moderation and do not exult in their success." In all likelihood, prudent Federalists were still a bit wary. It was not like Henry or Mason to take defeat gracefully. When the committee on amendments met the next day, there was a warm discussion over one proposal that curbed the power of Congress to levy direct taxes. The whole loaf had been lost, but this the Antifederalists salvaged in bringing out the committee report essentially in the form that Henry had first introduced the forty

[31] Spencer Roane to [?], June 26, 1788, Emmett collection, *NYPL*; Monroe to Jefferson, July 12, 1788, 13 *Jefferson Papers* 351–53.

alterations. The first part was a bill of rights, while the later twenty proposals ranged from prohibitions on a standing army to Mason's darling scheme to prevent a northern shipping monopoly.[32]

On the final day Federalists made a feeble attempt to deny their adversaries a consolation prize. Upset by the tone of the proposal on direct taxes, Federalists rallied around George Nicholas as he called for a vote to strike the obnoxious article. With Edmund Pendleton leading the way, enough Federalists saw no real harm in making this gesture, however, and the Antifederalists recorded their lone triumph only seconds before the convention adjourned.

Before the last vote on adjournment, Mason showed that he still had some fight left. He suggested that the Antifederalists meet in a public building and prepare "an address to reconcile the minds of their constituents to the new plan of government." Madison was suspicious, for he doubted that Henry and Mason would really work for something that was "of a peace making complexion." "I suspect the plan [of the Antifederalists] will be to engage 2/3 of the Legislatures in the task of undoing the work; or to get a Congress appointed in the first instance that will commit suicide on their own authority," Madison dolefully calculated.[33] Henry still had the state legislature under his thumb, as Madison well knew, and that body was beginning its session as convention delegates packed bags and boxes for homeward journeys.

It was typical of the Antifederalist rump session that something should go wrong. Mason, in a surly mood, had prepared an ill-tempered address that tended "to irritate, rather than to quiet the public mind." Most of the Antifederalist delegates came to the meeting with a less jaundiced view than Mason or Henry held, and many stalked out in disgust. Finally, Benjamin Harrison spoke against Mason's offering, and urged them all to observe the new Constitution in practice, hopeful that "those destructive consequences to their liberty . . . which the minority apprehended," might never appear. Mason became flustered, probably lamented the lack of spirit

[32] Robertson, *Debates of the Virginia Convention*, 471–75.

[33] *Virginia Independent Chronicle*, July 9, 1788; Madison to Washington, June 27, 1788, Madison papers, *DLC*.

his friends displayed, and "prudently . . . withdrew his address."[34] The address of the Pennsylvania minority, meant to be a clarion call, had been muted; but in Virginia, even the first notes had been too sour.

Defeat was bad enough, but salt was rubbed in the Antifederalists' wounds when Randolph sent the legislature Governor Clinton's two-month-old letter from New York that promised co-operation "with any sister State" in toning down the Constitution, "especially with one so respectable in point of importance, ability, and patriotism as Virginia."[35] Randolph had withheld the letter from the Convention on a technicality. When at last Mason saw Clinton's promise to work in unison for amendments, he reached the boiling point. Thereafter, Mason regarded Randolph as a treacherous soul and alluded to him as "young A[rnol]d."[36] At the moment, Mason ripped into the governor and unsuccessfully tried to pass a resolution that denounced Randolph's dilatory tactics. Randolph tried to prove that his intentions had been honorable, but no one seemed particularly anxious to give him an alibi. The comedy-of-errors in the Randolph-Clinton correspondence was not ended, however. In October the legislature sent its own belated reply to Clinton, seeking co-ordination on a call for a second federal convention. Even that message went astray. Months after the resolution had been posted in Richmond, it was still undelivered. Clinton and the leading Antifederalists thought they knew why.

In the midst of the shambles, it fell the lot of Richard Henry Lee to explain the failure to the New York Antifederalists. Lee bemoaned the failure of the Antifederalists to keep their communications lines in better repair, and he attributed their defeat to some mysterious "essential change in the minds of men." "The Constitution is to turn the world *topsy-turvy*," Inness had taunted sarcastically.[37] The Virginia microcosm of Henry and Mason and Lee was

[34] *Virginia Independent Chronicle*, July 9, 1788.

[35] Clinton to Randolph, May 8, 1788, Conway, *Life of Randolph*, 110–11.

[36] George Mason to John Mason, December 18, 1788, Mason papers, *DLC*.

[37] Richard Henry Lee to John Lamb, June 27, 1788, Ballagh, *Letters of Lee*, II, 475; Hugh B. Grigsby, *The History of the Virginia Convention of 1788*, I, 331.

indeed turned upside down. Voluntarily, Virginia had stepped from the leader's role back into the ranks with all the other states, big and small. They had fought to prevent that backward step. Their zeal and their makeshift plans were for naught. All of their late-hour conferences, tavern arguments, and hallway cajolery had not won the handful of precious delegates needed to stop the Federalists.

Trying to put their fingers on the ultimate cause of defeat, the Antifederalists always came back to the same answer. Despite an array that included Henry and Mason, the Federalists had "certainly the weight of talents. What must the individual be who c[oul]d thus oppose them united?"[38] Monroe was more explicit. The prospect of Washington as president had ruined their chances, he told Jefferson. "Be assured his influence carried this government."[39]

[38] William Nelson to William Short, July 12, 1788, Short papers, *DLC*.
[39] Monroe to Jefferson, July 12, 1788, 13 *Jefferson Papers* 351–53.

☆ XIV ☆

Willie Jones and the Bill of Rights

CAMPAIGN POLLYANNAISM, now a fixture of American politics, sustained the Antifederalists in 1787–88. Since that humiliating loss in Pennsylvania, they had persistently dismissed each subsequent failure as some kind of political fluke. Even after the Virginia debacle, die-hard Antifederalists admitted there were dark clouds elsewhere but saw silver linings overhead. Each reverse was belittled as having no meaning beyond the borders of the defecting state. Their reaction was unrealistic but vital, since hope is the politician's main asset. In the summer of 1788, Antifederalists lived on hope.

Indeed, instead of retreating, the last pockets of antifederal resistance defiantly ignored the facts and kept up their morale by solemnly assuring each other that a second federal convention was a virtual certainty. In Pennsylvania a few rural communities held meetings to discuss ways and means of revoking their state's ratification. More than seventy Antifederalists in Cumberland County formed a volunteer militia unit and signed "a private Article oblidging ourselves to oppose the establishment of the new Constitution at the risque of our lives and Fortunes." Deadly serious about the lengths they would go to keep the Constitution from operating, they reported their numbers were "daily increasing [and] all we want is arms." One Carlisle Antifederalist was incensed because local Federalists intimated "that none but such as had received a Colege [*sic*] education was capable to occupy any office or public trust." After Virginia ratified, a Northumberland Antifederalist expressed great surprise that the Constitution "is forceing on, against a great Majority of the people." He was convinced that "four fifths of the people here are against it."[1]

---

[1] William Petriken to John Nicholson, May 8, 1788; John Simpson to Nicholson, July 5, 1788, Nicholson Papers, Pennsylvania State Archives.

254

In the New York convention, adamant Antifederalists felt the same way. "I trust that our Deliberations will not in the least be affected or changed, in consequence of the State of New Hampshire & Verginia Acceeding to the Constitution," a firm Clintonian commented after the bad news from Richmond reached Poughkeepsie. DeWitt Clinton listened as his uncle reviewed the situation with other Antifederalists and decided the failure of Henry and Mason had made "no impression upon the republican members."[2]

Amidst great uncertainty the New York Federalists launched their attack at the Poughkeepsie convention. Chancellor Livingston upbraided the Antifederalists for depicting the Constitution as a federal dragon swallowing all the states. His remarks gave Antifederalists a chance to take their minds off the latest bad news. One by one they lambasted Livingston, and this byplay probably eased some tension. After the Antifederalists had taken their turns at chiding him, Livingston said he was "happy that he could say, with Sir John Falstaff, that if he had no wit himself, he had been the occasion of wit in others."[3] The session ended after Antifederalists introduced a draft of twelve amendments which the opposition mysteriously "suffered us to propose . . . without a word of opposition to them."[4]

With an overwhelming majority in their favor, the New York Antifederalists stumbled on the threshold of victory. Clinton's trump card—a conditional ratification that would help bring a second convention—was held aloft but never played. Meanwhile, his friends insisted everything was proceeding in good order. "I can tell you that the information from Virginia seems to have no effect on US," a smug Antifederalist commented. In contrast, Madison advised Hamilton to present the majority with an ultimatum for unconditional surrender. A conditional ratification, based on a right to withdraw at some future date if amendments were not made, would leave New York out of the Union. "The Consitution requires an adoption *in*

---

[2] Schoonmaker to P. Van Gaasbeek, July 2, 1788, Roosevelt Library, Hyde Park, New York; DeWitt Clinton to Charles Tillinghast, July 2, 1788, Clinton papers, Columbia University Library.

[3] Jay to Washington, [July 28?], 1788, *DHC*, IV, 394.

[4] Nathaniel Lawrence to John Lamb, July 3, 1788, Lamb papers, *NYHS*.

toto, and *for ever*." Madison's letter must have been waved under a few Antifederalist noses later that week. Hamilton knew how to use such an item as he reported that some Antifederalists perceived their anomalous position and were "desirous of a retreat." An exception was the governor himself.[5] Disturbed but apparently undaunted by events elsewhere, Clinton remained steadfast. With Lansing loyally supporting him, the governor stubbornly insisted that a second convention could be called.

While the convention business inched along, other New Yorkers gave vent to their feelings. At Albany, Antifederalists paraded into the heart of the city on July 4 and watched with approval as a copy of the Constitution was tossed into a bonfire. After they dispersed, a band of Federalists resurrected the charred Constitution and with much huzzaing began parading up a narrow Albany street. There they were met by an angry mob of Antifederalists. Accounts of what then happened varied—Federalists claimed a complete rout of bloody opponents, while Antifederalists reported six wounded men and twelve Federalist casualties. "A few of their ringleaders hid in dirty holes, were taken out & begged for mercy, which was granted them, although they illy deserved it," an angry Federalist fumed. One of the Antifederalist ringleaders, Abraham Lansing, looked back on the fray a few days later with great misgivings. Lansing laid most of the blame on rum rather than on principles. The battle "was unintentional on our side—and would not have happened had our Friends and their Antagonists not been heated with Liquor," he explained.

In Poughkeepsie, however, it was back and fill, back and fill. By July 7 it was obvious that the Clintonians favored a dilatory course not because it was planned but because of their own uncertainties. Each new day saw the introduction of more amendments, until Lansing finally brought in a proposed bill of rights. Jay was encouraged by the Antis' meandering course. "The Ground of *Rejection* . . . seems to be entirely deserted," he told Washington. Disturbing rumors from Poughkeepsie drifted upriver to Albany,

[5] Hamilton to Madison, July 2, 1788, Madison papers, *DLC;* Madison to Hamilton, July [8?], 1788, Hamilton papers, *DLC.*

where impatient Antifederalist leaders thought a forthright rejection of the Constitution should have been accomplished weeks earlier. Abraham Lansing was worried by reports of dissension among the delegates "respecting the Mode of introducing the amendments," which had a deeper significance and might even lead to "a total disappointment."[6] The Poughkeepsie newspaper contained "Cato's" warning to the Antifederalists who were dragging their feet. Ratification by the convention was no longer a matter "of speculation, but a question of expediency," the essayist (who had a Hamiltonian flair) announced. The Clintonians' insistence that the Union could not operate without New York was a policy of "madness" that if followed would make New Yorkers as contemptible as Rhode Islanders. That same day the Federalists, determined to let their inept opponents use every round of their oratorical ammunition, withheld their own fire. With some embarrassment, Antifederalists admitted they were still uncertain about the proper method for urging amendments "as conditional, explanatory or recommendatory . . . therefore they had *Nothing* at present to propose."[7]

While the Federalists were too worried themselves to really enjoy the opposition's dilemma, it was obvious that Clinton's firm grasp on the Antifederalists had either relaxed or slipped tremendously during the first week of July. The governor and those closest to him thought another federal convention was inevitable. To counter Clinton's plans, there were persistent hints that anything less than outright ratification would bring a secession movement from the city of New York. While the expiring Continental Congress went through the business of adopting machinery to put the new government in motion, Federalists contended that Clinton's crowd played a dangerous game that might result in "a cry of havock and the letting loose the dogs of war."[8] "The consequences of a rejection will be dreadful," a New York visitor observed, "nothing less, it is

[6] A. G. Lansing to Yates, July 9, 1788, Yates papers, *NYPL.*

[7] Notes on the New York Convention debates, July 8 entry, Hamilton papers, *DLC.*

[8] "Letter from a gentleman in Poughkeepsie, June 30," Providence *United States Chronicle,* July 31, 1788.

believed here, than a civil war" would follow such a rash antifederal act. "Governor Clinton is greatly blamed." Manhattan merchants claimed that procrastination at Poughkeepsie would ruin business, and might force Congress to move elsewhere; such an exodus would "be a fatal stroke to our Commerce & when it will end God only knows."[9] The uneasy businessmen calculated their probable losses at £100,000 annually if Clinton's tactics brought about that unhappy event.

The paucity of good news coming down-river bothered the New York Federalists. Patience was not the guide to their conduct. "The Southern District are determined on a Separation to join the union," General Samuel Webb confided, "and I do not believe the life of the Governor & his party would be safe in this place." It is always difficult to separate bluster from real intentions, but the Federalist talk of using the sword in New Hampshire if their plans went amiss and the threats from New York make it clear that the militant Pennsylvania Antifederalists had their counterparts. Headstrong Federalists seemed determined to show their defiance of Clintonian tactics as they scheduled a Constitutional procession for July 22, with or without good news from Poughkeepsie. Jefferson heard that Clinton probably would have his way, with the secession of Manhattan, "Straten [*sic*] and Long Islands" as a consequence.[10]

Clinton's political acumen failed to match his personal popularity, for he did not know how to call a bluff. The coffeehouse generals in New York thumped the table amidst warlike banter, but Henry Knox's insistence that the alternatives were ratification or civil war seems no more credible than his assertions during the 1786–87 winter that all western Massachusetts was aflame.[11] Moreover, the pressure which Federalists applied on Poughkeepsie delegates by circulating rumors about removal of the capital actually backfired, because it angered some Antifederalists who "treated it as a feint." Although, as often happens, some Federalist doubtlessly began to believe his

[9] Samuel Webb to Miss Hogeboom, July 13, 1788, Webb papers, Yale University Library.

[10] Francis Hopkinson to Jefferson, July 16, 1788, 13 *Jefferson Papers* 374.

[11] Knox to Washington, July 28, 1788, *DHC*, IV, 822–23.

associates' propaganda—the defection in Clinton's ranks seems to have been momentarily arrested by heavy-handed tactics. The arrogance of Federalists like Chancellor Livingston were reminders of that not-too-distant era when aristocrats had totally dominated New York. In order to make the Constitution acceptable to Antifederalists, enough of them needed to be convinced that they might have an equal opportunity in the postratification power struggle. As the historian George Dangerfield phrased it, the Antifederalists feared "a resurgence in state and national form of that privileged government which New York had experienced as a colony."[12] Compared with this threat of an elected elite, the rumblings about secession of the southern counties were of secondary concern.

In private meetings, the Antifederalists kept searching for a device that would provide a retreat if the second-convention scheme came to nothing. On July 10, Lansing proposed to burden the ratification with a hodgepodge of straddling amendments, some of them explanatory, some conditional, and others recommendatory. The Clintonian's inability to come forward with a forthright proposal seemed symptomatic of a fundamental weakness. Some Antifederalists even discussed another alternative—adjournment without taking any action at all. The aimless course, Jay reported, gave Federalists "Room for Hope." More and more, Antifederalists resembled a timid wagon driver who has struck dead center but fears going either backward or forward—so he does nothing. Jay's motion to adopt recommendatory amendments, as the Massachusetts convention had done, embarrassed the Antifederalists. The convention "is now wound up to a Crisis," DeWitt Clinton reported. Lansing emerged as the driving force behind the Antifederalists by propping up a straw man to block Jay's maneuver. Although Federalists saw Lansing's plan as a hydra-headed monster, the Clintonian coterie regarded it as "the ne plus ultra of anti concession."[13]

Lansing's concoction of amendments seemed to offer something to everybody. His ratification proposal was ladened with a bill of

---

[12] George Dangerfield, *Chancellor Robert R. Livingston*, 228.

[13] DeWitt Clinton to Charles Tillinghast, July 12, 1788, Clinton papers, Columbia University Library.

rights, an effort to clarify nebulous language in the Constitution, provisions limiting taxing powers, and qualifications on the power of the federal judiciary. The entire program was contingent on the call for a second convention. In effect, Lansing would have added a bill of rights to the Articles of Confederation, would have given Congress slightly more power than it had, and would have created a restricted federal court system. On these terms "our Represents. in Congress will be of service in calling another Convention." Melancton Smith, who believed one could skate on thin ice even in mid-July, praised the conditional features of Lansing's plan. However, Hamilton maintained it was full of nonsense, for Congress would not call another convention unless nine states applied for such a meeting. Thus conditional ratification was really a trap for every true friend of ratification even "tho' they do not intend it."[14]

Antifederalists seemed oblivious of repeated Federalist warnings that anything beyond recommendatory amendments would be unacceptable. Smith moved for a ratification that would be null and void if the first Congress failed to call a second convention.[15] Nearly in despair, Federalist Judge Hobart asked for an adjournment, but this failed to win antifederal support. "The Comercial [*sic*] people may—devise modes to meet their Northern Brethren," Hobart pleaded, meaning that the city interests might during a recess compromise with the agrarian elements. Lansing lashed out at the Federalists for their allusions to the northern and southern state factions, claiming that these remarks were improper since they hinted at a natural schism in New York interests. But Hamilton reminded delegates that the city of New York was overwhelmingly Federalist, and broadly suggested that the northern counties would find it "impracticable" to force the lower Hudson counties to join in rejection.

Antifederalist Williams admitted the quandary facing many on his side of the aisle by confessing that he could neither vote for outright rejection nor support unconditional ratification. Smith proved

[14] Gilbert Livingston, "Journal of Notes on the New York Convention, 1788," Manuscript, *NYPL*.

[15] Livingston, "Journal of Notes on the New York Convention, 1788," Manuscript, *NYPL*.

that the Clintonians were becoming restless when he began to back-slide. The important decision was whether to stay in the Union or separate, Smith said, as he recanted from his previous position. Smith's tone became more conciliatory as he suggested that they tentatively ratify the Constitution, await developments regarding a second convention, and remain "at liberty to withdraw."[16] Smith's idea had some immediate support. "The fedralists [*sic*] will agree," delegate Schoonmaker confided, because the plan was "the most favorable to them, and having no great hopes for a better—they say the lesser Evil of the two." The twenty-seven vote majority of a few weeks earlier seemed to have faded in morning mists along the Hudson. The same doughty Antifederalist lamented—"Our Difficulties and Embarrassments are very great, nay in a great Degree Unsurmountable as the Event of our Decision."

Antifederalist confidence began to crumble. There were dark whispers about Melancton Smith, who was "charged with some improper Steps." There was talk of a circular letter to the other states, inviting them to join in concerted plans for specific amendments. The governor himself apparently made little or no effort to unify supporters. The Antifederalists accordingly "seemed embarrassed," Jay reported, "—fearful to divide among themselves, and yet many of them very averse [*sic*] to the new Plan."

Shrewd Federalists in other states made their excuses in case New York rejected the Constitution, but their hedges were hardly necessary. By July 22, Governor Clinton had taken a back seat, relinquishing his leadership to Lansing at the moment when he should have been asserting it. Madison, as dignified as was his judgment unerring, marveled that the Antifederalists in such circumstances "were able to keep their numbers together in the opposition." "Now for the strength of nerves," an innervated Federalist exulted. "Upon the whole," an encouraged Hamilton told Madison, ". . . our fears diminish." The halls of the Continental Congress buzzed with rumors that Clinton's crowd sought only a graceful means of retreat. The news was good enough to bring the Federalists out in force for

---

[16] Schoonmaker to P. Van Gaasbeck, July 18, 1788, Roosevelt Library, Hyde Park, New York.

their procession, perhaps with the hope that glad tidings might come at any moment. The Federalist parade wound through the borough's narrow streets and headed for a grand feast at the bowling green, while "poar [*sic*] *antis* generally minded their own business at home; others, who were spectators at an *awful* distance, looked as sour as the Devil." Somehow the celebrants reached the green without a single fist fight breaking out, an instance so rare that witnesses held it nothing short of remarkable.[17]

Resistance by the Clintonian faction collapsed on July 23. Federalists claimed that the words "upon condition" prefacing the amendments would effectually nullify ratification. An Antifederalist moved that the phrase be replaced by "in full confidence." Clinton backtracked, refused to say anything against the motion, and sat down. Platt, Lawrence, Smith, Gilbert Livingston, Williams, and seven others chosen as Antifederalists in the down-river counties crossed over to the opposition when the question was called. The motion passed, thirty-one to twenty-nine.

If Clinton made any attempt to halt the defection, the evidence has not survived. Lansing showed more spunk as he came forward with a substitute resolution that would have reserved for New York the right to "withdraw herself from the Union after a certain number of years, unless the amendments proposed should previously be submitted to a general convention."[18] But a general ennui moved through the Antifederalist ranks. Jay and a few other Federalists had made conciliatory gestures regarding a circular letter that vaguely called for another convention. "The Scylla and Charybdis I would wish to avoid are non-conditional adoption & a disunion," DeWitt Clinton contended as he saw the majority frittered away.[19] By this time, young Clinton was as confused as his uncle. "The political sky is so frequently overcast and so variable to appearance that I am oftentimes at a loss what to think or what to say," he confessed.

[17] Madison to Washington, July 21, 1788, *DHC*, IV, 809; [?] to Samuel B. Webb, July 21, 1788, Webb papers, Yale University Library; Hamilton to Madison, July 22, 1788, Madison papers, *DLC*.

[18] Elliot, *Debates*, II, 412.

[19] DeWitt Clinton to Charles Tillinghast, July [23?], 1788, Clinton papers, Columbia University Library.

Smith laid antifederal opposition to rest with a funeral oration that gave them more of an excuse than a reason for their peculiar conduct. The alternative to ratification was to unleash those overworked "dogs of war," and risk secession of the southern counties, Smith said. Most historians of the convention have taken pains to show that this fear was the main cause of the Clintonian collapse. The chief defectors were themselves residents of southern counties, and they were attempting to save their political hides, not to mention their professional careers (since nearly all were merchants or lawyers).[20] This line of argument, however, fails to explain the governor's lame efforts or Clinton's failure to take advantage of his tremendous personal popularity. The governor's irresolution may have stemmed from his own grave doubts about the repercussions of nonaction, mingled perhaps with a conviction that a second convention was still a certainty. Indeed, Jay fed the latter hope by helping shape the sham compromise that was in fact a total surrender. The half-a-loaf-is-better-than-none type of reasoning apparently appealed to Clinton, who was now somewhat less than confident about the future and his place in it. "A precise history of his conduct is difficult to be written," Henry Knox wrote a few days later, "and must be left to time to explain."[21] Clinton obviously was as much of an enigma to his contemporaries as he has been to latter generations.

Another forty-eight hours passed before the Federalist triumph was secured. Jay saw little harm in a circular letter calling for another convention. He probably regarded this slight favor to Clinton as a small concession for the great gain promised. Thirty-two amendments were lumped together, echoing the Massachusetts and Virginia recommendations. Lansing attempted to rally support for con-

---

[20] Dangerfield, *Chancellor Livingston*, 231–32; Forest McDonald, *We the People* (Chicago, 1958), 284, 288n. McDonald accepts the account in William Dunlap, *History of the Netherlands* (New York, 1840), which reportedly was based on an eyewitness account of the secret caucus. John S. Jenkins, *History of Political Parties in the State of New York* (Auburn, New York, 1849), claims that Gilbert Livingston and Melancton Smith switched their votes "under the confidential advisement of the Governor [who] could not but foresee that a secession from the Union, at this crisis, would expose the State to imminent perils and dangers."

[21] Knox to Washington, July 28, 1788, *DHC*, IV, 822–23.

ditional surrender based on a second convention, but Jay insisted that the circular letter plan gave "the highest possible prospect of a convention for Amendments" without upsetting the whole constitutional cart.[22] "If there is so Strong an Interest to bring about a Convent[ion]," Lansing shot back, "our reservation will not affect our union." Hamilton, who feared the possibility of an adjournment "for no real end," moved that the circular letter be approved. When an Antifederalist complained that their majority had been whittled away by degrees, Hamilton countered that the Federalists had also stretched their principles.

Lansing's last-ditch stand, based on the right-to-withdraw proviso, ended on July 25 after Jay unfolded the much-discussed circular letter. Smith deserted the Clintonians, praising the circular letter "as a Middle Ground" in contrast to Lansing's motion which "would make the breach [*sic*] worse." The only consolation for the Clintonians was approval of a motion to prepare a bill of rights (thirty-seven to twenty-one), after the governor himself said that if this much could not be conceded a great deal of time had been wasted. A final vote on the whole ratification package, with its staggering list of recommended amendments, passed the convention on July 26 with a thirty to twenty-seven vote. Well aware that he had caught only the crumbs while the Jay-Hamilton-Livingston crowd had walked away with the cake, Governor Clinton avoided the gesture of even voting.

Perhaps Clinton really had great expectations for the circular letter, since Jay had overplayed things by permitting the use of fairly strong language that gave it a rather urgent tone. Union sentiment alone had kept New York from ratifying the Constitution without conditional amendments, the letter explained, but a second convention was vital. Many fears would be removed if such a body were called into session by the first Congress. "Even such of the states as may be content with every article" were asked to join in the call, as a harmonious gesture toward those citizens who believed amendments were needed.[23] What Clinton apparently overlooked

[22] Livingston, "Journal of Notes on the New York Convention, 1788," Manuscript, *NYPL*.

[23] Elliot, *Debates*, II, 413–14.

was that the efficacy of such a letter, no matter how well written, depended more than anything else on the power and prestige of the signer. The letter went to other governors bearing only Clinton's signature. The Federalist David had slain another Goliath. "The New York Ratification is not like[ly] to prove a Hermaphrodite as had been apprehended," a North Carolina delegate in Congress sighed. "Such have been the Effects of the weighty reasoning of the minority and *other* very weighty considerations."[24] One note of caution came from a Virginian in the Continental Congress, who feared the Antifederalists in their desperation would "get into Congress men who will promote the measure of a General Convention at too early a period." A colleague voiced a similar feeling—the Clintonians had done a good thing with a singular lack of grace. "They were not convinced of the propriety" of ratification, but simply recognized the expediency. Antifederalists themselves tried to rationalize their position. "Upon the whole I believe or *endeavour* to believe that it is best so both in a political and private light," volunteered Abraham Lansing.[25]

The sudden onrush of events had made the New York pro-Constitution parade of July 22 somewhat premature, but Federalists took the accounts from Poughkeepsie as signals for another celebration. Amidst the toasting and drinking, punctuated by an occasional skyward blast of a musket, a crowd began gathering near Thomas Greenleaf's printing establishment. Greenleaf, the "poor, thick-sculled creature" and doubtlessly the butt of many jibes by rum- or ale-soddened Federalists turned a deaf Antifederalist ear toward the merrymaking. As the day wore on, Greenleaf was warned that some spirited Federalists believed the lonely "Anti" printer needed a public lesson in humility. During the night a mob broke into Greenleaf's shop, upset the type cases, broke furniture, spilled ink, and scattered paper. Publication of the *Journal* was suspended temporarily. Greenleaf insisted that although his antifederalism had cost

[24] Hugh Williamson to James Iredell, July 26, 1788, Emmet collections, *NYPL*.

[25] Edward Carrington to William Short, July 26, 1788, 13 *Jefferson Papers* 414*n.*; William Irvine to William Alexander, July 28, 1788, *LCC*, VIII, 770–71; A. G. Lansing to Yates, August 3, 1788, Yates papers, *NYPL*.

him dearly, he had not been abandoned by "the patriotic part of the community."[26] Sixty cancellations by "illiberal subscribers" offered Greenleaf no balm, however.

After their first enthusiastic reaction to the New York ratification, a few Federalists had misgivings about the circular letter. The circular letter might prove troublesome, Madison thought, because it kept alive the prospective second convention. "The great danger in the present crisis is that if another Convention should be soon assembled, it would terminate in discord," Madison told Jefferson, "or in alterations of the federal system which would throw back *essential* powers into the State Legislatures." Madison wanted a cooling-off period that would dispel the fears "which have been artificially created by designing men and will at the same time point out the faults which really call for amendment." Most Federalists agreed with the Philadelphia essayist who counselled caution. "Heaven forbid any convention for a while! I dread the work of fifteen hundred reformers in the present fluctuation of sentiments. If we must at all amend, I pray for merely amusing amendments; a little frothy garnish." A less temperate view came from New Jersey, where the Clintonians were denounced as fit company only for "lawless Indians" since they had "not sense enough to frame or understand a system of government fit for a civilized nation."[27] The more the circular letter was studied by Federalists, the more they deprecated its potential—all bad.

Whatever discomfort the circular letter gave to Federalists, their adversaries up and down the coastline were more inclined to moan than feel consolation. Richard Henry Lee thought that a supplication for amendments was "neither wise or manly."[28] Mason retired to his arcadian retreat and abdicated his post as second-in-command of Henry's antifederal battalions.

Although the withdrawal of some Antifederalists was self-im-

[26] *New-York Journal*, August 21, 1788.

[27] *Pennsylvania Gazette*, July 15, 1788; *New-Jersey Journal*, August 13, 1788.

[28] Richard Henry Lee to General John Lamb, June 27, 1788, Ballagh, *Letters of Lee*, II, 475.

posed, the seclusion was not always voluntary. Colonel Oswald heard about the New York ratification while behind iron bars in a Philadelphia jail. The abettor of "Centinel" and "Philadelphiensis" had become entangled in a libel suit with the editor of the rival *Federal Gazette*. While under a one thousand dollar appearance bond, Oswald indiscreetly printed a thinly-disguised allusion to Chief Justice McKean in a commentary on the Fourth of July parade. The jurist had ridden in a high-wheeled cart dressed in scarlet robes "like the whore of Babylon." A contempt charge swiftly followed which landed Oswald in a dank prison cell. The demoralized Oswald was even rebuffed by brother printers, who agreed that he had gone too far. "Restrain the licentiousness," Oswald stormed, "and you in effect demolish the liberty of the press." As an Antifederalist, Oswald's main consolation was that the jailer even allowed him a pen and paper.

Bitter disappointment, mob violence, and a prison cell—the lot of Antifederalist editors required Job-like qualities. Edward Powars' fortunes with the Boston *American Herald* went from bad to ruinous, with New Hampshire ratification coming as a final, reeling blow. Taunted for months because of his political perversity, Powars finally decided to flee from the land of federal philistines. After printing the June 30 issue, Powars hauled his press overland to Worcester, modified his political opinions, and rejuvenated the *American Herald* there in August. Anyone searching for evidence that antifederalism collapsed in July, 1788, need search no further than the offices of the *New-York Journal*, the Philadelphia *Independent Gazetteer*, or the Boston *American Herald*.

Indeed, the fever and chilblains of the body politic were subsiding during the sweltering summer of 1788. The Continental Congress erected its own funeral pyre, while the untried constitutional machinery appeared free from tinkering, at least for the moment. Except for the New York circular letter and a few noisy Pennsylvanians, the agitation for a second convention seemed stifled. The wayward majority in Rhode Island pursued a reckless but harmless course, and the only other errant state—North Carolina—was finally getting down to business after a delay which local Federalists regarded as scandalous.

The handling of majorities—whether bare or overwhelming—by turning certain defeat into shattering triumph was by this time a Federalist tour de force. Hence in July, friends of the Constitution viewed the North Carolina situation with varying degrees of hope, despite the acknowledged power of Willie Jones in rough-and-tumble Carolinian politics. Jones (his first name was pronounced *wĭl'ĭ*) was another Antifederalist who did not fit the conventional mold. Reared in a wealthy family that possessed endless plantations, Jones had lost none of his democratic predilections despite an early training at Eton. With all his money and aristocratic background, Jones had returned to America and identified himself with the revolutionary radicals even though his high sense of honor prevented him from supporting extremist acts. During the Revolution, Jones had fought against the wanton confiscation of loyalist landholdings, at the risk of being tainted with "Toryism" charges.[29] Despite that one tilt with "the Saints in the Back Country," Jones was inclined to forgive the small landowners for their wartime rapacity. For all his thousands of acres of land, his famous stable of horses, and his dozens of slaves, Jones championed the cause of the common man. While others may have momentarily forgotten Jefferson's talents, Jones looked to the American in Paris as the main voice of agrarian America. Patrick Henry's ideas also found a ready, positive response in Jones. Jones thus embraced antifederalism wholeheartedly. While he controlled North Carolina politics, an unconditional ratification was impossible.

Standing behind Jones were a handful of self-made men who represented the back country in its continuous battle with seaboard interests. Timothy Bloodworth, David Caldwell, Lemuel Burkitt, and Judge Samuel Spencer looked to Jones as their champion. Thomas Person, a wealthy landowner and planter who was eight years Jones' senior, joined this company which Federalists regaled as a "blind

[29] Jones to Henry Eustace McCulloh, [1783?], quoted in Blackwell P. Robinson, " Willie Jones of Halifax," *The North Carolina Historical Review*, Vol. XVIII (January, 1941), 144–45.

stupid set, that wish Damnation to their Country."[30] "The truth is," a leading Federalist spouted, "that we have a set of fools and knaves in every part of the State, who seem to act as by concert; and are uniformly against any man of abilities and virtue. Lawyers of character are particularly obnoxious to them; but if they can find a profligate character at the bar, they caress him as one of themselves." Few lawyers wandered into the Antifederalist ranks, however, particularly after the hue-and-cry was raised along the seacoast against the back-country representatives who had pushed a paper-money bill through the state legislature a few years earlier. Almost to a man, these paper-money, pro-debtor men now congregated under the Antifederalist banner. Besides the paper-money issue there was the matter of federal taxation. Weeks before the Constitution had been completed, there was speculation that North Carolinians might fear "the expectation of heavy taxes when the Federal Government have sufficient power to compel payment. In that case we shall be opposed by a nest of hornets."[31]

Still another vexing matter to some of the land speculators (and most North Carolinians were either active or potential land speculators) was the Mississippi problem. Bloodworth, who had forsaken preaching and watchmaking for a career in the Continental Congress after the war, had a long record of opposition to northern plans to barter river rights for commercial favors. Late in 1786, Bloodworth had denounced Jay's proposed treaty. "Grant Congress the Power [of] occluding the Missecippey," Bloodworth warned, "and by parrity of reason, every other river in the United States must be at their Disposal, which appears an obsurdity, inadmisible."[32] Moreover, Bloodworth continued, "the partial advantages offered by the propos'd treaty, the Eastern States are to receive the benefits, by the sale of their fish and oile . . . and the Southern States are to pay the purchase, by giving up the Missecippey." The inevitable consequence

[30] Quoted in *A Plea for Federal Union, North Carolina, 1788* (ed. by Hugh Lefler), 9.

[31] Archibald Maclaine to James Iredell, August 29, 1788, Griffith J. McRee, *Life and Correspondence of James Iredell*, II, 178.

[32] Timothy Bloodworth to North Carolina Assembly, December 16, 1786, *LCC*, VIII, 521–22.

was "the Depreciation of the Vallue of the Lands on the Western Waters." The threatened loss of the Mississippi, along with troubles in the pseudo state of Franklin on the North Carolina frontier, made Antifederalists out of quaking citizens who believed that northern congressmen voted to weaken the South whenever possible.

Where other states had entrenched officers or paper-money advocates or western-land speculators, North Carolina had all of these anti-Constitution forces in one coalition. Pitted against such diverse interests, the Federalists, led by lawyers and their allies the town merchants, could make little headway. Mortified by the perversity of Antifederalists, friends of the Constitution believed that the average citizen meant well but was egregiously misled. "Some demagogues, a few persons who are in debt, and every public officer, except the Clerk of the County Court, are decidedly against any change," was the tired lament of Archibald Maclaine. The Antifederalists were a belligerent lot, moreover. William Hopper, respected signer of the Declaration of Independence from Orange County, dropped words for the use of stronger arguments with an Antifederalist. The patriot of '76, taking a Federalist side in an election campaign brawl, "came off second best, with his eyes blacked."[33]

These truculent, untutored yeomen looked to Willie Jones for leadership. Jones had elegant clothes and fine linen to prove that he had good taste and the money to support it. But Jones was a disciple of the democratic dogma—the aftermath of the Revolution had not disillusioned him. On the contrary, he still believed that the political instincts of the people deserved full play. Many of his neighbors raced, hunted, gambled in land deals, or sold crops on one hand, while on the other they attacked paper-money schemes as the handiwork of the shiftless. Jones listened to both sides without alarm. In debates he handled himself well enough. In legislative corridors or in private dining rooms, Jones was even more skillful. When Jones was "smoking his pipe, and chatting of crops, ploughs, stock, dogs, &c . . . [he] stole his way into the hearts of honest

[33] S. Johnston to [James Iredell], August 22, 1788, *ibid.*, 170.

farmers, and erected thrones for himself," a begrudging biographer admitted.[34] It was from that kind of throne that Jones directed the antifederal maneuvering in the North Carolina convention.

The North Carolina convention was scheduled for late July, when the Virginia decision would have certainly been reached. Jones appears to have regarded the interests of the two states as vitally entwined, and his admiration of Henry was no secret. During the preliminary skirmishing for delegates' seats, the North Carolina Antifederalists demonstrated their power convincingly. "Col. Geddy ... is a most furious zealot for what he calls *W. Jones's system,* which is indeed all he knows about it," harped one opponent. The Baptist clergymen raised the cry of "no freedom of conscience" till it echoed through the piney barrens and beyond. Dismayed Federalists complained that their opponents were "straining every nerve, to provent the new government [from] taking place." "All the low scoundrels in the county," a Wilmington Federalist reported, "and by every underhand means, are prejudicing the common people against the new constitution."[35]

In Dobbs County the electioneering finally grew violent. Bad feelings between two factions, apparently as much personal as political, finally erupted in a polling place melee. Witnesses said a Federalist lurched toward the polling bench swearing that he would pummel one of the inspectors. Candles tumbled, men fell in the darkness, and "many blows with clubs were instantly heard to pass." One luckless Antifederalist was overtaken, beaten by a mob, and left to scramble for his life before the hottest heads decided to finish the job. In the confusion, the ballot box was "violently taken away." As reports of the encounter were repeated, the story inevitably grew bloodier.[36] Another account had guns and axes brandished, with one Federalist killed and an Antifederalist critically wounded. Actually, no one

[34] McRee, *Life of Iredell,* II, 232.

[35] Davie to Iredell, January 22, 1788, McRee, *Life of Iredell,* II, 217; Archibald Maclaine to James Iredell, December 25, 1787, *ibid.,* 183; Archibald Maclaine to James Iredell, March 4, 1788, *ibid.,* 219.

[36] *New-York Journal,* May 17, 1788, quoting *North Carolina Gazette,* April 16, 1788.

appears to have been mortally wounded, but the local apothecary shop must have been a busy place the next day.

Federalists were dismayed but not startled by the election results, which was nearly an Antifederalist landslide. It was apparent that Jones and his followers had captured more than a two-to-one majority. Reviewing the debacle, friends of the Constitution frankly admitted that in Dobbs County "the federal-men, finding that they were in danger of losing their election, raised a riot . . . and destroyed the books." The Dobbs County returns were sure to be questioned, but Federalists countered that they had been robbed in another county where their candidate with 172 votes had been pushed aside by an Antifederalist with only 97 ballots because of a technicality. A distant observer condemned "club law" in North Carolina, which, added to the "State of Franklin" disturbances, seemed proof that a strong federal government was needed to quell such outbursts.[37] Unhappy opponents blamed the Antifederalist blight that had struck North Carolina on "3 or 4 designing Men, of influence in the back Counties." One man in particular was the most feared antifederal troublemaker.

Willie Jones made no secret of his strategy. Jefferson's letter which suggested that nine states adopt the Constitution and that the remaining four should hold out for amendments that would include a bill of rights became the nucleus of the Jones program. Confronted with Jones' popularity and almost certain defeat, the Federalists utilized a campaign technique that has in the twentieth century become known as the "big smear." Stories were circulated which first had Thomas Persons declaring "in substance *'that General Washington was a damned rascal, and traitor to his country, for putting his hand to such an infamous paper as the* new Constitution.'" Federalists were urged to see that the report gained wider currency through newspapers, but in the transition the offender's name was garbled until word-of-mouth reports placed the onus on Jones.[38]

[37] D. Witherspoon to James Iredell, April 3, 1788, McRee, *Life of Iredell*, II, 222; Archibald Maclaine to James Iredell, April 3, 29, 1788, *ibid.*, 221, 223; John Brown Cutting to Jefferson, July 11, 1788, 13 *Jefferson Papers* 331–32.

[38] Thomas Iredell to James Iredell, May 22, 1788, McRee, *Life of Iredell*, II, 224–25.

"Wilie [*sic*] Jones felt some mortification in finding himself in the company of Bloodworth and Persons," chortled one Federalist.

Meanwhile, huge bundles of pamphlets that had been sent to Jones and his friends by General Lamb's Federal Republican Committee in New York were somehow mislaid. A well-informed Federalist knew about the tracts and where they were destined on July 9, but General Person did not receive his parcel until July 23. Moreover, Person complained that his package had obviously been tampered with. Person also thought it extraordinary that it had taken the bundle some eight weeks to find its way southward—more than twice the time needed in ordinary circumstances.

Although the Antifederalists had been shaken by the turn of affairs in Richmond, Federalists knew their cause was hopeless when the North Carolina convention gathered on July 21 in Hillsborough. Arrayed against the twenty-two Federalist counties and boroughs were forty clearly dominated by Jones' friends and followers, with the demarcation line traceable between the coastal and back-country areas. Matters might have been even better, except that the Antifederalists lost their Dobbs County foothold because of the election-day riots, which caused the committee on elections to rule "no contest."[39]

Jones occupied a unique position. He was the only Antifederalist leader in the whole country who commanded a majority in the ratifying convention, who had a program, and who pursued it with dispatch. The success of Jones' initial mission certainly suggests that had the Antifederalists been as well-organized and well-led elsewhere, they would not have been in full retreat on nearly all other political fronts in July, 1788. Jones decided that the amendments which Mason and Henry had nursed through the Virginia convention would do well enough until something better came to hand. Fortified with both the Virginia recommendations and Jefferson's "let-nine-ratify-then-stop" letter, Jones had no intention of letting the Federalist minority do what they had done so successfully elsewhere—spell out the session, wage a war of attrition, and finally

[39] *Colonial and State Records of North Carolina* (ed. by William L. Saunders and Walter Clark), XXI, 10–11.

snatch victory from the tired, frustrated majority. Although some Antifederalists would have gone roughshod over the Federalists, that was not Jones' way. Antifederalists, rankled by the opposition's haughty procedures in Pennsylvania or Maryland, may have thought it prudent to give a demonstration on genteel majority conduct. Jones allowed the clause-by-clause debate motion to pass. Coupled with the report on Dobbs County, it was plain that the first round of the North Carolina convention had gone to the Federalists.

Appearances were misleading, however, for Jones continued to maintain a tight rein on the overwhelming antifederal majority. Although the Federalists showed their wares to great advantage, they elicited little support. Iredell knew only too well that most of the delegates had taken a strong anti-Constitution stand in the hustings, but he tried to budge them by twitting those who "arrogate infallibility to themselves." Iredell's point, that a man who changed his mind did nothing dishonorable, was followed by a rafter-ringing plea for the Union.[40] But the shoe which had been on the federal foot in Maryland was now worn by the adversary. The Federalists tried to draw out the opposition, but only encountered word-quibbling and sarcasm. Antifederalists took their cue from Jones, only interjecting a cryptic sentence on occasion. By a wave of his hand, Jones demolished a Federalist's syllogism.

It must have been obvious to the North Carolina Federalists that had a bill of rights been included in the Constitution their goal would have been easily accomplished. The failure to include guarantees for personal liberties was a recurring complaint of the Antifederalists, who insisted that such matters needed to rest "on a sure footing." Judge Spencer needled the Federalists by claiming that a simple sentence which declared that all the powers not specifically delegated to the federal government would be reserved for the states would have made a bill of rights unnecessary. Bloodworth kept dangling the Mississippi bauble before the delegates and in rebuttal to Iredell pointed out that northern congressmen had deviously offered to give up American rights on the western waterway. Whenever Bloodworth found an opening, he warned that the North would

[40] Elliot, *Debates*, IV, 14, 155, *passim*.

always be able to dominate the South through a majority in Congress—thirty-six northern votes against twenty-nine southern ones was his calculation. "They will always outvote us." The implication was plain. Citizens would lose their rights individually, while the South would lose its collective rights. Only drastic amendments could safeguard personal freedom or protect southern interests.

Near the close of the North Carolina convention, it seemed that the Antifederalists were indulging in a teasing game that they had not been able to play from the winning end elsewhere. The Federalists had finally exhausted their resources, however, and after nine days of going up the hill and marching down again, they called for ratification on the premise that needed amendments might be made "subsequent . . . and not previous to it." This maneuver forced Jones out of a long silence. Jones deprecated the dangers depicted by Federalists. Their cries of disunion were "merely ideal and fanciful." Rather, it was the delegates' duty not to approve the Constitution as it stood and to stipulate those amendments which would entice North Carolina into a regular ratification. Against a background of anguished moans, Davie appealed to Antifederalists "to act openly and aboveboard, adding that a contrary conduct on this occasion, was extremely despicable."

Jones denied that he had tried any trickery. On the contrary, he explained, he had patiently listened to the last oratorical bolts from the opposition. Iredell made Jones listen a bit longer as he recalled how the British had tried to break up the Union during the war by playing on sectional jealousies. Despite vigorous protests, Iredell denied that he was trying to smear the Antifederalists with the Tory brush, but the plain fact was that they had certainly endeavored to plant suspicions against their northern brethren. How really shortsighted they were, Iredell went on, for by staying out of the Union now they in fact increased the northern influence. The convention was in no mood for dire warnings, however. Jones' motion to place North Carolina in a state of suspended indecision—neither ratifying nor rejecting the Constitution—passed, 183 ayes to 84 nays.

The crushing vote told the Federalists that their orations and backporch conversations had availed nothing. Somewhat caustically,

Governor Johnston wondered aloud if the Antifederalists were waiting to hear what their friends in the Poughkeepsie convention had done. Even if the New York Antifederalists succeeded, Johnston said, North Carolina could expect little assistance from them, since "Her views are diametrically opposite to ours." As Johnston settled in his chair, Jones denied that the alternatives were ratification or ruin. Withholding approval and staying out of the Union— temporarily—was precisely what Jones wanted.

Jones became more explicit as he alluded to Jefferson's letter, which urged four recalcitrant states to use their objections as a lever for amendments. Jones candidly admitted that the amendments he favored were "word for word, the Virginia amendments, with one or two additional ones." Virginia would support her neighbor when the time came for North Carolina to ratify, and so would South Carolina and Georgia. "There is no doubt we shall obtain our amendments, and come into the Union when we please," Jones insisted. "For my part, I would rather be eighteen years out of the Union than adopt it in its present form."

Enamored with the idea of another federal convention, Jones was willing to peg all his hopes on that Antifederalist mirage. Obviously Jones had not seen any of Jefferson's second series of letters that reversed his earlier position by endorsing the Massachusetts amendments. What counted was that Jefferson's first thoughts had coincided precisely with Jones' own ideas. The work of another convention would take time, and many more months would be spent sending amendments to the states. So, Jones reasoned, why all the rush? Maryland had stayed out of the Confederation for years, but until she finally confederated she had been treated as a member of the Union in every way. Jones asked the Federalists if "twelve men, struggling under a heavy load, would refuse the assistance of a thirteenth man?"

On August 1, delegates read a long list of amendments that included one bombshell. This Jones-supported addition to the Virginia list denied federal control over paper money emitted by the states, "or in the liquidating and discharging [of] the public securities of any one of the states."[41] Other proposed curbs on the federal government revealed the suspicious antifederal approach toward a distant authority. Although the provision on the public debt must have caused a few Federalists an anxious moment, they were inclined to shrug off indications of North Carolinian parochialism. Sophisticated Federalists sarcastically declared the amendments "well worthy of the united band" gathered around Jones.

On the final day of the convention, Jones hurried things along. No wedges had been driven into the Antifederalists' ranks by the skilled orators, as in Boston, nor had there been any hints of bribery or corruption. There had been no wining and dining, as at Charleston, nor repeated allusions to Washington, as in Richmond. Instead of a party victory, however, the avalanche of nays that defeated the Federalists' ratification proposal was a personal triumph for Jones. Jones had also avoided that fatal error of Antifederalists elsewhere, for he never changed his original position. It was a lesson most Antifederalists never learned.

While Jones held the whip, he used it sparingly. He promised to recommend that North Carolina should collect tariffs similar to those imposed by Congress, and to send the funds "arising therefrom to the use of Congress." This promise he kept as a show of good faith toward the Union. Moreover, Jones supported a unanimous recommendation that the state speedily redeem all its outstanding paper money, as a further demonstration of good intentions. Finally, the governors of other states were to be informed of all their actions. In short, North Carolina offered to participate in any future amending convention which—as Jones confidentially assured friends—would materialize.

Without fanfare, with no bonfires or firing of muskets, or thirteen jubilant toasts, Jones' followers packed their saddle bags and headed homeward, certain that they had done the right thing. Jefferson had said so, Jones reassured them, and the long-winded Federalists had done well to keep their own convictions. The tidewater orators from law offices and countinghouses, cheek by jowl with those who had

[41] *Ibid.,* 244–47.

withered the opposition in Boston, only flushed out warm retorts in Hillsborough. Sensing trouble, the North Carolina delegation in New York had done its best to discount the Antifederalists' work back home by conspicuously avoiding the ratification celebration held by delirious Federalists on Manhattan island. Informed citizens believed that the ratification was all over now except for the shouting —of which there seemed to be a great deal. Even a few citizens who were extraordinarily well informed, however, made miscalculations. In far-off Europe, Jefferson longed for news from North Carolina but heard nothing. "But in such a case no news is good news," the American minister wrote, "as an unfavorable decision of the 12th state would have flown like an electrical shock through America and Europe."[42]

Jefferson had been abroad too long. Although the Antifederalists might have hoped their action would electrify the Republic, or at least galvanize the dissenting elements into some concrete program of action, the Federalists soon proved they had not lost their consummate ability to turn back bad news with good.

[42] Jefferson to Thomas Lee Shippen, September 29, 1788, 13 *Jefferson Papers* 642.

XV

The Second-Convention Fiasco

I F THE NORTH CAROLINA "Antis" intended to send a shock wave
rippling across the young nation, they were sorely disappointed.
Their action had a puzzling effect rather than an alarming one.
When the first surprise wore off, Federalists were inclined to heap
the blame on Willie Jones. Perhaps they would have been happier
if Jones had resembled the Antifederalist stereotype, but he did not,
and it was discomfitting to have a well-born, Eton-educated gentleman serve as spokesman for the anti-Constitution forces. For all his
endowments, Jones could still rub elbows with a dirt farmer. In fact,
Jones seemed to enjoy it immensely; and his political experiences
with men from all walks of life bred a mutual respect. Far from
being soured with the common man's capabilities, Jones readily became a practicing democrat. Federalists could not understand such
a man. In their haste to discredit the Hillsborough convention, they
tried to dab Jones with the brush of infamy.

The storm brewing among the frustrated North Carolina Federalists broke when rumors of the New York ratification were confirmed. They plunged into a newspaper war with vengeance. "A
Citizen and Soldier" blasted the Antifederalists for their noncom-
mital resolution at Hillsborough, which was patently the work of a
junto "determined upon the ruin of their country."[1] These wretched
men had a "dangerous and corrupted attachment" to paper money
and other fraudulent instruments. There was no more convincing
evidence of their crimes "than the strange, imprudent and outrageous
proceedings of the late Convention at Hillsborough." The Jones-
sponsored resolution was "an artful fraudulent evasion" practiced
by "wicked, abandoned and depraved" Antifederalists. As far away

---

[1] "To the People of the district of Edenton," Edenton *State Gazette of North
Carolina*, September 22, 1788, quoted in Lefler, *A Plea for Federal Union, North
Carolina, 1788*, p. 43.

279

as Boston, Jones was identified as *"his Satannick Majesty's Delegate to the Hillsborough Convention."*[2]

Jones undoubtedly knew that he was *persona non grata* with many of his neighborhood planters, but he remained even tempered and tolerated their remarks until the newspaper blast from "A Citizen and Soldier" appeared. Touchy on points of honor, Jones denied that he had impugned the motives of Federal Convention delegates or ever called Washington or Davie scoundrels. In fact, Jones explained, he knew as little of that august body "as this angry soldier (who perhaps never drew a sword in the service of his country) knows of me." Jones praised Washington as the first citizen of the world, and called Davie an honest and thoughtful citizen. In short, nothing exceeded his respect for those worthy gentlemen "unless it be my scorn and contempt for the 'CITIZEN and SOLDIER.' "[3]

Months passed but the Federalists' rancor did not abate as eleven other states prepared the makeshift Union for a spring launching. Friends of the Constitution complained that business was at a standstill while prospects were gloomy for the errant sister. *"And yet, with all these grievances under which an infant people with impotent Struggles laboured,"* Jones condemned the Federal Convention and had gone to Hillsborough "full of d—mns & G—d damns, blow [n] up an idle Fandango about Bills of Rights & Amendments, & what is still more infamous, throw[n] us altogether out of the Union. Was this a time to smoak a pipe, & suck the paw like a surly Bear, when your house was on fire?"[4]

Cast in the minority role, the North Carolina Federalists were uncomfortable and desperate. One bitter Federalist denounced the back-country elements which had supported Jones, and hinted that the seaboard might consider secession. The interest of the seaboard and the back country were irreconcilable, and since Federalists from

[2] *Massachusetts Centinel*, October 22, 1788.

[3] Willie Jones to Messrs. Hodge and Wills, October, 1788, quoted in *State Gazette of North Carolina*, October 20, 1788, and in C. C. Crittenden, "North Carolina Newspapers Before 1790," *James Sprunt Historical Studies*, XX, No. 1 (Chapel Hill, 1928), 68.

[4] George Sterling to G. Nicolson, December 14, 1788, quoted in Louise Trenholme, *Ratification of the Federal Constitution in North Carolina*, 202.

the coastal district had been unanimous in the Convention, "let us still stick together" rather than truckle to "the policy of our back country rules," even if it might bring on a clash of arms.[5]

More gall and wormwood for Federalists came from varied reactions to the political maneuver that Jones had engineered. A North Carolina delegate in the Continental Congress reported "extreme astonishment" there when the news was first announced. Federalists then took stock, attributed the surprise measure to a fondness for paper money, and were inclined to dismiss the whole incident as trivial. A friend of Madison's heard the news with amazement. "Good God what can they promise themselves!" The Virginian passed along the rumor (unconfirmed, he added) that Henry's influence had been at work in Hillsborough.[6] A New England politician feared the consequences of bad examples. He wondered whether "the Seeds of this degenerate vine" would cause brambles in the wheatfields, and concluded that other states would now shun North Carolina because "she hath gone a whoring after Strange Gods."[7]

In sharp relief against the Federalists' rage, the North Carolinians who sided with Jones took a calm view of the situation. Shortly after the convention adjourned, one of Jones' aides had reported to General Lamb's Antifederalist clearinghouse in New York. Thomas Person wrote that they might have easily rejected the Constitution outright, but had "conceived it more decent & moderate" to keep the main question dangling while making a strong pitch for the second convention. Meanwhile, Person added, they expected levelheaded men would prevail "in defiance of precipitation & some arts which I suspect tho' I cannot enumerate or trace them." Person had personal knowledge of one such art, however, for an important letter that he had written to Lamb had never been delivered; and Lamb's letter to Person (which took sixty-six days to reach him) bore evidence of tampering. If New York should adopt, Person speculated, there would be little chance of obtaining amendments unless the

---

[5] Lefler, *A Plea for Federal Union, North Carolina, 1788*, p. 72.

[6] John Swann to James Iredell, September 21, 1788, McRee, *Life of Iredell*, II, 240–41; Gordon to Madison, August 31, 1788, Madison papers, *DLC*.

[7] Jeremiah Hill to George Thatcher, August 29, 1788, Thatcher papers, *BPL*.

Antifederalists co-operated in sending men to the new Congress determined to "oppose every operation of the system until it is render'd consistant with the Preservation of our Liberties too precious to be Sacrificed to *Authority, Name, Ambition,* or *design*."[8] Jones' spokesman made it clear that the North Carolina Antifederalists were attached to the Union and believed their action would, in the long run, strengthen it.

Confident that their action had reflected the will of the majority, the North Carolina Antifederalists smugly proceeded in the direction of a second convention. When the state legislature convened, a resolution was passed which provided for a five-man delegation to another federal convention. The governor was empowered to pay their expenses once he had received the official convention call, which they believed would surely come. Five Antifederalists, including Person and Bloodworth, were named for the delegation by the Jones-led faction.

Beyond the North Carolina borders the real concern was not so much that the state failed to ratify, but that the hopes of the Antifederalists still flickered. The disappointment ranged from that of Jonathan Trumbull in Connecticut, who had hopes that the "shameless Prostitute"—Rhode Island—would "not be able to find an Associate in her Sins & Follies," to speculators in New York public securities who suffered financial reverses. "The North Carolina news lowered securities 6 *d*. in the £ *here*, too; but that is a short-lived business," Postmaster-General Hazard assured a Bostonian. Hazard might have even been a little relieved, for the din of ratification celebrations finally got on his nerves, and by mid-July he confessed, "I am sick of them."[9] Madison, caught in the tiresome and treacherous debate in the Continental Congress over locating the temporary capital, was in no mood for bad tidings. What troubled Madison was that the side step by North Carolina, which had the appearance of a rejection, would keep hopes for a second convention alive. The North Carolina maneuver, along "with the tendency of

[8] Thomas Person to John Lamb, August 6, 1788, Lamb papers, *NYHS*.

[9] J. Trumbull to Washington, June 20, 1788, *DHC*, IV, 716; Hazard to Belknap, September 9, 1788, *MHS, Collections*, 5th Series. III, 51, 62.

the circular letter from the Convention of N. York, has somewhat changed the aspect of things and has given fresh hopes and exertions to those who opposed the Constitution," Madison wrote Jefferson. The Antifederalists would certainly try "to effect an early Convention composed of men who will essentially mutilate the system," aiming most of their fire at the taxing powers of Congress. Madison frankly feared a second convention "in the present temper of America," because a short delay "would produce the double advantage of diminishing the heat and increasing the light of all parties." Madison thought a one-year cooling-off period while the Constitution was in operation would "probably suggest more real amendments than all the antecedent speculations of our most sagacious politicians."

At this stage Madison was not disturbed by the few late demonstrations of Antifederalist power, but rather by the petty sectional politics which were being exposed in the halls of Congress. The wrangling over a temporary seat for the new government turned into a power struggle between the North and South. To Washington, Madison wrote bluntly that the sectional skirmishes over the capital made it seem that the southern Antifederalists had been justified in sounding their dire warnings. Thus, northern delegates found the events in North Carolina less and less embarrassing as time passed. "That which at first appeared to be a misfortune, now appears to be a favorite Circumstance," Congressman Thatcher was told. The New England Federalist thought that if North Carolina had ratified it might have been "a material disadvantage to us at the northward in the arrangement of Matters under the new Government, & as matters now Stand we are upon par."[10]

Actually, the Antifederalists from both sections of the young nation might have been far more troublesome had the hopes for a second convention not been kept alive by the events in North Carolina and Governor Clinton's circular letter. Instead of trying to exploit the North-South rift in Congress to their own advantage, the Antifederalists kept looking beyond the congressional corridors to a second general convention. Madison lashed the New York circular letter as the Antifederalist chimera "from which mischiefs are

[10] Jeremiah Hill to George Thatcher, September 6, 1788, Thatcher papers, *BPL*.

apprehended." If it succeeded and another convention met, Madison predicted, the second body would either "terminate in discord" or urge many enfeebling amendments. Madison was peeved with Jay for having had a hand in the business, even though the circular letter had been a vital part of the Poughkeepsie compromise. "At present the public mind is neither sufficiently cool nor sufficiently informed for so delicate an operation."[11]

Antifederalist reaction to Clinton's circular letter was varied. Abraham Lansing believed the attempt to solidify the dissenting elements was not "altogether futil [*sic*] but the adoption is notwithstanding unconditional in every acception of the words."[12] Lansing had no great hopes for a second convention but pleaded for the concentration of antifederal energies so that friendly congressmen could be elected to "assist in bringing about the reformation we wish." In Rhode Island the state legislature eagerly seized the invitation for action by ordering copies of the letter printed and sent to the towns. The town meetings were asked to vote on the propriety of electing deputies for a second federal convention "or such other instructions as they deem conducive to the public good."

Governor Randolph went back to his wavering course when Clinton's dispatch arrived. Randolph forwarded the recommendations to the legislature, implying that he favored co-operation with the New Yorkers because the real point of another gathering was to "only incorporate the theory of the people with the theory of the [first] convention; and each of these is entitled to equal respect."[13] Randolph agreed with Madison that the proposed amendments aimed at limiting the federal taxation powers were suspiciously drawn. "But I can only endeavor to avert that particular evil, and cannot persuade myself to thwart a second convention merely from the apprehension of that evil," he explained.

When the jarring news from North Carolina was coupled with the reaction of governors in Rhode Island and Virginia, Federalist fears that antifederalism was far from moribund seemed justified.

11 Madison to Jefferson, August 10, 1788, 13 *Jefferson Papers* 497–98.
12 A. G. Lansing to Yates, August 3, 1788, Yates papers, *NYHS*.
13 Randolph to Madison, August 13, 1788, Conway, *Life of Randolph*, 117.

Madison gloomily read reports from friends and decided the circular letter had "a most pestilent tendency."[14] Unless the call for another convention could be parried, Madison maintained "that the system which has resisted so many direct attacks may be at last successfully undermined by its enemies." In retrospect, some Federalists thought it would have been better if New York had stayed out of the Union so that the new government "could have dissipated the fear which artifice had created, and the attempts resulting from those fears and artifices." Meanwhile, Henry was promoting the second-convention idea to willing confederates in Virginia, and nearly every mail seemed to bring in confirmation of Madison's worst apprehensions about Clinton's letter. Madison could hardly refrain from scolding Randolph for being even an unwitting partner in the scheme. The letter had become "a signal for concord & hope to the enemies of the Constitution every where," Madison admonished the governor, "and will I fear prove extremely dangerous." A second convention now would "be the offspring of party & passion . . . the parent of error and public injury."[15] Distressed to hear that Edmund Pendleton had professed himself a second-convention supporter, Madison urged that worthy to join him in a friendly watch-and-wait society. If only the Antifederalists would "wait untill some experience shall have taken place," Madison counselled, "the business will be conducted with more light as well as with less heat."

Tench Coxe assured Madison that Antifederalists in Pennsylvania were nearly inaudible but intransigent in their opposition. Federalists discounted the plans of several Pennsylvania counties to call a September convention, presumably to make amends for the unqualified ratification jostled through the Philadelphia gathering. The inland counties voiced impassioned pleas for a bill of rights, while the Philadelphia Antifederalists harped about direct taxes. The federal power to tax would doubtlessly "reduce the importance of the state governments," Coxe observed, which was the main

---

[14] Madison to Washington, August 15, 1788, Madison papers, *DLC.*

[15] Randolph to Madison, September 12, 1788, Madison papers, *DLC;* Madison to Randolph, August 22, 1788, Madison papers, *DLC;* Madison to Edmund Pendleton, October 20, 1788, *DHC,* V, 94.

reason local Antifederalists never tired of pulling out the tax bogeyman. Crocodile tears were thus shed in public over the taxing powers of Congress.[16] Coxe believed the central county partisans were dupes for the city Antifederalists, who "kept out of sight" their real motive for opposition "by putting the others forward." However, Coxe's friends doubted that the Harrisburg convention call came spontaneously from inexperienced Antifederalist hayseeds. The convention was not being held to discuss amendments but to plan the forthcoming election campaign and pick candidates for the legislature and Congress. Petty antifederal politicians in Philadelphia had seized Clinton's circular letter as a prop for their scheme, "A FREEMAN" charged, since that unfortunate document held out "the menacing alternative" of adopting amendments or plunging America into "the miseries of a civil war."

No Federalist was more upset by the Antifederalist rumblings than Madison. Madison aroused Washington by his speculations and cautioned that efforts to convert Rhode Island to Federalism might be sidetracked "till this new crisis of danger be over." Washington responded by sending a warning to New England that the circular letter was "intended to bring on a general Convention at too early a period, and in short . . . to set every thing afloat again." Reports of serenity on the Virginia political front hardly reassured Madison. "I rather think their conduct is intended to lull the friends to the new government into a state of security and then in the fall to make a violent attack," with Henry in the Antifederalists' vanguard. Upset by the congressional deadlock over locating the capital, Madison saw the need for tranquility at what appeared to be a critical moment; and each report of approbation for the circular letter or a general convention brought Madison pangs of discouragement. "An early Convention is in every view to be dreaded in the present temper of America," he informed Jefferson.[17] Having witnessed the discord

---

[16] Tench Coxe to Madison, July 23, 1788, Madison papers, *DLC.*

[17] Madison to Washington, August 15, 1788, Madison papers, *DLC;* Washington to Benjamin Lincoln, August 29, 1788, *DHC,* V, 34–35; Madison to Jefferson, August 23, 1788, 13 *Jefferson Papers* 540.

of the first convention, Madison added, he would "tremble for the result of a second."[18]

The strains of the long ratification campaign told on Madison. Among other things, his usually perceptive analysis of the situation suffered from his personal involvement in the North-South wrangling over the capital site. Unable to detach himself from the bickering that made southern Antifederalists seem better prophets than he once dreamed possible, Madison misinterpreted the effect of Clinton's letter and he miscalculated the damage done by the North Carolina Antifederalists. Thus Madison and other Federalists believed that there was a sudden upsurge of co-operation amongst the opposition. Vigorous measures might be needed to stamp out the antifederalism which had seemed crushed on July 26. But the "concord of opposition" that the Federalists thought they saw was a delusion, and within two months' time even Madison had to admit that they had been unduly upset.

The Antifederalists doubtlessly thought they could capitalize on the incessant chant for amendments by maneuvering the state legislatures into support of another general convention. When Mason saw the New York amendments, which he believed modeled on his Virginia list, his summertime disappointment gave way to new hopes. Indeed, the leading public men in Virginia were in rare accord as the Clinton letter drew public praise, helped by Governor Randolph's blessing. Randolph argued the point with Madison, insisting that the time was ripe for changes while the minorities were so large and respected. Was this not the precise moment when alterations should be made, the governor asked, before constitutional orthodoxy set in and "the spirit of amendments" would "be treated as heretical?" Randolph candidly confessed his "great distrust of some of those, who will certainly be influential agents of the government, and whom I suspect to be capable of making a wicked use of its defects." He excluded Hamilton from his list of suspects, but there were others whose conduct at the Federal Convention had created "A disgustful apprehension." For these characters salutary amend-

[18] Madison to George Turberville, November 2, 1788, Madison papers, *DLC*.

ments from a second convention would act as reins.[19] Not all Virginia Federalists agreed. "Lighthorse Harry" Lee saw the drift of things and became alarmed. The circular letter was "the standard, to which the various minoritys will repair, & if they should succeed in bringing quickly into action the objects of that letr., new & serious difficultys must arise, which will cross & may destroy the govt. in its infancy."[20]

While Henry organized Antifederalist affairs in Virginia, the Pennsylvania dissenters went their own way. Throughout August public meetings in Greensburg, Newton, Uniontown, Bedminister, and other communities selected delegates for the forthcoming Harrisburg convention. Discussions at these gatherings indicated that among plain citizens there was a consensus that a bill of rights ought to be the first business of the new government. These plain citizens suspected that smooth-talking Federalists would by "sullen and inactive conduct" prove that they never intended to support a bill of rights. Accordingly, they sent delegates to Harrisburg, expecting them to act jointly in support of a general revising convention. "We will [then] enjoy the supreme felicity of having assisted in snatching from slavery a once happy and worthy people," a Bucks County Antifederalist asserted. Perhaps it was levelheaded John Nicholson who persuaded the petition-writers to temper their remarks. At any rate, there was a conspicuous absence of saber-rattling, and loose talk about overt resistance to the Constitution was denounced as "the height of madness and folly."[21]

On the surface, the Harrisburg meeting seemed to be a genuine outcropping of the libertarian spirit. Some of the naïve gentry who gathered in the Dauphin County seat doubtlessly believed the Constitution was an engine of despotism that needed overhauling before its first trial. But, as well-informed Federalists had guessed, the impetus for the convention actually had come from a dozen Antifederalists who were already scrambling for positions in the forth-

[19] Randolph to Madison, September 3, 1788, Madison papers, *DLC*.

[20] Henry Lee to Washington, September 13, 1788, *DHC*, V, 50–51.

[21] James Hanna to John Vandergrift, *et al.*, August 15, 1788, quoted in John B. McMaster and Frederick D. Stone, *Pennsylvania and the Federal Constitution*, 553–54.

coming congressional races. A disappointingly small turnout of thirty-three delegates came from thirteen counties, with veteran politicians conspicuous in the Philadelphia contingent. Among the newcomers there was a young Swiss immigrant enjoying his first taste of political broth—Albert Gallatin.

From the outset the convention was dominated by would-be office-holders with little interest in high-sounding abstractions about the rights of mankind. Resolutions were duly adopted, and almost as swiftly forgotten. Their muted manifesto decried ambiguities in the Constitution, and was a compendium of the complaints heard at nearly every ratifying convention. The delegates also called for a "speedy revision" of the Constitution by a second convention. The whole affair was handled expeditiously, perhaps too much so, for the grass-roots clamor for a bill of rights somehow got lost in the Harrisburg shuffle.

In a few days it was obvious that the Harrisburg convention, instead of igniting a brush fire of protest, was much ado about nothing. The officeholders and office-seekers stumbled over each other until they all got tired and went home. A disappointed delegate from Carlisle looked back on the business and decided "our Harrisburg conference did more injury to our cause than all the strategems of our advarsaries [*sic*]."[22] Instead of working hard to get the Constitution amended, the delegates spent their time lining up support for their prospective candidacies. Conscientious Antifederalists thought their mission was "to form committees and associations and open a Chanel [*sic*] of communications through-out the United States." If this had been done, "the opposition would have appeared so formidable to the Federalists that they durst not have refused our demands." But short-sighted, office-hungry professional politicians had "defeated every salutary measure and we will perhaps never find the people in the same spirit again," delegate Petriken lamented, adding that "opportunitys once lost is not easily recovered." A Federalist might have summed up the Harrisburg fiasco with better grammar, but no more perceptively.

[22] William Petriken to John Nicholson, March 23, 1789, Nicholson papers, Pennsylvania State Archives.

When the Harrisburg convention was first mentioned, cautious Federalists thought that the Antifederalists had something shrewd up their sleeve. The circular letter had already been condemned as an impertinence which held out "the total annihilation of every useful and wise part of the constitution."[23] After the Harrisburg convention fizzled out, however, Federalists realized they had overestimated its importance. Madison heard that the attendance was skimpy and was pleased that its resolutions had "not rhyme[d] very well with those of the Southern advocates for a Convention; the objects most eagerly pursued by the latter being unnoticed in the Harrisburg proceedings."[24] It was the old story of Antifederalist ineptitude, accentuated in this case by bumbling would-be congressmen.

Whatever faint hope the Pennsylvania Antifederalists had of directing public attention toward a second convention through the Harrisburg affair was also thwarted by Federalist censorship of news. Outside of the regular Antifederalist newspapers, there was little disposition to print the Harrisburg proceedings. Antifederalists had not been prepared for the seeming indifference that greeted their tactics. A well-informed Philadelphia observer was startled by the aftermath of the Harrisburg conference. "Our Antifederalists have changed their Battery," he reported to Washington.[25] "They are now very federal. They want Amendments & they must get into the Seats of Government to bring them about—or what is better—to share the Loaves & Fishes." The Harrisburg convention "was a mere Election Jobb [*sic*] & no Harm is to be expected from it." Those few Antifederalists who were elected would "find it their Interest to support a Government in which they are Sharers tho' they may make a little Bustle."

By late September the flurry created by the circular letter appeared

---

[23] Quoted in Philadelphia *Independent Gazetteer*, August 16, 1788.

[24] Madison to Randolph, September 14, 1788, Madison papers, *DLC*. See also Paul L. Ford, *The Origin, Purpose and Result of the Harrisburg Convention of 1788* (Brooklyn, 1890) *passim*. The subtitle, "A Study in Popular Government," indicates Ford's viewpoint.

[25] Richard Peters to Washington, September 17, 1788, DHC, V, 65.

[26] Madison to Jefferson, September 21, 1788, 13 *Jefferson Papers* 624–25; Jay to Washington, September 21, 1788, *DHC*, V, 70.

to have spent itself. The Federal Republican Society in New York had temporarily suspended its activities. While the Continental Congress was split over the issue of a temporary capital, local Federalists tried to show New York in its best light, and perhaps Lamb's committee suffered from lassitude now that ratification was a *fait accompli*. Southern Antifederalists in the Congress voted for Philadelphia, Wilmington, Lancaster, Pennsylvania, and Baltimore in their futile attempt to keep the New Englanders from their choice of New York. When they finally lost, Madison was fearful that the northern victory would be trumpeted by southern Antifederalists "who have inculcated a jealousy of this end of the Continent." But on the credit side, Congress had voted to end its negotiations with Spain over the Mississippi, and Madison thought a permanent southern capital might ultimately be chosen when "the Western and South Western population comes more into view." In Madison's view, the boulders strewing the path of the new government could all be moved if only the opponents of the Constitution would drop their goal of "an *immediate* revision of it by another General Convention." John Jay surmised that many Antifederalists would have settled for a face-saving bill calling a second convention at some distant day.[26] There was good reason to postpone "the *Session* of such a Convention for three of four Years," Jay added, and he thought most Antifederalists "would be satisfied with that Delay."

In New England, the circular letter had been roughly handled wherever Federalists were in control. A committee in the Massachusetts legislature kept Clinton's letter bottled up until the time for effective action had passed.[27] The Rhode Island General Assembly was sympathetic enough, but the towns were so slow in responding to a call for instructions that, in the end, nothing ever came of it. In Connecticut, Clinton's letter was read to the general assembly where not even "the Champion of our Antis . . . had hardiness enough to call up the consideration of that Letter, or to mention one word of its subject."[28] After months of inactivity, the New York Federal Republican Society met at Fraunces' Tavern on October 30,

[27] Theodore Sedgwick to Hamilton, November 2, 1788, Hamilton papers, *DLC*.
[28] Johnathan Trumbull to Washington, October 28, 1788, *DHC*, V, 101.

pledged to work for a second federal convention and the election of George Clinton as vice president "to insure the adoption of the amendments."[29] Little enthusiasm greeted their announcement, however, as each day saw more news items reporting the election of senators and representatives for the first Congress. One of John Adams' backers for the Vice-Presidency confessed he was an Adams man not out of friendship but simply because Adams would help thwart another convention and the "alterations falsely and imprudently called by some of our state governors *amendments*." Hamilton, supporting Adams for the same reason, advised friends in New England to talk all drives for amendments to death. "The rage for amendments is in my *opinion* rather to be parried by address than encountered with open force," he hinted.[30]

In Maryland, personalities transcended abstractions about a bill of rights or direct taxes as the election campaigns progressed. "We have had the Devil to pay here for a few Days past," a weary Baltimore citizen complained. The voters were harangued, harsh words flew, and finally clubs and rocks were used to persuade. Several fashionable ladies lost their dignity in hair-pulling matches, "a few got broken heads, and one of the Principals had his windows demolished."[31] Samuel Chase, who was "running scared" for a house of delegates seat, claimed that recent party labels were suddenly outmoded. Antifederalists had been "against adopting it without previous amendments," but ratification had made the party names meaningless.[32] Baltimore voters seemed to disagree, as they rejected Chase amidst cries of electioneering frauds and violence.

Across the Potomac, Mason retired to Gunston Hall and left the Antifederalist burden on Henry's stooped shoulders, but the field was far from deserted. A Richmond Federalist was alarmed by

[29] E. Wilder Spaulding, *New York in the Critical Period* (New York, 1932), 269–70.

[30] Hamilton to Madison, November 23, 1788; Hamilton to Theodore Sedgwick, November 9, 1788, *Works of Alexander Hamilton* (ed. by Henry C. Lodge), IX, 451, 454–55.

[31] Otho Holland Williams to Dr. Philip Thomas, September 20, 1788, Williams papers, Maryland Historical Society.

[32] Baltimore *Maryland Gazette*, September 23, October 10, 14, 1788.

Henry's indefatigable efforts. Even the "staunchest friends of the new Constitution" had been persuaded "to close with N York & propose another convention to amend."[33] A week later the same citizen was certain that the "Cloven hoof begins to appear ... intrigue antifederalism and artifice go hand in hand." Again caught in a tug of war between his conscience and his vanity, Randolph decided to support Henry's drive for another convention. This latest twist amazed Federalists who saw great danger in the governor's enigmatic conduct. "He will injure his political Reputation by his doublings and turnings," Francis Corbin discerned. "He is *too Machiavelian* and not *Machiavelian Enough*." Antifederalists suspected Randolph too. Randolph's gyrations made Antifederalists watchful despite the governor's private remark that he would soon "retire from the Helm, and take a birth [*sic*] among the Crew—where he talks of Joining the mutineers either to trim the Ballast of the new Government or put the Ship about."[34]

In the full flush of power, Henry brushed aside suggestions that he go into the Senate. Instead, he decided that Madison must be denied any public favor that Virginia could bestow. Madison's plea for a waiting period before launching amendments was turned against him by Lee, who declared that the meaning of such words was "that abuse under the name of use shall be rivetted upon mankind." Lee promised to work for immediate reforms, cautioning that "the reference paid to established forms when supported by power has generally proved too strong for correction."[35] Early in November, Henry guided the senate nominations of Lee and Grayson through the assembly after warning delegates that Madison's election would bring "rivelets of blood throughout the land." It was also an open secret that Henry favored Clinton for the Vice-Presidency because the New York governor was the chief promoter of a second convention. Each move only confirmed Federalists in their belief that the

[33] George Turberville to Madison, October 20, 27, 1788, Madison papers, *DLC*.

[34] Francis Corbin to Madison, October 21, 1788, Madison papers, *DLC*; Theodorick Bland to Richard Henry Lee, October 1788, Lee papers, University of Virginia Library.

[35] Richard Henry Lee to William Cabell, October 15, 1788, Ballagh, *Letters of Lee*, II, 480–81.

powerful Henry intended to "throw into the Govt. every embarrassment he possibly can."[36] The wonder was that Henry had ever been
thwarted in the ratifying convention a few months earlier.

Citizens who tried to keep themselves informed about the changing political scene during that curious autumn of 1788 saw on one
hand state after state electing members to the new Congress, ready
to set the Constitution in motion, and on the other, a few cases of
die-hardism or outright efforts to make the Constitution creak and
groan from the start. Federalist and some erstwhile Antifederalists
looked upon Henry's tactics as reprehensible. Washington was assured that Henry's resolution for a second convention "contains a
direct and indecent censure on all those who have befriended the new
constitution holding them forth as the betrayers of the dearest rights
of the people." Early in November this resolution passed the Virginia General Assembly by an overwhelming eighty-five to thirty-
nine vote, causing a dejected member of the minority to declare,
"The triumph of Antifoederalism is compleat."[37]

Although Henry doubtlessly nursed a grudge against Madison
for the drubbing that he suffered at the convention in June, he
claimed that the ostensible reason for his effort to keep the bright
young man from Orange County out of the Senate was not personal.
Ignoring Madison's repeated promise to work on behalf of a bill of
rights, Henry insisted that Madison was actually against amendments. Henry knew that the way to beat Madison was to present the
matter emotionally. A vote for Madison, Henry warned, was a vote
against the second convention and against amendments. Monroe was
urged to campaign against Madison for a place in the House of Representatives after local Federalists began work for their absent friend.
With a suspicious nature that matched the most distrustful Federalist's forebodings, Henry charged that the opposition, "if they do
not manifest Enmity to public Liberty, yet shew too little Sollicitude
or Zeal for its preservation."[38] If a second convention were ordered

[36] Edward Carrington to Madison, November 9, 1788, Madison papers, *DLC;*
Henry Lee to Madison, November 19, 1788, Madison papers, *DLC.*

[37] Charles Lee to Washington, October 29, 1788, *DHC,* V, 101–103; George
Turberville to Madison, November 10, 1788, Madison papers, *NYPL.*

[38] Patrick Henry to Richard Henry Lee, November 15, 1788, Henry papers, *DLC.*

to meet in North Carolina, Henry admitted he might be tempted to go as a delegate. Delighted by the power Antifederalists had exhibited at Hillsborough, Henry claimed that in the counties along both sides of the Virginia–North Carolina border "at least 19/20ths [of the people] are antifederal & this . . . forms a great Map of Opposition not easy to surmount." Henry maintained that he believed in the Union, but he also thought "the American Union depends on the Success of Amendments."

As Henry hoped, Willie Jones kept the pot boiling in North Carolina. So confident were the North Carolina Antifederalists that the second convention would meet that they concentrated attention on the likelihood of a spring session, and ignored the feeble protests of local Federalists who urged the calling of another state ratifying convention. But as winter approached it was apparent that Henry and Jones were playing an isolated game. Madison, after his initial apprehensions, surveyed all the evidence and felt easier. Henry's schemes were "as impolitic as they are otherwise exceptionable," Madison avowed, because amendments would be more easily gained in the new Congress "than from attempts to bring about another Convention." The selection of senators in six states "known to be Bona fide friends to the Constitution" settled the matter in Madison's mind. Where he had felt qualms a few weeks earlier, the hardworking Federalist now believed the Antifederalists' dream of another convention was "a hopeless pursuit."[39] The "dark and threatening Cloud hanging over the Constitution" had disappeared.

As the eventful year of 1788 passed, it became obvious to all but the most hard-bitten Antifederalists that once again their plans had miscarried. Governor Clinton heard informally of Henry's tactics, but by mid-December he had not yet seen the official notice of Virginia's call for a second convention. After all the bad luck Clinton had experienced in communicating with Richmond, he was under-

[39] Madison to George Turberville, November 2, 1788, Madison papers, *DLC;* Madison to Henry Lee, November 30, 1788, Madison papers, *DLC;* Harry Ammon, "The Formation of the Republican Party in Virginia, 1789–96," *Journal of Southern History,* XIX (1953), 287*n.*, points out that the call for a second convention was "the only measure upon which the various [Antifederalist] elements were able to agree."

standably perturbed. The New Yorker suspected "that measures may be taken to retard delivery of it so as to defeat its utility."[40] Circumstantial evidence indicated that Clinton was actually too easygoing about the mail delays, but it was too late to do more than pout and ponder. Meanwhile, Henry's enemies claimed his highhanded methods would force people on the righteous path once they became "acquainted with the Conduct of their great high preist [*sic*]." A more moderate observer thought Henry had overshot the mark by supporting Lee and Grayson. "Thus may these Gentlemen verify their predictions of a bad Government, as effectually as the Physician may his who having foretold a Patient's death, is yet intrusted with administering his Physic."[41]

Elsewhere, only a few Antifederalists survived the Federalist juggernaut. Gerry was called from retirement by well-meaning friends who urged him to campaign for a place in the House of Representatives. Gerry harkened to the call by promising to work for amendments as proposed by the various state conventions. "To defeat amendments of this description," Gerry emphasized, "must be in effect to defeat the constitution itself."[42] Boston Federalists sent broadsides into Gerry's campaign, causing an old friend to castigate the "unprincipled Wretches who have persecuted you . . . as the Devil did Job."[43] Gerry won a seat in Congress and was thus committed to work for amendments but not bound to them as Abraham Yates wished. That tough-minded New Yorker demanded that Congress proceed immediately toward making alterations. Yates believed federal officers ought to withhold taking their oaths of office until amendments had been proposed by Congress. But "Rough Hewer" Yates, too extreme in his demands, confounded more than he convinced.

When the newly elected congressmen converged on New York

---

[40] George Clinton to J. Dawson, December 12, 1788, Conway, *Life of Randolph*, 114–15.

[41] George Turberville to Madison, December 14, 1788, Madison papers, *NYPL;* E. Pendleton to Nathaniel Pendleton, November 25, 1788, Pendleton papers, Yale University Library.

[42] "To the electors of Middlesex," in Austin, *Life of Gerry*, II, 92–93.

[43] Samuel Osgood to Elbridge Gerry, February 19, 1789, Gerry papers, *DLC.*

early in March, 1789, there was an evident mood of uncertainty. "I consider the first Congress as a second Convention," Samuel Osgood warned, "it is evident they must do some Acts relative to Amendments which will bear hard upon the Convention that formed the Constitution." But many who had served at the Federal Convention were taking places in the new Congress, and they had different notions about proper procedure. As the new government lurched forward, an experienced politician thought the congressmen were too cautious. He thought "there was no great prospect of a Convention, and when such men as father Sherman says 'try it first' do I much expect an early attempt at amendments."[44]

At least one Federalist, however, knew that watchful constituents would not tolerate any pussyfooting over a bill of rights. Madison defeated James Monroe after a hard campaign, and owed his victory to a pledge to work for amendments dealing with personal freedom— "particularly the rights of Conscience in the fullest latitude." Madison kept prodding his colleagues in Congress until they finally put the amending machinery in motion, but he could not please everybody. Mason mildly rebuked his son for assuming that Madison's proposals were in fact "proper Amendments." "The *Fact* was, Mr. Madis[on saw he wou]'d not be elected, without making some such Promises," Mason explained, "and to carry on the Farce, is now the ostensible Patron of Amendments." Mason dismissed them as "some Milk & Water Propositions . . . by way of th[r]owing out a Tub to the Whale." "Of important, substantial Amendments," he added, "I have not the least Hope."[45]

A meaningless resolution passed by the state legislature was the last gasp of antifederalism in New York. Only because of "an invincible Reluctance to Separate from our Sister States," the resolution recalled, had Antifederalists voted for the Constitution "without stipulating for previous Amendments."[46] The first Congress was

[44] Samuel Osgood to Elbridge Gerry, February 19, 1789, Gerry papers, *DLC;* Samuel A. Otis to Nathan Dane, March 28, 1789, Dane papers, *DLC.*

[45] Madison to George Eve, January 2, 1789, *DHC,* V, 141–43; Mason to John Mason, July 31, 1789, Mason papers, *DLC.*

[46] Copy of the "second convention" bill, dated February 5, 1789, Emmet collection, *NYPL.*

urged to call a second convention at the earliest moment. Backstage politics crowded their principles as skirmishes for Senate seats began. Melancton Smith was defeated because he "had disgusted many of the Antifeds. by acceding to the Ratification," Clinton admitted, and "his Choice w[oul]d. have been difficult." Clinton's main concern was to keep Chancellor Livingston hemmed in—and so in the negative way that politics sometimes works fortune smiled on Rufus King. After being disappointed in the shuffle for federal office in his native Massachusetts, King became a New Yorker without the onus of Livingston connections. Perhaps Clinton's glance fell on King because he expected the unaligned Federalist would help promote the governor's Vice-Presidential aspirations. If so, King proved a poor choice, but Clinton was far from finished as a political force. "They are trying to kill Clinton politically but wont [*sic*] succeed," a discerning Federalist predicted.[47]

Nothing better came out of Virginia, even though Henry had the state legislature at his bidding. "His edicts were registered by that body with less opposition than those of the Grand Monarque have met with from his Parliaments," a disgusted Federalist complained. Mason would not stir from Gunston Hall, but apparently still clung to the dream of a second convention. "*Your good friend* Col. Mason has not given up his opposition," a Virginia visitor observed with irony, "& I dare say will not so long as he is actuated by those *very liberal* principles which led him to oppose the system."[48] Representative Theodorick Bland had been Henry's choice to start the amendment movement in the House of Representatives, but Bland acted tardily. Bland finally submitted the Virginia resolution asking for another convention, but it was quickly sidetracked, ostensibly to await other similar requests from the states. Madison's insistence on direct action by Congress cut the ground from beneath Bland's efforts, moreover. "To the best of my Belief the true antis in the State do not wish to hear that Congress have adopted many of the modifications or alterations proposed" by the Jones and Henry factions, a

47 Samuel A. Otis to Nathan Dane, March 28, 1789, Dane papers, *DLC*.
48 Tobias Lear to John Langdon, January 31, 1789, Batchelor, *Early State Papers of New Hampshire*, XXI, 863–65.

seasoned observer reported from North Carolina. But another North Carolinian with his ear to the ground heard rumblings from Antifederalists who swore "that they will never forget Bland, Grayson and their other friends for suffering any business however important to be done in Congress prior to the subject of amendments."[49]

Federalists were reluctant to move toward amendments with anything approaching normal speed, and many Antifederalists were no more eager to tackle the ticklish assignment. Lee and Grayson, certain that Madison's amendments fell short of what they wanted, expected to waylay their opponent's proposals in the Senate where they would "effect, if possible, the wishes of our legislature." Grayson lamented that Madison's draft of amendments affected "personal liberty alone, leaving the great points of the Judiciary, direct taxation, &c., to stand as they are." Accordingly, Federalists would "go on coolly in sapping the independence of the state legislatures."[50] Aedanus Burke, a vociferous Antifederalist during the ratification campaign, thought there were other more pressing matters. And Gerry, whose election campaign had been based on the urgency of amendments, seemed to think political harmony was more important than the political safeguards.

Thus Washington's inauguration proved to be the wake of antifederalism. The bunting had hardly been removed before Antifederalists gave a hollow ring to much of the campaign oratory that had nearly prevented ratification. Each Antifederalist leader had been a party unto himself, with his particular version of necessary amendments varying from those of the man at his elbow. The farther apart Antifederalists were geographically, the further apart the philosophy behind their amendments. Although in the popular mind "amendments" meant something akin to a bill of rights, the Antifederalists—North and South—had irreconcilable versions. In

[49] Hugh Williamson to Madison, May 24, 1789, "Unpublished letters from North Carolina to James Madison and James Monroe" (ed. by Elizabeth E. McPherson), *North Carolina Historical Review*, XIV (1937), 162–63; Benjamin Hawkins to Madison, June 1, 1789, *ibid.*, 163–64.

[50] Richard Henry Lee to Patrick Henry, May 28, 1789, Ballagh, *Letters of Lee*, II, 487; William Grayson to Henry, June 12, 1789, Wirt, *Life of Patrick Henry*, III, 391.

their aimless wandering, and amidst wide differences of opinion, the Antifederalists finally went aground in a most predictable manner. Antifederalism collapsed in a wallow of confusion, sectional animosity, and downright insincerity. The federal Bill of Rights, instead of becoming a monument to the Antifederalists' devotion to principle, became the tombstone for their moribund party.

☆ XVI ☆

And Now, Domestic Tranquility

B Y AN EXTRAORDINARY DISPLAY OF INEPTNESS, the Antifederalists failed to exploit the public's desire for a bill of rights. Their
lukewarm position on amendments seemed to confirm Madison's
charge that their leaders were inmeshed in a "conspiracy agst direct
taxes . . . more extensive and formidable than some gentlemen suspect." Madison insisted that Antifederalists feared the power of
Congress to levy direct taxes more than anything in the Constitution.
"An abolition of that power," Madison asserted, "will re-establish
the supremacy of the State Legislatures, the real object of all their
zeal in opposing the system."[1] The indifference of leading Antifederalists toward the amendments which Madison introduced in
Congress seemed to prove that their outcries on behalf of personal
liberties had only been a campaign lure.

However grudgingly the Massachusetts Federalists may have
acted when drafting a set of recommendatory amendments, their
stratagem was in fact the master stroke of the ratification campaign.
Theophilus Parson's shrewd, calculating maneuver in Boston on
a frosty February morning had made ratification a certainty. In
retrospect, Richard Henry Lee regarded the Massachusetts plan as
a bold concession offered "as a most happy means" of saving both
the Union and the Constitution. "But now that they have gained
their point," Lee contended, "they are traducing the Men, and wish
to neglect the condition upon which probably their success was
founded."[2] By urging the first Congress to enact amendments, Madison kept the Massachusetts scheme from becoming an empty gesture.

While Madison's proposals were thrashed out in congressional
committees, northern Antifederalists were as gloomy as their south-

[1] Madison to Tench Coxe, July 30, 1788, *LCC*, VIII, 771–72.
[2] Richard Henry Lee to Samuel Adams, April 25, 1789, Ballagh, *Letters of Lee*,
II, 483–84.

ern counterparts. Joshua Atherton seemed dazed by the series of setbacks Antifederalists had so often encountered—all the more so because he was convinced their opponents had actually been "on the Brink of Failure." In bewilderment Atherton noted that the Federalists had somehow become champions of amendments, "and by a kind of duplicity often successful if not observed, are taking possession of the political Citadel under the Stile of Friends." Atherton had only apologies to offer the New York Antifederalists, for his preferred slate of electors (committed to Clinton for the Vice-Presidency) were routed.[3] With sad heart the leading Connecticut Antifederalist declined a judicial appointment rather than take an oath to support the new Constitution. "I have made no Secret of my Sentiments touching the Constitution," James Wadsworth grumbled, revealing his pessimism about the future of the new Republic.[4] Governor Clinton's personal popularity, which looked unshakable a year earlier, was jeopardized by Federalist onslaughts in New York. The Albany "Republican Committee, lately called the Anti-Federal Committee," appealed for votes on the grounds that a vote against the governor would make it appear "that we disapprove of his conduct" and were indifferent toward the calling of another general convention.[5]

Each day made the second convention a more distant mirage, until the idea spawned with such hope in 1787 was gently laid to rest in 1789. The last pockets of antifederal resistance collapsed slowly but irresistibly. In North Carolina, where high-toned Federalists believed Antifederalist delegates' "heads were no[t] otherwise of value than as they might be counted," there were still some misgivings about the Mississippi navigation and a fear of northern majorities in Congress.[6] However, Willie Jones' followers who went into the second state convention in November, 1789, with anything more than slender hopes courted disappointment. Madison's efforts

[3] Joshua Atherton to John Lamb, February 23, 1789, Lamb papers, *NYHS*.

[4] James Wadsworth to Governor Huntington, October 15, 1789, *Revolutionary War Records*, XXXVIII, 297, Connecticut State Archives.

[5] Handbill dated April 7, 1789, Peter Gansevoort, Jr., papers, *NYPL*.

[6] Rev. A. Iredell to James Iredell, October 6, 1789, McRee, *Life of Iredell*, II, 267–68.

in Congress plainly eased many of their earlier apprehensions. The best which the Antifederalists could salvage was approval of eight rather hopeless amendments. Despite pique at "tedious, trifling, and, I might add, absurd . . . objections" from Antifederalists, their opponents conceded that in defeat they had acted like sportsmen. Defeated 193 to 75, the Antifederalists appeared "perfectly satisfied since the decision, not because their doubts and fears have been fully removed, but because they have determined to acquiesce cheerfully in every measure which meets the approbation of a majority of their countrymen." "The Anties behave with great good humor on the occasion," was Governor Johnston's summary view.[7]

The situation in Pennsylvania, however, was confused and hardly humorous. Truculent Antifederalists continued to drill and bluster, bragging that on "saint Patricks night one of our Volunteers almost killed four stout young Feds without recieving [*sic*] the least damage."[8] But knowledgeable Antifederalists in Philadelphia would have none of the violent proceedings. They washed their hands of any bloodshed and went about their own quest of "the loaves and fishes" of federal office—usually without much success. The banner of resistance thus raised in western Pennsylvania was not easily furled, however. In a few short years it was unfurled in the Whisky Insurrection. It was no accident that Findley, Smilie, and Gallatin were Antifederalists in 1788 and antiexcisemen in 1791.

Diffident Rhode Island vexed her neighbors while she slowly pondered her next move. A northerner put matters in a Yankee perspective when he sent Governor Collins a reminder of some political facts-of-life. "The first measures of the new government are of great importance," Royal Flint observed, "and your cooperation with the other New England States, will be very beneficial." North Carolina could afford the luxury of not ratifying "because the southern Interest is already well supported in Congress."[9] The patience of Fed-

[7] William J. Dawson to James Iredell, November 22, 1789; Gov. Johnston to Iredell, November 23, 1789, McRee, *Life of Iredell*, II, 272.

[8] William Petriken to John Nicholson, March 23, 1789, Nicholson papers, Pennsylvania State Archives.

[9] Royal Flint to Governor John Collins, May 30, 1789, Lloyd W. Smith collection, Morristown National Historical Park.

eralists was not endless. Town merchants talked about a seccessionist movement if the country politicians did not awaken to their dilemma. After Congress passed the proposed bill of rights, the Rhode Island legislature assured President Washington that the fears of many good citizens had vanished.

The Rhode Islanders wanted to be coaxed into ratification, but their anomalous position was all too obvious when a ratifying convention finally convened in May, 1790. Sectionalism again came to the foreground when a few Antifederalists denounced the Constitution for its compromises on slavery. Delegate Job Comstock insisted there should be a *quid pro quo* from the South, since the northerners were asked to hide their feelings and accept constitutional protection of slaveholders' rights. When Comstock's tirade drew support, Jonathan Hazard reminded delegates that each state retained its right to abolish slavery. Northern states could clear their consciences, even though southern states propped up their economy with slavery. "We are clear of it," Hazard argued. "Let southern states act for themselves."[10] Further debate only proved the slavery issue was probably more dangerous than it first appeared. Finally, Federalists conceded a proposed set of amendments, including one that denounced the slave traffic as "disgraceful," and asked for the early prohibition upon slave importations. Still, the vote was perilously close—thirty-four to thirty-two. The death rattle of antifederalism came, significantly, because of one man's vote.

A propitious development of the ratification contest had been most Antifederalists' willingness to accept defeat gracefully even when they suspected their opponents of chicanery. As one New Englander observed, once the great question was decided, voters turned their attention toward local problems. The failure of the Harrisburg convention was further proof that most Antifederalists were prepared to give the Constitution a fair trial rather than to drag their feet, hoping for the worst. A Massachusetts newspaper lauded Federalists for their zeal in promoting the Constitution, but held that their wisdom was matched by "the virtue of its opposers in the candour and

[10] William R. Staples, *Rhode Island in the Continental Congress*, 645, 647, 655, 658.

good humor with which they have acquiesced . . . . They have discovered the most genuine principles of liberty and republicanism, in calmly submitting to the prevailing sentiment."[11] A young American serving abroad, who presumed he was an Antifederalist since he liked "much better the idea of *confederated states* than *consolidated states*," still urged those who shared his view to consider the alternatives. Events since the Revolution put the question "on a new ground—it is whether will America be in a worse condition by refusing or adopting the present constitution—& I think under that point of view we must determine in favor of it."[12]

Even the lingering distrust in the South gave way to a spirit of accommodation. William Nelson, a tidewater Antifederalist in Virginia, believed the distressed conditions had been overstressed so that "desperate remedies" would be prescribed. "The adoption of the new government is a case in point," he added, but though the ratifying majorities had been small, the Antifederalists "declare their determination to acquiesce, & use their influence with the people to promote it. No commotions are apprehended, unless any abuses should take place."[13] Overt acts were unthinkable, but Henry still played his role as the Antifederalist villain. He kept the Virginia legislature, which "met in Phrenzy," under his thumb for another year, and so permeated the house with his particularism that the assembly postponed final action on the federal Bill of Rights until December 15, 1791. When votes in the new Congress seemed to hinge on sectional bias rather than national interest, even so staunch a Federalist as South Carolinian Pierce Butler had grave misgivings about the value of the Union at any price. Senator Butler hoped for speedy ratification by North Carolina "as the only chance the Southern interest had to preserve a balance of power."[14] As a delegate at the Federal Convention who had urged southern concessions, Butler was already disillusioned to find the give-and-take had been mainly

[11] Springfield *Hampshire Chronicle*, June 25, 1788.

[12] William Short to William Nelson, May 30, 1788, Short papers, *DLC*.

[13] William Nelson to William Short, July 12, 1788, *ibid*.

[14] Edward Carrington to Knox, December 20, 1788, Knox papers, *MHS*; David Stuart to Washington, September 12, 1789, *DHC*, V, 205; Pierce Butler to James Iredell, August 11, 1789, McRee, *Life of Iredell*, II, 264–65.

a matter of southern "give" and northern "take." "I could not suppose that those concessions would be so soon abused and taken advantage of," he confided.

The turn of affairs in Congress had not disillusioned William Grayson but only confirmed his suspicions. The Constitution had shorn the South of its powers and turned the once-powerful region into "the milch cow out of whom the substance would be extracted" for northern prosperity. The Federalist tariff program that protected northern manufacturers was proof "that the idea of a difference between carrying States & productive States & manufacturing States & slave States is not a mere phantom of the imagination," Grayson asserted. Those amendments surviving the congressional conferences were in Grayson's judgment emasculated—"so mutilated & gutted that in fact they are good for nothing, & I believe as many others do, that they will do more harm than benefit."[15] In 1790 a North Carolinian still bemoaned ratification with a backward glance. "Had Virginia only stood out with us," he sighed, the two states might have tried to salvage some southern rights. As matters stood, the southerner reasoned, it was only a question of time until the North— united by economic interests, manners, and customs—"will form the laws of the General Government more to their own advantage and convenience." The consequence, he predicted, would leave the agrarian South "in a short time . . . reduced to indigence and extreme poverty."[16] Far from abating, this southern complex that made the North into an evil genius continued to grow until, seventy years later, it had worked itself into a militant obsession.

Still, with one Virginian as President and another pushing amendments along, the Antifederalists in both sections saw their dream of another convention fade. Another circumstance which helped topple the Antifederalists' hopes of a second convention was the business recovery of 1788–89. The story of how public security prices rose is familiar, but the upturn appears to have been widespread enough to help shippers, farmers, and merchants. Many property owners de-

---

[15] William Grayson to Patrick Henry, September 29, 1789, Henry papers, DLC.
[16] William Dickson to Rev. Robert Dickson, December 28, 1790, *The Dickson Letters* (ed. by James O. Carr), 37–38.

layed business decisions until ratification became a certainty. "When the Constitution is adopted," a shrewd Yankee counseled, "it is likely things will begin to settle to some fix'd point, & then a better judgment may be form'd of the value of that, as well as all other property."[17] "The commercial Affairs of the Country are in a more promising state than for some years," a New York citizen noted in 1789. Despite some smuggling that left official port figures unreliable, around Boston in 1790 there was an unmistakable increase in the business tempo. "The Increase of exports there is surprizing."[18] News of good times reached Washington, who relayed it to Jefferson. "Though the peril is not passed entirely; thank God! the prospect is somewhat brightening . . . Economy and industry are evidently gaining ground."[19] Prosperity produced as much political tranquility as the spotty depressions of earlier years had provoked discontent. When Pelatiah Webster noted a short time later that "the influence of merchants is the safest of any that can affect a government," he had proof of the maxim close at hand.[20]

The return of prosperity, the appeals for unity, and above all the democratic instinct that commanded obedience from the minority soon produced profound results. Rawlins Lowndes and Willie Jones withdrew from the political forums that they had known for a generation, perhaps more from fatigue than frustration. Jones was of that same breed as Mason—not unique in southern politics—with intense local loyalties and interests. The tumult of the new national politics passed him by. Mason, limping around Gunston Hall, had mellowed by the time Madison's amendments left Congress for the state legislatures. "Two or three further Amendments," Mason wrote, would find him "chearfully put[ting] my Hand & Heart to the new Government."[21] When death mercifully removed Grayson

[17] Jeremiah Libbey to Rev. J. Belknap, May 12, 1788, *MHS, Collections,* 6th series, IV, 405.

[18] Nathaniel Barrell to Jefferson, August 18, 1788, 13 *Jefferson Papers* 523.

[19] Washington to Jefferson, August 31, 1788, *ibid.,* 557.

[20] Pelatiah Webster, *Political Essays* (n.p., 1791), 443, quoted in Curtis P. Nettels, "The American Merchant and the Constitution," *Publications of the Colonial Society of Massachusetts,* XXXIV (1937–42), 26–37.

[21] George Mason to Samuel Griffin, September 6, 1789, Mason papers, *DLC.*

from the Senate where each day brought new disappointments, Henry's choice for his replacement was Mason. But Mason's intellectual powers, though undimmed, were burdened with a pain-racked body that forced him to decline. By 1792, Mason was in his grave, soon followed by Richard Henry Lee, so that neither lived to see their old chief—Henry—make the grand circle in logic and become in time a resolute Federalist. In that faster company, Henry joined a drove of former Antifederalists who had seen the new light. Samuel Chase and Luther Martin were among the most conspicuous converts. The attitude of a few Antifederalists softened when their investments paid handsome returns. Despite an acknowledged preference for a confederation, Virginian William Short had steadily purchased depreciated public securities which in 1791 had a face value of $66,439—convincing proof that life under a consolidated government was not a total loss.[22]

On the other hand, a few Antifederalists remained unconvinced and unyielding. Aedanus Burke, witnessing federalism at firsthand in the new Congress, was galled into a literary effort. Burke decided he would become the historian of the ratification struggle—"the late remarkable revolution in Government." The work was intended, so it seems, to be an exposé. Accordingly, Burke told a few leading Antifederalists of his plans, but enjoined them to secrecy.[23] Using that model of modern research, Burke had a questionnaire. Burke's model revealed his belief that the cries of anarchy in 1786 had been a Federalist ruse. He suspected that Washington had been exploited by a cabal that favored "a regal Govt. as at present." Burke wondered how active various professions and classes had been in the ratification campaign, and he sought information on the role played by "Cincinnati, Civil Officers, Monied men, Merchants, Lawyers, Divines, Men of Letters, Whigs, Tories, Women, Mechanics, Seafaring men, Creditors, Debtors," inhabitants of the "Middle Country, Sea Coast, Back Country," and "Foreigners." "Which of all these were instrumental, and to what extent, and from what views

[22] *Treasury Records*, National Archives, Loan of 1790, Virginia, Vol. 1110.
[23] Samuel Bryan to John Nicholson, November 21, 1789, Nicholson papers, Pennsylvania State Archives.

or motives for or against the system?" Burke asked. "Among those who were in opposition to the new system, was there any preconcert, correspondence or mutual understanding to act with unanimity? Or if not thro' what cause was it neglected or omitted?" Burke's questions implied much. Had the Post Office worked for one party and against the other? Had the printers been "under any . . . restraint to publish against the New System?" Clearly, Burke thought aristocrats had used Washington's prestige as a trojan horse to enter and overwhelm the republican household. Burke apparently never followed through with his projected history of how the "New System" came into being. None of the men closest to antifederalism ever got around to writing its eulogy.

Instead, there were many who wanted the antifederal corpse buried forthwith. Men who had long paid lip service to the notion that parties were "the greatest political evil of the time," forgot their old attachments as they formed new ones. In actual practice they learned that effective political action could result only from party organization and discipline. As an active political group the Federalists had enough influence and momentum to carry the new government from an idea into reality. The Antifederalists did not.

Never thoroughly co-ordinated in their program, the makeshift Antifederalist party fell apart rapidly. Provocative assumptions that gave the Antifederalists of 1787–88 links with the Jeffersonian Republicans of a decade later go aground on the facts. The political about-face which led to the conversion of Henry and Chase was matched by the eventual abandonment by Madison and McKean of their old moorings. The realignments lent truth to Madison's insistence that the Federalist–Antifederalist rivalry of 1787–88 expired with "the regular and effectual establishment of the federal government" in 1789.[24] The brilliant way that Madison maneuvered the Federalists into support of the amendments, more than any other single feat, erased the tenuous alignments in the first Congress.

[24] *Writings of Madison* (ed. by Gaillard Hunt), VI, 113, quoted in Noble E. Cunningham, Jr., *The Jeffersonian Republicans 1789–1801* (Chapel Hill, 1957), 23–24.

It was Madison's intellectual honesty, on the other hand, that soon forced him to admit that Antifederalists had told the truth during the ratification campaign about clashing sectional interests. After all his efforts "to abate the fears of an overbearing majority at this end of the Union," he confessed in 1789 that the votes of northern congressmen already confirmed the Antifederalists' warning.[25] Indeed, Madison was so chagrined by northern rapacity that he did not dare commit his feelings to paper. In the new setting, Madison learned that the particularism of Henry and Mason was matched by the provincialism of Fisher Ames and Rufus King.

Most Antifederalists accepted the Union as "the rock of their political salvation." A good many, however, insisted that the Union might have been saved without a drastic transfer of power from the state governments to a national government. With prejudiced hindsight, Mercy Warren chronicled their losing battle as a crusade waged on behalf of the people. The Antifederalists, she emphasized, were reasonable men who "were jealous of each ambiguity in law or Government, or the smallest circumstance that might have a tendency to curtail the republican system. . . . they also wished for the transmission of the enjoyment of the equal rights of man to their latest posterity." To historian Warren, the Constitution contained so many vague phrases that it might become putty in the wrong hands. Mrs. Warren's viewpoint was disputed by another New Englander who believed antifederal suspicions were based on ignorance rather than on democratic propensities. "The anti-federal [*sic*] think as they have been bred—their education has been rather indifferent—they have been accustomed to think on the small scale—they can think on no other without an enlargement of their minds," a Connecticut Federalist said.[26]

Perhaps there was a tinge of anti-intellectualism among the Antifederalists, but by their zealous endeavor they had actually performed a valuable service, as Washington himself admitted. "Upon

[25] Madison to Tench Coxe, September 18, [1789], Madison papers, *DLC.*

[26] Warren, *History of the American Revolution,* III, 360; *Connecticut Courant,* November 20, 1786, quoted in Allan Nevins, *The American States During and After the Revolution,* 234.

the whole I doubt whether the opposition to the Constitution will not ultimately be productive of more good than evil," the great man commented. By offering battle, the Antifederalists had aroused men to public exertions that they might otherwise have avoided. In the healthy contest between the two contending parties, the Antifederalists had helped shed new light "upon the science of Government, [*and*] they have given the rights of man a full and fair discussion."[27]

Federalists could be magnanimous, for they had taken a topsy-turvy political scene and set it aright, even though the majority was against them. Numbers alone counted for little against the superior art of practical politicians. The Antifederalists, an impassioned but essentially unorganized majority, lacked a bellwether of Washington's stature. Leaderless, they drifted into retreat, insisting all the while that an unconditional ratification in no way reflected public opinion. Outmaneuvered by the Massachusetts plan of recommendatory amendments, they branded that scheme as a mockery. But since they offered nothing better, the little glory they might have salvaged in the first Congress was snatched away by Madison.

The defeat of the Antifederalists, far from being a national tragedy, was soon interpreted as another in the series of providential acts that favored the new nation. Exulting over the ratification, Federalist Benjamin Rush gloried that it had come as "a triumph of knowledge over ignorance, of virtue over vice, and of liberty over slavery." The miracle was that the Constitution had been adopted without bloodshed.[28] Jefferson glowed when he surveyed the contest and its outcome. "There has been just opposition enough to produce probably further guards to liberty without touching the energy of the government," he commented, "and this will bring over the bulk of the opposition to the side of the new government."[29]

The domestic tranquility which the Constitution sought settled over the land. "Order is Heav'n's first Law," Pope had written, and Federalists in 1787 cheered the sentiment. "What was it brought

---

[27] Washington to Gen. John Armstrong, April 25, 1788, *DHC*, IV, 592.

[28] Benjamin Rush to Elias Boudinot [?], July 9, 1788, Butterfield, *Rush Letters*, I, 470–71, 475.

[29] Jefferson to Adm. J. Paul Jones, March 23, 1789, *DHC*, V, 167.

us from a state of nature to society, but to secure happiness?" asked Edmund Pendleton in the Richmond ratifying convention. The felicity that Pendleton saluted was that orderly state where every citizen was free to pursue his own goals, in a lawful (some would add, business-like) manner. "We are getting back fast to the system we destroyed some years ago" was not written by an angry American in 1788.[30] Thus the radicals of '76 had in many cases become the conservatives of '87—still willing to experiment provided the venture led back to the old pathways of safety and security.

The Antifederalists, on the other hand, venerated not order but local control. The proposed system smacked of an aristocracy, but it is noteworthy that even the wealthy Antifederalists had long identified themselves with the common people. For example, no delegate at the Federal Convention was ahead of George Mason in his plea for a broadened suffrage. Scorning the English example, which Mason thought Americans had been too prone to follow, he had then urged a wider enfranchisement for every man who had a "permanent common interest with Society." In short, a penniless father was entitled to vote because he had a stake in the future through his child, placing him on a plane with the banker whose interest in society was computed at ten per cent per annum.[31] To Antifederalists of Mason's bent, the citizen was a trustworthy guardian of his own future. The New York Antifederalists called this "republicanism" and practiced it by providing that all white male citizens over twenty-one, regardless of their property holdings, might vote for delegates to the 1788 ratifying convention. In short, the Antifederalists leaders of 1787–88 were not political pessimists, but rather they had a good deal of trust in the people.[32] With some disgust, a Federalist in the Virginia legislature that Henry dominated advised friends to adopt the epithet

---

[30] Francis Kinlock to Thomas Boone, May 26, 1788, "Letters of Francis Kinlock to Thomas Boone, 1782–1788" (ed. by Felix Gilbert), *Journal of Southern History*, VIII (1942), 103–105.

[31] 2 Farrand 203.

[32] For a diametrical viewpoint, see Cecelia M. Kenyon, "Men of Little Faith: The Anti-Federalists on the Nature of Representative Government," *William & Mary Quarterly*, 3rd series, XII, 3–43.

"True Democrats" because "Henry & his pack" preached the gospel of democracy.[33] Willie Jones subscribed to the same credo. Significantly, in the states where the Antifederalists were either dominant or nearly so, their strongest appeal was to the general electorate—in Massachusetts, Rhode Island, Virginia, New York, and North Carolina.

Why, then, did the Antifederalists fail? The evidence shows that the Antifederalists began their campaign for an amended Constitution without co-ordination, without a definite counterproposal, and without unified leadership. The bill of rights issue was their only common cry. Once they departed from that, as Federalists never tired of saying, the Antifederalists marched off in all directions. The one idea that was the great Antifederalist strength was also their great weakness—the cry of sectionalism. But where northern Antifederalists showed that the Constitution recognized slavery and thus was obeisant to southerners, their allies in Virginia and North Carolina contended that northern domination would surely result from an unconditional ratification. In the Mississippi treaty negotiations the North had already tipped its hand, southern Antifederalists argued. Fear of northern rapacity was the driving force behind antifederalism in the South. A stronger fear of disunion drove their opponents on to triumph.

The leading Antifederalists never had an unlimited view of the Union. Self-reliant themselves, they believed the strength of the republic rested in the powers possessed by each state as it struggled to meet its own problems. Trained in the art of local politics, they were convinced that a remote, impersonal government could scarcely be democratic in tone. The immediate future was not worrisome, but they fretted about "unborn generations." They feared that under the Constitution Americans would owe their allegiance to some distant Colossus where the emphasis would be on ceremonies and forms rather than a better life for the people. Much depended on the leadership, as Richard Henry Lee noted. Although the Constitution had faults, "the honor and safety of the U. States" might

---

[33] Francis Corbin to Madison, November 12, 1788, Madison papers, *DLC*.

still be preserved by enlightened men.[34] The Antifederalist party soon dissolved, but the political faith it aroused was only temporarily submerged. Its chief tenet—that the people must be trusted—has found adherents in every subsequent generation.

[34] Richard Henry Lee to John Lamb, June 27, 1788, Ballagh, *Letters of Lee,* II, 475–76.

Bibliographical Note

THE MANUSCRIPT COLLECTIONS used and cited have been supplemented by printed collections of letters and public papers. The works of Jonathan Elliot, Max Farrand, and Julian Boyd have already been noted. Other valuable collections are: *The Writings of George Washington,* ed. by John C. Fitzpatrick (Washington, 1931–44); Kate Mason Rowland, *The Life of George Mason* (Philadelphia, 1892); *The Letters of Richard Henry Lee,* ed. by James C. Ballagh (New York, 1911–14); W. B. Reed, *The Life and Correspondence of Joseph Reed* (Philadelphia, 1874); Charles E. L. Wingate, *The Life and Letters of Paine Wingate* (Medford, Massachusetts, 1930); *Correspondence and Journals of Samuel B. Webb,* ed. by Worthington C. Ford (New York, 1893); James T. Austin, *Life of Elbridge Gerry* (Boston, 1828–29); *The Letters of Benjamin Rush,* ed. by Lyman Butterfield (Princeton, 1951); Edwin S. Delaplaine, *Life of Thomas Johnson* (New York, 1927); *The Works of John Adams,* ed. by Charles F. Adams (Boston, 1850–56); Richard Henry Lee, *Life of Arthur Lee* (Boston, 1829); Moncure D. Conway, *Forgotten Chapters in the Life of Edmund Randolph* (New York, 1888); *The Bland Papers,* ed. by Charles Campbell (Petersburg, Virginia, 1840–43); Griffith J. McRee, *Life and Correspondence of James Iredell* (New York, 1858); *Correspondence and Public Papers of John Jay,* ed. by Henry P. Johnston (New York, 1890–91); *Writings of James Madison,* ed. by Gaillard Hunt (New York, 1900–10); Harry A. Cushing, *Letters of Samuel Adams* (New York, 1904–1908); *Works of Alexander Hamilton,* ed. by Henry C. Lodge (New York, 1904); William Wirt, *Sketches of the Life and Character of Patrick Henry* (Hartford, 1852); *Life and Correspondence of Rufus King,* ed. by Charles R. King (New York, 1894–1900).

Useful public documents for this period are printed in: *Public Records of the State of Connecticut,* comp. by Charles J. Hoadly and Leonard W. Labaree (Hartford, 1894–19—); *Records of the Colony and State of Rhode Island,* ed. by J. R. Bartlett (Providence, 1865); *Early State Papers of New Hampshire,* ed. by Albert S. Batchelor (Concord, 1892);

Colonial and State Records of North Carolina, ed. by William L. Saunders and Walter Clark (Raleigh, 1886–1914); *Debates and other Proceedings of the Convention of Virginia,* comp. by David Robertson (Richmond, 1805). The observations of some participants in the ratification struggle are available in *Pamphlets on the Constitution,* ed. by Paul L. Ford (Brooklyn, 1888); *Essays on the Constitution,* ed. by Paul L. Ford (Brooklyn, 1892); *A Plea for Federal Union, North Carolina, 1788,* ed. by Hugh T. Lefler (Charlottesville, 1947); Mercy Otis Warren, *History of the Rise, Progress and Termination of the American Revolution* (Boston, 1805); William Manning, *The Key of Libberty,* ed. by Samuel E. Morison (Billerica, Massachusetts, 1922); "The Diary of John Quincy Adams," Massachusetts Historical Society, *Proceedings,* 2nd Series, XVI (1902); Ebenezer S. Thomas, *Reminiscenses of the Last Sixty-Five Years* (Hartford, 1840); Theophilus Parsons, *Memoir of Theophilus Parsons* (Boston, 1859).

Valuable secondary accounts of this period include: Hugh B. Grigsby, *The History of the Virginia Convention of 1788* (Richmond, 1890–91); Louise Trenholme, *Ratification of the Federal Constitution in North Carolina* (New York, 1932); Samuel B. Harding, *The Contest Over Ratification of the Federal Constitution in Massachusetts* (New York, 1896); Clarence E. Miner, *The Ratification of the Federal Constitution in New York* (New York, 1921); John B. McMaster and Frederick D. Stone, *Pennsylvania and the Federal Constitution, 1787–1788* (Lancaster, 1888); William R. Staples, *Rhode Island and the Continental Congress* (Providence, 1870); J. A. Munroe, *Federalist Delaware 1775–1815* (New Brunswick, 1954); E. Wilder Spaulding, *New York in the Critical Period* (New York, 1932); Richard P. McCormick, *Experiment in Independence New Jersey in the Critical Period, 1781–1789* (New Brunswick, 1950); Joseph B. Walker, *A History of the New Hampshire Convention* (Boston, 1888); Allan Nevins, *The American States During and After the Revolution, 1775–1789* (New York, 1924); L. M. Miner, *Our Rude Forefathers* (Cedar Rapids, 1937); George Dangerfield, *Chancellor Robert R. Livingston* (New York, 1960). Specialized works that are useful include: Noble E. Cunningham, Jr., *The Jeffersonian Republicans 1789–1801* (Chapel Hill, 1957); *Essays in the Constitutional History of the United States 1775–1789,* ed. by J. Franklin Jameson (Boston, 1899), with particular attention to Edward P. Smith's article, "The Movement Towards a Second Convention."

Index

Abingdon, Va.: 193

Adams, Henry: 216

Adams, John: 41, 45, 160; seeks Vice-Presidency, 292

Adams, John Quincy: 80, 111–12, 119–20

Adams, Samuel: 33, 76–77, 81–82, 94, 214; role in state convention, 67, 96–97, 99, 103, 110

Albany, N.Y.: 205, 206, 302; antifederal newspaper sought, 139; local support for Clinton, 141, 204; Fourth of July riot, 256

Albany County, N.Y.: 204, 206

Ames, Fisher: 310

Anglican Church: 192

Annapolis, Md.: 155, 159, 185; Convention of 1786, 8

Anne Arundel County, Md.: 155–56

Antifederalists: 4–6; in Pa., 20, 25, 51–59, 62–64, 143–50, 254; in Md., 28, 149–59; in Va., 37, 141–42, 169–98, 218–34, 245–53; in Mass., 22–25, 66–68, 74–82, 92–114, 214–16; in Conn., 82–86; in Ga., 87; in N.Y., 30, 83, 139–41, 199–209, 235–44, 255–65; in N.H., 117–22, 210–13; in R.I., 124–27; in S.C., 162–69; in N.C., 268–79; lack definite plan, 208–209, 311; democratic leanings of, 312–14; newspaper supporters, 37–38, 72–73, 128–30; printers harassed, 135–39, 148–49, 165, 265–66, 267, 309

Armstrong, John: 63

Articles of Confederation: 3–4, 6, 15, 22, 38, 83, 141, 143, 173, 202, 216, 228; revisions planned, 8; discredited by Federalists, 10

Ashley, John, Jr.: 79

Atherton, Joshua: 117, 210, 213, 236–37; role in state convention, 118–20, 123, 211–12; explains Antifederalist collapse, 302

Augusta *Georgia State Gazette:* 87

Austin, Benjamin ("Candidus"): 68

Bailey, Francis: 131

Baldwin, Simeon: 122

Baltimore, Md.: 67, 123, 130,

317

Platt, Zephaniah: 207
Portland, Me. district: 113
Portland *Cumberland Gazette:* 77
Portsmouth *New-Hampshire Spy:* 216
Postal service: 128, 309; criticized by Antifederalists, 62, 128–34, 137
Poughkeepsie, N.Y.: 125, 162, 212–13, 235, 239, 255, 258, 265
Powars, Edward: 22–23, 73, 99, 130; feels Federalist financial pressure, 138; continued financial troubles, 267
Powhatan County, Va.: 194
Presbyterians: 55
Prince Edward County, Va.: 180, 189
Prince Frederick Parish, S.C.: 167
Providence, R.I.: 67, 104, 119, 126, 213; newspaper quarrels, 136
Providence *United States Chronicle:* 72
"Publius": *see* Alexander Hamilton and James Madison

Quakers: 54

Ramsay, David: 7
Randall, Benjamin: 95, 98
Randolph, Edmund: 25, 32, 34, 36, 70, 76, 116, 124, 127, 141, 171, 176–77, 179–81, 183–89, 190–92, 194–95, 197, 202,

209, 224–25, 252, 284, 287; works at Federal Convention, 11–16; explained Antifederalist leanings, 141–42; attends state convention, 229–30, 248; breaks with Antifederalists, 228; his indecision condemned, 293
Rehoboth, R.I.: 73
Revere, Paul: 81
Rhode Island: 124–27, 160, 216, 282, 286; opposed federal revenue system, 6; legal-tender acts denounced, 9–10; legislators attack Society of Cincinnati, 45; refuses to call convention, 124–26; rejects Constitution, 126–27; legislature favors second convention, 291; delayed ratification, 303–304
Richmond, Va.: 148, 162, 188, 193, 197, 224–25, 229, 238, 245
Ridgely, Charles: 151, 156
Ridgely, Charles of William: 151, 156
Roane, Spencer: 142, 250
Robin Hood Society (of Richmond, Va.): 188
Rush, Benjamin: 27, 58, 149, 161, 311; spurious letter attributed to, 130–31
Russell, Benjamin: 73, 81, 111; defends postal service, 133
Rutledge, Edward: 36

The Ordeal of the Constitution has been set on the Linotype in
11½-point Caslon Old Face, a faithful rendering of the original
William Caslon types. Foundry Caslon Italic has been selected to
preserve the continuity of type design in the rich Caslon tradition.
The book is printed on paper which bears the watermark of the
University of Oklahoma Press, with an effective life of
at least three hundred years.

UNIVERSITY OF OKLAHOMA PRESS
Norman

(-16 Levis, Davi
Q-15 Lee, Sungi
Q-15 Lee, ... Dino
R-28 Patel, Ken
R-28 Parham, Jac
R-27 Palmer, Ric
R-26 Oliver, Ro
R-25 Northern, Mic
R-24 Mullins, Mic
R-23 ...